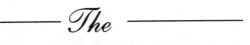

The

NEW
PORTABLE
MBA

The Portable MBA Series

The Portable MBA Series provides managers, executives, professionals, and students with a "hands-on," easy-to-access overview of the ideas and information covered in a typical Masters of Business Administration program. The published and forthcoming books in the series are:

Published

The New Portable MBA (0-471-08004-7) Eliza G. C. Collins and
    Mary Anne Devanna

The Portable MBA Desk Reference (0-471-57681-6) Paul A. Argenti

The Portable MBA in Economics (0-471-59526-8) Philip K. Y. Young and
    John McCauley

The Portable MBA in Entrepreneurship (0-471-57780-4) William Bygrave

The Portable MBA in Finance and Accounting (0-471-53226-6)
    John Leslie Livingstone

The Portable MBA in Management (0-471-57379-5) Allan R. Cohen

The Portable MBA in Marketing (0-471-54728-X) Alexander Hiam and
    Charles Schewe

New Product Development: Managing and Forecasting for Strategic Success
    (0-471-57226-8) Robert J. Thomas

Real-Time Strategy: Improving Team-Based Planning for a Fast-Changing
    World (0-471-58564-5) Lee Tom Perry, Randall G. Stott, and
    W. Norman Smallwood

The Portable MBA in Strategy (0-471-58498-3) Liam Fahey and
    Robert M. Randall

Total Quality Management: Strategies and Techniques Proven at Today's Most
    Successful Companies (0-471-54538-1) Stephen George and Arnold
    Weimerskirch

Market-Driven Management: Using the New Marketing Concept to Create a
    Customer-Oriented Company (0-471-59576-4) Frederick E. Webster

Forthcoming

The Portable MBA in Global Business Leadership (0-471-30410-7)
    Noel Tichy, Michael Brimm, and Hiro Takeuchi

The Portable MBA in Investment (0-471-10661-5) Peter L. Bernstein

Negotiating Strategically (0-471-01321-8) Roy Lewicki and Alexander Hiam

Psychology for Leaders (0-471-59538-1) Dean Tjosvold and Mary Tjosvold

The

NEW
PORTABLE
MBA

Eliza G. C. Collins
Mary Anne Devanna

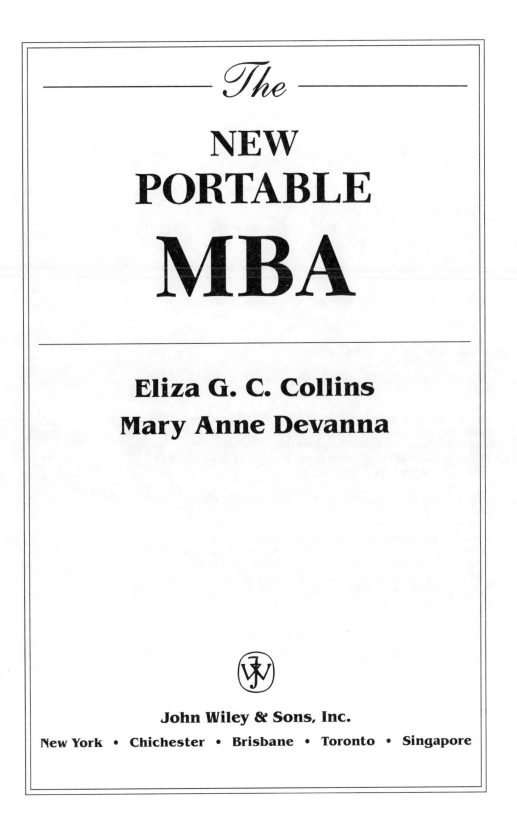

John Wiley & Sons, Inc.
New York • Chichester • Brisbane • Toronto • Singapore

CONTENTS

PART THREE MANAGING CHANGE

INTRODUCTION: THE NEW WORLD OF BUSINESS AND THE NEW MBA

Eliza G. C. Collins

The first edition of *The Portable MBA* is only five years old, and yet we, and the editors at John Wiley & Sons, think not only that we need a new edition now but also that we will probably need a third in the year 2000. Few books on business these days have a truly useful shelf life of more than five years. This generalization may not apply to perennially useful books that illuminate the history of business or that present the intriguing ideas of innovative thinkers such as Peter Drucker or Alfred Chandler. It is never amiss to learn how we got where we are. Nor is obsolescence inevitable for books that instruct in a professional area such as accounting or finance, although as conventions change, these too become out of date. However, virtually any book that purports to inform on the state of the art in leadership, technology, or the strategic uses and organizational impacts of information systems needs constant rethinking and attention.

The Portable MBA is no exception although, the purposes of the new edition remain the same—to offer readers:

- *An opportunity to learn the language of business.* If you want to participate in the life and culture of another country, you need to know its language and customs. Business is no different. It has a language all its own, and *The New Portable MBA* will provide you with a basic understanding of important business functions, accounting, finance, marketing, the strategic planning, and more, giving you a common business vocabulary and the information to develop managerial literacy, regardless of your professional background or present position.

- *A framework for making reasoned business decisions and judgments.* You won't, for example, be an expert in accounting after reading this book, but you will understand the role cash flow statements and balance sheets play in a business. Nor will you be a strategy guru, but you will recognize the importance of developing and implementing a strategy for an organization. *The New Portable MBA* offers you the resources to understand how a business fits together: why a decision in marketing may have serious impact on a company's strategy; or why your human resource practices may affect your company's competitive position in its industry.

- *An opportunity to learn from faculty members in a broad range of leading MBA programs.* Most of the chapters in the book have been written by experts from leading business schools: Columbia, Dartmouth (the Tuck School), Harvard, Wharton, George Washington, McGill, Babson, Boston University, University of New Hampshire, American University, and Cranfield Institute of Management in the U.K. New to this edition is a nonacademic look at the purpose of business by a business observer from a top daily newspaper, the *Boston Globe*.

Despite having the same purposes, however, the tenor of the book and its overarching concerns have changed. They reflect what has happened and what continues to happen at an astounding rate in the real world of business—a total shake-up of every conventional wisdom, from who's the boss to who's the customer, to what marks a successful business career.

What are these changes and what impact are they having on organizations? Aren't we exaggerating just a bit? Not if the massive retooling of MBA programs at top business schools to address these changes is any indication. In the Introduction, we will briefly consider these changes and the business school responses, and then outline how this book will address these issues without sacrificing its basic purposes.

A number of different forces from different arenas have combined to create our new world of business. If the upheavals came from only one direction, we might say that the present turbulence is temporary. But it is the systemic nature of the changes and their universality that leads most business thinkers to agree that what we're experiencing is revolutionary:

- Information technology is becoming so sophisticated and immediate that it is virtually changing the rate at which things happen, the people who make things happen, the shapes of organizations in which things happen, and what happens itself.

- Organizations that used to be hierarchical and designed along military and control principles focusing on the CEO are swiftly downsizing to become flatter learning structures oriented toward the customer.

- The number of competitors in most industries is growing and so are the numbers of service and product options they offer customers. In return, customers with ever-greater expectations are driving organizations to respond at faster and faster rates.

- The markets that most businesses serve are expanding and are now global. Companies not only have to serve more and more defined markets but are competing against other companies with more and more defined competencies.

- The workforce that enters organizations today is both so intolerant of the strictures of hierarchy and so diverse in its background and competencies that it almost defies structural attempts at organization, leaving it, by yesterday's standards, almost ungovernable.

If you were a manager in a traditional organization, you might throw up your hands and tender your resignation. Nothing you had ever learned about how things happen in your company and what you ought to do and think would work anymore. And in your secret managerial heart you'd see these changes as problems. And this may be the biggest problem business today faces: the understandable reluctance of managers to see these eruptions as opportunities, not problems. If we apply old ways of thinking, they are problems because the tools and models we would use can't deal with them. Rigid hierarchies simply don't respond well to rapid change either within or without the company.

What is needed are new models of how companies work most effectively considering all the pressures and demands made on them by the changes—and our list is not exclusive by any means—we've outlined. We know what doesn't work; what we don't know is what does. But therein lies a critical fallacy. In asking that question, we presume that there is a single model that works. What is becoming increasingly plain is that there isn't one model that works. What works must fit the situation at hand and what the people on hand need to accomplish to do the job. In other words, what works is what will allow organizations to meet customer demands faster and better than anyone else. If that is the criterion, then business needs to respond with organizations that can change shape and priorities on a dime. The model then becomes a flowing, shifting conglomeration of people focused outward, not inward. This is enough to give nightmares to a hierarchy buff.

What does all this mean for a real manager in a real business? Are we talking about issues that impact business life today, or are they mostly theoretical problems, worthy of interest for business researchers, but not for real practicing managers? Let's say you're a manager in a mail-order company, and you sell camping equipment. Your competitors, other mail-order companies also selling camping equipment, are outperforming you at every turn. You look at your products and see that they are virtually the same as theirs. What else do you look at? You do a quick survey and find that a major difference is the time it takes for your competitors to fill their orders compared with the processing time in your company. How do they do it? While your company order receiver takes an order, for example, for a pair of men's fishing boots, and then passes the order on to the order-fulfilling department head, who passes it over to the person in charge of the boot division, who forwards it to the head of the men's boot department, who delivers it to the shipping room head, who presents it to a clerk, your competitor's order goes from the order receiver straight to the shipping room clerk who packs the boots. You decide to copy this system and discover that, although this is a very simple-sounding undertaking, it has within it all the makings of an organizational upheaval.

First, to facilitate the order's passage through the company, the strict boundaries between the different business functions, such as marketing, manufacturing, and finance, will have to come down. By virtue of its existence, the information system that takes the order straight to the shipping department and checks the inventory along the way will pierce the boundary to some extent, but what if the shipping department and the order-taking department are at loggerheads, why would the shipper pay attention to the order?

To ensure cooperation and understanding of the importance of that order's fulfillment, the second thing your competitor has done is to eliminate all the functions of the business and instead structure it along the processes that the company performs, such as order fulfillment, product and service creation, and innovation. In this company, everything is organized toward what the customer needs and wants. Anything that doesn't serve the customer directly, such as accounting or finance, is taken care of in small staff offices.

In addition to developing an information system to replace the functional structure, your competitor also has put people into self-managing teams that form a lattice across the company keeping it focused outward rather than upward. When the customer makes new and different demands, it is the team— the order taker, the shipper, and all the other team members—that makes the decision. Even more boundary smashing, your competitor has actually formed alliances with some suppliers, making them part of the team as well. The CEO has also worked out a reciprocal deal with another direct competitor to direct customers to each other rather than lose them to a third firm.

This is all well and good you say, but what does your competitor do? Now that all the real decisions that affect the customer are made by people in teams across the company, what's the CEO's job and boundaries of authority? In your competitor's company, the whole idea of what it means to be a leader has changed; in fact, it looks as if your competitor thinks the job of management is to create an environment in which the members are able to learn and adapt quickly to the customer and ensure that all the company's systems—from rewards to information—are geared to supporting the people who face the customer.

In this company, control has been replaced by learning, functions have been replaced by processes, people are not defined by tasks but by the team they belong to, rewards go to teams rather than to individuals, and at no time does the company have a preordained shape or size.

Creating and leading such companies are the jobs that face future graduates of business schools. And most business school MBA programs are not currently able to adequately prepare their students for these tasks. Business schools' MBA programs have generally been designed to reflect traditional organizations, along functional lines. Faculty members in traditional programs work in an area such as marketing or finance and teach courses that focus on a problem as, say, primarily a marketing or finance issue. Understandably, some graduates of these schools will take too narrow a perspective to be effective in the new world of business. Even schools that historically have championed the general manager point of view and, teaching through the case method, have required students to see the big picture and accept the primacy of context, find that the functional structure just may not prepare students properly for the open-ended ambiguous situations in which they will make decisions less often than they will articulate the decisions of others.

Currently most leading business schools are redesigning their MBA programs. Some have completely done away with the functional structure and focus instead on processes such as how to scan the environment or design a new product or service. Others are proceeding more slowly, retaining the functional structure but requiring that teachers introduce ideas from outside the discipline to broaden students' perceptions of problems and provide the information they need to address them.

In conceiving the *The New Portable MBA*, we've taken the middle road. Believing that it is critical that managers have the functional building blocks firmly in place, we've retained the functional structure that formed the core of the first edition. Even in that edition, however, we made room for some cross-functional issues that would concern all managers, such as how to think like an executive and how to manage both numbers and people across an organization. In this edition, we've gone even further in embracing the cross-functional/processes of organizations while retaining the core. Each function chapter has been revised to help managers broaden their focus when considering an issue and bring different paradigms to bear on their judgments.

Part One of "The Foundations of Management," begins with a new chapter, "What Is Business About?" In this chapter, David Warsh considers various schools of thought about the nature of business and its role in our society. As we've discussed, more and more businesses are taking a true marketing position and orienting themselves to the customer and what the customer demands. But is this what business should be doing? Is this wasteful? In a free market economy, should business supply anything the customer wants? Is profit the only purpose of business? Will this change as the markets become more global?

Chapter 2, "How to Think Like an Executive," by Leonard Schlesinger, outlines the tasks that any general manager needs to perform to assure an effective operation, from building a positive work environment, to allocating resources strategically, to creating excellence in operations and execution. An additional task has been added, consistent with the new thrust of this book: managing with a broader perspective toward just about everything, from the span of control to the people you must influence in developing the company's expanded agenda.

The basic tools available to the manager are unchanged; they are still the building blocks of the behavioral sciences, quantitative analysis, and economics. In Chapter 3, "Managing People," Allan Cohen focuses on an issue that has preoccupied both organizational theorists and practitioners for the past 75 years—how to motivate employees to deliver their best. Current thinking has moved away from the notion that the art of Japanese management had its roots in an essentially collaborative culture and would be difficult to replicate in the West. Indeed, productivity and quality of Japanese-managed plants in the United States that are staffed by American workers equal or exceed that of comparable plants in Japan. Excellence is not culture bound, but it does require a deep-seated understanding of human behavior and the ways an organization can encourage or discourage people from doing their best.

In Chapter 4, "Quantitative Tools," Brian Forst explains various ways that numbers are useful for improving the performance of the business. While revenues, costs, and operating budgets have long been in the domain of the "number crunchers," much of the current emphasis on quality control, accurate forecasting, and efficient resource allocation requires a basic understanding of statistics and quantitative techniques to support production management, marketing, finance, research and development, and corporate planning.

Managerial economics provides guidelines for choices and decisions the organization makes in the marketplace. It is the basis for the environmental scanning that has become a large part of the strategic planning process in many organizations. In Chapter 5, "Managerial Economics," Frank Lichtenberg examines the impact that government interventions on behalf of the public good as well as the impact of different market structures—monopoly versus many competitors—have on the organization's field of choices. New to this edition is a section on global economics with a concise discussion of, among other things, the theory of exchange rate determination, international capital mobility, and the trade balance, all critical to an understanding of how a company can fare in the global economy.

In Part Two, "The Functions of a Business," we show how the building blocks are used in combination with the expertise each of the business functions offers. Each function has a role to play, but it is less and less an organizational, structural role and more and more an informational, perspective one. In each chapter in this section, the authors acknowledge the interdependence of the functions and their sublimation to the greater goal—the effective management of the processes that define the business.

Chapter 6, "Marketing Management," by Frederick Webster, goes beyond the normal distinction between a market-driven company that provides what the buyer wants and a product-driven one that tries to sell what it already makes to focus on the customer-driven company. In a truly customer-driven company, the company not only responds to the customer but also is organized with the customer as its focal point. The difference might seem theoretical, but as our mail-order company example shows, it is anything but. Manufacturing companies can learn a lot from service firms that already have the customer as their reason for being.

Whereas the dramatic changes the marketing concept has undergone in the past few decades are documented in Chapter 6, Chapter 7, "Information Technology," would not have existed if this book had been written, say, 25 years ago. Yet, the development of such technology has catapulted organizations from the manufacturing-product-oriented age to the customer-oriented information age. N. Venkatraman documents the challenges that emerge as information technology is linked to strategic management including the impact on changing industry boundaries, business definitions, sources of competitive advantage, and new business opportunities. Perhaps most far-reaching are the effects that information technology has on the very shapes and sizes of organizations, which will influence who works on what, where, and with whom.

Although everyone acknowledges the importance of information technology, it is still people who make a business work. How they are brought into an organization and then rewarded and developed assumes more, not less, importance in this era of high technology. In Chapter 8, "Human Resource Management," Mary Anne Devanna provides us with a look at the role a sophisticated human resource function plays in leveraging organizational performance in the way it attracts and retains, evaluates, rewards, and develops its human resources.

This function, which started as record keeping, is now at the heart of most organizations' efforts to develop a new diverse workforce that increasingly will work in self-managed teams in boundaryless organizations.

Even with the best technology and people in place, a business still needs to have a system for getting products and services "out the door." Linda Sprague, in Chapter 9, "Operations Management," looks at the operations function, which is responsible for output and, therefore, for productivity and quality as well as cost and delivery performance. In a globally competitive world, an effective operations function is an essential part of the competitive arsenal. Superior R&D capability can never be fully realized if an organization cannot produce goods and services faster and with fewer quality problems than its competitors. Critical to achieving that aim is making a company's processes central to its organization. Productivity and quality issues need to be viewed as integral to the processes, not as things in themselves. Only in this way will the total quality management goal of all production operations be reached.

Measuring and accounting for all these people and business activity provide the focus for Chapters 10 and 11. In Chapter 10, "Accounting and Management Decision Making," John Leslie Livingstone provides insight into the role that accounting plays in management control, planning, and financing a business, as well as how to test your business for short-term and long-term solvency and current profitability. The manager is also reminded, however, that just as critical as using the right tools is measuring the right things; measurements in and of themselves can establish priorities that may run afoul of the company's overall processes.

In Chapter 11, "Financial Management," there is a crash course on the terminology that sets the financial wizards apart from the rest of the organization; John Leslie Livingstone and James Walter also help us understand the rationale behind the financial headlines that result from the interaction between organizations and the financial community. These include the equity and bond markets that provide cash for expansion as well as for merger and acquisition activity.

The functions are managerial tools for formulating and implementing the organization's strategy. In Chapter 12, "Strategic Management," Liam Fahey brings us full circle. Writing that "the conflict between the demands of the present and the requirements of the future lies at the heart of strategic management," Fahey outlines three core strategic management tasks: managing strategy in the marketplace; managing the organization; continually reconfiguring it; and practicing strategic management, *viz.*, monitoring and improving the ties between the market strategy and what people actually do in a company or firm. Strategy is no longer simply planning. It is executing and organizing. It is as intricately tied up with how the organization works.

In this edition, we've added a whole new section: Part Three, "Managing Change." The constant is change, and in order to be effective, managers need to understand that the relative stability of the 1960s, 1970s, and 1980s is gone for good and has been replaced by a world of immediacy and instant responses. Chapter 13, "Organizations for the Year 2000," William Halal describes the design and structures of organizations to come. These will be competitive enterprise networks of empowered individuals responding quickly and regrouping and disbanding as the market dictates.

Finally, in his chapter on "Leadership for the Year 2000," Jay A. Conger explores two critical issues: First, what makes some people leaders and others not? Is it background and experiences or genes that are the determining factors? Second, what do leaders need to do that sets them apart from managers, especially in this rapidly changing competitive environment in which even the most sacred of leadership positions, the board of directors, is up for grabs if its policies and postures don't help a company be more customer responsive?

The manager's job is now a challenge beyond previous imaginings. Where once the analytical specialist was the ideal manager, now it is more often the person who can juggle the many influences and needs of all the parties who affect a customer. It is a job that requires great artistry in creating new and different solutions to new and different problems every day. We hope that this book will provide readers with not only the tools for the job but also a sense of its great importance for our futures.

PART ONE

THE FOUNDATIONS OF MANAGEMENT

Before a manager deals with any of the problems described in the Introduction, he or she must face a completely different set of issues, more personal. Before you chose a business career, what did you think about? For example, if you were going to become a pianist you would have—it is hoped—some natural talent with keyboard instruments. If you were going to send yourself off to art school, you would most likely have shown some skill with drawing, mixing, and applying color, or creating three-dimensional objects. But it's not so readily obvious what you should be good at and enjoy doing and thinking about if you're going to embark on a career in business. What are, if you will, the foundations of management?

Why business and not architecture or medicine? One of the reasons people enter a business career is an issue of values. Business has purposes that serve and reflect the society in which we live. In choosing a business career, you may not be explicitly aware of all the effects of business or agree with some people's interpretations of them, but you have your own beliefs, strictly formulated or not. Your idea may be simply to make money. Or it may be to make an idea you have tangible. Or it may be to create goods that better the world. Regardless, you have a view as to the purpose of business. What your view is and how it fits with what you do is an important issue for you to resolve, especially if you are going to manage others. In Chapter 1, David Warsh looks at how others have decided the issue and points to factors you should consider in determining for yourself what kind of career you will pursue.

Another reason you might choose a business career, and eventually succeed at it, is that you're gifted at managing. Individual performers—pianists, artists, computer wizards, super salespeople—as a rule, are neither interested nor very good at structuring the environment to help others do what they need to do, at organizing how work gets done, or at finding and portioning out resources. Some people are very good at it.

1

Most have some talent but need help in perfecting it. Leonard Schlesinger, in Chapter 2, "How to Think Like an Executive" discusses the point of view a manager should adopt to succeed in today's organizations and outlines the seven tasks a manager must perform. Allan Cohen, in Chapter 3, "Managing People" focuses on an issue that has preoccupied both organizational theorists and practitioners for many years—how to motivate employees to deliver their best.

Finally, once the will and the way are in hand, a manager needs to be able to speak the languages of business. Regardless of how successful a manager is with people, success in the marketplace will come down ultimately to numbers. Are you outperforming your competitors and how can you tell? In Chapter 4, "Quantitative Tools," Brian Forst provides an overview of the tools and the kinds of problems they can help managers solve. In Chapter 5, "Managerial Economics," Frank Lichtenberg explores how the decisions managers make are affected by forces outside their direct control; namely, the microeconomy (the behavior of individuals and industries) and the macroeconomy (the behavior of the economy as a whole, including the global economy).

1 WHAT IS BUSINESS ABOUT?

David Warsh

From the quarterdeck of a newspaper office,° bucking on a sea of constant change, it is amazing to reflect on how quickly fads and fashions about the nature of business come and go. In the 1960s, for example, a career in business was popularly thought to be a bore. In the 1970s, it was seen to be something of an obligation ("Plastics!") or at least a right. In the 1980s, it had an exaggerated reputation as a kind of self-fulfillment, thanks to business poets like George Gilder. And in the 1990s—well, perhaps it is still too early to tell about the 1990s, but the signs are promising. So far, the most striking fad seems to involve something called "management by open book."

Looking back, it is possible to discern a long and orderly tradition of thinking about business—about the business system in general. For more than two centuries, since Adam Smith, some of our deepest thinkers have hashed over the question of how it works and why, and how it *should* work.

All the while, pioneers, magnates, inventors, tycoons, proprietors, entrepreneurs of all sorts have given these professional students plenty to think *about,* producing miracles of organization and innovation faster, often, than they can be cataloged, much less explained.

In the end, practitioners and researchers have achieved a certain degree of consensus that is far more durable the latest management fad. Properly assimilated, made into a part of your mental filing system, their collective wisdom should last a lifetime.

° The author is a business journalist with *The Boston Globe.*

3

For the benefit of the prospective manager, then, herewith a newspaperman's whirlwind tour of respectable thinking about business—from *The Wealth of Nations* to *The Portable MBA*.

ABOUT THIS BUSINESS OF "BUSINESS"

Virtually the entire apparatus for our thinking about business comes from Adam Smith, prices and taxes; the role of capital, labor, know-how and the rent of land; the significance of foreign trade; inflation and unemployment; monopolies and other market failures; consumer sovereignty; the very idea of the economy as a self-ordering system: they are all there. They all receive their clearest early treatment from him.

This great Scottish economist, who lived from 1723 to 1790, learned his trade traveling in England and France as a tutor. He was famously absent-minded, yet his writing is filled with the most penetrating sorts of insights ("People of the same trade seldom meet together, even for merriment and diversion, but the conversation ends in a conspiracy against the public, or in some contrivance to raise prices.") He called his *magnum opus*, "An Inquiry Into the Nature and Causes of the Wealth of Nations" was published the same year as the Declaration of Independence. It still makes great reading.

Smith built his edifice on a foundation of self-interest. "It is not the benevolence of the butcher, or the baker, that we expect our dinner, but from their regard to their own interest. We address ourselves not to their humanity, but to their self-love, and never talk to them of our necessities but of their advantages." Here is the rationale for all business, large and small. "Every man thus lives by exchanging, or becomes in some measure a merchant."

This conviction that people usually can be counted on to do whatever they think is in their self-interest gave rise to Smith's most famous image, that of all the economic agents in the world unknowingly presided over by an "invisible hand" of competition. Each person is driven by the desire to make profits, said Smith; he therefore employs his skills, and his capital, to achieve the highest possible return. This freedom to pick and choose makes a kind of feedback mechanism. If a person charges too much for the work he does, the bread he bakes, the money he lends, others will enter the market and drive prices down toward the cost of production, where no excess profits exist.

In this "system of natural liberty," as Smith called it, capitalists will sniff out new opportunities, channeling investment in labor and lands into areas where their profits are greatest. Consumers, with their dollar "votes," will govern the system as a whole by making their individual choices of what to buy and sell, bidding up prices (and profits) in one area, driving them down in another, while the unwitting capitalist does little more than strive to anticipate or keep up with changing tastes. "He generally, indeed, neither intends to promote the public interest, nor knows how much he is promoting it. . . . He intends only his own gain, and he is in this, as in many other cases, led by an invisible hand to promote an end which was no part of his intention."

In the *Wealth of Nations*, government is to be found at the back of the book. In a section called "Of systems of political Oeconomy," Smith attacks what he labels the "mercantilist" system of heavy government regulation of commerce and trade. In a section called "Of the Revenue of the Sovereign or Commonwealth," he describes in some detail what he considers to be the proper tasks of government—defense, justice, public works like highways and schools—and discusses the various taxes with which we pay for them. Smith was no libertarian; he saw plenty of opportunities for government to improve market processes. But his real enthusiasm was reserved for what we have come to call private enterprise.

This was, after all, the period of the industrial revolution, the "years of miracles" when a wave of continuous improvements in transportation and manufacturing methods swept over England and brought with it a transformation of society from rural to urban. In a much overlooked passage at the front of his book, Smith asserts that "the division of labor is limited by the entent of the market," meaning that specialization and broad markets, low prices and big profits go together hand-in-hand.

Sure enough, canals were making it easier for farmers and manufacturers to send their products to market; power looms and high-tech waterwheels were making it easier to spin cotton into cloth. The Boston merchant Francis Lowell visited Manchester in 1810 and memorized the plans to the Cartwright loom; within a few years the revolution had spread to America.

Yet low prices and high volume were not the only way to make a fortune in the eighteenth century. Smith's friend Josiah Wedgewood did very well out of the pottery and porcelain craze by keeping his prices relatively high. Every new technique, every new design that Wedgewood brought to market was quickly copied by his competitors, and often at prices equal to half his own. Yet Wedgewood was able to establish a worldwide market for his mass-produced wares. How? By advertising. He assiduously positioned himself as supplier to royalty, aristocracy, and beautiful people generally; mass taste followed, as he understood it would.

It was in these years that England became the center of the commercial world. Victory in the Napoleonic Wars insured that the center of finance shifted to London from Amsterdam. Private banks sprouted; merchant bankers flourished, buying "anything, everywhere" that it was good and cheap, and selling it at a profit; investment banks proliferated, selling government debt and speculative railroad bonds.

Then, too, financial journalism got its start in England. The *London Times* appointed its first financial editor in 1817, Thomas Alsager, a business-man with wide interests. His job was to comment on markets, offer advice, criticize the Bank of England. For many years, he was a lone voice warning that the railroad boom was about to collapse. As Richard Fry says, "The Times lost a great deal of advertising revenue but the proprietors were high-minded and Alsager was proved right." A few years later, in 1843, "The Economist" magazine was born.

After Adam Smith, the next voices who gave us concepts with which to analyze what business is about were David Ricardo and Thomas Malthus. Best friends, these two gloomy fellows vied with each other in the years between 1810 and 1820 to predict the bigger disaster in aftermath of the Napoleonic Wars—in Ricardo's case, stagnation arising from the exhaustion of the land; in Malthus' case, overpopulation. Both these thinkers were given to an ambitious (and usually spurious!) precision based on abstract models of the economy, rather than the sort of reasoning from historical example that characterized the approach of Adam Smith.

Eventually this propensity to reduce matters to the simplest underlying mechanisms imaginable became known as the Ricardian Vice. Indeed, it was preoccupation with Ricardo's "law of diminishing returns"—that is, with the gradual exhaustion of opportunities of all sorts—that led economics to be la-beled in the 1840s "the dismal science." A growing band of professional stu-dents of the economy gathered round, determined to make a science of their subject. But anybody who had a view was entitled to his or her opinion.

And so for a few happy decades in the nineteenth century, business, finance, financial journalism and economics were Shavian worlds, accessible to all.

MARGINALISM AND VALUE

The next big thing that happened to economics was a movement called "marginalism." It unfolded beginning in England and Europe in the 1870s and reached its flood tide in America around the turn of the century. The prestige of physical science was at its height, but as much as anything, marginalism can be understood as a reaction to Karl Marx, who for the 20 years before, returned to the sort of story-telling style of Adam Smith in order to paint economics as a kind of ideology, nothing more.

By ignoring markets, Marx guaranteed his analysis eventually would collapse; too bad that it took 125 years. But his aggressive attack on economics from the outside did contain many tantalizing glimpses of a deep truth: in particular, that changing technology had much to do with both economic growth and people's experience of it. And Marx did spur economists to try harder to understand how their markets worked. The main result was marginalism.

Why were pearls expensive and water cheap? Thinking systematically about this problem of "value" had preoccupied economists for 100 years. By 1870, they knew a lot about the costs of production and what they called "the labor theory of value," that is, about the rough determinants of the supply of goods and services in the economy. But something crucial was missing from their cogitations. With marginalism economists finally began incorporating the idea of demand in their analysis.

Value became a subjective, interpersonal thing. No longer did economists think that pearls were valuable simply because men dived for them; rather, men dived for them because pearls were thought to be valuable. Economists formalized this intuition of a vast, interdependent world of bid and offer by employing the concept of utility, or satisfaction, which all economic actors were seeking to maximize; the principle that equal extra (or marginal) increments of utility-producing means (a glass of beer, a stream of dividends, another book) produce diminishing increments of satisfaction gave them a basis for representing the economic activity of all of society in great long systems of equations—"mathematical psychics." And the shared conviction that this was the proper path to a truly scientific economics in turn slowly led to the excommunication of businesspersons from the circles of professional economists (though social scientists with an explicit religious sensibility were the first to go).

Businessmen didn't care. They were having the time of their lives making the modern world. Sometime during the decade of the 1840s, the global capitalist system had taken off, spurred, as much as anything, by advances in ocean-shipping; by the 1870s it was in high gear. In the United States, Jay Gould was attempting to corner the telegraph system. Cyrus McCormack was inventing the power reaper, Alexander Graham Bell the telephone, Thomas Edison the electric system.

But invention was no sure passport to wealth and power; Andrew Carnegie introduced the Bessemer and open-hearth methods to steelmaking only after his rivals had proved them more efficient, and John D. Rockefeller built his Standard Oil Trust through shrewd monopolistic practices. Fortunes were as various as the entrepreneurs who make them. In time, the great Victorian economist Alfred Marshall would describe supply and demand as operating like the twin blades of a scissors, with price determined at their intersection. It was a truth any businessman might recognize in his bones, but it was hardly necessary to know more.

There is a somewhat embarrassing distinction between theory and practice. It is a truism among historians of science that thermodynamics learned a lot more from the steam engine than the steam engine ever learned from thermodynamics. Steam engines were powering river steamers, cross-country locomotives and high-powered pumps long before Sadi Carnot and James Joule got into the disagreement about limits to engines' efficiency that led to the two great laws of thermodynamics. Practitioners are often miles ahead of the scientists who come along afterwards to articulate the general principles that underlie the tinkerers' successes.

It seems safe to say that once an area of investigation is identified as promising, the scientists eventually catch up; chemists, after all, were the brains behind the explosion of possibilities in dyestuffs, petrochemicals, and pharmaceuticals after 1900; university departments of aeronautical engineering took over from the heirs of the Wright brothers when it was time to go to the moon; physicists and electrical engineers in the 1930s finally went far beyond what even the most gifted electronic experimentalist was able to produce at his bench. It was theoretical understanding, not accidental discovery, that led to the creation of the atom bomb, the semiconductor, the laser. In field after field, theory has become indispensable to practice.

No practical person will linger long wishing that he had been born at a time when his business were no longer an art but a science, however. Business leaders of the late nineteenth and early twentieth centuries roared ahead, while reformers reformed and economists studied. Henry Ford raised the assembly line to a new level of sophistication and made the automobile a central element in American life. J. P. Morgan himself acted as a central bank until the Congress authorized the creation of the Federal Reserve Board to coordinate banking policy and serve as lender of last resort. Pierre DuPont, finding himself owning both the family chemical business and, after a fortuitous investment, a controlling interest in General Motors Co., invented the modern managerial corporation, with its characteristic departments reporting to an executive committee.

As the complexity of business grew, so did the sense that additional skills were necessary to manage modern enterprises. Hence the demand for business education. Joseph Wharton opened his school in conjunction with the University of Pennsylvania in 1881 for the express purposes of educating the children of the well-to-do to carry on their family businesses. When the Harvard Business School was founded 25 years later, it borrowed heavily from the pedagogy of Harvard's Law School, in an effort to make its curriculum appear to be as serious as possible. Emphasis was placed on case studies and practical knowledge of disciplines such as accounting, finance, and marketing.

Moreover, the new century brought a fresh spurt of development for the business press. The financial commentators of daily newspapers had long been stars in their own right; finally one of them, B. C. Forbes, quit the *New York Tribune* in 1917 to start a magazine of his own. He brashly capitalized his own name, and his habit of showing up for interviews wearing striped trousers and morning coat endeared him to the big businessmen he sought as readers and advertisers.

Forbes' remarkable success in the long boom of the 1920s led Henry Luce to launch *Fortune,* and the McGraw brothers to launch *Business Week*—both just in time for the depths of the Great Depression. Together with older competitors like *The Wall Street Journal* and *Barron's,* the business magazines became important contributors to the formation of respectable opinion about business.

The arrival of the Great Depression brought a raft of questions of the most fundamental sort. Did the economists know what they were talking about? Were the business schools really only servants of the ruling class? What about the successes of the Russian Revolution? Was it possible to manage a nation like the Soviet Union as though it were a single enormous firm? In the early 1930s, there were a cacophony of contending voices speaking to this question. One voice eventually rose above the rest, that of an English economist named John Maynard Keynes.

THE KEYNESIAN REVOLUTION

It was World War II that untangled the problem of the Great Depression, and put workers in every corner of the globe back to work. It was only afterwards that the great public relations battles took place with respect to what actually had happened during the 1930s. The first of these was the Keynesian Revolution. The second, more decisive campaign went barely noticed. It had to do with the further formalization of economics.

The 1920s and 1930s had seen a big economic migration to America. Continental scientists in touch with the latest probability techniques in the physical sciences sought refuge in American universities, bringing with them Continental ambitions for a more intellectually ambitious and logically correct economics. It was to be a "general equilibrium" approach, in their parlance, in which changes were to be traced through to their farthest-flung (and often least-anticipated) effects, as opposed to the rough-and-ready "partial equilibrium" approach favored by British economists and their American cousins, which was sometimes described as being the method of "one thing at a time."

These teachers mixed with the brilliant kids who, in their twenties, were reading Keynes' 1936 manifesto, "The General Theory of Employment, Interest, and Money" with its "over-saving" explanation of the severity of the Great

Depression powerful case for government responsibility for the management of the economy as a whole, to make an exciting intellectual revolution. The dogma of laissez-faire was in a few years nearly completely overturned. Together in Chicago during World War II, where a key group of economists worked together on war-related tasks, the young Keynesians cooked up a recipe for post-war policy designed to forestall the sorts of Depression that had followed the end of World War I and that had plagued the 1930s. When the war ended, this "new economics" was ready to pop out of the oven.

Ahead lay the 1950s, an era of unrivaled growth and prosperity. Much of the rest of the world lay in ruins. The United States led a new wave of internationalization of business, sponsoring through the Marshall plan the "German miracle," through General Douglas MacArthur's occupation, the much less-noticed "Japanese miracle" as well. Both were designed to forestall communism. The Russian and, soon-to-be, the Chinese specter, remained powerful spurs to enterprise, giving the American economy a competitive big kick. President Dwight Eisenhower resolved to spend $90 billion to build the interstate highway system—a fortune in those days, nearly 20 times the annual revenues of the Big Three automakers. Quite aside from its military might, to the rest of the world, America was oil companies, steelmakers, chemical concerns, and heavy manufacturers of all sorts.

It was with the election of John F. Kennedy that the New Economics really triumphed. Kennedy brought to Washington men like MIT's Paul Samuelson and Robert Solow and Yale's James Tobin. He was the first to actively embrace Keynesian "demand management" techniques to try to manipulate the business cycle—including the famous stimulative tax cuts that were enacted in the year after his death. Kennedy might have had a kitchen cabinet of business folk to whom he turned for advice, but he kept them out of sight. It was economists who were out front, leading the way. Indeed, today it is often noted that Japan's economic success has been inversely proportional to the influence of its economists; then, there were only a few troubling portents, as when Kennedy collided with US Steel's Roger Blough when the nation's foremost steelmaker decided to put up prices. "My father always told me that businessmen were SOBs," Kennedy was overheard to say.

Just as Kennedy's administration showcased the economists, so the war in Vietnam brought to national prominence for the first time the MBA degree. Robert McNamara, Harvard Business School class of 1939, was Kennedy's Secretary of Defense. He had won his spurs as one of the World War II "whiz kids" at the Army Air Corps Statistical Control Branch, presiding over a corps of 3,000 Harvard Business School-trained procurement officers by V-J Day. The same faith in measurement and analysis carried him to the top at Ford Motor Co., then over the top in Vietnam. McNamara symbolized the mystique of corporate management, which had been celebrated in influential books about the business culture by Peter Drucker (*The Concept of the Corporation*) and John Kenneth Galbraith (*The New Industrial State*). His defeat by the tenacious Vietnamese was the first faint foreshadowing of the age to come. But thanks at least in part to McNamara's reputation as a managerial wizard, enrollments in business schools boomed.

Some time in the late 1950s, for reasons that are still unclear, all this began to come apart. The economy began to overheat after its eight-year boom, and the Vietnam War came to be seen as lost. The American government lost its resolve in its responsibilities to the international currency system, not maintaining the convertability of dollars to gold. On Wall Street, the late 1960s came to be known as "the go-go years"; their emblematic figure was off-shore mutual fund swindler Bernie Cornfeld, who would begin his pitch to his unsophisticated victims, "Do you sincerely want to be rich?" What in those days was a business for? To many of those who were caught in this first wave of post-war merge mania in the late 1960s, the answer was painfully obvious. It existed to be bought and sold. *Welcome To Our Conglomerate, You're Fired!* was the title of a best-selling book.

ACQUISITIONS AND TAKEOVERS

During the 1970s, the world of business experienced something of a crisis; so did the world of economics. If anything, the crisis of economics was more acute.

Corporations began the 1970s with a reputation for invincibility. Harold Geneen, among other things as a graduate of the advanced management program at the Harvard Business School, replaced Robert McNamara as the world's most famous MBA. The slightly sinister-seeming genius who had put International Telephone & Telegraph together in an endless series of acquisitions, was rumored to travel nowhere unless accompanied by whole trunks of data. Geneen made a fetish of "managing by the numbers," ruthlessly buying and selling companies on the basis of their quarterly earnings.

Another central focus of the "planning" movement in the 1970s was General Electric (GE) Co. This blue-chip conglomerate, the direct descendant of the companies of Thomas Edison, in the 1950s had a famous strategic planning department where economists and MBAs came and went, promulgating semi-secret doctrines whereby great corporations were expected to be managed. GE chief executives enjoyed their reputation as among the most sagacious business statesmen. Even the corporate pitchman, the veteran actor Ronald Reagan, had possessed a certain unusual appeal. (When Reagan began to get politically active in the early 1960s, however, GE fired him.) Royal Dutch Shell, with its "scenario planning" methods of peering into the future, was another example of this supposed corporate superiority; its intellectual technology had permitted it to prepare for the new world in which the Organization of Petroleum Exporting Countries (OPEC) reigned capriciously over all the rest.

But no citizen of the business world exemplified the 1970s better than the little strategy boutiques that had begun to spring up to capitalize on various fads that were sweeping out of the business schools like storms from the high plains of Canada: management by objective, portfolio matrix management, scenario planning, zero-based budgeting, and so on. The most famous of these was the Boston Consulting Group, with its two-by-two growth share matrix in which the universe of business possibilities was divided into cash-cows, dogs, stars, and wildcats. Year after year in the 1970s, BCG's Bruce Henderson hired the top-ranking graduates of the top-most business schools and sent them out into the world to preach a simple-minded relationship between market share and profitability. (Twenty years later, Scott Armstrong of the University of Pennsylvania's Wharton School would run a complicated intellectual experiment on a sampling of MBAs who had mastered the BCG matrix. Given a choice among competing possibilities, of those who actually *used* the matrix in their analysis, 87 percent chose the less profitable investment.)

NEW GROWTH ECONOMICS

Then at the end of the 1970s, everything in the firmament of business somehow changed: Margaret Thatcher, Ronald Reagan, Paul Volcker, Lech Walesa, and others. One moment eco-pundit Robert Heilbroner was confidently predicting that socialism lay just around the corner. The next, a decisive "turn to the right" had begun, toward markets and democracy and away from hierarchies and planning. Nor was it just in the West that this evolution took place: China began sending its best and brightest to earn Ph.D.s in economics and MBAs; so did Mexico, Mongolia, India, and eventually, even Russia.

In a way, you could say that the 1980s was about the rediscovery of Adam Smith, by best-selling writers as disparate as George Gilder (*Wealth and Poverty*), Tom Wolfe (*Bonfire of the Vanities*), and Michael Porter (*Strategy and Competition*). The reputation of the author of *The Wealth of Nations* even staged a come-back in technical economics, where a "new growth" economics concerned with the determinants of technical change emerged to elbow aside the old Keynesian preoccupation with "demand management" of the business cycle.

It was in these years that the popularity of the MBA degree surged. Universities churned them out in increasing numbers. *Business Week* began its famous survey of the reputations of various schools. Europe, which had assimilated the practice of management education from the Americans after World War II, accelerated its acceptance of the custom. Even Oxford and Cambridge started MBA programs.

Moreover, an apparent revolution in finance, emanating from the business schools and propagated by commercial and investment banks, resulted in the creation of enormous "risk markets" in Chicago and around the world. These markets for future, options, swaps, and the like—derivatives, as they are known, in contrast to the securities on which their markets are based—soon spread until they reached into every nook and cranny of the world of Big Business—and therefore to the world of government, too. All that money being made (and lost) was the strongest evidence yet that finally there was something of practical value to be learned in the nation's business schools and economics departments.

Meanwhile, the 1980s also saw the rise of a whole new universe of electronic and electronically based media. No longer was business and finance the province solely of *The Wall Street Journal;* indeed, if anything, the *London Financial Times* threatened to knock it off its perch, by managing to be a dependable step quicker to report the most important news affecting world markets. A bond trader from Solomon Brothers turned a bond price-quoting machine ("the Bloomburg box") into the world's fastest-growing wire service. And an old news service, Reuters, became the world's biggest purveyor of electronic markets, by dint of a superior understanding of the possibilities of the new computers. Bright young kids armed with masters degrees from the London School of Economics are the new pundits, publishing their analyses on computer money market wires.

Most telling, perhaps, was the rise of the little guy. The world of business was no longer seen as the exclusive preserve of a relative handful of giant corporations. The entrepreneur was once again seen to be the agent of economic change. Again and again were told the stories of how young Bill Gates of Microsoft bested IBM Corp., of how Craig McCaw outwitted not only AT&T with cellular phones, but also humbled the Baby Bells; of how the tabloid king Rupert Murdoch brought the television networks to their knees. The freedom of smaller entrepreneurs to undertake great tasks was celebrated, too. Perhaps there is no more telling observation to be made about the 1980s than to note that one of the more intelligent and successful magazines in America during those years—*Inc.,* for the successful small-business entrepreneur—was written by a cadre of staffers many of whom had spent their college days in the 1960s as members of Students for a Democratic Society. Even Harold Geneen, whose fabled IT&T had been just another casualty of miscalculation on the corporate battlefield during the 1980s, returned to prominence at the age of 80, reincarnated as—what else?—the owner of a small business. What else is there to be said about the power of Adam Smith's invisible hand?

THE PRESENT DAY

What goes on today in business schools? Plenty! The research apparatus is simply enormous. Professors are researching every conceivable topic. To be sure, some are spouting a lot of hyperconfident nonsense. But the baseline of knowledge continues to accumulate. And here and there is discovered a grain of substantially new truth.

After 200 years of serious thinking about the business system, there is no doubt whatsoever that we possess much knowledge about how it works that is both dependable and valuable. As the editors note in the introduction, what *The New Portable MBA* has tried to capture in a practical way is that evolving knowledge about the business system.

HOW TO THINK LIKE AN EXECUTIVE: THE ART OF MANAGING FOR THE LONG RUN

2

Leonard A. Schlesinger

Effective management is much more than the production of immediate results. Effective management includes creating the potential for achieving good results over the long run. The manager who as president of a company produces spectacular results for a 3- to 10-year period can hardly be considered effective if, concurrently, he or she allows plant and equipment to deteriorate, creates an alienated or militant workforce, lets the company develop a bad name in the marketplace, and ignores new product development.

Dealing with current or impending problems is a key reality of managerial behavior in almost all modern organizations. Coping with complexities associated with today and the immediate future absorbs the vast majority of time and energy for most managers. This chapter sets the stage for the rest of the book by placing management in a longer time frame. How do managers develop their organizations to assure the potential for facilitating organizational effectiveness in the long run?

THE LONG RUN

Most managers will readily admit that their ability to predict their company's future is limited. Indeed, with the possible exceptions of death and taxes, the only thing entirely predictable is that things will change. Even for the most bureaucratic company in the most mature and stable environment, change is inevitable.

Over a period of 20 years, it is possible for a company, even one that is not growing, to experience numerous changes—in its business, product markets, competition, government regulations, available technologies, labor markets—and its own business strategy. These changes are the inevitable products of its interaction with a world that is not static.

Growing organizations tend to experience even more business-related changes over a long period of time. Studies have shown that growing businesses not only increase the volume of the products or services they provide but also tend to increase the complexity of their products or services, their forward or backward integration, their rate of product innovation, the geographic scope of their operations, the number and character of their distribution channels, and the number and diversity of their customer groups. While all this growth-driven change is occurring, competitive and other external pressures also increase. The more rapid the growth, the more extensive the changes that are experienced.

These types of business changes generally require organizational adjustments. For example, if a company's labor markets change over time, it must alter its selection criteria and make other adjustments to fit the new type of employee. New competitors might emerge with new products, thus requiring renewed product development efforts and a new organizational design to support that effort. In a growing company, business changes tend to require major shifts periodically in all aspects of its organization (see Tables 2-1 and 2-2).

The inability of an organization to anticipate the need for change and to adjust effectively to changes in its business or in its organization causes problems. These problems sometimes take the form of poor collaboration and coordination; they may involve high turnover or low morale. Always, however, such problems affect the organization's performance—goals are not achieved and/or resources are wasted.

Because change is inevitable and because it can so easily produce problems for companies, the key characteristic of an effective organization from a long-run viewpoint is its ability to anticipate needed organizational changes and to adapt as business conditions change. Anticipatory skills can help prevent the resource drain caused by organizational problems, while adaptability helps an organization avoid the problems that change can produce. Over long periods, this ability to avoid an important and recurring resource drain can mark the difference between success and failure for an organization.

A CASE OF ORGANIZATIONAL DECLINE

To fully appreciate the importance of anticipatory skills and adaptability in the long run, consider this somewhat extreme case. The company involved was founded in the late 1940s, primarily through acquisitions. It was created as the response of an entrepreneur to a variety of changing market conditions. Over a

TABLE 2-1   Greiner's summary of required changes in organization practices during evolution in the five phases of growth

Category	Phase 1	Phase 2	Phase 3	Phase 4	Phase 5
Management focus	Make and sell	Efficiency of operations	Expansion of market	Consolidation of organization	Problem solving and innovation
Organization structure	Informal	Centralized and functional	Decentralized and geographic	Line-staff and product groups	Matrix of teams
Top management style	Individualistic and entrepreneurial	Directive	Delegative	Watchdog	Participative
Control system	Market results	Standards and cost centers	Reports and profit centers	Plans and investment centers	Mutual goal setting
Management reward emphasis	Ownership	Salary and merit increases	Individual bonus	Profit sharing and stock options	Team bonus

Source: Larry E. Greiner, "Evolution and Revolution as Organizations Grow," *Harvard Business Review*, July–August 1972, p. 45.

TABLE 2-2 Summary of changes during three stages of organizational development

Company Characteristics	Stage I	Stage II	Stage III
The Business:			
1. Product	Single product or single line	Single product line	Multiple product lines
2. Distribution	One channel or set of channels	One set of channels	Multiple channels
3. R&D	Not institutionalized—oriented by owner-manager	Increasingly institutionalized search for product or process developments	Institutionalized search for *new* products as well as for improvements
4. Strategic choices	Needs of owner vs. needs of firm	Degree of integration. Market share objective. Breadth of product line.	Entry and exit from industries. Allocation of resources by industry Rate of growth
The Organization:			
1. Organization structure	Little or no formal structure—"one man show"	Specialization based on function	Specialization based on product/market relationship
2. Product/service transactions	Not available	Integrated pattern of transactions: A→B→C→Market	Not integrated: A B C ↓ ↓ ↓ Market
3. Performance measurement	By personal contact and subjective criteria	Increasingly impersonal, using technical and/or cost criteria	Increasingly impersonal, using *market* criteria (return on investment and market share)
4. Rewards	Unsystematic and often paternalistic	Increasingly systematic with emphasis on stability and service	Increasingly systematic, with variability related to performance
5. Control system	Personal control of both strategic and operating decisions	Personal control of strategic decisions, with increasing delegation of operating decisions based on control by policies	Delegation of product/market decisions within existing businesses, with indirect control based on analysis of "results"

Source: Adapted from Bruce Scott, "Stages of Corporate Development," Boston: *HBS Case Services*, 1971.

5- to 10-year period, he established an enormously successful venture. In its market, it became the largest and most profitable organization of its kind.

Historical records do not reveal how much, if anything, the entrepreneur did to develop the company's long-run organizational adaptability. Two facts, however, are known. First, the ongoing operations were so profitable that he submitted to the demands of the national union just to avoid a disruption of operations. This resulted in the establishment of innumerable "work rules" and the entry of first-line supervisors into the union. Second, he did almost nothing to bring in or develop mid- or top-level managers. As an extremely talented person capable of making a large number of effective business decisions himself, he saw no need for assistance from others.

In the mid-1960s, the entrepreneur died. His brother took over as president and tried to maintain the company's existing policies and profitability. For the first few years of his tenure, everything seemed to work well.

However, the company's industry, like many others, began to undergo significant changes. These changes occurred gradually but continuously over at least a 10-year period. During this time, the company made very few organizational adjustments to adapt to these changes, for a number of reasons. First, the few people who had any real decision-making authority in the company did not seem to see a need for many changes. They simply did not have the information that would have shown them what was happening in their industry and in their market area. Second, when they did have information on the changes that were occurring, they had difficulty deciding how to adjust to them. They were, for example, completely unaware of the typical development sequences shown in Tables 2-1 and 2-2. The intuitively brilliant leadership supplied by the original entrepreneur was gone, and nothing had taken its place. Finally, when they did identify a change and saw what response was needed, the managers were generally unable to implement it. For one thing, union rules prohibited a great deal of change; for another, there was no middle management to help them implement it. The firm was not at all flexible.

Some of the company's competitors were successful in identifying and reacting to the industry and market changes. As a result, the rate of increase of this company's sales and profits began to decrease. At the same time, problems with employees and the union began to surface.

The company's president initially focused his efforts on trying to stop the profit decline. In this endeavor, he was somewhat successful, yet in slowing the profit decline, he was forced to hold salaries and maintenance budgets down, thereby adding to the problems with his employees and the union. A climate of antagonism and distrust developed.

Between 1976 and 1985, the company's real (noninflated) annual growth in sales declined from 5 to 0 percent. Its profits leveled out and then fell to a net loss in 1985. By that time, the company's stock price was so low that a larger corporation successfully acquired a controlling interest. This corporation brought in its own top management group (which included a number of extremely successful managers) and predicted a quick turnaround.

The company resumed profitable operations in 1989 and, with the exception of one year, has remained profitable to this time. Nevertheless, its profitability levels remain below the industry average, and its 1993 sales were, in real dollars, about the same as in 1985. It has gone through two more presidents since 1985, and the current one has been quoted in the business press as saying that the job of organizational "renewal" that is ahead of them remains extensive.

CHARACTERISTICS OF AN EFFECTIVE ORGANIZATION—FROM A LONG-RUN POINT OF VIEW

It is possible to infer the characteristics that contribute to long-run effectiveness by looking for what was missing in the previous example. The picture that emerges is one of an organization where (1) changes in its business are anticipated or quickly identified, (2) appropriate responses are quickly designed, and (3) the responses are implemented at a minimum cost. This behavior would be possible because the company is staffed with talented managers who are skilled at organizational analysis, as well as having relatively adaptable employees. Informal relations among these people would be characterized by trust, open communications, and respect for others' opinions. The formal design would include effective integrating devices, sensitive and well-designed measurement systems, reward systems that encourage adaptability, and selection and development systems that help support all other characteristics (see Table 2-3).

Unlike the declining company described earlier, an organization with the characteristics listed in Table 2-3, as well as other characteristics that specifically fit its current business, could successfully respond to growth, industry changes, top management turnover, and virtually anything else that came its way. Its adaptability would allow it to continue changing the organization to fit its changing business, and it would survive and even prosper over long periods.

BUREAUCRATIC DRY ROT

Very few companies or nonprofit businesses have organizations with characteristics even close to those described in Table 2-3. This fact has been emphasized by a number of social scientists who, in the past decade, have expressed serious concern over what they call *bureaucratic dry rot*. We all pay a heavy price, they

**TABLE 2-3   Characteristics of a highly effective organization:
A long-run point of view**

Employees:

1. The company is staffed with more than enough managerial talent.
2. Managers are skilled at organizational analysis and understand typical stages of organizational development.
3. A large number of employees are relatively adaptive and have skills beyond a narrow specialty.
4. Employees have realistic expectations about what they will get from, and have to give to, the company in the foreseeable future.

Informal Relations:

1. There is a high level of trust between employees and management.
2. Information flows freely, with a minimum of distortion within and across groups.
3. People in all positions of responsibility are willing to listen to, and be influenced by, others who might have relevant information.

Formal Design:

1. The organizational structure includes more than enough effective integrating mechanisms for the current situation and relies minimally on rules and procedures.
2. Measurement systems thoroughly collect and distribute all relevant data on the organization's environment, its actions, its performance, and changes in any of these factors.
3. Reward systems encourage people to identify needed changes and help implement them.
4. Selection and development systems are designed to create highly skilled managerial and employee groups and to encourage the kinds of informal relations described above.

note, for the large, bureaucratic, nonadaptive organizations that are insensitive to employees' needs, ignore consumers' desires, and refuse to accept their social responsibilities.

Existing evidence suggests that although most contemporary organizations cannot be described as adaptive, many managers nevertheless appreciate the benefits of adaptability. When polled, managers often respond that "ideally" they would like to have the kind of organization suggested by Table 2-3, but they also admit that their current organization does not have all or even some of these characteristics.

At least five reasons account for the inflexibility and shortsightedness of most contemporary organizations. The first and most significant is related to resources. Creating a highly adaptive organization requires time, energy, and money. In the case of the company that went into decline, creating an adaptive organization early in its history might have required:

- Hiring, assimilating, and training a management team, both at the top and in mid-level ranks.

- Selecting and training all other personnel.
- Concentrating efforts from the managers to develop integrative devices, measurement systems, and the like.
- Developing and maintaining good, informal relationships among managers and their employees.

The organization may not have had the resources to invest in these systems. Had it tried, the company might have been compelled to divert resources from some of its current operations. If its competitors did not choose to follow its lead but continued to invest as heavily as possible in current operations, perhaps the company would have lost market share and income and even gone out of business long before it could enjoy the benefits of its long-term investment in adaptability.

A second reason for the nonadaptive and bureaucratic behavior of modern organizations is that their managers are not very skilled at producing the characteristics of an effective organization in the long run. Organizations generally invest resources in current operations and not in producing adaptive human systems. The on-the-job education of managers is usually focused on current operations, not on producing adaptability. Generating the characteristics shown in Table 2-3 requires skills that have to be developed and nurtured.

Still a third reason for the inflexibility of many contemporary organizations is that some people clearly benefit from a static situation. The entrepreneur who established the nonadaptive organization described earlier thoroughly enjoyed the way he ran the company. It is doubtful that he would have invested resources in developing a management team, or developed one even had it cost him nothing. Furthermore, financial backers approved of how he ran the business, which included passing on a large share of the firm's earnings in dividends. Had he tried to cut the dividends to invest more in something as intangible as adaptability, they undoubtedly would have protested.

A fourth reason for nonadaptive behavior also is evident in the case of decline. Once an organization reaches a certain size, if it has not developed a certain minimally adaptive human organization, it becomes very difficult to turn things around without a gigantic infusion of resources. Considerable effort is required simply to overcome the "organizational entropy" that makes the organization even more nonadaptive and rigid.

A fifth reason more companies do not have organizational characteristics like those in Table 2-3 is their management's decision that such characteristics are unnecessary. Based on their projection of what the future has in store for their company, management estimates how much adaptability they will need and then invests their resources to produce only that level of adaptability. If the company is growing very quickly or if it is in a volatile market and management expects rapid changes to continue in their business, they would invest considerable resources in creating an adaptive human organization. However, if the company is not growing, if it is in a stable market, and if management feels the future will not demand many changes of them, they generally invest relatively few resources.

In short, the forces that prevent organizations from developing a high level of adaptability are strong. The forces that can push successful organizations into decline are numerous as well. As a result, one of the most difficult of all management tasks involves developing an organization that has *enough* adaptability to promote effectiveness in the long run.

SEVEN TASKS OF THE MANAGER WHO MANAGES FOR THE LONG RUN

If a manager's goal is to create a lasting, high-performance company, focusing on the seven key tasks that constitute the "basics" of the manager's job in any company is one way to achieve that elusive goal. These seven basic tasks cut across the issues raised in all the chapters in this book and include (1) building a positive work environment, (2) establishing strategic direction, (3) allocating and marshalling resources, (4) upgrading the quality of management, (5) organizing effort, and (6) creating excellence in operations and execution, and (7) maintaining a broad perspective.

Nothing should be surprising about this list; the fundamentals of the job should sound familiar. What makes it important is that it cuts the job down to size. The vast majority of the activities that managers perform in any situation can be grouped into these headings. The tasks help a manager define the scope of the job, set priorities, and see important interrelationships among the six areas.

Task 1: Building a Positive Work Environment

Every company has a particular work environment that dictates to a considerable degree how its managers respond to problems and opportunities.

A company's work environment is partly a heritage of its past leaders. However, shaping that environment is a critically important part of every incumbent manager's job, regardless of what he or she inherits from the past. This includes small companies, medium-size ones, and giants like General Motors and General Electric. Over time, most managers exert influence on their work environment by taking three types of actions: (1) establishing goals and performance standards, (2) establishing values for the organization, and (3) establishing business and people concepts that are consistent with their goals and values.

The basic goals of the company provide a unifying force to channel efforts in chosen directions and to elevate performance standards. Individually, they provide direction in selected areas. Collectively, they influence the way people act in a company. Specific, action-oriented goals describe an aggressive and demanding work environment and influence the way people respond to strategic opportunities and business problems within the company. Conversely, a company with no specific goals or vague or undemanding ones is much more likely to drift, be bureaucratic, or tolerate unexciting results.

Successful managers typically set high standards across the whole business. High standards are reflected in many ways, including (1) the relative quality of the company's functional strategies and its market leadership; (2) the detailed end results that are sought and achieved, as compared with relevant competitors; (3) the quality of written plans and oral presentations that people make, both in terms of substance and style; (4) the relative quality of managers at all levels; (5) rising productivity in all functions of the business, particularly as compared with major competitors; and (6) consistent product quality and reliability.

Values reflect the relative concern that an organization has for its employees, customers, investors, suppliers, and other stakeholders. Values help define not only the manner in which business will be conducted (how these stakeholders will be treated), but the types of business in which an organization will engage. The "fit" between an individual and an organization is often determined by these values.

Business concepts reflect an organization's values, such as (1) the kinds of products or services the business will offer; (2) the company's position or role in its industry; and (3) structural devices, including levels of organization, methods of communication, and planning processes to be employed in conducting business.

Policies that support such values include (1) the stress on internal growth from operations; (2) emphasis on hiring from within; (3) the way performance is judged and rewarded; (4) emphasis on fairness in dealing with people; and (5) the importance of candor, integrity, and high ethical standards in relationships.

In any organization, the manager's personal style influences associates for better or worse. If the manager insists on long memos or frequent meetings, these usually will be the order of the day throughout the organization. A "hands-on" style will be widely copied. The cost-conscious manager results in cost consciousness throughout much of the organization. If the manager favors complex systems, this too will usually have a "ripple" effect throughout the company. Other managers take their cues from the manner in which their manager responds to others' successes or failures.

The manager's style influences the ethical tone of the business. The manager's actions tell associates far more than words. A manager who lacks integrity, fairness, or a sense of commitment quickly creates confusion and cynicism in the organization. Conversely, managers who set high standards in these areas usually find their associates following their lead. The importance of consistency between what general managers say and how they act in creating a sound working environment hardly can be overstated.

Managers can be most effective if they have an all-encompassing theme for the working environment. The theme can range from converting a slow-moving company into a dynamic business to becoming our industry's innovative merchandising leader to becoming a blue chip company. Successful leaders frequently use such broad themes to help focus the working environment on one overriding purpose.

Task 2: Establishing Strategic Direction

Whether the manager is the main architect of the company's strategy, he or she is responsible for ensuring that a process is in place for strategic planning. There is no universally accepted definition of what constitutes a good strategy. Some companies make elaborate efforts to spell out what they mean by a strategy; in others, the strategy consists largely of ideas contained in the manager's head. In any case, the manager is the executive who must decide whether or not the business will be run on the basis of an explicit, formalized strategy and, if so, the process to be employed in developing, reviewing, and implementing it.

A commonly accepted framework for strategy formulation and appraisal highlights the following elements: (1) the task, including the environment and concept of the business, its definition, mission, competitive position, and functional goals and efforts; (2) available resources including leadership, human, financial, technological, customer franchise, stakeholder relationships, and working environment; and (3) structure including organization, controls, systems, standards, rewards, policies, processes, and values.

A starting point in the process of strategy formulation and appraisal is an understanding of the task facing the business. Devices such as Michael Porter's "five forces analysis" can be useful here. Just as important is an understanding on the part of the manager of the way a business runs and the important factors in its success or failure. An *operational* understanding of the business is critical.

Managers typically face several issues in organizing people's efforts to develop and review strategy including (1) those who will be directly involved and in what role; (2) the format of the plans; (3) the mechanisms needed to gain input, understanding, and commitment of key managers as plans evolve; (4) the nature of the review and approval process; and (5) the manager's individual role in the process.

During the process of strategy formulation and review, the manager is faced with a sequence of important decisions that determine the effectiveness of the strategy. Successful strategies usually start with good ideas and evolve over time as they are exposed to the realities of the market place.

The scarce resource in strategy development often is bold, innovative ideas, those that provide a new vision for the business rather than a slight alteration of existing strategy. Hence, managers must stimulate everyone, including themselves, to think creatively and to be willing to consider fresh approaches. This is true whether the manager does most of the thinking personally or serves more as the prime mover for the process.

Task 3: Allocating and Marshalling Resources

Successful strategies require resources to convert them into reality (including both "hard" resources such as cash, plant and equipment, and offices, and "soft" resources such as people and technology).

The manager's unique role in resource allocation stems from three distinctive features of the job. First, the manager is the only person who can commit resources across the entire business. Since nearly every major strategy entails cross-functional commitments, the manager is normally the only executive empowered to make these commitments.

Second, the manager must be the chief decision maker of trade-offs among key projects and functions competing for limited resources. Since most businesses lack the resources to do everything that is proposed, this is usually a major responsibility.

Third, once a decision is made to pursue a strategy, the manager assumes the responsibility for marshalling the resources needed to ensure success.

Marshalling resources often involves the manager in a series of negotiations with external entities (financial institutions, major investors, government agencies, and labor unions) as well as internal constituents.

While strategy decisions have an important influence on resource allocations, managers also routinely allocate resources to operate the business. It is important for a manager to be sure that both kinds of resources—strategic and operational—are productively employed.

Task 4: Upgrading the Quality of Management

Many managers contend that the selection, development, and deployment of people are the most important responsibilities. They also feel it is a satisfying part of the job to see managers grow and the organization strengthen as a result of their efforts. Managers who attach a high priority to this activity usually find their associates do also.

In addition, most skillful managers personally involve themselves in (1) defining and supervising the process for selecting and developing the company's senior and upper-middle management (such as stressing individual evaluations and development assignments), (2) seeing that each function periodically analyzes its skill requirements and people needs and has a strategy to fill those needs, (3) setting job requirement standards (at least at top levels), (4) making sure that outstanding managers have challenging, timely development assignments that effectively utilize their talents, (5) ensuring that compensation programs are both competitive and rewarding for managers who meet assigned goals, and (6) making sure that entry-level management jobs are sufficiently challenging to attract the best people.

Task 5: Organizing Effort

Because of their cross-functional responsibilities, managers normally play a dominant role in designing the company's organization. This function usually includes three important activities:

1. *Defining the organizational concepts for the company.* This means deciding (in light of the company's competitive and general environment) the appropriate level in the organization at which important business decisions should be made, how tightly or loosely controlled the business will be operated, and the role that measurements, controls, and policies play in running the business.

2. *Deciding on the organization structure at the top.* Important questions to be addressed here include, What is expected of each key functional area? Where does it report? What subunits will it contain? How will each function work together? What are the necessary line and staff relationships? What role will the general manager play?

3. *Defining interfunctional relationships.* In most organizations, the manager is the only executive who can be held responsible for coordinating major functional relationships. Moreover, how the manager defines and supervises these important relationships usually determines how smoothly functional groups work together.

Organizations are naturally dynamic. They change with shifts in competitive conditions, strategic thrust, or the talent available to the general manager. Therefore, the process of organization design, staffing, and coordination is nearly always an ongoing, high-priority concern of the manager.

Task 6: Creating Excellence in Operations and Execution

Typically, the manager influences day-to-day operations in three major ways: (1) by his or her style, (2) by the management processes used (consistent with that style), and (3) by the way time is allocated. If the manager is a direct, personal leader, things will usually be done in a direct, personal way. Less direct leaders may rely on a consensus-driven approach. Whatever the style, the manager is responsible for understanding day-to-day operations and for establishing the processes that govern them. The manager will typically be involved in (1) operational planning, including the development of annual plans and efforts to see that they are met; (2) coordination among the direct-report functions, with special concern that functional units work together so that proper trade-offs are made, parochial departmental interests do not dominate, and inevitable interfunctional conflicts are resolved; (3) decision making, with primary emphasis on cross-functional matters and major commitments; and (4) problem identification and solution, whether through direct involvement or setting in motion a process for the purpose.

The manager's responsibilities cover a wide range of activities. Individually, they may not be as important or as interesting as the development of a business strategy. Taken together, however, they keep the business going effectively, meeting its short-term sales and profit goals. Without an understanding of day-to-day operations, a manager will have difficulty identifying important elements of the strategic task facing the firm.

Task 7: Maintaining a Broad Perspective

The pace of changes impacting organizational performance is on an ever-accelerating cycle of what social scientist Peter Vaill labels "managerial whitewater." Beyond the direct confrontation of bureaucratic dryrot, managers must become increasingly willing to address the continuing application of rules of thumb that have become increasingly inapplicable. Consider, for example, the models of management that guide many of today's service organizations. These models worked well in the post-World War II economy characterized by an abundance of labor, rapid market growth, and an ability to pass on cost increases to consumers. However, today's service firm must challenge important economic, chronological, and labor force shifts that call traditional models into question.

Managers must regularly question the fundamental premises on which their organizations and strategies are based. Three questions are critical to the maintenance of the desires perspective:

1. Why? All too often established rules, procedures, policies, and practices remain in place simply because they have never been questioned.
2. What if? This question assists managers in addressing the imagination of employees in evaluating a wider range of alternatives.
3. What will it take? This final question engages the organization's members in addressing the implementation issues associated with any of their ideas.

Using these questions in sequence provides the manager with a simple, yet powerful, tool kit designed to force their organizations to be increasingly intolerant of the status quo.

CONCLUDING REMARKS

These seven basic tasks of the manager represent an arbitrary selection. Nevertheless, they represent discrete and broad responsibilities important to the successful performance of the manager's job in most companies.

A primary skill of the manager is to pick the specific areas where his or her involvement will have the greatest impact on business results. The scope of the job is such that a manager nearly always faces many more problems and opportunities than he or she can possibly deal with personally. The manager may decide to put greater emphasis on strategy formulation; at another time, the focus will be on the development of people or the working environment. Knowing what to emphasize, when to emphasize it, what and when to delegate, and to whom to delegate are crucial decisions.

Success as a manager isn't solely a function of focusing on these key tasks. Some managers are simply better leaders than others. Some bring a personal package of experience or style that is especially suited to a particular situation.

However, whatever leadership skills or personal package a manager brings to the job, he or she still must decide specifically how to focus efforts that will fundamentally improve the business. Therefore, the key tasks come into play in nearly every situation.

A skillful manager usually is the most important contributor to an organization's success over time. Those contributions are most effective when efforts are concentrated in the six areas described within this chapter.

FOR FURTHER READING

Bennis, Warren, and Burt Nanus, *Leaders: The Strategies for Taking Charge* (New York: Harper & Row, 1985).

Cohen, Allan R., *The Portable MBA in Management* (New York: John Wiley & Sons, 1993).

Fahey, Liam, and Randall, Robert, *The Portable MBA in Strategy* (New York: John Wiley & Sons, 1994).

Itami, Hiroyuki, *Mobilizing Invisible Assets* (Cambridge: Harvard University Press, 1987).

Kimberly, John C., and Robert E. Quinn, *Managing Organizational Transitions* (Homewood, IL: Irwin, 1984).

Kotter, John P., *The Leadership Factor* (New York: Free Press, 1988).

3 MANAGING PEOPLE: THE R FACTOR

Allan R. Cohen

None of us are working in the same ways we did 10 years ago. There have probably been more changes in the nature of work in the past 10 years than in any previous decade since the industrial revolution.

The employee of 10 years ago may have sat at a similar desk, but he or she worked very differently. In the interim, the employees of many of the successful companies have switched from independent to team-based work. Many have far less in the way of direct supervision and control. For many, evaluations and rewards are no longer based on individual performance against internal business standards. The performance that counts now is likely to be the work of a team or the output of a business process. The standards used to judge that work are likely to be external instead of internal—what impact the work has on customer attitudes, how it affects bottom-line profitability for the business unit, or whether it exceeds world-class benchmarks.

This shift from internal to external yardsticks of performance is perhaps the hardest of the changes for the people of the new businesses. David Whitwam, Chairman of Whirlpool Corporation, explains that as his company adopted total quality management (TQM) methods, they "had a most difficult time changing the internal focus of our people, who love to compare themselves to their own prior performance." It was difficult to convince employees, in Whitwam's words, that "all our tasks and processes must be focused externally on the real customer, the consumer."[1]

A great deal of attention is given to the new tools used by employees. The employees of a decade ago would find the tools and charts of total quality management unfamiliar. They would not have heard of business process reengineering and would probably scoff at the possibility of self-directed work teams. Today's employees need to learn a larger and more varied set of tools, to be sure. But beyond this change, something more fundamental has happened to their work. If you compare similar jobs of a decade ago and of today, the most uniform change is in the extent and importance of interpersonal interaction. The new management methods and tools bring with them a new, high-contact style of work. Regardless of the job or company, today's employees are likely to spend far more time in team meetings, cross-functional problem-solving projects, and the like than they did 10 years ago. The importance of people, their motivations, performance, and interactions, is paramount to the newly evolving organization. The ability to understand and modify people's behavior is essential to the manager in this new organization.

Before we turn to concepts for understanding and modifying people's behavior, it is helpful to look at the many changes associated with the new directions in business and to examine their impact on managing people. A survey of U.S. businesses by the Olsten Forum on Human Resource Trends indicates that three-fourths of them are increasing their efforts to improve the quality of their goods and services. Quality improvement activities such as employee training, program communications, and performance incentives are more often the responsibility of the human resources department than any other department. And the human resources department is also involved in activities that are the responsibility of senior management and its quality staff, such as program design and management of performance measurement. There is heavy involvement of human resources in all aspects of quality improvement processes. And this involvement makes sense when you consider that new quality-centered management practices require significant changes in employee attitude and motivation, along with shifts in workplace behavior. The adoption of any major change in a company is a challenging application for the people skills of the MBA program.

A survey of U.S. and European businesses, this one by the Conference Board in 1994, indicates that quality improvement is only one of a range of changes sweeping businesses today. Change may be motivated by one or more of a half-dozen causes, each having significant implications for employees and the way they are managed. These causal factors are:

1. Significant increases in competition.
2. A major shift in company or industry financial performance.
3. Introduction or adaptation to new technologies.
4. Expansion into global markets.
5. Entering into partnerships or strategic alliances.
6. Entering into mergers or acquisitions.

These factors have pushed a large majority of midsize and large firms to adopt formal or informal change efforts since the beginning of the decade. Of the 178 firms in the Conference Board's sample, 160 or 90 percent were in the midst of significant changes. The results of these changes are far-reaching, touching everything from customer satisfaction and production processes to bottom-line financial performance. But for many firms, the largest impact is in employee behavior. Table 3-1 indicates the percentage of companies from the Conference Board's survey that report high levels of impact on specific aspects of employee behavior. More than half have seen big changes in the areas of attention to quality, awareness of customer needs, and productivity.

The data in Table 3-1 mean there has been a dramatic level of change in employee behavior in just the first half of this decade. Change management efforts, regardless of their specifics, always boil down to one thing: changing the behavior of managers and employees. Thus while managers once had only to concern themselves with maintaining an internal standard of behavior for themselves and their staff, now they must concern themselves with rapid modification of those behaviors in response to the imperative of a fast-changing competitive environment.

All of the skills covered by a good MBA program are important for effective management, but when businesses must change rapidly, the key skills relate to managing people. And as organizations become more process-oriented in the pursuit of flexibility and rapid improvement, the people factor becomes more vital to success. Caterpillar, for example, undertook what many experts viewed as a model quality program in the 1980s. It trained thousands of workers and gained union support for more flexible, process-oriented work rules. But it failed to reap the benefits of these initiatives because management clashed with unions and the company fell into a series of destructive strikes and labor disputes. Employee behavior never changed as management wished, and management behavior toward employees failed to change as the unions had hoped it

TABLE 3-1   Results of change management since 1989—Impact of changes on employee behavior

Aspect of Employee Behavior	Percentage of U.S./European Firms Reporting High Impact
Attention to quality	64%
Customer awareness	55
Productivity	50
Adaptability	35
Commitment	33

Source: Change Management: An Overview of Current Initiatives, The Conference Board, 1994, p. 41.

would. Many of the potential benefits of the quality process were derailed by the problems Caterpillar encountered in managing its people.

The sad truth is that within an organization, employees will not all view problems in the same light. As a manager, you may find yourself in pursuit of changes and improvements that do not seem as pressing to your employees or colleagues. Even direct subordinates may resist your orders when they are convinced you are wrong and will certainly drag their heels if they are afraid of proposed changes. Others whom you do not supervise, including your boss and colleagues, may be downright ornery, if not hostile. Yet your ability to get your work done, let alone change the work of others, depends on all these people. Fewer and fewer decisions can be made or implemented in isolation in the modern business organization.

The news is not all bad, however. As organizations move toward management of processes across multiple functions, it becomes simpler to align the interests of individuals with the team's objectives. Someone from sales and marketing is more likely to share an engineer's viewpoint if both work together on a cross-functional product development team, for example. Processes that are made up of interrelated tasks and involve the people who are responsible for those tasks can help reduce the turf wars that drive managers crazy. The traditional problems tend to be replaced by new ones: complaints about the performance of a team member, disagreements about how to reach a consensus decision. The modern manager must apply people skills to the jobs of getting people to pull together, use their talents, and do whatever is required to satisfy customers, increase productivity, and keep learning and changing at an accelerating rate.

Are the traditional tools of the MBA curriculum up to these new challenges? Yes and no. The fundamentals of diagnosing and managing behavior still apply, and we will examine these in detail in the rest of the chapter. But the applications to which the traditional tools are applied have changed, and we will need to explore some of these new applications as we go.

Being part of an organization inherently means being interconnected with many others—for worse *and* better. Sometimes those who refuse to cooperate actually have valuable knowledge or abilities; they may even be indispensable to your success. "Managing others" is not only about gaining their compliance, but also about learning from and accommodating them, when appropriate.

We will approach the enhancement of managerial capacity in these areas by focusing first on *diagnosis*—understanding what causes people in organizations to behave as they do. Then we will consider how to alter this behavior. Taking appropriate action is easier, although seldom automatic, when the diagnosis is solid; at the least, careful diagnosis prevents foolish errors. In any organization, there are daily occurrences of managers leaping before looking, causing unforeseen consequences they later regret. Even worse, managers can cultivate a mountainous problem where a mere molehill previously existed.

A manager chews out a subordinate who arrives late for the third time, without realizing that the subordinate had worked several nights on a big project. Another manager demands a faster pace from a work team without anticipating the effect on their concern for quality. A third manager, who in the past has accomplished great results through kindness, falls behind schedule because a subordinate needed constant reminders and close monitoring. All these managers share the problem of taking action without understanding the particular circumstances. We begin by offering a way of sorting through the complexities of ongoing organizational life to understand the forces causing behavior.

PERSONALITY AND SITUATION

A preliminary cut at explaining behavior in organizations is to differentiate between forces within the behaver's *personality* and "everything else," that is, the forces in the *situation* surrounding the person. Most Americans are psychologically oriented, so the natural tendency is to resort to explanations of behavior that are within the person. "He needs to be in control." "She is a perfectionist." "They are a bunch of mavericks." Even when such observations may be correct in some way, they are usually incomplete, therefore misleading, and not easily amenable to managerial action. Even extended psychotherapy has a poor record of changing personality, and managers are not trained therapists. While it is helpful to understand something about the forces inside people, usually more leverage results from special attention to diagnosing the external forces.

If an employee's manager criticizes every action, the equipment is designed wrong for the work, the organization pays the lowest possible wages, and fellow workers refuse to talk to anyone who produces at a high rate, we will be helped very little by diagnosing a poor performer as "lazy" or "stupid." Although that could also be true, a valid conclusion is unlikely when so many organizational conditions are stacked against conscientious performance. The person may well be clever in figuring out "how the game is played" in this organization; in another more favorable setting, that cleverness might lead instead to greater investment and higher performance.

Personality is often cited as a problem when process improvement teams run into conflict. It is common, for instance, for managers to hear team members complain, "Joe doesn't listen. He thinks he knows best and doesn't care what the rest of the team thinks." Or the manager may learn from team members, "Ann is uncooperative. She is so critical about our work, but does not do the work we assign to her." Are these behavior problems really the result of negative personal traits? If so, then your options as a manager are severely limited—to replace Ann and Joe with more cooperative people might seem like the best course, but it would be a difficult and costly one. More likely, however, Joe and Ann have legitimate beefs that reflect their experiences on this or a previous team. Perhaps Joe has been burned by a past experience with an incompetent. And perhaps Ann's supervisor does not count her team contribution when he does her regular performance appraisal. Aspects of each team member's situation may be key in explaining their behavior toward the team.

The individual's personality and internal motivation do come into play but seldom are sufficient to explain observed behavior. Therefore, we will examine external forces extensively and look for ways in which they interact with personality. Indeed, an important working assumption is that all significant behavior has *multiple causes* which reinforce each other. In that sense, most behavior is overdetermined, with several causes. If you can sort the causes out, then you will be in the best position to determine where to intervene and what the likely consequences of that intervention will be.

THE NEED FOR A CONCEPTUAL MODEL

Because the realities of individuals and organizations are so complex, a conceptual scheme for simplifying and ordering is desirable. Using *any* model provokes the dangerous temptation to treat the model's abstractions as if they were the whirling reality—or alternatively, the temptation to dismiss the model as mere jargon. We will treat the model as a tool, a walking stick to help us navigate difficult terrain, rather than as an end in itself. It should be relied on only insofar as it is useful in guiding attention and uniting many factors that together cause behavior.

With only a bit of stretching and poetic license, we can fit an abundance of social science research and theory into a conceptual scheme where all key words begin with "R."

R FACTORS: THE SITUATION

Although we will discuss one factor at a time, note that all situational R factors interact with each other (and with individual factors) to shape behavior. Together they send powerful messages to individuals about what is expected, right, good—even possible. Although different individuals may vary their responses according to their personalities, a consistent set of situational R factors will often produce similar results among a wide range of individuals.

The situational R factors we will examine are *roles, relationships, rewards,* and *rites.* (See Figure 3-1.)

FIGURE 3-1 R factors affecting behavior in the *situation*

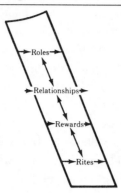

Roles

Roles are positions in an organization defined by a set of expectations about behavior of any incumbent. Organizational roles have attached to them a required set of tasks and responsibilities (often, but not always, spelled out in a job description). The *formal* role tells its occupant what activities are expected, and often what results are desired. Since salaries are paid in return for performance of the role, roles have a powerful effect on behavior. Roles can also evolve *informally,* creating expectations that are not official, but that strongly influence behavior. Both formal and informal roles can have "requirements" about both tasks and interactions. The role tells the person who holds it not only what tasks to carry out but also with whom to interact in carrying out the tasks. Though the requirements of the role may never be written, they will be conveyed to the occupant and more or less enforced; in any event, they strongly influence behavior. The following example illustrates these ideas.

Formal Role

Dan Alighieri is a quality control manager in a large plant. He is responsible for seeing that the products leaving the plant are produced to customer specifications within certain tolerances. His job requires that he apply statistical sampling techniques and high standards to ensure that work at every stage of manufacture is done appropriately. His colleagues at the plant have divergent roles; they want to manufacture quickly with minimal rework, and ship everything that has been completed. Dan feels obligated by role to be critical and suspicious; if he were not, substandard parts might be shipped by his people. Yet customers are increasingly demanding.

Dan's colleagues, the managers of manufacturing, engineering, and sales, consider him a royal pain since his stance at meetings is perpetually negative. Even on subjects unrelated to quality control, he usually focuses on limitations, weaknesses, and dangers. They joke (behind his back) about his being a "sadistic s.o.b." and a "black cloud." Yet when Dan coaches his son's Little League team, he is warm, patient, and supportive. The issue at work is not his personality, but his role, which signals him about expected behavior. In fact, Dan sometimes carries over the critical set appropriate to his job into problem-solving sessions where it interferes, but not because he is inherently negative.

The Evolution of an Informal Role

Compounding the problem is the emergence in Dan's peer group of an informal role—group skeptic—that has evolved for Dan. As the group began to notice Dan's critical approach, they came to expect that on any issue he would point out the pitfalls. In turn, they stressed the positive. Dan interpreted their consistent stance as a sign that if he did not exercise extra caution, they would go off half-cocked. Soon, everyone left to Dan the job of looking for negative possibilities, and the role of group skeptic became his. This item did not appear on his job description, but the expectations were no less powerful. Although the group complained about Dan's negativity, he often prevented their leaping before thoroughly looking and occasionally rescued them from impending disaster.

The Impact of Tasks on Roles

Whether a role is formal and written, or emerges from informal interaction with others, expectations draw behavior from the person who holds the role. However, roles also shape behavior in other, less direct ways.

The nature of the tasks assigned to a role have an impact on the feelings of the occupant about how hard to work, depending on whether the tasks are simple or complex, repetitive or varied, stationary or mobile, concentration-intense or not, equipment/technology-oriented or not, and so on. In general, researchers have found that increasing numbers of individuals respond with greater commitment and effort when the tasks of their job provide stimulation and challenge. The exceptions are those individuals whose skills and aspirations are so low that they do not respond to challenge—a declining breed in developed economies.

The Connection between Roles and Relationships

Tasks assigned to roles impact behavior because they determine with whom the occupant will have contact. Some organizational tasks are performed alone, but most are carried out in *relationship* to others. With whom a role-holder is required to interact, how often, and toward what end, all have important consequences. One of the basic laws of behavior is that, in general, greater interaction (especially among relative equals) will lead to greater liking; in turn, greater liking usually leads to more frequent interaction. It is hard to develop liking for those with whom we have no contact, and we tend to seek out those we like. As a result, people in organizations develop connections—friendships or "acquaintanceships"—with those to whom their job leads them. (Sometimes no interaction is *required*, but geographic proximity promotes it, with similar results.)

The relationships resulting from interaction can impact behavior. When the relationships are with single individuals, the pair will develop ideas about what is expected from one another, how to view the company, how much effort to put into work, and so forth. Strongly developed friendships may become more important in shaping behavior at work than the formal tasks or the individual's personal inclinations.

Relationships That Become Self-Sealing

When relationships with colleagues are positive, work is more enjoyable, information flows more freely, disagreements are more readily resolved, and greater trust evolves. On the other hand, negative relationships among peers can result in great unhappiness and poor ability to accomplish work requiring cooperation or collaboration.

When two individuals develop a negative working relationship, they often do so because the actions of each causes the other to produce more of the behavior irritating to the other, which in turn provokes the first person, and so on. This self-sealing reciprocity can be extremely frustrating to the parties caught in it, as well as to those working around them.

For example, Joan Jeffries and Kirk Rulon were colleagues in a professional services firm. Joan recruited Kirk to head a newly established research unit; within a year she was at war with Kirk. Joan was a creative, enterprising wheeler-dealer who had an excellent reputation with clients. Her motto was, "It's easier to beg forgiveness than to obtain advance permission," and she constantly bent rules to accomplish her goals. Kirk, on the other hand, was careful, systematic, and a bit plodding. A skilled bureaucratic infighter, he was a master of budget procedures and organizational rules as a means of achieving his projects.

When Joan and Kirk had to deal with one another, each drove the other wild. Joan would be too busy to answer memos or attend planning meetings; at the last minute, she would have a brainstorm and want to have input. Kirk would say, "Gee, you had a chance but didn't say anything, so now it's too late." Joan would hit the roof, railing about Kirk's rigidities; in turn, Kirk would point out reporting lines, published deadlines, and so on. Kirk's repeated inflexibility provoked Joan to avoid him, prompting her to miss more meetings and deadlines. Around they went, until Joan resolved to eliminate Kirk—who was working on transferring to another unit where Joan could not hamper him. Their battles frustrated their colleagues and boss, who liked both of them, but could not determine how to motivate them to pool their talents.

Relationships Develop Informal Norms

Even more powerful influences can be the groups that form at work. Whether a formally designated work team or an informal group that develops out of casual interaction, mutual interests, or outside connections, groups develop *norms*—ideas about how members are supposed to behave. In a well-developed group, the norms will be extensive and well-enforced. Norms about how much to produce, how hard to work, how to treat other members, how to talk to managers, how to relate to nongroup members, even how to dress, are common features of groups at work.

For the individual member, these norms can feel like powerful "requirements" of the job and constitute price of admission to membership. Following the group's norms is necessary to be a member in good standing, and groups enforce the norms in a variety of ways. In a classic study of a workgroup, the punishment for breaking a norm was "binging," a sharp rap on the arm. In higher-level work teams, norms may be enforced by kidding remarks ("Nice jacket, Kim; was there a polyester glut at your tailor's?"), by direct disapproval ("Design engineers are supposed to represent the customers, Chris, not their fellow designers"), or by subtle hints ("I didn't see you at the office when I was here on Saturday, Sandy; is everything OK?").

When a member does not conform to a group's norms, increased interaction is addressed to that person in an attempt to bring him or her into line; if that fails, the group gradually ignores the person. Only a very determined individual, or one with one or more satisfactory memberships in outside groups, can long resist a group working to enforce its norms. The signals sent by work teams to its members can strongly influence behavior; if the team's norms are different from the person's task requirements, as often happens, the team may well be the greater influence.

One exception to the tendency of greater interaction leading to greater liking is when the interaction required is between people of acutely opposing values or status. Those with differing values (e.g., "I live to work" versus "I work to be able to live well") may find that more contact only clarifies their differences and drives them to reduce contact, even if the job requires it.

People of highly unequal status also may wish to avoid one another to minimize potential discomfort arising from the inequality. Although North Americans tend to downplay status differences, it is still likely that the president of a large company will not seek out his or her driver beyond those times when work requires it. The president may be overtly friendly, but probably not engage in personal conversation or revelations. The driver is likely to be polite and, if highly confident, may exchange a bit of banter, without presuming friendship. This reticence in no way suggests that one is a better, more worthwhile person than the other; the differences in organizational power usually work to create barriers and distance, however politely each pretends none exists.

These same impulses push some managers to avoid social contact with subordinates, even when previously they have been friendly as peers. North Americans are so uncomfortable with the idea of status creating distance that they work to deny status differences. For example, when the oldest member of a team of MBA whiz kids is perceived by his peers as aspiring to become the group's liaison with management, they deny there is any need for the role, despite the company president's interest. A manager seeking openness or closeness with subordinates will have to work hard to overcome this universal recognition of the impact of unequal status, making life in flatter organizations a challenge.

The traditional manager applies an understanding of formal and informal roles by taking note of the roles his or her subordinates play in their various interactions. Observing these roles can help diagnose apparent personality conflicts such as Joan Jeffries and Kirk Rulon experience. Role conflicts may be behind complaints about fellow employees or supervisors. And employees can be encouraged to examine and modify their own roles over time.

What of the modern manager, someone involved in a quality, reengineering or other change process, or perhaps someone who has to combine two groups of employees from merged companies or departments? This manager is faced with a different kind of challenge, but an understanding of roles is equally useful.

Role conflicts and confusion arise when staffs are combined. There are often parallel roles in the two groups of employees, even when formal job descriptions do not overlap. And when managers have to facilitate a large number of quality or process improvement teams, they need to be conscious of the fact that every new team must go through a "norming" process in which members adopt a shared set of norms and find productive roles for themselves. The manager who understands that productive team performance only comes *after* norms and roles are established will have far more success in facilitating teams. And employees who are encouraged to self-diagnose role related problems will do far better in the modern team environment, where after all they may be required to develop and play many more roles because of their membership in multiple teams over time.

Relationships Upward: The Impact of Leadership

We have already begun to discuss the ways relationships affect behavior; one of the key relationships is with the person's direct supervisor. A few extremely independent people behave the same no matter what their bosses do, but most people are affected by the relationship the boss creates (or allows to be created).

Does the subordinate want personal closeness, and will the boss give it? Does the subordinate know the work so well that it can best be done without close supervision, and will the boss allow that? Or, is the work so complicated that more attention is needed (or so boring that constant watching is required), and will the boss provide that? Does the subordinate have valuable contributions toward setting methods or solving problems, and does the boss listen? Does the subordinate need to cooperate with people in and outside of the work unit, and does the boss support those kinds of relationships?

A number of conditions yield high performance and commitment when the boss manages tightly; other conditions require greater latitude and participation by subordinates. Performance can be harmed by a bad fit between the complexity of the tasks, the manner in which the employee desires to be supervised, and the leadership style. In general, when inexperienced, dependent subordinates are engaged in simple, routine tasks, tighter supervision produces better performance; with complex, changing tasks, knowledgeable, mature subordinates perform best when leadership style is participative and warm. Some dilemmas complicate these issues:

1. A style that fits may yield performance in the short run, but how can subordinates and tasks be developed to make new styles appropriate. In today's complex organizations, fewer organizational tasks are simple and unchanging, fewer subordinates are uneducated and submissive. Can directive styles continue to achieve high performance? Can managers afford to be heroic, to disseminate all the answers, to keep total control and responsibility? Where will talented people come from if current members are not developed?

2. Individual and collective satisfaction may not match performance. There is no necessary correlation between satisfaction and performance; happy employees can be productive or unproductive, as can unhappy ones. Does employee satisfaction matter then? Does it matter only when unemployment is low, allowing dissatisfied people to easily leave and obtain other jobs? Or in the long run, is a satisfied workforce needed to retain good people and keep them growing as the environment changes?

3. How will employees learn if managers fail to provide challenge and autonomy? How can the managers be sure the employees will do the right things well?

The way in which an individual's manager resolves these relationship issues has profound effects on the person's behavior. Managers are also someone else's subordinates, so their relationships with their bosses are likely to affect the way they deal with their subordinates.

Rewards

Discussing leadership must include the subject of *rewards,* both formal and informal. It is not exactly startling news that people tend to do what they are rewarded for, although organizations sometimes have difficulty implementing that truth. Identifying the desired tasks or behaviors is challenging, as is measuring their accomplishments and attaching appropriate rewards. Furthermore, individuals may find very different things to be rewarding, so a uniform system may not touch everyone as intended.

Whatever the difficulties of establishing a reward system that performs as planned, all organizations have them. The particular nature of the system contributes to individual behavior. Is salary fixed, no matter what the performance? Is it partly or totally contingent on performance, as with commissioned salespeople? Are there performance bonuses; are some or all levels eligible for them; are bonuses individual, group, departmental, or total-organization based? How easily can good performance be measured? Are decisions about who to reward perceived as fair, objective, or subjective? Do actual rewards match what top management says is important?

No one reward system works for every situation, but whatever is in place will affect individual behavior. Consider the impact on behavior of a plant that produces hazardous chemical gases, claims to be safety conscious, yet posts the volume per minute produced by each shift. Although operators are paid a fixed wage, the competition engendered by the charting of volume produced (combined with lax supervision) is one factor that led to sloppy performance and contamination of the plant on the third shift one night. Other organizations have found that rhetoric about quality, diversity, excellence, or innovation fall on deaf (or cynical) ears unless accompanied by concrete rewards for those who contribute to those goals.

In addition to the impact of formal reward systems, it is useful to identify the rewards that have evolved informally within the organization. What behaviors help people get ahead (or get along)? Many of these are products of the group or team to which a person belongs (as discussed above), but some reflect the mores of the wider organization.

These methods can vary widely; in some fast-growing high-tech firms, the aggressive, innovative person receives rapid promotions and recognition; in some more traditional firms, hard work, sincerity, and "fitting in" lead to advancement. In fact, at one such bank it was believed that "the tallest weed is cut down first," so no one wanted to take big risks; at a computer company growing 40 percent a year, anyone who saw a problem or opportunity and avoided taking initiative was frowned on. These informal rewards lead to quite different behavior.

Rewards play a key role in transforming modern companies. Employee suggestions are recognized when they contribute to quality or productivity improvements. Employees are encouraged to modify their behavior from individual to team focus through recognition of team contributions and team accomplishments. A recent study of noncash award programs at U.S. companies concluded, "recognition, ceremony and symbol are important underpinnings to the successful functioning of a total quality management process," and reward "reinforces the cultural and behavioral change TQM requires."[2] The modern manager must become expert at devising new ways, formal and informal, to reward desired changes in employee behavior and performance.

Because the modern business emphasizes external over internal performance yardsticks, managers are shifting their emphasis to externally oriented rewards. For example, many companies now emphasize award programs for business units, instead of individuals or teams. And they model these awards on external standards such as the Malcolm Baldrige National Quality Award, sponsored by the U.S. Department of Commerce, the British Quality Award, the Deming Prize in Japan, and the European Quality Award. While many smaller rewards are given to individuals and teams, the greatest emphasis may now be on the yearly competition between business units for a quality award based on one of these national standards. IBM, Bausch & Lomb, Whirlpool, and many other companies now use these quality awards to encourage change and improvement.

Rites

As suggested by the discussions of informal rewards, organizations can differ dramatically in their cultures—the unspoken assumptions about proper behavior. The culture usually reflects a combination of the organization's size, founders(s), particular industry, current leadership, and key crises and events in the history of the organization. The organization's resulting *rites*—its routines, rituals, and general "way we do things"—also impact individual behavior.

Just as a small group's norms "direct" members about what it takes to be in good standing, an organization's culture directs appropriate behavior, and its rites reinforce ideas about how to behave in many circumstances. For example, are people expected to follow orders, or challenge anything illogical? Is hierarchy rigidly respected or played down? Do new members receive formal training in the organization's practices, or are they left to fend for themselves? Do Friday afternoon beer-busts reinforce informal connections across levels and units (as at many Silicon Valley companies), or do members rarely socialize? Does customer satisfaction really matter or is it only a buzzword? Are divisions or units autonomous or centrally controlled? Do long-run considerations take precedence over short-term gain (increasingly rare in American industry) or vice versa?

The nature of the industry contributes to the answers to these questions. All siding salesmen may not behave as unethically as those depicted in the movie *Tin Men*, but because of industry practices, most are probably closer to that image in reality than are IBM salespeople or trust officers at traditional banks.

Reinforcement

Although it is necessary for clarity to discuss factors one at a time, in reality, the factors interact and reinforce one another (or conflict with each other, sending confusing signals to organizational members). The pressures from the tasks in a role may be formally rewarded while the relationships that arise create a different set of informal rewards. The organization's rites may encourage a different kind of behavior or align with the other factors. The interaction of these factors allows a total situation to emerge, with its resultant impact on the individual.

Reinforcement issues come to the fore in any change management process because change does not happen across all the factors that affect employee behavior at once. A new emphasis on self-management through self-directed work teams may be intended to empower employees to solve problems on their own. But will they really change their behavior? Will they really believe that senior managers will not penalize people who make mistakes and take risks? Not if other factors still encourage traditional employee behavior. For example, what if the company still allocates spaces in the parking lot based on status, giving top managers covered spots near the door and regular employees open-air parking far from the building? This kind of glaring symbol of the hierarchy reinforces traditional power relationships, signaling to employees that the old management roles are not gone and may resurface if something goes wrong. In trying to change employee behavior through the transformation of reinforcements, managers need to keep track of all the reinforcements employees perceive as important, for example, through informal employee attitude surveys and watercooler chats with trusted confidants.

R FACTORS: THE INDIVIDUAL

Most behavior is shaped by factors outside the individual. However, personality does matter, and it shapes responses to the various factors in the situation.

FIGURE 3-2   R factors affecting behavior in the *individual*

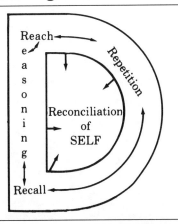

Thus, the next part of the scheme deals with individual internal factors brought to any organizational situation. The factors relate to each other, organizing the person's self-view. We will discuss each of the factors in turn: *recall, reach, reasoning, repetition,* and their overall configuration: *reconciliation of self.* (See Figure 3-2.)

Recall

One of the key influences on how we see ourselves and our organizational situation is *recall* of our past experience. Experiences provide the skills and competencies that shape what people are willing to tackle or like to do (and may overrely on). Experiences also shape attitudes about work, people, and organizations.

How does the person feel about his or her skills? What are a person's experiences with those in positions of authority? They may explain current reactions to his or her boss. Has work usually been enjoyable or a burden? Has the person been supported by peers or found them to be nasty competitors? Has the person learned that new skills are readily mastered or cause fumbling and confusion?

Not only does recall of general experiences impact how a person behaves, but recall of key incidents in the particular organization often determines his or her attitude toward current issues. Both kinds of experiences help shape how open a person is, how trusting, how willing to be a committed organizational member. Often, when someone is reacting oddly, it is worth exploring what related experiences the person recalls since the behavior may be logical when the source is revealed.

Reach

Another powerful determinant of behavior is the person's *reach*, his or her goals or values. Goals are the objects or events for which a person strives to fulfill needs. Goals may be realistic or unrealistic, depending on the person's talents and the opportunity inherent in the organization; in either case, most of the interesting behavior in organizations is goal-driven.

Values are more fundamental than goals; they are beliefs about what is important in life, conceived as ultimately unobtainable ideals. Examples of values include:

1. Always do one's best.
2. Never put work above friendship.
3. Always be honest with others.
4. Never deliberately hurt anyone's feelings.
5. Win at all costs.

Notice that it is unlikely anyone could perfectly live up to each of his or her values, and that an individual may well hold contradictory values for some situations. For example, the person who holds values 3 and 4 could easily come into conflict when faced with a nice but weak colleague who fears he has insufficient skills for a job and requests "an honest opinion."

Because values are global, they can easily conflict with a person's specific goals. This clash creates inner tensions; how they are resolved helps to shape the person and may result in alteration of either the goals or values. For example, Bill Flynn took a job as a systems analysis trainee, determined to enhance his computer skills. Shocked by the rigorous, competitive program and the management's strictness, he gradually broke the program's rules to succeed. Although he thought of himself as honest, eventually he shuffled through his boss's desk late one night to read the trainee evaluations that were unavailable to the trainees. Afterward, he could barely justify his action to himself or his friends, and he struggled to reconcile his values with his goal of successfully completing the program. In such experiences, identity and self-image are formed.

Reasoning

In addition to goals and values, people *reason*—develop beliefs—about the world, other people, organizations, and more. These beliefs form a cognitive pattern that also shapes behavior. If a manager (we'll call her Kim) believes, for example, that all managers in the division would walk over their parents to get ahead, Kim is likely to be on guard when dealing with them. Indeed, Kim may take any opportunity to disparage them as a defensive tactic against their "aggressiveness." Is it a surprise, then, that Kim's colleagues become increasingly nasty due to their beliefs that Kim is a vicious competitor, thus "confirming" to Kim the validity of the original views?

Beliefs make it possible to function since they provide guides for unforeseen situations (imagine trying to act if you lacked beliefs about how people react, organizations work, bosses behave, and so on), but beliefs can become self-fulfilling prophecies, as they did for Kim.

This cycle complicates diagnosis. Organizational members act on beliefs they do not always articulate and often are certain their beliefs are correct because others behave accordingly—even though the causes of others' behavior are actually contrary to what is assumed.

Because human beings prefer to have explanations for what they see around them, they are prone to "explain" the behavior of others by attributing motives. When Mark Bennett, president of a high-tech company, failed to inform Jacque Laroux, the chairman and founder, about several important issues, Jacque was upset. He felt increasingly excluded from daily operations and unappreciated for his many technical contributions. Puzzled that "any reasonable president would cut me out," he attributed to Mark unpleasant motives: jealousy, ambition, and fear. In fact, Mark believed that Jacque's loose style of interacting with technicians and scientists at all levels of the organization was disruptive, and Mark wanted to keep him from "messing up the organization." But Jacque was so sure of his attributions that he was convinced of the futility of asking Mark why he was holding Jacque off, so he never asked. Instead he convinced the board to fire Mark.

In general, people act on their beliefs as if they were true; it is therefore useful to explore what another's beliefs are when trying to understand that person's behavior.

Repetition

Many aspects of behavior are no longer consciously intended, but are rote *repetition*. Habits form (often based on what worked to solve a problem at some earlier time) and persist independent of their appropriateness to current situations. Some habits are harmless, amusing, or only mildly annoying—such as the manager who automatically reacts negatively to new ideas before asking any questions about them—and are not especially significant in understanding behavior.

Other habits can be equally automatic but more significant in consequence. Based on early experiences, managers develop favored ways of dealing with sticky situations that they automatically repeat in vaguely similar situations, even when the behavior is essentially ineffective. *Repetition* of a particular response builds the manager's skill, so that its frequent success reinforces its automatic use. The strength then becomes a weakness because it is overused, even when not appropriate.

Ted Chatham, for example, was trained as an actuary. Brilliant and analytical, he rose through the ranks in his insurance company relatively rapidly. Then he plateaued, much to his consternation. Peers, to whom he felt intellectually superior, were selected for senior vice-presidential posts he coveted. The problem was that he had overdeveloped his analytical skills and used them in situations where compassion or intuition was needed. He could not deal with less brilliant subordinates or peers, especially when they were upset or tackling ambiguous problems. The dispassionate analytical skills that advanced him early in his career had been so often repeated that they were automatically called into play even when totally inappropriate.

When examining puzzling behavior, try the hypothesis that the person is acting out of habit rather than from careful situational diagnosis. The notion that the behavior may be an overused strength can lead to useful understanding.

Reconciliation of Self (Self-Concept)

The individual components, *recall, reach, reasoning,* and *repetition* have been discussed as if they were separate elements, but they interact within the person as well. Together they form the person's self-concept (*reconciliation of self*)— the way the person sees himself or herself. The goals, values, and beliefs arising from experience converge to form a view of self that in turn shapes behavior. Once such a self-concept is formed, people strive to maintain that concept by engaging in behavior consistent with it. Thus, a person who sees herself as ambitious and honest can aggressively confront a boss she believes to be blocking her career advancement, while one who sees herself as ambitious but inexperienced and powerless will tolerate managerial ineptness that the first person would readily tackle.

Perhaps the most useful observation about self-concept is that viewed from within a person, even behavior that an outsider might find strange usually makes sense. Bill Flynn, who bewildered his friends by searching his boss's desk in the middle of the night, did not see himself as dishonest; rather, he saw himself as ambitious and determined in a situation where pertinent information was being unreasonably withheld. He *recalled* earlier experiences in which assertive, harmless actions had helped him. His *reach* for success in becoming a systems analyst and broadening his computer experience was shared by colleagues. His *reasoning* told him bosses and companies inconsiderate of employees did not deserve blind obedience. Finally, the resourcefulness he had used to get through college and find good jobs was *repeated* as, "on impulse, Bill let himself into [his boss's] office and closed the door."

Diagnosing the elements of individual behavior, *recall, reach, reasoning,* and *repetition,* and their combination to form a *reconciliation of self,* increases your understanding of the behavior of individuals in organizations. When combined with the situational R factors, enough of behavior is understandable to determine possible leverage points for change.

These lever points are all applicable in the traditional or modern business, but one of them is especially useful in modern businesses. Think about what makes a company embarking on radical change unique, and you will be able to guess which of these levers is especially important. Any change management effort must be predicated on a powerful new vision of the organization, usually at odds with the old vision. Senior managers lead a quality improvement or process reengineering effort by asserting a new vision of their company, usually one that emphasizes rapid change and improvement based on a heightened customer focus and greater participation by all employees. This means the manager's job now must include the difficult task of sharing a new vision with all employees. New personal goals, such as continuous learning or the delivery of service so good it surprises customers, need to be tapped or added to each employees' personal reach, the set of goals and values that guide behavior. Old goals and values such as "satisficing" or doing the minimum needed to satisfy work requirements would have to be altered because of the obvious conflict with the new goal of providing world-class quality that many companies are now adopting.

Reinforcement (Again)

Just as the situational R factors reinforce each other, individual R factors overlap and reinforce each other (or send contradictory, mixed messages about behavior). Careful analysis of each particular situation is required to see whether, and how, the factors unite to shape behavior that at first glance may be puzzling if attributed only to personality or a single situational factor. As stated at the beginning of this chapter, most behavior has multiple causes and cannot be explained by a single factor.

Situation Refracts Through Self-Concept

All of the situational R factors are interpreted through the individual's self-concept, as if they were light waves *refracted* through water to shine on the pond's interior. The same set of factors may have differential impacts on individuals with different views of themselves, although, as noted earlier, perhaps less often than is usually assumed.

The following example illustrates the interconnections among R factors. The sales manager at Healthco, Inc., had a problem. The turnover rate in his sales force was too high, and far too many of those who left were women. Knowing his own good intentions about employing women, he assumed that selling to male-dominated groups of physicians and hospitals was probably difficult for women and that they needed more sales-skill training.

This preliminary diagnosis leapt from a problem (turnover) to the conclusion that one situational factor (poor sales skills) was the cause. The sales manager was thus ready to begin a training program.

Fortunately, he was persuaded to allow a more thorough diagnosis. To his surprise, numerous other situational factors were identified:

- Women were assigned easier territories by considerate intention, but as a result they could not prove their worth to their supervisors. If the woman succeeded, the performance was discounted as an easy sale; if she did not do well, no further support was offered.

- From the assumption that women would not want to travel, many territories were not offered to them. Then others believed that the women were inflexible.

- Male salespeople met for drinks and, while together, informally traded information and sales tips. They assumed the women would not want to go drinking, so did not invite them. As a result, women were inadvertently excluded from important learning.

- Secretaries at headquarters flirted and chatted with the unmarried male salespeople, so they knew the men better and readily helped them in preference to the female salespeople.

- The organization had traditionally been male in its orientation, which provoked some supposedly innocent joking and teasing that professional women found insulting.

Indeed, when those women who left were tracked, the survey revealed that many of them had obtained even better sales jobs and were performing successfully. Thus, it was unlikely that chauvinist customers or lack of skills were the causes. The roles, relationships, rewards, and rites were inadvertently stacked against women who wanted to stay.

Not every female salesperson had left, however. A few were challenged by the situation, believed strongly in their ability to overcome the situational obstacles, and did not want to work elsewhere. Despite the general response of female salespeople, one or two had self-concepts that counterbalanced the situational forces.

Results

The reader, like the sales manager at Healthco, is probably interested in *results* of individual behavior in producing more successful behavior or alteing unsuccessful behavior. Figure 3-3 summarizes the R factors that affect behavior.

What results are managers interested in? There are at least five important dimensions to pay attention to:

1. *Productivity.* How much does the person produce, for how much input? Does the work get done? Does the right work get done?

2. *Growth/learning.* Is the person learning new skills, developing greater ability to contribute to the organization in the future?

3. *Satisfaction.* Does the person enjoy the work, fellow workers, and the organization?

4. *Commitment.* Does the person genuinely care about the organization and its success? Does he/she want to do what is good for the organization?

5. *Competitive capability.* As a result of the previous four dimensions, does the person's behavior help the company compete better against its rivals, serve customers better, and keep costs down?

FIGURE 3-3   All R factors conceptual scheme

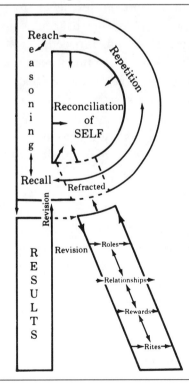

Any combination of results on these dimensions is possible. Individuals can be ecstatically happy while unproductive; productive at present but learning nothing (and therefore less likely to be productive as tasks, technology, or requirements change); highly committed but frustrated; and so on. Rarely does any set of circumstances produce highly positive results simultaneously in all five dimensions, although that is the goal of many organizations. If trade-offs are necessary, realistic managers try to balance short- and long-term objectives, and realize that over time, attention may have to shift if one dimension falls off too far.

REVISION/REFORM

What can managers do about results below their standards? Unsatisfactory results usually prompt an attempt to *revise* some or all of the culprit situational and individual factors. A group of workers is choosing to use its technical discovery to finish work early rather than to produce more; a new MBA is productive but her style disturbs her supervisor and co-workers; experienced and new supervisors are at war against each other, affecting productivity; a group of engineers has low morale and slipping productivity; or a newly appointed president of an acquired company finds enormous resistance from his predecessor and the vice-presidents he will have to manage—what can be done? How does the manager who wants to alter current results proceed?

First, it is necessary to do a careful diagnosis, as suggested previously. Since it is easier to change situational R factors than personality R factors, all the possible causes related to *roles, relationships, rewards,* and *rites* need to be identified. Then those that are most readily in your control can be addressed first. If, for example, tying people's rewards to measures of quality (or other indicators such as safety or customer complaints) will achieve the desired results, much aggravation may be avoided.

Often, however, the situational factors are complex and interwoven, so that one simple change will not achieve the desired results—or worse, it moves performance in the wrong direction. Many grand schemes for change, including the latest and hottest fads, produce unanticipated results because they ignore the interconnected strands that are causing current behavior. Introduction of new technology, for example, does not merely alter a few tasks; it often affects opportunities for interaction, existing social relationships, skills required, status attached to different roles, long-standing rites, and so on. Just look at the impact of companywide E-Mail, which sounds merely like an efficient way to send messages, but suddenly allows anyone at any level or location to communicate with anyone else. Similarly, any attempt to move from a functionally organized company to one that is organized by processes, requires far more than redrawing the boxes on the organization chart. The roles employees are required to perform, the others with whom they must interact, the way they are measured and rewarded, and the rites that will inevitably be affected, are all going to have to change. The barriers to such change include the sheer complexity of understanding how things actually work now, so that the new design will both address the important activities for success and overcome resistance to implementing it.

Care in understanding all the R factors is not just a nuisance dreamed up by behavioral scientists; it is necessary if change is to be successfully accomplished. What is often seen as resistance to change may not be resistance to all change, (unexpected salary bonuses, for example, are seldom resisted). However, expect resistance to appearing unintelligent before peers while learning new skills, to the breakup of established relationships, or to group norms that pressure people not to produce so much that weaker members appear inadequate. Helping those affected by change gain needed competence is beneficial. In general, a close understanding of the web of R factors that are causing behavior and that will be affected by the proposed change, is needed before plunging in; therefore, planning must proceed accordingly. Some ways of approaching the problem follow.

Behavior changes when there is dissatisfaction with the status quo, a vision or model of how things could be better, and a process or pathway for getting to the improved state. This concept was written as a formula by a consultant, David Gleicher, as

$$\text{Change} = (\text{Dissatisfaction} \times \text{Vision} \times \text{Process}) > \text{Cost of change}.$$

We will examine each component in turn.

Managing Dissatisfaction

Dissatisfaction is a motivator for change. This statement not only refers to the manager who wants to change someone else's behavior, but also to those who are the targets of change. People are most responsive to learning when they are moderately dissatisfied; too little, and they don't want to bother; too much is paralyzing. Therefore, if you want to increase a person or group's readiness to change, you need to manage their dissatisfaction. In practice, that often requires finding ways to increase dissatisfaction (suggesting that a happy worker is not always the best worker). This strategy can be accomplished in several ways:

1. Provide data from, or direct contact with, those who use the person's or group's services or products. Whether the "customer" is outside the firm or employees from other departments, they can show how performance needs to be better.

2. Provide other kinds of data on how performance falls short. These can be quantitative and impersonal, or qualitative and personally delivered; however, the data should demonstrate important gaps in performance. Effective managers learn to give timely, concrete feedback in a supportive, useful, nonpunitive manner. Most employees want to please their bosses and co-workers; direct feedback provides the information they need to see what is necessary.

3. Create educational programs to broaden perspectives or teach new skills.

4. Arrange for people to see better ways of doing things in other departments, divisions, or outside companies.

5. Create an exciting vision of some future state in which performance is higher or better quality, satisfaction is greater, and so on.

Creating Vision

The creation of vision can in itself help raise dissatisfaction to increase readiness for change, but vision is also necessary as a natural part of the change process. Without a clear view of the new, desired behavior and conditions, it is hard for even very dissatisfied people to change. The manager needs to create the paradox of a tangible vision that is futuristic but vivid enough so the targets of change can understand and be excited about it. The tangible vision needs to be sold to affected members of the organization.

Vision does not simply descend from above. The creation of vision comes from a considerable amount of exploring, analyzing, and rooting around in the territory of the problem. Firsthand data, from spending time with the people involved, is almost always needed, along with the more quantitative, impersonal data acquired for analysis. Small experiments or pilots are often helpful, especially if they are genuinely observed for learning and modification, rather than treated as ultimate solutions disguised as "just experiments" so no one will object.

"Getting to know the territory" can provide a clearer picture of what is desired. This knowledge would clarify whether the manager could induce the work group to use its technological discovery to increase productivity; whether the new MBA figured out how to gain the support of old-timers; and not only whether the experienced supervisors taught the new supervisors the ropes but also whether they were stimulated by their own fresh ideas; and so on.

Specifying Process/Procedures

People may be dissatisfied with the present and excited about a future state when all is better, but if they lack the knowledge to get there, frustration increases, and often cynicism sets in. Therefore, it is crucial to create and identify the pathways to achieve the vision. This process entails thinking through a number of issues and acting accordingly.

One place to start is by analyzing (for any particular change) who has an interest in it, who is a stakeholder in some way. For example, if your boss wants you to start using the computer, you are clearly a stakeholder, but so may be your co-workers, the department that receives your work, your boss's boss, the information systems manager, and so forth. Often, the number of stakeholders is far greater than is at first apparent; the manger of a regional office in a federal agency was astounded when, using this tool, she identified 236 stakeholders on a key issue she was trying to resolve. To visualize the concept, place a brief label for the change in the center of a blank page, and draw a circle around it. Then, one at a time add spokes to link it to the name of each possible stakeholder.

Once all the possible stakeholders are identified, then try to determine the following for each:

- What exactly are their stakes in the issue?
- What are their needs/desires in relation to the issue?
- What are their resources in relation to the issue? Information? Allies? Funds or supplies?
- Exactly how will they be affected by the change? Finances? Relationships with others? Status? Influence? Reputation? What might cause them to resist?
- Is their cooperation or goodwill necessary, desirable, or unimportant?

Having done this analysis for each stakeholder, do the same for yourself. What do *you* bring to the issue? Then prioritize those stakeholders most critical to your success. Your attention should first be directed to figuring out what you can offer them from your resources that would fit with their needs or desires, in return for whatever you need from them. Before initiating action, however, try to trace through all the possible implications for all the stakeholders, and plan accordingly. This can be tedious, but it saves aggravation later. Too many good ideas for change have been sunk because the well-intentioned manager did not anticipate who would be affected and how to deal with them.

After the stakeholders have been identified, part of planning is to determine how the resistance of key people (including those directly targeted for changed behavior) can be overcome. For some, clear and accurate information about your plans, progress, and problems will reduce uncertainty. Since no change plan leads to guaranteed results, there is always uncertainty, so anything that can reduce unnecessary uncertainty will be useful.

Another practical way to reduce resistance is to increase the amount of control in the hands of those affected. This end is often best achieved by encouraging their participation in diagnosing the problem(s) and devising solutions. The level of expertise regarding the particular change and the degree to which the change depends on their cooperation, determine how appropriate will be their participation in shaping it. Occasionally, the targets of the change lack relevant expertise and are replaceable if they do not cooperate, but as education levels rise and organizations become more complex, that situation is less often the case. The need is increasing for managers to share responsibility with their subordinates, often as a team. Furthermore, organizational stress occurs when individuals do not have control over much of their life at work. The resulting stress can lead to passivity, overt resistance, or even physical illness and burnout. This negatively affects not only implementation of change, but even everyday work.

As suggested earlier, since almost any change in behavior will require new knowledge or skills, and since most people are embarrassed about appearing awkward while learning, plans need to be made for training and support of learning. Providing training in advance allows time for trial and error, time for peers also to be in the learning situation, and time to identify unanticipated skill gaps that need to be addressed.

If the change involves more than a few people in one area, there may be need for a demonstration project, utilizing participants who are primed for the change, capable of learning what is needed, and eager to cooperate. It is always useful to load early attempts for success (although managers sometimes erroneously begin with their toughest audience, believing that once the change works with them it can work anywhere). Early wins and successes spur future efforts and overcome skepticism.

Another important part of planning is the anticipation of what other changes in related R factors will be necessary to support the change. Given a group of disenchanted engineers, for example, a new committee to allow their input on decisions may require other changes to make it work: new access to information, new tasks, or even altered performance measures. Accurate diagnosis of R factors helps identify the related changes that need to be made.

Again, for complex change projects, creation of a transition management structure addresses all these issues, coordinates this change with others in progress, links to higher management for support or resources, and in general guides the change effort during its introduction while regular work continues. It is difficult to put on new athletic shoes and tie them while running in a marathon, but that feat is analogous to making changes while keeping the work flowing. In fact, the current pace of change makes some feel that organizational life is like running the marathon while *manufacturing* your running shoes. And every mile is Heartbreak Hill! A special temporary management structure can ease the overload. All the methods mentioned so far minimize the costs of change.

CONCLUDING REMARKS

Careful diagnosis and planning aid in managing people. Without the understanding of situational forces acting on individuals, the internal factors that determine how the forces are interpreted, or the action steps available to alter behavior causing undesirable results, effective management is only an accident. Yet, managing others requires skill and art as well as careful analysis. Whatever natural talents you have will be enhanced by extensive practice at putting yourself in managerial situations, and a willingness to subsequently reflect on your own behavior to learn from it. Your self-concept, your own attitude and sensitivity toward other people, needs to be open enough to permit constant alterations in your own behavior. You need to view management as an ongoing attempt to find mutual interests and make modifications, not as a test of how much power you have or to what extent you are correct.

No one book can teach you all the skills vital to management, such as to listen carefully to what is important to those with whom you work, to give honest feedback to aid their learning, to judge appropriate times to build consensus from below or to take strong initiatives, to find ways to link your interests to others and the organization, to look carefully before leaping yet be comfortable leaping when an absolute outcome cannot be predicted; and to mix challenge and support. Nevertheless, you need to acquire these skills.

Perhaps a final R factor should be added to the already lengthy list: *reflection.* If you can learn *to learn* from your experience, and practice *revision* on yourself as well as those you want to manage, no single mistake will matter for long. Changing yourself is usually the best way to begin changing others. In your managerial pursuits, my best *regards.*

FOR FURTHER READING

Bennis, Warren G., and B. Nanus, *Leadership* (New York: Harper & Row, 1985).

Bradford, David L., and Allan R. Cohen, *Managing for Excellence: The Guide to Developing High Performance in Contemporary Organizations* (New York: John Wiley, 1988).

Cohen, Allan R., *The Portable MBA in Management* (New York: John Wiley, 1993).

Cohen, Allan R., and David L. Bradford, *Influence without Authority* (New York: John Wiley, 1990).

Herzberg, F., "One More Time: How Do You Motivate Employees?" *Harvard Business Review 46,* 1968, pp. 53–62.

Kanter, Rosabeth M., *The Changemasters: Innovation for Productivity in the American Corporation* (New York: Simon & Schuster, 1983).

Kanter, Rosabeth M., *Men and Women of the Corporation* (New York: Basic Books, 1977).

Kotter, John, and James Heskett, *Corporate Culture and Organizational Performance* (New York: Free Press, 1993).

Manz, Charles, and Henry Sims, *Business without Bosses: How Self-Managing Teams Build High-Performing Companies* (New York: John Wiley, 1993).

Mintzberg, Henry, *The Nature of Managerial Work* (New York: Harper & Row, 1973).

Pfeffer, Jeffrey, *Managing with Power: Politics and Influence in the Organization* (Boston: Harvard Business School Press, 1992).

Whyte, W. F., *Street Corner Society* (rev. ed) (Chicago: University of Chicago Press, 1955).

QUANTITATIVE TOOLS: NUMBERS AS THE FUNDAMENTAL LANGUAGE OF BUSINESS

4

Brian Forst

Numbers are the fundamental language of business—the bottom line on the income statement is a number. Efficiency on the production line is expressed numerically; numbers can be improved through statistical analysis and can, in turn, powerfully affect the bottom line. The business plan is expressed specifically as numbers on the operating budget, numbers that may derive largely from statistical projections of revenues and costs. Decisions to invest in assets that can accelerate the growth of the business are usually based on numbers that reflect the expected profits and risks of each alternative use of invested funds. Success and failure of the business or any of its parts typically comes down to numbers.

The radical changes sweeping business today are reflected in the numbers used to manage business. In the past, managers often focused on internal issues, and their statistics reflected this focus. The traditional sales forecast builds on previous years' numbers, for example. But managers must now also emphasize numbers that give them insight into the fast-changing business environment. They may now collect numbers on another company's shipping, order processing, manufacturing, or customer service process to compare it with their own and benchmark any aspects that are superior. And this means a shift from numerical analysis of functions or departments to analysis of whole business processes so that they can be compared with others and improved to become more competitive. Similarly, forecasts now reflect more data concerning the business environment: new technologies, competitors, and trends that may alter sales fundamentally from previous years' patterns. The greatest changes are seen in the measurement of quality. Where businesses used to treat quality control activities as a cost center, now they consider quality improvement to be a major source of both cost savings and competitive benefit. Despite these radical changes, managers continue to work with a common set of numerical tools. Applications are shifting, but the fundamental quantitative skills required for good management are the closest thing to a constant in the MBA curriculum.

While it is unnecessary to learn the intricacies of statistics and applied mathematics to gain control of the numbers and improve them, executives and managers stand to gain significantly from knowing that many of their real-world problems can be solved with tools that work with numbers, the tools of quantitative methods. Such knowledge empowers the manager to make the best possible decision of where to turn and what to expect from the computer programs and experts that carry out the detailed problem-solving calculations. This knowledge is bound to improve the business and make the manager more successful.

This information becomes critical especially in the company of the 1990s and beyond, both profit-making and nonprofit. Knowing how to use quantitative tools is no longer an expertise located somewhere high up in a corporate office of strategic planning or a production logistics unit. The reduction and elimination of corporate hierarchies means that this knowledge must now be understood and acted on by people involved in the production of goods and in the delivery of services, people directly responsible for satisfying the wants of customers and clients. Powerful quantitative tools are now available for personal computers and local area networks, but many who need them often fail to recognize that some of their most aggravating problems are actually manageable ones that have been faced for centuries. Exposure to the application of the tools of this chapter to a variety of real-world problems can empower the manager to recognize that a new problem is actually of a certain type that, properly formulated, has an accessible solution.

This chapter provides an overview of these tools and the kinds of problems that they help managers solve. The six sections—statistical estimation and the control of quality, root cause analysis, regression analysis as a tool for explaining statistical associations, statistical forecasting, decision analysis, and operations research—use a hypothetical company to illustrate how each tool can improve the bottom line.

STATISTICAL ESTIMATION AND THE CONTROL OF QUALITY

It has been well established that quality is the key to long-run growth in revenues. A time-tested way to control the *quality of goods* is by inspection as they proceed through the production line, keeping track of the rate at which defects occur. Control of the *quality of service* is achieved by asking customers about the service they have received, keeping track of the proportion who are dissatisfied and why.

However, measuring quality isn't enough. Controlling the quality of production in a manufacturing plant or the quality of customer service by inspecting and measuring goods and customer satisfaction does not eliminate the need for commitment-to-excellence programs, thorough training of production and service personnel, and preventive maintenance of equipment.

If quality begins with a commitment to excellence, it ends with something much more prosaic—measurement. And measurement usually requires sampling. When defective products are capable of imposing grave costs on users, as in the case of faulty automobile brakes, *all* the products must be carefully inspected. Most goods and services, however, do not require 100 percent sampling to ensure that quality is properly controlled. The testing itself may destroy the product, as in the case of foods, disposable goods, and explosives; 100 percent sampling would leave no products for the customer.

In the traditional approach to quality, the problem is this: How can we minimize the total cost of inferior-quality goods and services, taking into account both the cost of inferior quality and the cost of a quality control program?

In a time of intense worldwide competition in the quality of goods and services, this is no academic issue. It is of particular importance to our example company, Power Tools, Inc. You have been appointed to manage this company during the course of this chapter. Power Tools enjoyed industry dominance during the 1950s and 1960s but has gradually lost business to Asian and European competitors ever since. Your marketing people are sure of the primary cause: The quality of the products made by foreign competitors has surpassed that of your goods, and the customers know it. The marketing vice president supports this claim by a compelling fact: 3 percent of Power Tool's chain saws and 2 percent of its power drills are returned under the one-year warranty, while the rate of return for your leading competitor is only 1 percent for each of the two products.

To remedy the problem, your engineers disassemble and carefully examine the competitor's chain saw with a view to understanding and correcting the leading cause of your warranty claims: the central gear assembly. The basic design of the competitor's gear assembly is the same as yours; that finding leaves as a leading candidate for the cause of the problem excessive variability in the dimensions of the gears (length, outside diameter, tooth height, tooth width, etc.) in your products. To validate this suspicion, you compare the variability of a sample of 20 of their gears with 20 of yours. Table 4-1 presents the measurement for the outside diameter of the largest gear in the sample.

Gear variability can be measured in several ways. The simplest measure is the *range,* the difference between the largest and the smallest value in the distribution. For Power Tools, the range is 0.007 (1.158 − 1.151) and for Brand X

**TABLE 4-1   Distribution of gear diameters:
Power Tools and leading
competitor**

	Power Tools	Brand X		Power Tools	Brand X
1.	1.155	0.976	11.	1.153	0.973
2.	1.157	0.972	12.	1.156	0.973
3.	1.151	0.974	13.	1.156	0.974
4.	1.153	0.974	14.	1.157	0.972
5.	1.158	0.970	15.	1.157	0.973
6.	1.154	0.974	16.	1.152	0.975
7.	1.157	0.973	17.	1.155	0.972
8.	1.151	0.974	18.	1.152	0.972
9.	1.158	0.972	19.	1.158	0.974
10.	1.151	0.971	20.	1.153	0.973

it is 0.006 (0.976 − 0.970). That seems fairly close, but the Power Tool gear is slightly larger to begin with, and range does not adjust for that. More important, the range is a limited measure in that it considers only two values out of the entire distribution, in this case, ignoring the variability of the other 18 gears in each sample. Other measures of variability (or dispersion) take all 20 observations into account. Three widely used measures that do this are the *standard deviation, variance,* and *coefficient of variation.* The standard deviation is commonly used in quality control problems; the variance, which is the square of the standard deviation, is more commonly used in inquiries into the causes of variability; and coefficient of variation is used to standardize variability by the mean value of the distribution. The formulas for calculating these statistics and their values for this example are shown in Table 4-2.

All the measures of variation other than the range reveal the diameter of the Power Tools' gear to be substantially more variable than that of the competitor's. The standard deviation, as estimated from the sample, is 82 percent larger; the estimated variance is over three times larger; and the sample coefficient of variation is 53 percent larger. The probability that the competitor's gears are in fact as variable as ours—that the observed differences could be due only to randomness for samples of size 20—is virtually zero.

Note also in Table 4-2 the three measures of central tendency or "average" value of the distribution: *mode, median,* and *mean.* the mode is the most commonly observed value in the distribution; the median is the middle value when the observations are sorted; and the mean is the sum of the values divided by the number of values. (The term *average* is perhaps best avoided because it is ambiguous; sometimes it connotes any measure of central tendency, and sometimes it connotes the mean in particular.) The mean is the generally preferred

TABLE 4-2 Basic descriptive statistics and their values for Power Tools and brand X

Statistic	Definition	Power Tools	Brand X
Fundamental Measures:			
Sum	Σy	23.094	19.461
n	Number of observations	20	20
Measures of Central Tendency:			
Mode	Most common value	1.157	0.974
Median	Middle value	1.155	0.973
Mean	$\bar{y} = \Sigma y / n$	1.15470	0.97305
Measures of Dispersion:			
Range	Maximum − minimum	0.007	0.006
Standard deviation	$s = \sqrt{\dfrac{\Sigma y^2}{n} - (\bar{y})^2}$	.002472	.001359
Variance	$s^2 = \dfrac{\Sigma y^2}{n} - (\bar{y})^2$	.0000061	.0000018
Coefficient of variation	$s/\bar{y}$	.002141	.001397

measure of central tendency, although for most applications it doesn't hurt to report all three.

Your primary concern, however, based on analysis of the numbers in Table 4-2, is dispersion around the mean. To improve the quality of your products, you purchase gears from a new vendor with more reliable specifications, modernize the production line, and retrain your production crew. Now you wish to set up a quality control system that will improve your ability to find inferior products before they come into the customer's hands. You set up various quality control tests all along the production line. One is a vibration test of finished goods: The production process should produce chain saws that operate with about 0.06 millimeter of wobble, with a standard deviation of 0.01 millimeter.

Because this test is more labor intensive than other tests and is one of several, you don't test every unit—only a random sample of five units every two hours, which a quality control expert recommends to you as a sensible balance between the cost of random error associated with small samples and the cost of sampling. Any chain saw that exceeds 0.10 millimeters of wobble will be disassembled, adjusted, reassembled, and retested. Any sample of five that exceeds the 0.06 production line standard by more than two standard deviations (an arbitrary limit that leads to the rejection of just under 5 percent of all samples) will call for a production process adjustment that will delay production for about an hour.

The standard deviation for the distribution of means for samples of size n is given by the formula $s_n = s/\sqrt{n}$. Since the standard deviation for a single product is 0.01, for our sample of five, two standard deviations beyond the production line standard of 0.06 will give a boundary of acceptable products of 0.06 + (2) [(0.01)/$\sqrt{5}$], or 0.0689.

This result can be displayed on a *quality control chart,* a useful tool to monitor the quality of products by graphing the results of periodic samples of products. If the production line runs from 8:00 A.M. until 6:00 P.M., and five units are sampled during each two-hour period, the quality control chart for Power Tools, Inc., for one week will look like Figure 4-1.

The quality standard of 0.0600 is shown as the horizontal line at the center of the chart, and the lines above and below represent variations of two standard deviations from that level in either direction. In many production processes, parts are rejected if they fall outside either of the two standard deviation boundaries, since uniformity of part size is usually the primary objective; in this case, we are concerned only if the wobble exceeds the top line, at 0.0689 millimeters.

How likely is it that a sample will exceed that limit? Let's rephrase this question in more specific terms, so that the answer can be more clearly derived: If we take repeated samples of five per sample and measure the mean wobble for each sample, what will the distribution of those mean values look like, and what fraction of the distribution will have mean values that exceed 0.0689?

First, how will the distribution look? Under a basic proposition known as the *central limit theorem,* the distribution of repeated samples will take on the shape of the familiar bell-shaped *normal distribution,*[1] regardless of the shape of the distribution of items taken one at a time (which in this case is also normal). The distribution for this example, with a mean of 0.0600, a standard deviation for the parent distribution of 0.010, and $n = 5$, is shown in Figure 4-2.

The probability that a sample will exceed the 0.06894 boundary is the proportion of the curve that is shaded. To find the area under a normal curve, we can go to a book of standard statistical tables or to a computer program that gives areas under a special normal curve—one that is standardized with mean = 0 and

FIGURE 4-1   Quality control chart

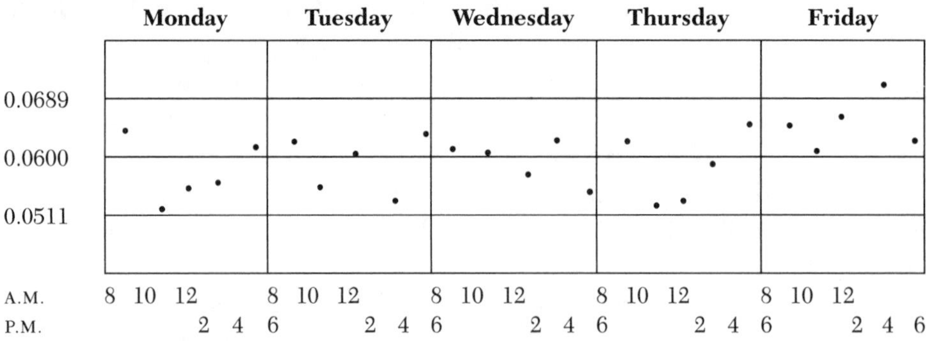

	Monday	Tuesday	Wednesday	Thursday	Friday

| A.M. | 8 10 12 | 8 10 12 | 8 10 12 | 8 10 12 | 8 10 12 |
| P.M. | 2 4 6 | 2 4 6 | 2 4 6 | 2 4 6 | 2 4 6 |

FIGURE 4-2 Distribution of mean values from repeated samples
(*y* = 0.060; *s* = 0.01; *n* = 5)

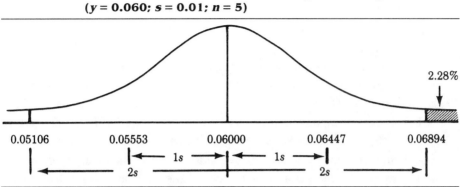

standard deviation = 1. Doing so yields the following information: 15.87 percent of the curve lies beyond the one standard deviation mark above (or below) the mean, in this case beyond the value 0.06447, and 2.28 percent lies beyond the two standard deviation mark, 0.06894. Therefore, we can expect over 2 percent of all samples of five chain saws to have a mean wobble of more than the 0.06894.

Should we assume that such occurrences are just due to luck of the draw, or *random error,* with no need to adjust the production process? Absolutely not. When the production process is working properly, it will produce samples with values that *exceed* the acceptable limit 2 percent of the time, but *the production process does not always operate at that standard!* Some errors are *nonrandom.* A commonsense look at the data shown in Figure 4-1 suggests that Friday's production process was operating above the 0.060 standard all day, and quite possibly was an extension of a trend that started the previous day, not just a stroke of bad luck for the period from 2:00 to 4:00. Five successive samples above the standard for an entire day suggests that something else may be going on. Such patterns are often caused by factors that are well known to the staff on the production line: excessive pressure to meet accelerated end-of-week production schedules, key people out sick, beer-soaked TGIF lunches, and so on. Regardless of the underlying causes, simple descriptive statistics, properly organized, can be potent tools for ferreting out the patterns that, when known, provide the basis for action.

REGRESSION ANALYSIS AS A TOOL FOR
EXPLAINING ASSOCIATIONS

The data graphed in Figure 4-1 reveal some random fluctuations and the prospect of a nonrandom "Friday" effect, but a closer look suggests more: A daily cycle is also evident. The midday products tend to be better than those produced at either the start or end of the day. But you are viewing only one week's data. By retrieving data for several weeks, you could establish more conclusively the existence of both a daily cycle and the Friday phenomenon. Such findings could induce you to inquire into the causes of these patterns. In the meantime, you can use the data graphed in Figure 4-1 and reported in Table 4-3 to test both the Friday and midday effects.

Here is how: You speculate that the amount of wobble is determined in part by whether the day is Friday, in part by whether it is midday (between 10:00 A.M. and 4:00 P.M.), and in part by random forces. Then you designate the amount of wobble as the variable y, the day of the week as x_1 ($x_1 = 1$ if Friday, $x_1 = 0$ if any other day), and the time of day as x_2 ($x_2 = 1$ if midday, $x2 = 0$ if either before 10:00 A.M. or after 4:00 P.M.); and you write the linear equation

$$y = a + bx_1 + cx_2 + \text{r.e.} \tag{1}$$

where a, b, and c are coefficients you want to estimate with your data, and r.e. represents random error, a factor assumed to be normally distributed with a mean of zero.

This equation is your model of the relationship between vibration and three hypothesized determinants of vibration: the Friday effect (you think it may increase vibration), the midday effect (you think it may decrease vibration), and the random effect (all the other factors that affect vibration). The variable being explained or predicted, y, is called the *dependent variable,* and the variables used as explainers or predictors, x_1 and x_2, are the *independent variables.* In this case, the independent variables are *binary* (often called "dummy") *variables,* that is, variables that can assume only the values zero or one. You use a linear equation both because you have no compelling reason to believe the relationship is nonlinear and because a linear equation is simpler to estimate than other equations.

If you can now imagine this equation as a plane in a space containing the 25 dots that represent the observations of one week, any number of planes can "fit" your 25 data points reasonably well; but statisticians have developed the *least*

TABLE 4-3   Quality control data for one week of production

Time	Monday	Tuesday	Wednesday	Thursday	Friday
8–10	.0641	.0618	.0612	.0618	.0641
10–12	.0522	.0552	.0605	.0529	.0612
12–2	.0552	.0604	.0575	.0535	.0659
2–4	.0559	.0545	.0621	.0588	.0699
4–6	.0612	.0629	.0559	.0639	.0621

squares criterion, under which you should choose the plane with the coefficients that minimize the sum of the squared vertical deviations from each observation to the plane. Your 25 data points to be used for estimating the equation of this plane are shown in Table 4-4.

To estimate the parameters (the true coefficients of the relationship, as distinct from the coefficient values obtained from the sample) of Equation 1, you enter the data points into a computer that can perform *regression analysis.*

Regression analysis was once done either on a large mainframe computer or with some effort using a calculator and a pad of paper; today, it can be done easily on a personal computer with any modern spreadsheet program, such as Lotus 1-2-3®, or standard statistical analysis software. For the data in Table 4-4, the linear equation with the least squares property is

$$y = .060681 + .006067x_1 - .00351x_2 \quad r^2 = .461$$
$$ (.003427) \quad (.001713) \quad\quad (.001399) \tag{2}$$

Or using words, you can estimate the amount of wobble by taking the constant .060681, adding .006067 to it if the saw was produced on Friday (don't subtract .006067 if it was produced on another day), and then subtracting from it .00351 if the saw was produced between 10:00 A.M. and 4:00 P.M. The r^2 statistic is the *coefficient of determination;* it can be interpreted as follows: 46.1 percent of the variance in y is accounted for (or explained) by the variables x_1 and x_2. The numbers in parentheses below the estimated regression coefficients are *standard errors of estimates* which are needed for testing whether the coefficients themselves are "statistically significant"—that is, whether they are different enough from zero to allow you to say that it is just too unlikely that such differences are attributable to chance alone. You can determine whether a

TABLE 4-4   Data for regression estimate to explain variation in quality

	y	x_1	x_2		y	x_1	x_2
1	.0641	0	0	14	.0621	0	1
2	.0522	0	1	15	.0559	0	0
3	.0552	0	1	16	.0618	0	0
4	.0559	0	1	17	.0529	0	1
5	.0612	0	0	18	.0535	0	1
6	.0618	0	0	19	.0588	0	1
7	.0552	0	1	20	.0639	0	0
8	.0604	0	1	21	.0641	1	0
9	.0545	0	1	22	.0612	1	1
10	.0629	0	0	23	.0659	1	1
11	.0612	0	0	24	.0699	1	1
12	.0605	0	1	25	.0621	1	0
13	.0575	0	1				

TABLE 4-5   t Statistics and corresponding significance levels

Degrees of Freedom	Significance Levels		
	.10	.05	.01
10	1.81	2.23	3.17
20	1.73	2.09	2.85
30	1.70	2.04	2.75
40	1.68	2.02	2.70
50	1.68	2.01	2.68
100	1.66	1.98	2.63
∞	1.64	1.96	2.58

coefficient is significant by dividing the coefficient by its standard error, thus getting the *t statistic.* Some sample t statistics and their significance levels are shown in Table 4-5. The *degrees of freedom* are the number of observations (n) minus the total number of variables in the regression equation. For your problem, there are 25 observations and 3 variables in the regression equation, yielding 22 degrees of freedom.

To establish the effect of time of day and day of week on the quality of your chain saws, you obtain t statistics of 3.54 for the day-of-week effect (.006067/.001713) and −2.51 for the time-of-day effect (−.00351/.001399). From Table 4-5, with 22 degrees of freedom, we can see that these results are significant at .01 and .05, respectively.

Here is what the figures mean: If there were no day-of-week effect, you would obtain a statistical association between product vibration and day of week as strong as you did less than 1 percent of the time just due to randomness and, if there were no time-of-day effect, you would obtain this same association less than 5 percent of the time just due to randomness. If you are not yet convinced that the patterns are real rather than random and if you perceive that the value of further investigation exceeds the cost, you can retrieve data from additional weeks and analyze them the same way to see whether higher levels of statistical significance result.

How Much Quality?

One of the most basic quality control issues is this: How much quality control is enough? Earlier, it was suggested that the right amount takes into account both the cost of controlling quality and the cost of inferior quality. Specifically, the right amount is the point at which the cost of additional quality control *begins* to exceed the additional benefit of higher quality. To know that level, you must know not only the cost of the quality control program—which includes the labor cost of the program, the cost of destroying materials in sampling, and the cost of production downtime associated with quality control improvements—but also the benefit of higher quality (or the cost of inferior quality) and the relationship between the quality control program and product quality. The benefit of higher quality should show up in subsequent revenues, as we will see in the next section. Other factors are bound to influence revenues too, factors that may be related to the quality control program, making it more difficult to isolate the effect of the program on revenues. For example, a new manager may introduce a quality control program and a host of other stimulants to revenues at the same time, in which case one could easily make the mistake of attributing higher revenues to the quality control program rather than the new manager or his or her other programs. Alternatively, one could assess the benefit of a quality control program using a measure more directly related to quality than revenue, such as the rate of customer complaints or product returns, and regressing that variable on the cost of the program and its other measurable characteristics in earlier periods.

ROOT CAUSE ANALYSIS AND THE CREATION OF QUALITY

So far, we have explored quantitative methods in the context of a traditional approach to quality. The traditional approach, termed quality control, focuses on improving quality by catching and correcting errors. Your approach at Power Tools, Inc., is a good example of quality control. For instance, you performed an analysis of the distribution of gear diameters, found that there was more variation in your gears than your competitors', and rejected your supplier in favor of a new one. Further, you added a vibration test at the end of the production process, since off-spec gears cause chain saws to vibrate. When your quality control engineers find a sample of saws that vibrate too much, they know there is a gear problem and can go back to the supplier and ask them to tighten up their operations. They can also alert the assemblers to be more careful, because occasionally the problem is in the way the gears are assembled as well. For instance, sometimes the assemblers forget to add a small washer to the gear assembly.

These steps have reduced the number of warranty clams from 3% to 2%, but the new approach costs more money and you doubt it is worth the cost to try to cut claims down to 1% or less. The larger or more frequent your samples, the more time and effort required. The more thorough your quality control, the more saws will land on your scrap and rework piles. The costs of catching and controlling such errors, along with the costs of selecting and training new suppliers, and handling returns, warranty claims, and your staff of inspectors, plus handling customer complaints from out-of-spec products that slip through the controls, probably make up 30% or so of Power Tools' total manufacturing costs.

When quality control is increased, total manufacturing costs rise. And prices or profit margins will have to reflect these changes.

Breaking the Cost-Quality Link

For companies like Power Tools, Inc., competition is tough because new competitors put pressure on prices as well as quality. Customers expect Power Tools to increase its quality and reduce its costs at the same time—an unrealistic combination unless you can somehow break the link between quality and costs. Fortunately, you can. To do so requires a shift in approach, from quality control to process improvement. And a new set of analytical methods have been developed to help cut costs and increase quality simultaneously. These tools use similar numbers, but in different ways. They are associated with total quality management and continuous process improvement methods, and employees in many companies are now receiving special training in how to use them. They are typically used by a team made up of the people who "own" a process, since they are the ones who understand the process intimately enough to redesign it effectively. At Power Tools, Inc., such a team might focus on the gear problem with the goal of reducing variation in the gear. And it might include designers from the engineering function, a shift supervisor and production workers from the manufacturing line, and perhaps someone from sales or marketing to represent the customer's perspective.

The team's mandate would be to analyze the entire gear design and production process to identify the root causes of deviation from specified measures. Root cause has a formal meaning in this usage: It means a potential cause that is shown to have a significant, quantifiable influence over the result, to be at the beginning of the chain of causal links if any such chains exist, and to be present in the process in question.

When the team first starts thinking about what causes the variation in gears, they will generate a long list of potential causes. Some of these will be explained by factors that in turn cause *them* and thus are not at the root of a chain of effects. Obviously, it is more productive to look at the root causes than other variables driven by them. Other potential causes will turn out to be latent causes, meaning they could cause the result if present, but they can be shown to be absent in the specific process in question. And finally, some potential causes will turn out to be null causes, meaning they are not capable of causing the effect.

Why distinguish among multiple definitions of causes? Because when trying to prevent the occurrence of a costly quality problem, you must focus on root causes. In practice, many improvement teams waste their time on latent or null causes and produce no improvement in the process. To be sure your team has identified root causes, you can use the first of the new quality improvement tools: the *with/without study*. It attempts to artificially generate the problem (gear variability in the Power Tools example), both with and without the root cause being present. To use it, you must set up an appropriate experiment and collect the same data used in the previous quality control example. Compare two samples, one generated with and one without the hypothesized root cause being present. Collect the same measures detailed in Table 4-2 (fundamental measures, measures of central tendency, and measures of dispersion). If the differences between the two samples are not dramatic, you may need to apply statistical methods to determine whether they are due to chance or likely to reflect real differences (the previous discussion of t statistics provides a general framework for this task, and most companies have in-house quality control engineers capable of more sophisticated analyses).

If a significant difference in the frequency of the quality problem is found, this result shows not only that you have isolated a legitimate root cause, but also allows you to estimate the importance of that cause. Let's say that in the normal process you have a 1 percent occurrence of the problem, but that in the experimental process you find the problem occurs only .25 percent of the time. You can make an initial estimate that the root cause under study explains 75 percent of the problem. (Later in the chapter, we will review regression analysis, which forms the basis for more advanced approaches to this analytical problem. Again, it is probably enough to know that advanced tools exist, so that you can order them from a resident or consulting quality engineer if needed.)

The end result of the team's brainstorming of potential causes, followed by analysis to isolate the legitimate root causes from their list, is likely to be a shorter list of between 5 and 10 root causes. Even though these are all root causes, the team will get nowhere if it tries to fix all of them at once. Some have a stronger influence over the variation in gear size than others. The 80-20 rule of thumb generally applies; that is 20 percent of the causes are likely to explain 80 percent of the result. Therefore the next quantitative method the team needs is the Pareto chart, a vertical bar chart that shows the frequency of root causes or the percentage of variation explained by them. As a practical matter, such information can just as easily be presented in tabular format, but it is helpful to be able to see the data. Generally, one or a few of the root causes explain most of the occurrences of the problem, and show up as dominant in the bar chart display. The largest of these should be the focus of the team's first improvement effort. See Figure 4-3 for a Pareto chart analysis of the problem at Power Tools.

The team's analysis and experiments determined that most of the problems with gears can be traced to poor quality gears shipped from the supplier. The change of suppliers helped reduce the number of bad gears received, but in spite of this effort, the supplier's lack of quality control is still the major root cause. The team made a note to make this its highest priority problem. The next

FIGURE 4-3   Pareto chart, causes of vibration

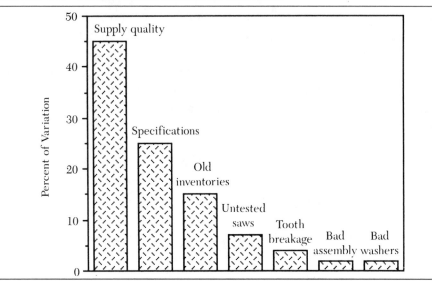

most important problem was revealed in discussions with people at the supplier company: The specifications they receive from Power Tools' engineering department are not realistic in all respects. Power Tools' engineers do not fully understand the constraints of the steel used, the type of machines the supplier uses to cut it, and so forth. Poor communication produces specifications that are inherently difficult for the supplier to meet. The team decides to tackle this problem once they have solved the first one. Finally, the team notes that the third most important problem is that Power Tools has a large, valuable inventory of gears in its warehouse, as well as a smaller but also significant inventory on the production floor. Even when bad gears are found through the control charting and vibration tests you instituted, the shift supervisor has little choice but to keep drawing gears out of the inventory. No one wants to throw away the entire inventory because a few bad gears were found, but you suspect the quality of gears in inventory is low.

What can the team do to eliminate these high-priority root causes? The temptation is to start making changes right away. That is a mistake—the relationships between the many controllable factors are not well understood. The team cannot see the forest for the trees. The team needs to flowchart the entire process as it is currently performed in order to gain a systems perspective. In flowcharting, each step is drawn as a box, arrows link each box with the steps that flow from it, and decisions, where choices of path are made in the process, are drawn as sideways diamonds. Figure 4-4 is a process flow diagram for the

FIGURE 4-4   Process flow diagram, seventeen-step process

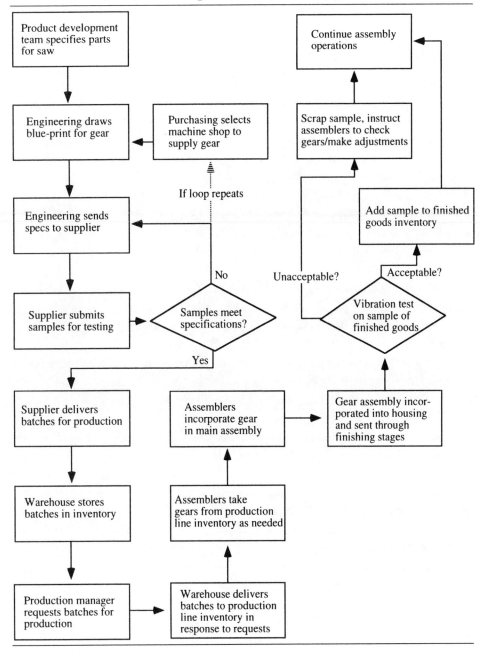

process of designing, specifying, sourcing, receiving, and using gears in the production of chain saws at Power Tools.

Redesigning the Process

This process diagram reflects the two fixes you have already made as a result of your prior quantitative analyses. It shows the process of selecting a new supplier, the first fix you tried. Unless your team eliminates the problems with the new supplier, the process will inevitably return to this step and you will bounce from supplier to supplier—a prospect that seems unlikely to cut errors or costs. The process flowchart also shows the vibration testing process you instituted at the end of the production line.

This process flowchart helps the team understand why these two fixes did not increase quality as much as they had hoped. The vibration test is too far downstream from the three most important root causes. It does nothing to eliminate the production of poor quality gears by the supplier, nor does it help improve the specifications engineering produces for the supplier. And it does not address the inventory problem either. In fact, all it does is to increase the amount of rework and scrap, thus raising costs without eliminating root causes. The team's first decision is therefore to eliminate the vibration test completely and focus instead on process improvements that address root causes. You wonder whether this is wise but eventually agree with the team's conclusion that the best strategy is to eliminate all bad gears, rather than try to catch them after saws are assembled.

The next step the team takes is to look closely at the supplier's quality control efforts. The team realizes that the current process leaves quality to the supplier and provides no support or rigorous requirements. No wonder the supplier delivers defective gears! The team agrees that the supplier needs to be integrated into Power Tools' quality improvement process and invites representatives of the supplier to join the team. This results in a new focus on the supplier's production line, and one of Power Tools' engineers agrees to spend a month at the supplier company to help them learn how to use quality control charts and analyze their own process.

The team feels it has taken steps needed to address the first root cause. But it recognizes that the second root cause, poor specifications, is related to the first from the supplier's perspective. It elects to keep redesigning the process until this cause is eliminated too. In examining the files, the team discovers that complaints about specifications are most often due to poor communications among the different people and groups involved. The flowchart shows that the product development department, the engineering department, the purchasing department, and a supplier are all involved in the first four steps of the process.

The team is emboldened by the benefits it has already seen since inviting the supplier's representative to join it. Why not create a cross-functional design team that eliminates the need to pass the design from function to function? The team redraws the first four steps of the process, deciding in the future to use a cross-functional design team that can iron out all the issues in one step.

Next the team realizes that the two changes it has made eliminate the need for the supplier to submit samples for testing. The supplier is now an integral part of the design team, and Power Tools has an engineer on-site at the supplier's production facility, so you are no longer worried about the supplier's quality. You know the team can work hand-in-hand with the supplier to develop on-site processes and tests that will ensure high quality at the supplier's plant. The team is having fun now and wants to keep working until the third root cause is addressed as well.

The third root cause is the large inventories of gears in two different locations at Power Tools. The process flow-chart shows that gears are currently delivered in large, infrequent batches, at the convenience of the supplier, and placed in a Power Tools warehouse remote from the production line. This means the production manager must request gears from Power Tools' warehouse, which is not always cooperative, so the production manager keeps extra gears in another inventory on the production floor. The team decides that the new, cooperative relationship with the supplier makes it possible to eliminate the in-house inventories completely and instead ask the supplier to deliver just enough gears every morning for the saws Power Tools plans to make that day. Power Tools' production manager always works from a one-week plan but has never shared that plan with the supplier before. From now on, the team will deliver the weekly plans to the supplier.

Now the team has a simpler process in which many unnecessary hand-offs between functions are eliminated. The responsibility for quality has been pushed upstream to the supplier, and Power Tools now collaborates with the supplier to eliminate the errors resulting from poor design and specifications, and from lack of controls on the supplier's production line. The team has also eliminated the vibration test at the end of Power Tools' line. Its final fix is to train all its assemblers how to draw a sample of gears from the daily inventory each morning, measure them, and plot the measurements on appropriate control charts. This means assemblers now know, in advance of using gears, whether the daily inventory is perfect or not. You doubt there will be many problems, but it seems prudent to check for a while, at least until the new supplier quality processes have proven adequate.

What if the assemblers find faulty gears? They will be unable to make saws, as there will be no other inventories of gears on site. The team worries about this at first, then realizes it will create the desired emphasis on eliminating root causes of errors. You estimate that the line may have to be shut down for a day several times each year, but a quick calculation shows that this will cost Power Tools far less than the current inferior quality costs. It turns out to be far cheaper to invest in a process that never produces a bad saw than to try to catch bad saws after they have been made.

The new process is shown in Figure 4-5. Note that it has 13 steps, compared with 17 in the previous process flowchart. The new approach to quality has reduced steps while increasing quality (such changes might typically be

FIGURE 4-5 Process flow diagram, thirteen-step process

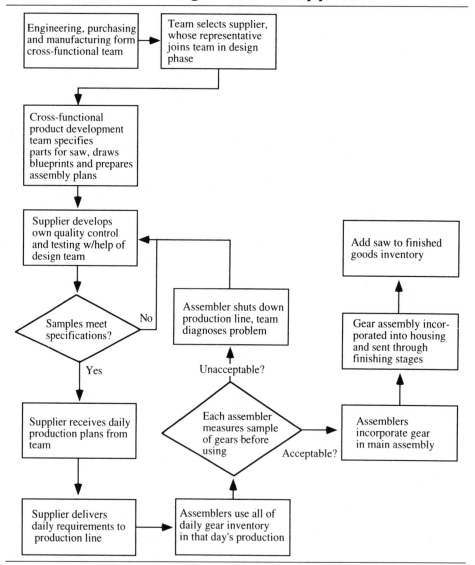

associated with cuts in warranty claims from 2 percent to .02 percent in a typical manufacturing plant). And when a process is shortened, its costs decrease. This reflects the fact that two kinds of costs drive the overall costs of any process, whether in manufacturing or service businesses: time and money spent. The redesign at Power Tools cut time spent by eliminating steps. And it cut money principally by eliminating the need to hire quality control inspectors and by cutting gear inventory from months' worth to a single day's worth at most. Further, by helping the supplier do a similar process redesign, Power Tools' new quality team will probably cut costs from the supplier and will be able to share this savings by obtaining a cut in gear price.

The final quantitative method in the new toolbox is the cost-time profile, which is used to compare the cost and time expenditures required for different processes. It is a simple graph in which the vertical or y axis represents costs to the company, and the x axis represents time. Figure 4-6 shows the cost-time profiles as calculated by the team for the old and new processes at Power Tools. Note that the profile is shorter and lower after the process is redesigned. To create these two profiles, the team had to collect and organize data on costs incurred and the timing of these costs. Each of these paired data points show where the profile will jump upward on the graph. Time elapsed between these cost expenditures is drawn as a horizontal line.

The pursuit of higher quality at lower cost makes use of many of the same, simple measurements and computations that you learned in the previous section, "Statistical Estimation and the Control of Quality." The difference is that these quantitative methods are used for a different purpose. By adding root cause analysis and process flowcharting, and by using the tools in the

FIGURE 4-6   Cost-time profile, gear sourcing and assembly

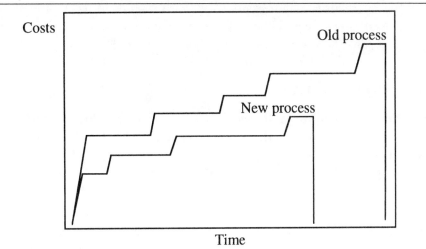

context of a cross-functional process improvement team, you can obtain very different results. In many cases, managers and employees can achieve competitive breakthroughs by applying the same, basic set of quantitative methods in new, creative ways. Measures and statistics can be used to answer many questions, and some of these questions are more profitable than others. Now we will turn to the subject of forecasting which, like statistical estimation, consists of methods that once learned can be applied in both traditional and creative ways.

STATISTICAL FORECASTING—USING DATA TO ANTICIPATE THE FUTURE

We have seen that regression analysis helps to *explain* relationships among variables. When we can state a plausible theory in terms of an equation with a dependent variable and a set of explanatory independent variables, the least-squares method of regression analysis offers a tried-and-true way to estimate the parameters of the model and draw useful inferences about the factors that cause the dependent variable to take on specific values. Until you examined Figure 4-1 and ran the regression analysis to validate what the graph suggested, it might never have occurred to you that Friday and the start and end of each work day were problems that deserved scrutiny.

We may, after all, have been incorrect about the structure of the model. It may not be linear; it may consist of more than a single equation; and the explanatory variables in the model may be stand-ins for other variables that are not measured. In our example, the variable "Friday" stands in for certain behaviors of the people working on the production line, behaviors that are related to Friday and perhaps to other events. Even with such distorted representations, the regression model may serve as an extremely useful way of explaining relationships among those variables for which we do have data.

Predicting Quality

Regression analysis is useful for more than explaining relationships among variables of interest as we saw in the previous section; it is useful also for *prediction*. At a time of extraordinary and unpredictable changes, it turns out that some things in business actually change less than others; many facets of business are quite predictable. To the extent that we can know how to identify predictable patterns in demand and in the availability of resources and extend them into the future, we can put the information to use to manage more effectively.

To return to our quality control example, if you had no other basis for predicting the result of the quality control test for product vibration by time of day and day of week, the regression result of Equation 2, $y = .060681 + .006067 \cdot x_1 - .00351 \cdot x_2$, could be used as a basis for predicting next week's test result; that prediction is shown in Figure 4-7.

Of course, more than a week of data would be better. Just as more data improve our ability to explain relationships among variables more reliably, data also improve our ability to predict or forecast values of dependent variables more accurately. Additional data tend to improve the accuracy of predictions by reducing both random and nonrandom errors. The greater the amount of data, the less the random error because the estimate becomes more *precise*—the variance of the distribution of predicted values tends to decline as the number of observations used to produce the regression increases. Additional data can also reduce nonrandom error by producing estimates that are less *biased*. In our example, there may be a quality cycle within the month or year, such as a month-end or a seasonal effect, that we cannot learn about with one week's data. Our regression result, based on one week of data, will produce biased parameter estimates for a week that happens to be in a different phase of a monthly or seasonal cycle.

Forecasting Sales

You have worked hard now to analyze and improve the quality of your products so that your market share could expand, and now you wish to bring the same analytic power to help you forecast revenues, so that you can develop your operating budget for the coming year. Suppose that you have been tracking your sales now for five years, and wish to forecast sales for the next four quarters. Your numbers for the past 20 quarters are shown in Table 4-6.

You can project sales for the next four quarters by estimating the parameters of the regression equation

$$y = a + bx_0 + cx_1 + dx_2 + ex_3 \qquad (3)$$

FIGURE 4-7 Quality control prediction

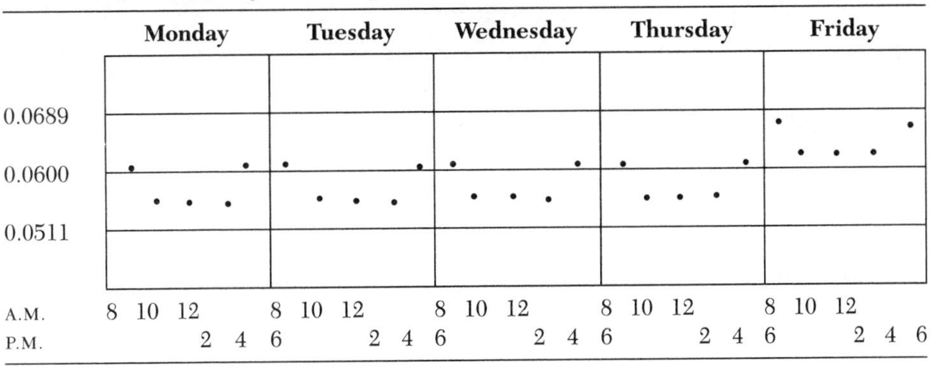

	Monday	Tuesday	Wednesday	Thursday	Friday
0.0689					
0.0600					
0.0511					

A.M.	8 10 12	8 10 12	8 10 12	8 10 12	8 10 12
P.M.	2 4 6	2 4 6	2 4 6	2 4 6	2 4 6

TABLE 4-6 Power Tools, Inc. revenues by quarter ($000's)

Quarter	19X5	19X6	19X7	19X8	19X9
Q_1	331	802	1827	2685	3096
Q_2	392	1253	2005	3212	3412
Q_3	466	1393	2441	3230	3618
Q_4	468	1485	2258	3118	3270

where y is the quarterly sales for Power Tools, x_0 is the year (from 1 to 5, historically), x_1 is a binary variable representing the first quarter (1 if first quarter, 0 otherwise), and x_2 and x_3 are corresponding binary variables for the second and third quarters, respectively. The result is

$$y = -189450 + 769750x_0 - 371600x_1 - 65000x_2 + 109800x_3 \qquad (4)$$

with $r^2 = .970$, which means that this model explains all but 3 percent of the variance in quarterly sales. (We don't show the standard errors or t statistics here; those are more useful for models designed to explain relationships than for those designed to predict values of a dependent variable.) From this result, you are able to forecast the sales for the coming year by quarter (in thousands of dollars):

Q_1	Q_2	Q_3	Q_4
4057	4364	4538	4429

You might be able to improve these forecasts and learn something useful along the way with different data. The model we have just estimated is a naive model—it ignores all causal factors that may influence your firm's sales. It provides a rough-and-ready basis for projecting sales. In this case, however, explaining sales is also critical, especially to your marketing people.

One factor that you strongly suspect will influence your revenue statistics is the quality of your products, as reflected by the proportion of your products that are returned under the one-year warranty in the previous quarter; let's call this x_4. Another factor you are pretty sure will drive your sales is the health of the construction industry. Therefore, you find a statistical almanac and obtain the construction industry component of the quarterly data on the gross national product (x_5, in $billions). Your revenues by quarter are still y. The data are shown in Table 4-7.

Note that the year and quarter variables used in the previous model are excluded here. You exclude them because the construction data already contain both the annual trend and the seasonal variation that influence your sales figures, and because you have only 20 observations and wish to preserve degrees of

TABLE 4-7   Data for regression estimate to predict quarterly revenues

	y	x_4	x_5		y	x_4	x_5
1	331	.027	30.1	11	2441	.015	50.7
2	392	.028	38.5	12	2258	.013	35.8
3	466	.027	41.2	13	2685	.012	39.8
4	468	.025	29.5	14	3212	.010	49.9
5	802	.024	32.2	15	3230	.011	55.0
6	1253	.020	41.7	16	3118	.009	41.1
7	1393	.021	43.0	17	3096	.010	42.6
8	1485	.018	32.3	18	3412	.010	54.4
9	1827	.017	37.3	19	3618	.008	59.2
10	2005	.015	46.6	20	3270	.009	42.4

freedom. You then put these numbers into your electronic spreadsheet and obtain the following regression result:

$$y = 3,459,989 - 146,444,000x_4 + 23,410.8x_5 \qquad r^2 = .987 \qquad (5)$$
$$(138,005) \qquad (6,017,816) \qquad (4907.0)$$

With this result, you have reduced the unaccounted-for variance in y from 3.0 percent to 1.3 percent; along the way, you learn that product quality and construction industry revenues drive your own revenue numbers, both having t statistics well above 4. Then, by predicting that your product return rate will remain at 0.9 percent all year and plugging trade association forecasts of next year's construction industry component of GNP (48.0, 57.9, 61.5, and 47.9, respectively) into Equation 5, you get a more modest (because you are assuming an end to the improvement in quality) set of sales projections for next year (in thousands of dollars):

Q_1	Q_2	Q_3	Q_4
3267	3497	3581	3262

An important element of this forecast is that it serves to remind you that you have some control over the success of your business. Unlike the naive models of Equations 3 and 4, this result says that you can increase revenues by $146,444 per quarter for each 0.001 reduction in the rate at which customers return your product: Improve quality and you will improve sales.

Time Series Forecasts

Even though they offer little by way of explaining causal relationships among variables, naive models can still be extremely useful for forecasting. Models that forecast a variable based strictly on past patterns of movement of the variable over time are naive models known as *time series* models. The central idea of time series forecasting (or time series analysis) is that data ordered over time can be decomposed into three distinct parts: an underlying trend (up, down, or flat); cycles (daily, weekly, seasonal, etc.); and irregular fluctuations. Equations 3 and 4 exemplify how a regression model can decompose the variance: x_0 is the trend variable; x_1, x_2, and x_3 are aspects of a cycle; and the unexplained (or residual) variance is the third part.

Another method of time series analysis is the *moving average* time series method. This approach differs from the regression approach, which is calculated in a single operation, in that it proceeds in stages: First, measure and project the trend, then smooth the data to measure the cycle, and finally adjust the initial projection to account for the average cycle.

Let's see how this works with your last 20 quarters of sales data, shown in Table 4-7. First, the trend is estimated by fitting a regression line to the 20 sales values:

$$y = a + bx \tag{6}$$

where y is your firm's quarterly sales and x is the corresponding quarter number ($x = 1, 2 \ldots 20$). The least squares result is

$$y = 42563 + 190051x \qquad r^2 = .966 \tag{7}$$

By plugging x values from 21 through 24 into Equation 7, you can project sales for the coming year unadjusted for the quarterly cycle:

Q_{21}	Q_{22}	Q_{23}	Q_{24}
4034	4224	4414	4604

Next you isolate the quarterly cycle using a four-period moving average. The moving average technique smooths the data so that an adjustment factor can be calculated for each phase of the cycle. The worksheet for carrying out this exercise is shown in Table 4-8.

In Columns 3 to 5, we create the smoothed data. Since each number in Column 5 is based on exactly one year's worth of data, the result is purged of the cycle; since each is based on four observations, much of the unaccounted-for variation is dampened as well. In the last four columns, the ratio of the actual to the smoothed number is created for each phase of the cycle; these ratios are then averaged to provide the four adjustment factors at the bottom of the worksheet.[2] The four unadjusted quarterly projections are then divided by these adjustment factors to create the final projections. Here is the end result:

Q_{21}	Q_{22}	Q_{23}	Q_{24}
3901	4758	4567	4354

TABLE 4-8   Estimating the quarterly adjustment factors using the moving average method

(1)	(2)	(3) 4 Qtr Moving Sum	(4) 4 Qtr Moving Average	(5) Centered Moving Average	(6)	(7) Adjustment Factors (Column 2 / Column 5)	(8)	(9)
Qtr	Sales				Phase 1	Phase 2	Phase 3	Phase 4
1	331							
2	392							
		1657	414.3					
3	466			473.13	0.98494			
		2128	532.0					
4	468			639.63		0.73168		
		2989	747.3					
5	802			863.13			0.92918	
		3916	979.0					
6	1253			1106.13				1.13278
		4933	1233.3					
7	1393			1361.38	1.02323			
		5958	1489.5					
8	1485			1583.50		0.93780		
		6710	1677.5					
9	1827			1808.50			1.01023	
		7758	1939.5					
10	2005			2036.13				0.98471
		8531	2132.8					
11	2441			2240.00	1.08973			
		9389	2347.3					
12	2258			2498.13		0.90388		
		10596	2649.0					
13	2685			2747.63			0.97721	
		11385	2846.3					
14	3212			2953.75				1.08743
		12245	3061.3					
15	3230			3112.63	1.03771			
		12656	3164.0					
16	3118			3189.00		0.97774		
		12856	3214.0					
17	3096			3262.50			0.94897	
		13244	3311.0					
18	3412			3330.00				1.02462
		13396	3349.0					
19	3618							
20	3270							
				Means:	1.03390	0.88777	0.96640	1.05739

Other Forecasting Techniques and Applications

Regression analysis and moving average method of time series analysis are two of the most commonly applied forecasting tools used in business,[3] largely because they are robust yet easy to use. However, they are not the only ways to forecast the numbers that are critical to the success of the business. Other forecasting techniques range from qualitative approaches, such as juries of expert opinion and subjective estimates of the sales staff, to highly sophisticated statistical methods of time series analysis, such as the Box-Jenkins and spectral analysis methods.

We have seen how such techniques can forecast quality and sales, but they are also useful for estimating future levels of a host of other factors that influence the success of the business. They are important in strategic planning to project consumer demographics that can be critical to your ability to anticipate future consumption patterns. They are useful in marketing—to estimate the effects of changes in pricing policy on sales volume and market share. They can be used in accounting—to provide a basis for estimating reserves for bad debts based on the company's history of uncollectables by the characteristics of the products, services, and customers.

DECISION ANALYSIS

Your actions to improve the quality of Power Tools products have helped to increase the company's revenues, and your improved projections of future business have strengthened the company's planning and budgeting performance, but you can continue the turnaround of the company in several other areas.

One critical area is the need to expand. Your production facility in Atlanta has started generating profits, but it is now operating at full capacity, unable to satisfy the current demand. Your markets in the West have begun to grow faster than your other markets. With this in mind, you have narrowed the list of candidate sites for building or purchasing a facility in that region to Phoenix and Los Angeles. You have determined that it is much less expensive to purchase and convert an existing facility than to build a new one. The estimated capital and operating costs of the two prospective sites are ready to review—the present values of those costs over a 25-year horizon amount to $15 million for Los Angeles and $12 million for Phoenix. You also estimate the future stream of gross profits for the two facilities under a best case scenario, a most likely case scenario, and a worst case scenario. The present values of gross profits in each case and their accompanying probabilities are shown in Table 4-9.

A sound basis for deciding what to do is provided by a set of techniques known as *decision analysis*. Problems that lend themselves to solution by

TABLE 4-9   **Present values of gross profit streams ($ millions): Two prospective sites and three scenarios**

Scenario	Probability	Los Angeles	Phoenix
Best case	.20	$25	$20
Most likely	.60	20	17
Worst case	.20	9	9

decision analysis are ones in which a decision maker confronts two or more alternative courses of action, each action having measurable outcomes that are contingent on forces beyond the decision maker's control. When the decision maker can assign probabilities to the contingencies, decision analysis offers a framework for selecting among the options. The problem at hand has all of the ingredients for solution by decision analysis.

The basic procedure of decision analysis is to lay out the set of available courses of action and contingencies in the form of a *decision tree* (Figure 4-8), calculate the *expected value* of each available option, and then select the option that offers the largest expected return (or smallest expected loss) to the decision maker.

The present value of profit figures in Figure 4-8 result from subtracting the present value of capital and operating costs for Los Angeles ($15 million) or Phoenix ($12 million) from the corresponding present value of gross profit figures shown in the last two columns of Table 4-9. For example, the best case scenario for Los Angeles is $25 million minus $15 million, or $10 million. An *expected value* is defined as an amount times the probability of that amount occurring; the expected value of the best case scenario for Phoenix is the amount

FIGURE 4-8   **Decision tree for site selection problem**

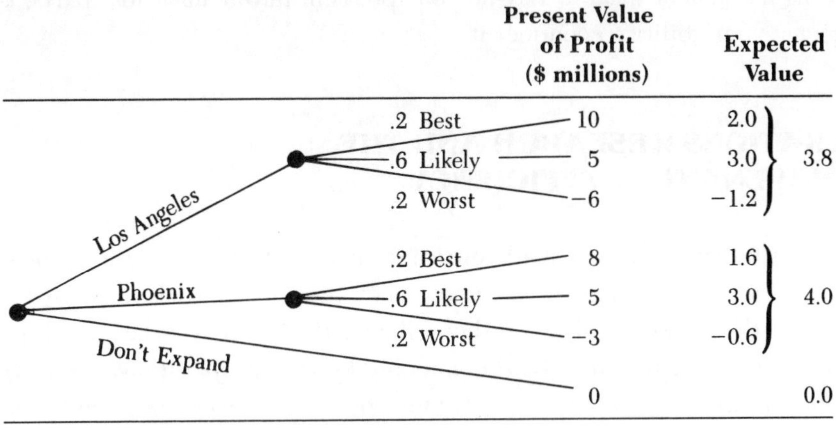

$8 million times the probability of obtaining that amount, .2, or $1.6 million. The expected value of any alternative course of action is the sum of the expected values of all possible outcomes; the expected value across all contingencies is $4 million for Phoenix, $3.8 million for Los Angeles, and $0 for the status quo, no expansion. If expected profit were all that mattered and if you were indifferent to incurring risk,[4] your choice would be to set up the facility in Phoenix, since you could "expect" the equivalent of $200,000 more profit in Phoenix than in Los Angeles. If, on the other hand, you were a risk taker drawn to the larger profit for Los Angeles under the best case scenario, or if you had a nonpecuniary attachment to Los Angeles that was worth more than $200,000, you would be inclined to select Los Angeles for your second production facility.

Your ability to make decisions under conditions of uncertainty can be enhanced significantly by making each essential aspect of the decision problem explicit in a decision tree, assigning probabilities to contingencies beyond your control that affect the final result, and calculating the expected value for each available option under your control. If you don't like the result, you can ask yourself why you don't—you may have left out an important factor or factors to which you might assign a dollar value equivalent (e.g., the amount that your firm would be willing to pay for a twofold reduction in pollution or in the risk of labor unrest) and then include that explicitly in the analysis.

Decision analysis becomes increasingly useful as the problem grows more complex. You could, for example, analyze whether to spend $50,000 to conduct surveys in Los Angeles and Phoenix that would improve your estimates of the probabilities and the contingent outcomes by certain amounts; you could consider sites other than Los Angeles and Phoenix; you could explicitly account for a host of intangible factors by assigning equivalent dollar amounts to advantages and disadvantages of each site (weather, access to athletic and cultural activities, etc.); you could build in your aversion to risk; and so on. Decision analysis derives power from its ability to assist you in dealing with such complexity by following an ancient maxim: Divide your problem into manageable parts, thus enhancing your ability to conquer it.

OPERATIONS RESEARCH AND THE IMPROVEMENT OF EFFICIENCY

The quantitative tools we have been using thus far to improve the company's performance are grounded in *statistics;* they have to do with drawing *inferences* from the data to inform and thus enhance decisions. Another set of quantitative tools, belonging to a field commonly known as *operations research,* is grounded in *applied mathematics;* these tools help to solve problems *deductively.* Just as you don't have to be a statistician to know what kinds of problems lend themselves to solutions involving statistical methodology, neither do you have to be a mathematician to know what kinds of problems lend themselves to solutions involving operations research methods.

Inventory Management Models

One widely used class of operations research models aims at more efficient inventory management. For firms that have large amounts of capital tied up in inventory or that frequently lose sales because their inventory keeps running out, more efficient inventory management can result in substantial increases in profit. Inventory includes raw materials, work in process, and finished goods; *inventory management models* deal primarily with the problems of how often to order more raw materials and how much to order, and how many goods to produce during a period to keep the finished goods inventory at the right level.

What levels are the right levels? You should aim for the *economic order quantity*, the level that balances two kinds of inventory costs: *holding (or carrying) costs*, which increase with the amount of inventory ordered, and *order costs*, which decrease with the amount ordered. (See Figure 4-9.)

The largest components of holding costs for most companies are the cost of space to store the inventory and the cost of tying up capital in inventory, capital that could otherwise be used either to obtain assets that increase profits or to pay off debt that imposes interest costs on the firm. Other components of holding costs include the labor costs associated with inventory maintenance, insurance costs, and costs associated with deterioration, spoilage, and obsolescence.

The costs of more frequent orders include lost discounts for larger quantity purchases; labor and supply costs of writing the orders, paying the bills, and

FIGURE 4-9   The economic order quantity

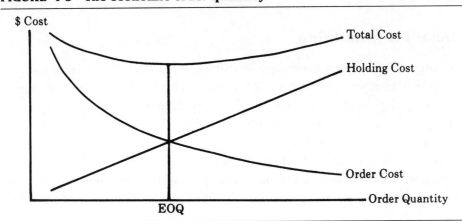

processing the paperwork; associated telephone and mail costs; and the labor costs of processing and inspecting incoming inventory.

Notice that the economic order quantity—the size of order that minimizes the total of holding and ordering costs—is the amount at which holding costs equal order costs. The economic order quantity (EOQ) can be expressed in more detailed terms:

$$EOQ = \sqrt{\frac{2UO}{H}} \tag{8}$$

where U is the number of units used annually, O is the order cost per order, and H is the holding cost per unit.[5]

This inventory management model can help you at Power Tools. Your raw materials inventory for chain saws has averaged $500,000, with a $1 million purchase every six months to satisfy the annual demand for 40,000 saws. You have calculated that it costs a total of $20 to hold the raw materials for one saw per year and $50 to place an order for more material. So your economic order quantity for chain saws is

$$EOQ = \sqrt{\frac{2 \times 40{,}000 \times 50}{20}} = \sqrt{200{,}000} = 447 \tag{9}$$

How much of an improvement is this amount over your current practice of an order for parts for 20,000 saws every six months? Currently, your costs come to $200,000 of holding costs (10,000 of average inventory times $20 in holding cost per saw) plus $100 of order costs (two orders at $50 per order), or $200,100 of total cost annually for your raw materials inventory. Under the EOQ ordering policy, your costs will come to $4,470 of holding costs (223.5 of average inventory times $20 in holding cost per saw) plus $4,470 of order costs (89.4 orders—about seven orders every four weeks—at $50 per order), or $8,940 of total cost annually—a cost reduction of $191,160. It's not called the economic order quantity for nothing!

Linear Programming

You can produce further economies by using other operations research models. One widely used class of such models comes under the heading of *linear programming*. Developed around 1950 as a way of maximizing some desirable quantity (or minimizing an undesirable one) that is subject to one or more constraints, linear programming is useful for a variety of problems: allocating scarce resources to jobs, finding the best mix of inputs in accomplishing some objective, routing resources through a complex network, and determining the least cost flow of goods from a set of production facilities to a set of warehouses or retail outlets. When a measurable objective to be maximized or minimized and a set of quantifiable constraints can all be expressed as linear algebraic statements, with at least as many unique statements as variables in the system, we have the fundamental elements of the linear programming problem.

Optimal Mix Problem

Suppose, for example, that the two Power Tools, Inc., production lines at your Atlanta facility can be set up for power saws or power drills; that production line A has 36 hours of time available for saws and drills this week while production line B has 30 hours of available time; a power saw takes 2 hours to go through each production line while each power drill requires 2 hours on production line A and 1 hour on line B; the marginal profit is $50 per saw and $30 per drill; and your company can sell as many of each product as it can produce this week. Your problem is to determine how many of each product to produce. If we let

$$x_1 = \text{the number of saws}$$

and

$$x_2 = \text{the number of drills,}$$

your objective is to maximize profit, $50x_1 + 30x_2$, subject to the constraints:

$$2x_1 + 2x_2 \leq 36 \text{ for production line A}$$

$$2x_1 + x_2 \leq 30 \text{ for production line B}$$

and

$$x_1, x_2 \geq 0$$

The last equation states that you can't produce negative amounts of either saws or drills.

A standard way of solving this problem is by graphing the constraints, shading the resulting polygon that represents the area of all feasible solutions, and then observing the value of the *objective function* (the expression being maximized or minimized; in this case, the profit line $50x_1 + 30x_2$) as it passes through each corner of the polygon. This process and the optimal solution are shown in Figure 4-10. The objective function passes through the polygon of feasible solutions at an infinite number of points. Figure 4-10 shows the function for the profit levels $200, $400, and $600. However, the firm's profit is maximized at one point: $x_1 = 12$ and $x_2 = 6$. By producing 12 saws and 6 drills, your firm will satisfy the capacity constraints for both production lines and produce a profit of $780, higher than for any other feasible combination of saws and drills.

FIGURE 4-10   Graphical solution to an optimal mix problem

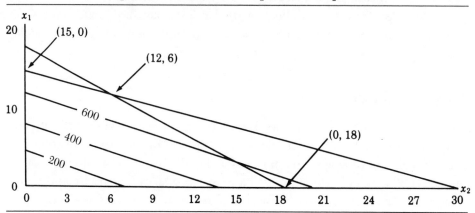

Transportation Problem

Another major area of Power Tools, Inc.'s, business that has potential for improvement is transportation costs. Your firm's increase in revenues has brought with it a substantial increase in transportation costs. The company has grown to the point where your production facilities in Phoenix and Atlanta are now shipping finished goods to three warehouses—in Los Angeles, Chicago, and New York, and you suspect that your system of routing goods to the warehouses is inefficient.

Your sales projections indicate the need for 8,000 power drills next year in Los Angeles, 8,000 in Chicago, and 10,000 in New York. Your production facility in Phoenix can make and distribute up to 15,000 drills, and your Atlanta facility can produce 13,000 drills per year, assuming last year's mix of drills and saws.[6] The cost of shipping a drill from each production facility to each warehouse is shown in Table 4-10.

If you let

x_{pl} = the number of drills shipped from Phoenix to Los Angeles
x_{pc} = the number shipped from Phoenix to Chicago
x_{pn} = the number shipped from Phoenix to New York
x_{al} = the number shipped from Atlanta to Los Angeles
x_{ac} = the number shipped from Atlanta to Chicago and
x_{an} = the number shipped from Atlanta to New York

TABLE 4-10   Shipping costs per drill shipped

To From	Los Angeles	Chicago	New York
Phoenix	$1	$4	$5
Atlanta	5	2	4

your problem is to minimize the total shipping costs:

$$x_{pl} + 4x_{pc} + 5x_{pn} + 5x_{al} + 2x_{ac} + 4x_{an}$$

subject to the demand requirements:

$$x_{pl} + x_{al} = 8,000 \qquad \text{for Los Angeles}$$

$$x_{pc} + x_{ac} = 8,000 \qquad \text{for Chicago}$$

$$x_{pn} + x_{an} = 10,000 \qquad \text{for New York}$$

the supply constraints for your two production facilities:

$$x_{pl} + x_{pc} + x_{pn} \leq 15,000 \text{ for Phoenix}$$

$$x_{al} + x_{ac} + x_{an} \leq 13,000 \text{ for Atlanta}$$

and the nonnegativity constraints $x \geq 0$ for all routes.

There are a variety of techniques for solving transportation problems of this kind, most of which involve developing an initial *feasible* solution (one that satisfies *all* the constraints) and improving on it until an *optimal* solution (one that cannot be improved on) is reached. As a practical matter, these problems are most efficiently solved using linear programming software on a computer (including the personal computer, except for extremely large problems). Here is a common method for producing an initial solution manually that is virtually always close to optimal: Allocate as many units as possible to the routes that are the lowest cost for both a source and a destination, and then allocate to the remaining lowest cost alternatives in a commonsense manner until the source and destination constraints are satisfied.

For the problem at hand, the routes that have the lowest cost for both a source and a destination are Phoenix to Los Angeles and Atlanta to Chicago—you can satisfy Los Angeles's demand for 8,000 drills by sending them all from Phoenix, leaving 7,000 in Phoenix to satisfy part of the remaining demands, and you can satisfy Chicago's demand for 8,000 drills by sending them all from Atlanta, leaving 5,000 in Atlanta to satisfy the New York demand. Then, since the cost of satisfying New York's demand for 10,000 drills is $1 cheaper for each unit sent from Atlanta rather than from Phoenix, you use up Atlanta's remaining inventory of 5,000 and fill the remainder with 5,000 drills from Phoenix. This solution, displayed in Table 4-11 is optimal; no other routing arrangement produces

TABLE 4-11   Solution to transportation problem

To From	Los Angeles	Chicago	New York	Excess Supply	Total Supply
Phoenix	8,000	0	5,000	2,000	15,000
Atlanta	0	8,000	5,000	0	13,000
Total demand	8,000	8,000	10,000	2,000	28,000

a lower cost solution. By multiplying each of the six primary cell values shown in this table by the transportation cost per unit for the corresponding cell shown in Table 4-10 and calculating the sum of all the resulting products, you obtain the total transportation cost for this solution: $69,000.[7]

Simulation Models

Many quantifiable business problems are just too complex to lend themselves to solution through a linear programming or other optimization technique. For such problems, it is often more effective and less costly to use a *simulation* model. Simulation models solve complicated problems by allowing the user to characterize a real-world situation as a system of formulas that reflect the relationships among the various components of the situation, including the uncertainties and dynamic interdependencies that make the problem difficult to solve in the first place. The uncertainties are simulated with the use of random numbers, and the dynamic interdependencies are dealt with through the use of explicit formulas stating the relationships. By testing different structures (e.g., what if we reconfigured the production line?) and converging on values of the factors over which you have control (what if we kept production in operation for nine hours rather than eight?) that maximize system performance or minimize system cost, you can solve problems that defy solution using more elegant analytical procedures.

Simulation models have become especially attractive as computers have become so capable and accessible. The marriage of simulation models and computers permits brute force "number crunching" solutions to complex problems that not very long ago could be addressed only by simplifying the problem to the point where it bore little resemblance to reality. For many applications, simulation models today are much more efficient than analytical models and infinitely more efficient than running tests on the system itself.

You begin the simulation process generally by defining the problem, and proceed by identifying the most important variables; constructing the simulation mode; specifying the alternative structures of the system and values of the variables to be tested; running the model and examining the results; modifying the model as appropriate; and, when you are satisfied with the modifications, selecting the course of action that works best.

One common application of simulation modeling in business is that of determining how many servers (e.g., checkout counters, telephone operators, maintenance stations, tollbooths) to use in situations where the demand for service is random. This is called the *queuing problem.* The queuing problem is solved by estimating the demand for service (the average number of arrivals per unit of time) and the average time required to serve each customer or unit, making assumptions about the distributions of demand and service time, and testing the effects of alternative structures—how many servers and queue discipline (e.g., first-come first-served vs. separate lines for each server)—on system performance and cost. System performance is often measured in terms of the ability to satisfy demand for service, the amount or percentage of idle time of servers, and the average waiting time of customers. As a general rule, it doesn't hurt to translate those factors into dollars.

The telephones at Power Tools are often swamped with calls, and you would like to get a better grip on how many operators you should have handling them. Calls arrive at a rate of 120 to 240 per hour, depending on the time of day and day of week. On average, it takes 10 seconds to process a call. You would be willing to pay $5 to prevent each minute of a caller's waiting. Operators cost $10 per hour. How many operators should you have during the peak hours? During the lowest calling rate hours? What should your decision rule be for the other times?

You can begin by thinking of this problem in the same terms as the inventory problem: Having either too many or too few operators is analogous to having too much or too little inventory on hand. In this case, you'd like to know the number of operators that minimizes the total costs of waiting for telephone service, where the two principal components of cost are the cost of operators and the cost of having callers wait. As you add operators, the cost of callers waiting declines and your labor costs increase. Your total costs can be expressed as:

$$\text{Total costs} = \text{Operator costs} + \text{Caller waiting costs}$$

This is very much like the model displayed in Figure 4-9 (substituting the number of operators for the order quantity on the x-axis), except that it is a good deal easier to express the inventory order cost component in terms of the number of units ordered than it is to express the waiting cost in terms of the number of operators, a feature that makes the problem of optimization more complex in queuing models than in the standard inventory model. For your problem, the total costs are the sum of your operator costs of $0.167 per operator per minute plus your waiting costs of $5 times the average number of minutes each caller waits for an operator times the number of callers per minute.

To estimate how the average wait per caller declines with the number of operators and the resulting effect on costs, you can either make some simplifying assumptions about the distributions of arrivals and service time and use queuing formulas that apply to your unique situation, or you can use a computer spreadsheet to build a simple simulation model, such as the one displayed in Table 4-12. This table shows the results of selected one-hour simulations on a second-by-second basis, varying the number of operators from one to four and the arrival rate from two calls per minute to four. At an arrival rate of two

TABLE 4-12   Simulation of waiting costs and operator costs*

Four Calls Arrive per Minute, One Operator:

Second Number	Random Number	No. of Calls	No. in System	No. on Hold	Costs		
					Waiting	Operator	Total
1	.8081	0	0	0	$0.000	$0.003	$0.003
2	.0650	1	1	0	0.000	0.003	0.003
3	.4598	0	1	0	0.000	0.003	0.003
4	.8836	0	1	0	0.000	0.003	0.003
5	.0301	1	2	1	0.083	0.003	0.086
⋮	⋮	⋮	⋮	⋮	⋮	⋮	⋮
3600	.9447	0	1	0	0.000	0.003	0.003
				Totals:	$49.367	$10.000	$59.367
				Costs per minute:	$ 0.823	0.167	$ 0.989

Four Calls Arrive per Minute, Two Operators:

Second Number	Random Number	No. of Calls	No. in System	No. on Hold	Costs		
					Waiting	Operator	Total
1	.5382	0	0	0	$0.000	$0.006	$0.006
2	.0729	0	0	0	0.000	0.006	0.006
3	.7171	0	0	0	0.000	0.006	0.006
4	.0243	1	1	0	0.000	0.006	0.006
5	.8414	0	1	0	0.000	0.006	0.006
⋮	⋮	⋮	⋮	⋮	⋮	⋮	⋮
3600	.3400	0	0	0	0.000	0.006	0.006
				Totals:	$9.633	$20.000	$29.633
				Costs per minute:	$0.161	$ 0.333	$ 0.494

calls per minute, the model simulates an arriving call when the random number is between 0 and 0.0333; at a rate of four calls per minute, the model simulates an arriving call when the random number is between 0 and 0.0667. Waiting costs show up at a rate of 8.33 cents for each second a caller is put on hold. The model calculates the sum of waiting costs and operator costs in the last column.

You can organize and display the results of these simulations in a graph to see more clearly the effects of variations in arrival rates and the number of operators on total costs. Such a graph is shown in Figure 4-11.

This graph makes it clear that you minimize costs by having two operators, regardless of whether calls arrive at the rate of two or four per minute. Further use of the model indicates that it will be time to use a third operator when the arrival rate goes above 4.5 calls per minute. As your business continues to grow and calls arrive at higher rates, you can simulate further to help decide when to add still more operators.

FIGURE 4-11   The effects of arrival rate and number of operators on total costs

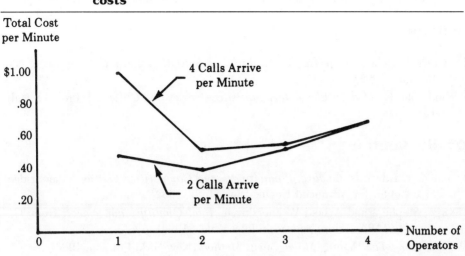

CONCLUDING REMARKS

Effective management is much more than just a matter of working with numbers. The successful manager relies on common sense and intuition; sensitivity to human factors that defy quantification; and creativity that transcends the numbers. (It didn't take a quantitative genius to realize that the waiting costs at the Hudson River tollbooths in New York City could be cut in half with virtually no loss in revenues by doubling the fares of the eastbound booths and eliminating the westbound booths altogether.) When the numbers send up a red flag, the successful manager looks beneath them to find out what is going on.

Most successful managers also know that the business cannot thrive without close attention to the numbers, and that tools designed to work with the numbers can be indispensable. Today's successful manager understands that quantitative methods can be powerful agents for solving the problems of human institutions and human beings.

FOR FURTHER READING

General

Gallagher, C. A., and H. J. Watson, *Quantitative Methods for Business Decisions* (New York: McGraw-Hill, 1980).

Markland, Robert E., and James R. Sweigart, *Quantitative Methods: Applications to Managerial Decision Making* (New York: John Wiley, 1987).

Tilanus, C. B., O. B. DeGans, and J. K. Lenstra, *Quantitative Methods in Management: Case Studies of Failures and Successes* (New York: John Wiley, 1986).

Statistics

Downing, Douglas, and Jeffrey Clark, *Business Statistics*, 2nd ed. (Hauppauge, NY: Barron's, 1992).

Freund, John E., *Modern Elementary Statistics* (Englewood Cliffs, NJ: Prentice-Hall, 1988).

Quality Control

Deming, W. Edwards, *Quality, Productivity, and Competitive Position* (Cambridge, MA: Center for Advanced Engineering Study, 1982).

George, Stephen, and Arnold Weimerskirch, *Total Quality Management*, from The Portable MBA series (New York: John Wiley, 1994).

Walton, Mary, *The Deming Management Method* (New York: Putnam, 1986).

Regression Analysis

Draper, Norman, and Harry Smith, *Applied Regression Analysis* (New York: John Wiley, 1981).

Wonnacott, Thomas H., and Ronald J. Wonnacott, *Regression: A Second Course on Statistics* (New York: John Wiley, 1981).

Forecasting

Box, George E. P., and Gwilym M. Jenkins, *Time Series Analysis: Forecasting and Control* (Oakland, CA: Holden-Day, 1976).

Wheelwright, Stephen C., and Spyros Makridakis, *Forecasting Methods for Management* (New York: John Wiley, 1985).

Decision Analysis

Brown, Rex V., A. S. Kahr, and C. R. Peterson, *Decision Analysis: An Overview* (New York: Holt, Rinehart and Winston, 1974).

Raiffa, Howard, *Decision Analysis: Introductory Lectures on Choices under Uncertainty* (New York: Random House, 1986).

Operations Research

Hillier, Frederick S., and Gerald J. Lieberman, *Introduction to Operations Research* (San Francisco: Holden-Day, 1980).

Taha, Hamdy A., *Operations Research: An Introduction* (New York: Macmillan, 1987).

Wagner, Harvey M., *Principles of Operations Research* (Englewood Cliffs, NJ: Prentice-Hall, 1975).

5 MANAGERIAL ECONOMICS: GUIDELINES FOR CHOICES AND DECISIONS

Frank Lichtenberg

In capitalist economies such as that of the United States, Canada, and the countries of Western Europe, managers of firms are continuously faced with numerous choices. How much output should they produce? What techniques should be employed to produce this output? How many workers should the firm employ, and how much should the firm spend on new plant and equipment in a given year? (In a command economy such as that of the former Soviet Union, managers of enterprises do not make these decisions—they are dictated by a central government authority.) One of the central objectives of economic analysis is to provide answers to these questions. Managers of firms are assumed to have certain objectives, such as the maximization of profits or shareholder wealth, or the minimization of the cost of producing a given level of output. Economics provides managers with a set of *decision rules* that tell them what choices they should make (how much output to produce, how many workers to employ) to best achieve these objectives under a given set of conditions (the extent of demand for the firm's product or the level of prevailing wages). These rules also indicate how the manager should *change* the choices he or she makes when economic conditions change, for example, how the rate of investment should respond to interest rate changes.

Because managers (and consumers) are pursuing their own private interests and decisions are made in a decentralized manner (rather than by a central planner), a very important question concerning the *coordination* of economic activities arises. Thousands of firms are autonomously choosing which products to produce, how much they will produce, and how they will produce them. At the

97

same time, millions of consumers are autonomously choosing how much of various products and services they will purchase. Is there any reason to believe that these decisions independently formulated by millions of firms and households will be mutually consistent? Is there any guarantee that firms will decide to produce the goods consumers wish to purchase, and in the appropriate quantities? Will the total number of workers that firms wish to employ equal the number of people willing and able to work, so unemployment will be eradicated?

Until the late eighteenth century, economists saw little reason to believe that the multiplicity of actions and decisions taken in a decentralized, free-market economy would be mutually consistent and harmonious. Indeed, they suspected that only chaos could result from the operation of such an economy. They argued that a detailed system of government regulations was required to ensure the coordination of the diverse activities of producers and consumers. Such regulations might require, for example, that all adult men wear wool caps on Sundays to ensure sufficient demand for wool to maintain the employment of the nation's shepherds. The need for a detailed system of economic regulations was an important part of the doctrine of *mercantilism.*

In 1776, the same year a political revolution occurred in England's American colonies, the Scottish political economist Adam Smith launched an ideological revolution by publishing *The Wealth of Nations.* Smith argued that the coordination and integration of diverse economic activities did not require detailed government regulation, that this function could be performed much more efficiently without human intervention by the operation of a *price system.* Producers would be guided as to which products to produce, in what quantities, and by what techniques of production, by *prices* established in the marketplace. Similarly, decisions by households about how much of various commodities to consume and how much labor to supply would be based on prices (including the wage rate which is the price of labor services). Smith argued that under many circumstances the prices established in competitive markets—markets with a large number of both buyers and sellers—would induce firms to produce, and households to consume, the *socially optimal* quantities of various goods and services. In other words, a system of unregulated markets and prices would, as if guided by an "invisible hand," ensure that society's limited resources yielded the maximum possible satisfaction of wants.

How are prices determined in competitive markets, and how do prices influence firms' decisions about what and how to produce? How do changes in government policies (e.g., taxes), technology, and other market conditions affect price, output, and the number of firms in an industry? What is the theoretical justification for the government's pursuit of antitrust policy, the policy to promote competition and prevent monopolization? One of the two main branches of economics, *microeconomics,* seeks to provide answers to these and related questions. Microeconomics is concerned with the behavior of individual households, firms, and industries. The other branch of economics—*macroeconomics*—focuses on the behavior of the economy as a whole. Some of the questions central to macroeconomic inquiry are: Why do modern capitalist economies often fail to achieve the goals of full employment and price stability? (In other words, what are the causes of unemployment and inflation?) Can the government's monetary and fiscal policies be used to help the economy realize these goals? Is there an inescapable trade-off between unemployment and inflation—to achieve lower inflation, must we accept higher unemployment? Why has the U.S. economy grown more slowly since 1973 than before? Why is it growing more slowly than some other economies and faster than others?

This chapter provides brief introductions to both branches of economic analysis. Although we discuss the two branches separately, it is important to recognize the important connections and similarities between microeconomics and macroeconomics. Both analyze how prices and quantities of goods and services are determined within the context of supply-and-demand models. In the case of microeconomics, the quantity and price are those of specific commodities (such as bicycles or floppy disks), whereas *aggregate* output (the *sum* of the quantity produced of all commodities) and aggregate price (the average of all prices) are the concerns of macroeconomics.

Both branches of economics have *positive* as well as *normative* objectives. The positive objective is to *explain* what has happened in the past and to *predict* what will happen in the future, without making value judgments about these events. (Why was the unemployment rate so high in 1982? Will interest rates rise after the 1996 national elections?) The normative objective is to evaluate alternative economic decisions and policies in terms of their consequences for economic welfare, and thereby to facilitate rational decision making. (Should the government attempt to prevent hostile takeover of U.S. companies, or do the latter contribute to economic welfare? Should the income tax be replaced by a tax on consumption?)

Despite the connections between microeconomics and macroeconomics, for many years, microeconomists and macroeconomists were happy to conduct research in relative isolation from one another. This is no longer the case. Today, macroeconomists recognize that in order to understand the relationships among key economic aggregates such as income, consumption expenditure, interest rates, and the inflation rate, they must have carefully constructed theories of the behavior of individual households, firms, and markets. One of the most important developments in economic thinking in recent years has been the construction of *microfoundations of macroeconomics.*

MICROECONOMICS

Microeconomics seeks to provide a general theory to explain how the quantities and prices of individual commodities are determined. The development of such a theory will enable us to predict the effects of various events, such as industry deregulation and oil price shocks, on the quantity and price of output. For concreteness, we will consider a hypothetical market for wine, and pose the question "How is the quantity (number of bottles) and price (per bottle) of wine determined?"

We assume the existence of a *market demand curve* (or schedule) for wine, which indicates the total number of bottles consumers are willing to purchase at different possible prices of wine (Figure 5-1). Assumption: Wine is a perfectly homogenous commodity—there is no distinction between Thunderbird and Chateau Lafite Rothschild. For two reasons the demand curve assumes a downward slope—the higher the price, the lower the quantity demanded. First, as the price of wine increases, wine becomes more expensive *relative* to possible *substitutes* for it, such as beer, spirits, and soft drinks, so consumers will demand less wine and more of the substitutes. Also, the real income, or purchasing power, of consumers falls as prices of consumer goods rise, so consumers purchase smaller quantities of almost *all* goods. These two effects of a price change on demand are known as the *substitution effect* and the *income effect.*

The demand curve considerably narrows the possible values for the quantity and price of wine—only points on the line, not those off the line, could

FIGURE 5-1   The market demand curve for wine

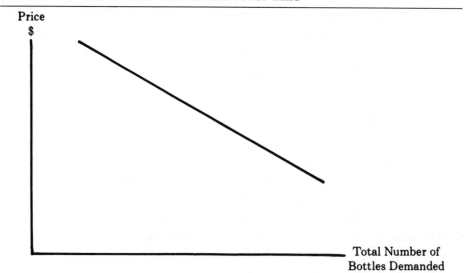

prevail (in the absence of government interference such as rationing or pricing ceilings). But to uniquely determine quantity and price, we need to also consider the "supply side" of the market—wine producers.

Suppose that there are 100 wine producers. For simplicity, assume that they have identical facilities, costs of labor, capital, and technology—they are simply clones of one another. Each producer is therefore faced by the same *cost function*—the relationship between total cost of production and quantity produced. Total cost is assumed to be a strictly increasing function of output: To produce more, the firm will have to hire greater quantities of inputs (land, labor, machinery, and so on), thus increasing costs. In the following analysis, we will need to make use of another relationship, the *marginal cost* curve, which can be derived from the (total) cost function. Marginal cost (MC) is simply the *additional* cost of producing the *last* unit of output. For example, if it costs $20 to produce 10 bottles of wine and $23 to produce 11, the marginal cost of the 11th unit is $3. The marginal cost *curve* is the relationship between the number of units and the marginal cost of the last unit. Again for simplicity, we will assume that MC is strictly increasing. The MC schedule in Table 5-1 will be used for illustrative purposes.

We assume that each producer's objective is to maximize his profit, where profit is defined as revenue minus cost. Revenue is the number of units sold times the price per unit. For the moment, we also assume that each producer considers himself to be a "price taker": He can sell as many units as he likes at a price determined by the market, and his output decision has no influence on the price. (We relax this assumption later when we consider the case of monopoly.)

Under these conditions, the producer can maximize profit by producing the quantity of output at which MC = P, where P denotes price. Suppose, for example, the price were $6, and the MC schedule is given in Table 5-1. Then the profit-maximizing level of output is 3. (Actually, the firm is indifferent between producing 2 and 3 units). If the firm increased production from 3 to 4 units, its revenue would increase by $6 (= P) but its costs would increase by $7

TABLE 5-1   Total and marginal cost schedules of typical producer

Number of Units Output	Total Cost	MC of Last Unit
1	$ 3	$ 3
2	7	4
3	13	6
4	20	7
5	28	8
6	38	10

(the MC of the fourth unit); hence, its profits would decrease by $1. Similarly, if the firm reduced production from 3 units to 1, it would save $10 in costs but would lose $12 in revenue, so its profits would decline by $2. At P = $6, the firm cannot do better than a profit of $5 by producing 3 units. This analysis reveals that *the supply curve of the firm*—the relationship between price and profit-maximizing quantity—*is identical to its marginal cost curve.* That is, we can determine from the marginal cost curve, the number of units of the goods the firm would be willing to supply at different possible prices.

The *market* supply curve is the ("horizontal") sum of all the individual firm supply curves. It indicates the total quantity that *all* firms in the market would be willing to supply at various prices. If there were 100 firms in the market, each faced with the cost schedule in Table 5–1, then the market supply curve would be

Price of Output	Quantity Supplied by All Producers
3	100
4	200
6	300
7	400
8	500
10	600

The market equilibrium price and quantity of wine—the price and quantity that would occur in a competitive market—are determined by the intersection of the market supply and demand curves. In Figure 5-2 this is the point (Q_o, P_o). P_o is the only price at which the quantity of wine producers are willing to supply is equal to the quantity consumers are willing to purchase. At prices above P_o, there is *excess supply* of the product. If one producer tried to charge a price above P_o, other producers would find it profitable to charge a slightly lower price $(\geq P_o)$ to draw away his customers. Competition among producers ensures that the market price is driven down to P_o.

This exercise is a *short-run* analysis, in the sense that we have assumed that the number of producers in the industry is fixed. In the *long run*, however, new firms may enter or existing firms may exit the industry. Whether or not entry and exit will occur depends on how the rate of profit earned by firms in the industry compares with that earned by firms elsewhere in the economy. Suppose that $P_o = \$7$, so that each firm is producing 4 units and earning $8 [= (4.7) − 20] in profit, and that each producer has invested $100 of capital in his firm; his rate of profit is therefore 8 percent. If the rate of profit available

FIGURE 5-2   Determination of market equilibrium quantity and price

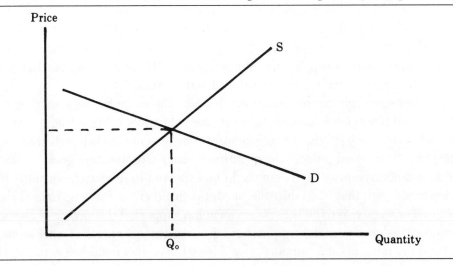

elsewhere in the economy is only 5 percent, in the long run, new producers will enter the industry, shifting out the market supply curve, driving down the market price, output, and profits of each producer. Entry will cease once the profit rate in this industry is equal to the economy-wide profit rate.

One of the most important properties of the competitive market equilibrium is that the quantity produced is the *socially efficient* quantity: The cost of producing the last unit of output just equals consumers' marginal willingness to pay for it. Any level of output below Q_0 would be inefficient since it would cost less to produce the marginal unit than consumers would be willing to pay for it. Since all firms receive the same price for the product, the distribution of output across firms is also efficient. Instead of assuming that all firms have the same marginal cost schedules, suppose that there are two types of firms, "high-cost" and "low-cost." Because of poor land or access to water, high-cost firms have a greater MC at every level of output. Because both high- and low-cost producers equate their MC to the price (uniform across producers), low-cost firms operate at a higher level of output. This arrangement is socially efficient: If both types of firms were producing at the same rate, total costs of production could be reduced by transferring production from high-cost to low-cost firms. As noted, the tendency of a competitive market to produce the socially efficient quantity of a good and to allocate production efficiently across firms, without the direction of a central planner or coordinator, is an example of the operation of the "invisible hand"—a term immortalized by Adam Smith.

The supply-and-demand framework just outlined enables us to analyze or predict the effects of various events and government policy changes on the price and quantity of wine. Suppose that advances in biotechnology result in increased grape yield—more grapes can be grown with given amounts of land, labor, and capital. This hypothesis implies that each producer's MC schedule will be shifted down—the MC of producing any given level of output has declined. Consequently, the market supply curve shifts down, and there is a reduction in price and an increase in total quantity produced and consumed.

Even seemingly remote events can have an impact on the wine market. At many social functions, wine and cheese are served together, suggesting that they are *complementary* goods. If two goods are complementary, then an increase in the price of one good reduces the quantity demanded of the other good. Hence, an increase in the price of cheese might be expected to reduce the quantity of wine demanded, that is, to shift the market demand curve for wine toward the origin. For many years, the U.S. government has supported the income of cheese producers (dairy farmers) by purchasing enormous quantities of cheese and other dairy products at a "support price" above the market equilibrium price. At the end of 1984, the government had accumulated stockpiles of over 1.4 billion pounds of cheese, butter, and nonfat dry milk, amounting to more than 40 percent of the total production of cheese and butter in that year. If the government were to sell its stockpiles, it would drive down the market price of cheese, which would (assuming complementarity of wine and cheese) increase the demand for wine, thus raising the price and quantity of wine. Wine producers might not lobby for the sale of government dairy stockpiles, however, since such sales would probably also depress the price of milk; if milk and wine are *substitutes* in consumption, a fall in the milk price would trigger a decline in wine demand. The net impact of the government's action on wine demand would depend on the relative strength of the cheese and milk price effects.

The final scenario affecting the wine market is the imposition by the government of a $1 per bottle tax on wine, payable by suppliers. This tax acts to shift up by $1 the MC schedule of the typical producer, since in addition to paying factors of production (workers, suppliers of materials), the producer must make payments to the government. Now, the marginal cost *to the producer* of the fourth unit of output, for example, is $8 rather than $7. The *social* cost or value of the resources used to produce the fourth unit is still $7, however; the additional $1 is a *transfer* from the producer to the government.

Since each producer's MC curve is shifted up by the tax, the market supply curve is also shifted up (see Figure 5-3). The equilibrium quantity will fall from Q_0 to Q_1. In discussing the effect of the tax on the price of wine, we must be careful to distinguish the *gross* price (inclusive of tax)—the price paid by the consumer—from the *net* price (exclusive of tax)—the price received by the producer. The gross and net prices may be denoted P_g and P_n and are related by the equation $P_g = P_n + 1$. Figure 5-3 shows that as a result of the tax, the price paid

FIGURE 5-3   Effect of a $1 per bottle tax on the wine market

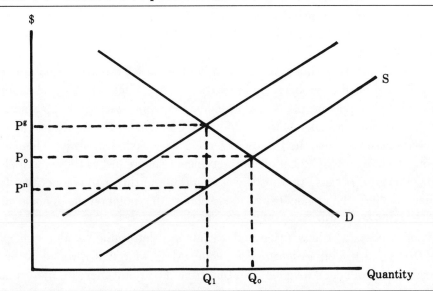

by consumers will increase, but by less than $1, and the price received by producers will decrease, also by less than $1. The "burden" of the tax is shared by consumers and producers; the fraction of the burden borne by each group depends on the slopes of the demand and supply curves.

The amount of revenue the government raises is equal to the equilibrium quantity (Q_1) times the tax per unit ($1). The flatter the demand curve—the more price sensitive consumers are—the less revenue will be raised by imposing the tax, since consumers will reduce purchases more (shrinking the tax base) in response to the tax-induced price increase.

Q_1, the amount of wine that is produced and consumed after imposition of the tax, is not a socially efficient quantity. Suppose $Q_1 = 500$. Consumers would be willing to pay more—but less than $1 more—for the 501st unit than the value of the resources required to produce it; therefore, it should be produced. However, in the presence of the tax, they would have to pay the full dollar above the resource cost, which they are unwilling to do; hence, the 501st unit will not be produced. The tax, by driving a "wedge" between the price paid by consumers and the price received by producers, causes an insufficient quantity of the good to be produced, reducing economic welfare (even though the resources appropriated by the government via the tax are presumably used to increase the output of some other product or good). The sum of the losses borne by consumers (in the form of reduced consumer welfare) and those borne by producers (in the form of reduced profits) exceeds the government's gain in tax revenue.[1] Using taxes of this sort to transfer income or resources from one use to another resembles using a leaky bucket to transfer water; some of the intended benefits of the transfer are dissipated due to imperfections in the transfer mechanism.

We conclude our analysis of the hypothetical wine market, and our brief sojourn into microeconomics, by investigating the effects of monopolization of an industry's supply on price, quantity, and economic welfare. Suppose all the productive capacity (firms) in the industry were under the control of a single decision maker (monopolist) whose objective is to maximize profits. The market demand curve and MC schedule of the typical firm are just as they were before. Now, however, because there is (by assumption) no threat of competition from other suppliers, the monopolist is free to choose that point on the demand curve that maximizes profit.

To understand how price and output are determined under monopoly, we first need to define *marginal revenue* (MR). Marginal revenue is the increase in a producer's revenue resulting from a one-unit increase in output. If a producer is maximizing profits, he will produce output up until the point at which the marginal profit earned on the last unit equals zero. Since Profit = Revenue − Cost, the condition that marginal profit equals zero is equivalent to the condition MR = MC. Thus, the general condition for profit maximization is that the firm produce the level of output at which MR = MC. Recall that in the case of a competitive firm, we assumed (because the firm is "small" relative to the market) that the firm could sell as much output as it wanted without influencing the market price; the firm was a "price taker." Hence, marginal revenue is identical to price (MR = P) and the condition MR = MC reduces to P = MC. (This equality between price and marginal cost was one reason we found the competitive market to be efficient.) In contrast, because the monopolist controls the entire industry supply, he is *not* a price taker—he is a price setter. The demand curve facing the monopolist is the *market* demand curve. The monopolist recognizes that if he wishes to increase the quantity of output that he sells he will have to lower the price of *every* unit of output. Suppose that two points on the market demand curve are

Price	Quantity Demanded
$10.00	9
9.50	10

If the firm sells 10 units, the price of the tenth unit (and of the first nine) is $9.50; however, the MR of the tenth unit is $5 [= (10 × 9.50) − (9 × 10.00)]. The firm lost $.50 on each of the first nine units when it lowered its price to enable the tenth to be sold. Because demand curves slope down, the MR curve always lies below the demand curve (see Figure 5-4). Indeed, MR can easily be negative, as it will be if demand is very *elastic* (price sensitive). The quantity produced by a monopolist, therefore, is always lower than that which would be produced in a competitive market, and the price will be higher. In Figure 5-4, the output produced is equal to Q_M and is determined by the intersection of the MC and MR schedules. This number is lower than the competitive output level Q_o, which we argued is the socially efficient level. The value to consumers of units of output $Q_{M+2}, \ldots, Q_o$ exceeds the cost of producing them, but given the incentives facing the monopolist, he or she is (rationally) unwilling to produce more than Q_M units.

This theoretical demonstration that monopolists tend to restrict output below the socially desirable level has long been a cornerstone of antitrust policy, which attempts to ensure that industries do not become monopolized. But some prominent economists, notably Joseph Schumpeter, have made a case that monopolies (or more generally, firms with "market power" (the ability to influence price) are not necessarily entirely, or even mostly, bad for economic welfare. Schumpeter maintained that, in the long run, economic well-being depends as much on "dynamic efficiency" (the rate of introduction of new and improved products and processes) as it does on "static efficiency" (efficiency in the sense just discussed). Moreover, he claimed that large firms with command over extensive resources are more likely to produce important innovations than smaller, more competitive firms. This latter claim is quite controversial and largely untested. Nevertheless Schumpeter's critique of the standard (static) theory of monopoly is worth noting.

FIGURE 5-4 Output and price determination under monopoly

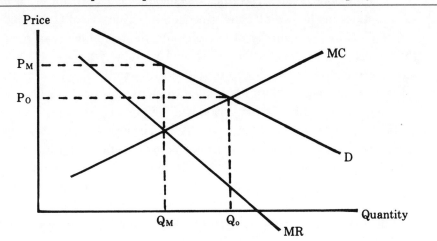

MACROECONOMICS

We have indicated that microeconomics is concerned with the issue of how the quantity and price of output of individual firms or industries is determined. In contrast, macroeconomics addresses the determination of the *entire economy,* or *aggregate* output and price. Economists are often more interested in analyzing the *changes* or *rates of growth* of aggregate output and price than they are in analyzing their *levels.*

The most widely used measure of aggregate output is *gross national product* (GNP)—the market value of all final goods and services produced in an economy within a given time period. (The market value of a good equals the quantity produced of the good times its price.) Since GNP in each year depends both on that year's quantities and that year's prices, the change in GNP from 1986 to 1987, for example, was due partially to a change in quantities and partially to a change in prices. It is important to distinguish between these two sources of change. We can do so by calculating what GNP *would have been* in 1987, if prices had remained at their 1986 levels, and comparing this with actual GNP in 1986. That is, we will use the *same year's* (1986) prices to compute the value of output in both years. The increase in GNP we calculate when we use a constant set of prices (base year prices) is called an increase in *real* GNP. The increase in GNP we calculate when we use a changing set of prices is called an increase in *nominal* GNP. The difference between nominal and real GNP growth is due to *inflation,* that is, to a change in the average level of (or *index* of) prices:

$$\text{Inflation rate (percentage increase in average price level)} = \frac{\text{Nominal GNP}}{\text{growth rate}} - \frac{\text{Real GNP}}{\text{growth rate}}$$

One of the major challenges in macroeconomics is to explain—and *predict*—fluctuations in the overall rate of economic activity (real GNP) and in the price level. (In the remainder of this chapter, the term GNP will refer to *real* GNP, which will be denoted by the symbol Y.) Table 5-2 presents data on the annual growth rate of GNP during the period 1970 to 1986. Several features of the data are noteworthy. GNP has tended to increase over time: The mean rate of increase during this 16-year period was 2.6 percent per year. However, the growth in aggregate output is far from steady: The growth rate ranged from a minimum of −2.5 percent in 1982, to a maximum of 6.4 percent just two years later. These data also point to the existence of *business cycles:* Years of below average (2.6 percent) growth in GNP (indicated by a minus sign in the last column of Table 5-2) tend to be bunched together, as do years of above-average growth (indicated by a plus sign). The path of GNP over time can be described as cyclical fluctuations around a long-term upward trend. In order to explain or

TABLE 5-2   Annual growth rate of real U.S. GNP, 1970–1986

Year	Percentage Change in GNP from Previous Period	Below (−) or Above (+) Average Growth
1970	−0.3	−
1971	2.8	+
1972	5.0	+
1973	5.2	+
1974	−0.5	−
1975	−1.3	−
1976	4.9	+
1977	4.7	+
1978	5.3	+
1979	2.3	−
1980	−0.2	−
1981	1.9	−
1982	−2.5	−
1983	3.6	+
1984	6.4	+
1985	2.7	+
1986	2.5	−
Average, 1970–1986	2.6	

predict movements in GNP, we will need to answer two questions: (1) Why does GNP have an upward trend, and how is the magnitude of this trend determined? (2) Why are there sizable short-run fluctuations of GNP around this long-term trend? The first question is of primary concern to economists studying *long-run economic growth,* the second to economists concerned with *short-run economic fluctuations* or business cycles.

To answer these questions, it is useful to define the concept of *potential GNP* and to contrast it with actual (observed) GNP. Parents and teachers sometimes complain that students are "underachievers"—that their actual level of performance falls short of their potential for achievement. Similarly, economists postulate that during certain periods (lasting up to several years) less output may be produced than an economy is capable of producing. The economy's potential output (like the potential achievement of a student) is usually not directly observable—it must be inferred indirectly on the basis of available data. To infer an economy's potential output, we need to make use of a fundamental economic relationship known as a *production function.* A production function is a relationship between output and input (labor, capital) that indicates the maximum amount of output it is possible to produce from given quantities of input, using available technology. Potential output is defined as the level of output that would be produced if the labor and capital resources available in the economy were "fully employed." Hence, the economy is operating at potential if, and only if, resources are fully employed. What does full employment mean? Let us consider the issue of full employment of labor. In 1983, there were 174 million persons 16 years of age and over in the U.S. population. Does "full employment" mean that all 174 million should be working? No, some of these individuals were in school, retired, ill, taking care of families, or otherwise not interested in working for pay. Only 112 million people were in the civilian *labor force*—either employed (101 million) or unemployed (11 million). The unemployed are people who are not working, but who are seeking work. The *unemployment rate* is the ratio of the number of people unemployed to the number of people in the labor force (the sum of the employed and the people seeking work). Should "full employment" of labor mean that the entire *labor force* is employed, that is that the unemployment rate is zero? While this might seem sensible, economists do not think zero is the value of the unemployment rate that corresponds to full employment of labor. It is natural and even desirable for some individuals, such as people changing jobs and new entrants into the labor market (e.g., high school graduates), to be unemployed for a time while they search for an appropriate job. Thus, even an economy producing at its potential would have a positive amount of unemployment. The appropriate value of the natural or full-employment rate is a matter of considerable debate among economists. The consensus value of the natural rate of unemployment (denoted U^*) in the 1980s for example was about 6 percent. If the actual unemployment rate (denoted U) exceeds the natural rate, less than full utilization of the economy's labor resources occurs, and actual output falls below potential output. These data indicate that in 1983, the unemployment rate was 9.6 percent, 3.6 percent above the natural rate.[2]

When the unemployment rate exceeds the natural rate, some fraction of the output the economy was capable of producing will not be produced. Economists refer to this fraction as the *output gap* (YGAP).

> YGAP < 0 if the economy is below full employment
>
> YGAP = 0 at full employment
>
> YGAP > 0 if the economy is above full employment

In addition to noting that YGAP and the unemployment rate U are inversely related, we need to know *how much* YGAP will decline (increase in magnitude) when U increases 1 percentage point—from 6 to 7 percent, for example. On the surface, it might seem that there should be a one-for-one (inverse) relationship between U and YGAP—that lowering the utilization rate of the labor force by 1 percent (a 1 point increase in U) should cause 1 percent less output to be produced. However, as demonstrated by the late macroeconomist Arthur Okun, the slope of the relationship between U and YGAP is close to -3:

$$YGAP = -3 \, (U - U^*)$$

This relationship is referred to as *Okun's Law.* Therefore, a 1 percentage point increase in U is associated with a 3 percent reduction in output. For several reasons, output falls dramatically when the unemployment rate rises. First, when U increases, the labor force contracts, since some workers who otherwise would have searched for jobs become discouraged and drop out of the labor force. Second, average weekly hours of work tend to be lower during periods of high unemployment (recessions), partially because employers cut back on the use of overtime. Third, labor productivity (the average amount of output produced per hour of work) is lower during recessions than it is during periods of high unemployment, because the pace of work is slower.

The cost to society of unemployment, in terms of the amount of output forgone, is high. Okun's Law implies that if the economy had been at full employment in 1983 (if U had been 6 percent rather than 9.6 percent), almost $400 billion worth of additional output would have been produced. As a benchmark, this is slightly greater than the total purchases of goods and services by all state and local governments in that year.

Why does unemployment occur, that is, why do modern industrial economies sometimes fail to fully utilize available resources and realize their potential for producing output? Is there anything the government can do to reduce unemployment? If so, does the reduction of unemployment entail sacrifices with respect to other economic goals, such as maintaining a low rate of inflation? These are some of the fundamental questions that macroeconomics attempts to answer.

Providing complete answers to these questions is beyond the scope of this chapter; we will instead sketch some answers using a simple model of supply and demand. Some crucial differences, however, distinguish the model we will develop here from the one used previously in the section on microeconomics. There the quantity and price determined by the model were those of a single commodity (wine). Here, the quantity refers to real GNP—the sum of the quantities of all goods and services produced—and the price refers to the aggregate price level—an average (or index) of the prices of all goods and services. (The Consumer Price Index is probably the most familiar example of a price index.) When quantity and price are defined in this way, the supply and demand are referred to as *aggregate supply* (AS) and *aggregate demand* (AD) curves.

The AS = AD model is depicted graphically in Figure 5-5. We shall consider the AS curve first. In contrast to the usual (microeconomic) upward-sloping supply curve, the AS curve is *vertical,* and it is vertical at the value Y^*. This orientation signifies that the amount of output producers wish to supply does not depend on the (average) price level, and this amount is equal to potential output. Why does the aggregate supply of output not increase when the price level rises? The supply remains constant because the price level is an

FIGURE 5-5   AS-AD model of real GNP and price-level determination

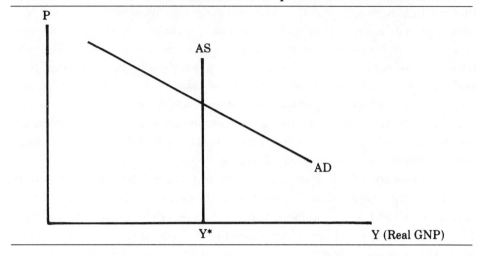

average of *all* prices, including prices paid by producers for inputs (e.g., materials and labor). When the price level goes up by, for example, 5 percent, we assume that all prices increase 5 percent, and that *relative* prices remain unchanged. If the prices of a producer's output and inputs go up by the same percentage amount, the producer's profit-maximizing level of output remains unchanged. The reason the microeconomic supply curve derived earlier sloped upward was that we implicitly assumed that when the price of output increased, the price of inputs remained unchanged, so that the *relative* price of output increased. Since relative prices are assumed to remain unchanged when the aggregate price level P changes, the quantity of aggregate output supplied is independent of P.

Now we turn to the AD curve, which shows the total amount of output that consumers, investors, the government, and foreigners would want to purchase at different values of P. Like the microeconomic demand curve, the AD curve slopes down, *but for different reasons.* One reason the microeconomic demand curve had a negative slope was that reductions in price were assumed to reduce the *relative* price of the good, inducing substitution toward the good; in the AS = AD model, relative prices are unaffected by changes in P. Why, then, does the AD curve slope down? The descent is due to the effect of changes in P on the *real stock of money* in circulation, hence on *interest rates,* hence on the desired amount of *investment.* Let us briefly consider these linkages. Investment, which includes purchases by businesses of buildings and machinery, and by households of houses, is a very important (and volatile) component of aggregate demand. The amount of investment (I) that businesses and consumers wish to undertake is sensitive (and inversely related) to the level of the market interest rate (R), since the latter determines the cost of borrowing. (The rate of investment in residential housing is particularly sensitive to interest rate fluctuations.) The level of the interest rate—which may be thought of as the *price* of (borrowing) money—depends in turn on the *quantity* of money in circulation. It is the *real* quantity, or purchasing power, of money, not simply the number of dollar bills in circulation, that determines the level of interest rates. Suppose the (nominal) amount of money in circulation (M) is $1 million. If the price level is 2, that money would purchase only half as many goods and services as it would if P were equal to 1: Money would be scarcer, and the interest rate would be higher to "ration" the smaller supply. For a given nominal stock of money, then, the higher P is, the lower the real stock of money; the higher is the interest rate, the lower is desired investment, and the lower is desired total spending. This relationship can be summarized as:

$$P \uparrow \rightarrow \frac{M}{P} \downarrow \rightarrow R \uparrow I \downarrow \rightarrow Y \downarrow$$

It is this effect of P on interest rates and investment that accounts for the negative slope of the AD curve.

We can now use the AS = AD model to explain how real GNP and the price level are determined, and consequently why output may deviate from its potential level. Suppose that the AD curve were initially at the position indicated by AD_0 in Figure 5-6, and that the price level were equal to P_0, the price at which the quantity of output demanded equals the quantity supplied; the economy would be at full employment. Suppose further that there were a sudden downward shift (to AD_1) of the AD curve; there is a decline in the quantity

FIGURE 5-6   Effect of a decline in aggregate demand on output and price

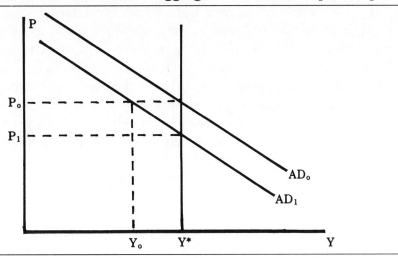

of output demanded at any given price level. Such a decline could occur as a result, for example, of a severe downturn in the stock market (like the one that occurred in October 1987) which might cause consumers to feel poorer (due to capital losses) and more apprehensive about the future economic outlook, and therefore to curtail expenditures, particularly on "big-ticket" items such as automobiles and major appliances. What impact would this kind of AD "shock" have on real GNP?

Observe that if the price level were to immediately fall to P_1, then the quantity of output demanded would again be equal to $Y*$, and the economy would remain at full employment. If P were extremely *flexible,* tending to fall rapidly whenever demand declined, then the decline in demand would not cause output to fall below potential; YGAP would remain equal to zero, and U would remain equal to $U*$. According to the "classical" school of economic thought (which prevailed throughout the nineteenth and early twentieth centuries until the Great Depression of the 1930s), there was every reason to believe that prices *were* extremely flexible. In the face of a general decline in demand, producers would lower their prices enough so that full employment would be maintained. Price flexibility essentially guaranteed that the economy would continuously remain at full employment.

The problem with this view of the macroeconomy became apparent in the early 1930s, when it was grossly at odds with the facts. Between 1929 (the year of the historic stock market crash) and 1933, real GNP declined almost 30 percent. Moreover, it was clear that this collapse was due to a decline in demand (and an increase in the magnitude of YGAP), not due to a reduction in potential output. The unemployment rate increased from 3 percent in 1929 to 25 percent in 1933; by 1940, it was still as high as 15 percent. The British economist John Maynard Keynes observed that these facts were blatantly inconsistent with the hypothesis of flexible prices. Such high and persistent unemployment, argued Keynes, could only be explained by the tendency of prices and wages to be *downwardly rigid.* Keynes believed that workers would refuse to accept wage reductions, even if failure to do so would result in mass layoffs. Producers would not reduce the prices of their products unless their labor (and other) costs declined. The consequences of price rigidity may be seen in Figure 5-6. If the price level remains "stuck" at P_0 after AD has shifted from AD_0 to AD_1, output will fall from $Y*$ to Y_1: The economy enters into a recession (or even a depression) and operates below its potential. Moreover, *deflation,* a decline in the price level, could not be counted on to eliminate unemployment. Although prices and wages might ultimately fall, Keynes was fond of saying that "in the long run, we're all dead."

Keynes rejected the classical doctrine that price flexibility could be relied on to "automatically" keep the economy at full employment. He did not, however, believe that society had to simply accept the existence of prolonged periods of unemployment. Full employment could be achieved, not as a result of automatic price adjustment, but by deliberate and intelligent use by the government of *monetary policy* and particularly *fiscal policy*. Monetary policy refers to the government's control of the nominal stock of money, fiscal policy to its control over government expenditure and taxation. In terms of Figure 5-6, the basic idea is that when AD shifts down from AD_0 to AD_1 and the price level is stuck at P_0, by judicious use of fiscal and monetary policies, the government can shift AD *back* to AD_0, thus restoring full employment. When the AD curve is located at AD_1 and the price level is P_0 there is *insufficient demand* to keep the economy's resources fully employed. There are three ways the government can attempt to increase demand for goods and services. The first, and most direct, is for the government to increase its expenditures on highways, education, national defense, and other items. The second is by lowering taxes on consumers (thus increasing their disposable income) or on firms (thus increasing their after-tax profits); such tax reductions would tend to increase consumption and investment expenditure, respectively. (Either increasing government expenditure or lowering taxes could also have the undesirable side effect of increasing the government's budget deficit, the excess of expenditures over tax revenues.) The third way is to increase the nominal money supply. As discussed earlier, if P remains fixed at P_0 this measure would result in an increase in the real money supply, a fall in interest rates, and an increase in desired investment expenditure. Keynes believed that an increase in government spending was likely to be the most effective of the three techniques for stimulating aggregate demand.

Keynesian macroeconomic theory amounted to a revolutionary advance over previous thought, but there have been many further important developments since Keynes published *The General Theory of Employment, Interest and Money* in 1935. The classical and Keynesian models adopted completely polar assumptions about the process of price adjustment: In the first model, prices are perfectly flexible; in the second, they are perfectly rigid (at least in the downward direction). An intermediate view of price adjustment (in some sense a synthesis of both extreme views) underlies much contemporary macroeconomic analysis. According to this *"sticky price"* model, prices are rigid in the short run—they do not decline immediately in response to a decline in AD—but they are flexible in the long run—they tend to gradually decline when the economy is below full employment. They do not decline immediately because some individuals (such as workers and firms covered by collective bargaining agreements) have previously signed long-term contracts that lock them into price and wage levels. As time passes, however, those contracts expire and new wage and price negotiations can take account of changes in economic conditions.[3] As prices decline, the real stock of money increases, interest rates fall, and investment and output increase, until output has returned to potential. As in the Keynesian model, the economy has undergone a recession (due to the failure of prices to instantaneously fall), but in the sticky price model, the recession was temporary, and the economy recovered from it without intervention by the government. This is not to say, however, that government intervention would not have been desirable. Although the recession was temporary, it was not painless—output was lost during the period of adjustment to the new, lower price level. In principle, the government could have reduced the duration and depth of the recession by appropriate use of its fiscal and monetary policies.

In practice though, it may be difficult for the government to provide the right amount of stimulus at the right time so as to keep the economy at full employment. While the scenario of a one-time downward shift of the AD curve is a convenient one for illustrating how GNP is determined, in reality the AD curve is constantly (and unpredictably) shifting up and down as the economy is buffeted by various economic and political disturbances. Consequently, the target that economic policymakers are (or should be) aiming for is moving rather than stationary. Moreover, it takes time for changes in policy, such as expansions in the money supply, both to be implemented and to have an effect on the economy. There is evidence, for example, that the peak effect of changes in the money supply on GNP takes about 1½ to 2 years to occur. Suppose the AD curve shifted down from AD_0 to AD_1, and the government increased the money supply to combat recession, but that AD for unrelated reasons (an increase in investor confidence, for instance) quickly shifted back to AD_0. The monetary stimulus would eventually cause the economy to "overshoot" full employment as AD shifts past AD_0 and prices are stuck temporarily at P_0. The problem with going above full employment (YGAP > 0), as indicated by the price-adjustment equation, is that inflation will result. The recognition that the position of the AD curve is highly unstable and that it takes considerable time for fiscal and monetary policies to have an effect on aggregate demand has made many contemporary macroeconomists more skeptical about policymakers' ability to *fine tune* the economy (maintain it continuously at full employment) than Keynes was half a century ago.

The last aspect of macroeconomic fluctuations considered here is the existence (or lack thereof) of a *trade-off between unemployment and inflation*. Although the costs to society of a high rate of inflation are less obvious and amenable to measurement than the costs of high unemployment, inflation is regarded by policy makers and the public as just as serious an evil as unemployment. Two pieces of legislation (both lacking enforcement provisions)—the Full Employment Act of 1946 and the Humphrey Hawkins Act of 1978—commit the federal government to the twin goals of *full employment* and *price stability* (absence of inflation). The question is whether these objectives are consistent: Can they be simultaneously achieved or does greater achievement of one entail less achievement of the other?

The price-adjustment equation given implies that there *is* a long-run trade-off between unemployment and inflation: Society can achieve a permanently low rate of unemployment by maintaining a permanently high rate of inflation, and vice versa. We can see this relationship by substituting for YGAP in the price adjustment equation, using Okun's Law:

$$\eta = -3f(U - U\circ)$$

For a given value of $U\circ$, the higher U is, the lower the inflation rate η. Prior to the early 1970s, this theoretical relationship "fit" observed data on unemployment and inflation very well: The inflation rate tended to be low (or even negative) during years in which unemployment was high. The inverse relationship between U and η was first established empirically by A. W. Phillips using British data spanning many years; for this reason, this relationship has come to be called the *Phillips Curve*. Taken at face value, the Phillips Curve indicated that (1) it would be difficult or impossible for the economy to simultaneously achieve low unemployment and low inflation, and (2) policymakers could bring about a low rate of unemployment by maintaining a high rate of inflation—by adopting a policy of rapid monetary growth, for example.

In the early 1970s, however, the Phillips Curve relationship began to break down—it no longer fit the data. In 1975, the unemployment rate reached 8.5 percent, the highest rate since the Depression, and the inflation rate reached 9.3 percent, the highest rate since the late 1940s. Contrary to the dictates of the Phillips Curve, the economy was experiencing a period of both stagnation (low output) and inflation: *stagflation*. Economic theory had to be reformulated to attempt to explain this new and unpleasant phenomenon.

It turns out that a relatively simple reformulation (generalization) of the price-adjustment equation can account for the existence of stagflation and other aspects of observed macroeconomic behavior. Though simple, this reformulation has dramatically different implications concerning the nature of the unemployment-inflation trade-off and the effectiveness of economic policy in fighting these two scourges. This reformulation, proposed independently by Milton Friedman and Edmund Phelps, consists of respecifying the price adjustment equation as:

$$\eta_t - \eta_{t-1} = f \cdot YGAP_{t-1}$$

YGAP is now related to the *change* in the rate of inflation, rather than the *level* of inflation, as it was in the original price adjustment equation. This revision implies that if YGAP = 0, the rate of inflation will be *constant*—it will not, in general, be *zero*. If the economy is below full employment (YGAP < 0), the *inflation rate* will decline, but the *price level* will not necessarily decline. (If the inflation rate falls from 7 to 5 percent per year, prices are still increasing, but at a slower rate.)

The revised price adjustment equation implies that there is *no long-run trade-off between unemployment and inflation, only a short-run trade-off.* The absence of a long-run trade-off is signified by the fact that *as long as* $\eta_t = \eta_{t-1}$ (the rate of inflation is constant), $\text{YGAP}_{t-1} = 0$ (the economy is at full employment), *regardless of the level of* η_t. If the economy had a permanent 10 percent rate of inflation, it would have no less unemployment (or more output) than it would if it had a permanent rate of inflation of zero—in both cases, the economy would be at full employment. The existence of a short-run trade-off is due to the fact that $(\eta_t - \eta_{t-1})$ is proportional to YGAP_{t-1}. For *disinflation*—a reduction in the rate of inflation—to occur, the economy must undergo a recession. The greater the desired extent of disinflation, the deeper the recession required. Suppose that f = 2, each percentage point reduction in YGAP_{t-1} reduces the inflation rate by 2 percentage points. If the rate of inflation in year t − 1 is 10 percent and policy makers want to reduce it to 4 percent in year t, then they will have to use fiscal and/or monetary policies to force output 3 percent below potential in year t − 1.

Policymakers "engineered" a recession to lower the rate of inflation in the early 1980s. In 1979 and 1980, the rates of inflation were respectively 13.3 and 12.4 percent—considered too high by the administration and many Americans. The government allowed the unemployment rate to rise from 5.8 percent in 1979 to 9.7 percent—a postwar high—in 1982, primarily via tight monetary policy. By 1983, the inflation rate had fallen to 3.8 percent. Once the "inflation dragon" had been tamed, the economy was allowed to gradually return to full employment, and the rate of inflation remained moderate.

We observed two salient attributes of the growth of real output: an upward long-term trend, and cyclical fluctuations around this trend. Economists postulate that the tendency of actual output to increase in the long run is due to steady growth in potential output, and that the cyclical fluctuations are due to transitory deviations of actual from potential output. The preceding discussion explains why such temporary departures from full employment may occur. We now provide a brief introduction to evidence and theory pertaining to long-run growth of potential output.

Table 5-3 presents data on the average annual rates of real output growth of the United States and of five other countries during four intervals of the period 1870 to 1984. During the first two intervals, the United States experienced the highest rate of output growth, but it had the second lowest rate in interval III. Every country experienced a sharp acceleration in output growth from interval II to interval III, and a dramatic slowdown from interval III to interval

TABLE 5-3 Real output average annual growth rates, six countries, 1870–1984

Country	Period				Acceleration from Period II to Period III	Slowdown from Period III to Period IV
	I (1870–1913)	II (1913–1950)	III (1950–1973)	IV (1973–1984)		
United States	4.2	2.8	3.7	2.3	+0.9	−1.4
France	1.7	1.1	5.1	2.2	+4.0	−2.9
Germany	2.8	1.3	5.9	1.7	+4.6	−4.2
Japan	2.5	2.2	9.4	3.8	+7.2	−5.6
Netherlands	2.1	2.4	4.7	1.6	+2.3	−3.1
United Kingdom	1.9	1.3	3.0	1.1	+1.7	−1.9

IV. How can we account for these substantial differences across both countries and time in the rate of economic growth?

To begin to answer this question, it is useful to define the notion of *productivity*. The general definition of productivity is the quantity of output per unit of input:

$$\text{Productivity} = \frac{\text{Output}}{\text{Input}}$$

Beyond this general definition, two more specific concepts or measures of productivity differ with respect to the definition of input. First, *labor productivity* is defined as output per unit of labor input:

$$\text{Labor productivity} = \frac{\text{Output}}{\text{Labor input}}$$

The conventional measure of labor input is the total number of hours worked by all persons employed. Recall that according to the production function, another input besides labor—capital—determines the quantity of output produced. Hence, labor input is only a *partial* measure of the amount of resources utilized in production, and labor productivity is a partial productivity measure. The second concept of productivity is *total factor productivity* (TFP), which is defined as output per unit of total input (the terms factor and input are synonymous):

$$\text{TFP} = \frac{\text{Output}}{\text{Total input}}$$

Total input is a weighted sum of the quantities of labor and capital employed, similar to the way in which GNP is a weighted sum of the quantities of all of the commodities produced in the economy. TFP is the best measure of the productive efficiency of the economy: If TFP increases, more output can be produced with the same quantity of input (or a given level of output could be produced with less input).

To facilitate our discussion of long-run economic growth, adopt the following notation:

$$Y = \text{Output}$$
$$L = \text{Labor}$$
$$K = \text{Capital}$$
$$T = \text{Total input}$$
$$\theta = \text{Total factor productivity}$$

Since $\theta = Y/T$, then

$$Y = \theta \cdot T$$

The amount of output produced is determined by the quantity of total input times total factor productivity (output per unit of total input). This is a relationship among the *levels* of Y, θ, and T. However, we are primarily concerned with the *growth rate* of Y and its determinants. Let a dot over a variable denote the growth rate, or percentage rate of change, of that variable; for example, $\dot{Y}$ denotes the growth rate of output. The previous equation implies the following relationships among growth rates:

$$\dot{Y} = \dot{\theta} + \dot{T}$$

This means that output growth is the *sum* of total input growth and total factor productivity growth.[4]

We are close to having a simple model that can account for long-run output growth. To complete the model, one more point must be addressed. It concerns the definition and measurement of $\dot{T}$, the rate of growth of total input. Economists have shown that the correct way to define $\dot{T}$ is as follows:

$$\dot{T} = \lambda\dot{K} + (1 - \lambda)\dot{L}$$

where λ is the ratio of capital costs to aggregate costs of production, and $(1 - \lambda)$ is the ratio of labor costs to aggregate costs of production. $\dot{T}$ is therefore a *weighted average* of the growth rates of capital and labor input, weighted by their relative importance in the production of output. For the U.S. economy as a whole, λ is approximately equal to 0.3: Capital accounts for 30 percent, and labor the remaining 70 percent, of total production cost. We will therefore set λ = 0.3. Substituting this value into the previous equation and rearranging terms,

$$\dot{T} = \dot{L} + .3(\dot{K} - \dot{L})$$

The growth in total input may be expressed as the sum of labor input growth $(\dot{L})$ and the growth in capital per unit of labor $(\dot{K} - \dot{L})$ multiplied by capital's share in production costs. Substituting this expression for $\dot{T}$ into the output growth equation, we obtain our final model of output growth:

$$\dot{Y} = \dot{L} + .3(\dot{K} - \dot{L}) + \dot{\theta}$$

This equation reveals three sources of output growth in the long run: (1) growth in labor input; (2) growth in capital-intensity, that is, increase in the amount of capital employed per worker; and (3) growth in total factor productivity or efficiency. Let us briefly consider each of these sources of output growth in turn.

Population increase is the major reason for long-run growth in labor input. Between 1950 and 1973, for example, the U.S. population increased at an average annual rate of 1.4 percent, from 152 million to 212 million. However, labor input growth also depends on changes in the *labor force participation rate* (the fraction of the population in the labor force) and in average weekly hours of work. The participation rate remained essentially constant between 1950 and 1973, although it has increased somewhat since, due to the increased presence of women in the labor market. Average weekly hours of work declined fairly steadily during 1950 to 1973, at an average annual rate of -0.3 percent. The average growth rate of labor input was therefore about 1.1 percent (= population growth rate + growth rate of average hours). This figure is well below the output growth rate of 3.7 percent reported in Table 5-3, and implies that labor productivity—output per hour of work—was increasing at a rate of 2.6 percent.

One reason for the high rate of growth of labor productivity was that during this period, the amount of capital per worker was increasing at a rate of almost 2.2 percent per year. Society was saving and investing enough to provide each worker with more machinery and other capital with which to work, not merely enough to equip a growing labor force with the same average amount of capital per worker. As indicated by the last equation, to determine the contribution of capital accumulation to output growth, we multiply the increase in capital per worker by 0.3, which reflects the relative importance of capital in production. Thus "capital-deepening"—the increase in capital intensity—was responsible for about 0.7 percent per year of the growth in output. The *sum* of the contributions of labor input growth and capital deepening to output growth is 1.8 ($= 1.1 + 0.7$) percent. This is only about half of the 3.7 percent rate of increase of output during the period. About half of the increase in total output was due to an increase in efficiency (total factor productivity), rather than an increase in the amount of capital and labor employed.

Economists have identified a number of the sources of this growth in efficiency; two important sources are investment in education and investment in research and development (R&D). Education tends to increase the quality, or skill level, of the labor force; the effective quantity of labor input depends on the skill level of persons employed as well as on the number of persons. The average level of educational attainment of the labor force has increased substantially over the long run. For example, the fraction of workers employed in manufacturing who had at least some college education increased from 17 percent in 1960 to 27 percent in 1980.

Investment in R&D contributes to efficiency and output growth by adding to the stock of useful knowledge and by yielding new and improved processes and products. Abundant evidence indicates that industries that perform the most R&D per dollar of sales tend to have the highest rates of TFP growth.

Unfortunately, the rate of TFP growth has fallen substantially since the early 1970s. The rate declined from 1.9 percent during the period between 1950 and 1973, to 0.5 percent during 1973 to 1984. In fact, the entire slowdown in output growth documented in Table 5-3 can be attributed to this deceleration of productivity. A large number of studies have attempted to determine why the productivity slowdown occurred. They have investigated the role of such factors as the sharp energy price increases of the 1970s, the increase in environmental regulation, and a possible decline in the rate or efficacy of industrial innovation. For the most part, however, these studies have failed to provide a compelling explanation for the post-1973 slowdown. The decline in the rate of productivity growth remains a mystery waiting to be solved by future research.

EXCHANGE RATES AND THEIR RELATIONSHIP TO DOMESTIC AND FOREIGN INTEREST RATES

We have sketched out a framework for understanding how two of the most important macroeconomic variables—real GNP and the price level—are determined. But in the 1990s, as the trade and investment flows between the United States and other economies increase, there is another variable of great concern to businesspeople and policymakers: the exchange rate. The exchange rate E is the number of units of foreign currency (e.g., Japanese yen) that can be purchased for $1. (The reciprocal of the exchange rate is the price of foreign currency: for example, if $E = 100$ yen/\$, then $1/E = (1/100)$ \$/yen $= 1$ cent/yen.) The exchange rate can change substantially—by a few percent—in a single day. We conclude this chapter with a brief discussion of the theory of exchange rate determination.

The basic premise of this theory is that capital is internationally mobile: investors can invest their funds in a number of different countries and will invest in the country where they expect to receive the highest return—taking into account future expected exchange rate movements. We use a simple example to illustrate this point and its implications.

Suppose that the American interest rate R (paid by the U.S. government on its Treasury bonds) is 5%—$1.00 today yields $1.05 in one year—and the Japanese interest rate R_J (paid by the Japanese government on its Treasury bonds) is 3%—100 yen today yields 103 yen in one year. An American investor has $1 to invest for one year, and seeks the highest return on that investment. On the surface, it might appear that there are no circumstances under which the investor would want to purchase a Japanese bond. But that is not the case: Under certain conditions (a sufficient expected decline in the exchange rate), the Japanese bond is the superior investment.

Suppose that the current exchange rate E_0 is 100 yen/\$, and that the investor expects the exchange rate in one year E_1 to be 95 yen/\$: she expects a 5% depreciation of the dollar. How many dollars will she expect to receive a year from now if she invests in the Japanese bond? To invest in that bond, she must first use her $1 to purchase 100 yen today on the foreign exchange market, since the Japanese treasury will not accept foreign currency as payment for its bonds. As noted previously, the Japanese treasury will pay her 103 yen in one year for investing 100 yen today. Because she expects the exchange rate to be 95 yen/$ at that time, she expects to receive about $1.08 (= 103 yen/95 (yen/$)), whereas the American bond would have yielded only $1.05.

It can be shown that the expected return (in dollars) on the Japanese bond is higher, whenever the difference between the two interest rates $(R - R_J)$ is smaller than the expected rate of exchange rate depreciation $((E_0 - E_1)/E_0)$. Stated differently, the expected returns on the two securities are equal if the difference between the interest rates is equal to the expected currency depreciation:

$$R - R_J = (E_0 - E_1) / E_0$$

This equation is known as the *interest-rate parity* (or interest-rate arbitrage) condition. It says that, for an investor to be indifferent between the securities of different countries, the difference between the two interest rates must be equal to the expected rate of exchange-rate depreciation (which is not, in general, zero). For the investor to be indifferent between an American bond paying 5% interest and a Japanese bond paying 3% interest, she must expect the dollar to depreciate against the yen by 2% (from 100 to 98).

The interest-rate parity condition is (merely) a *hypothesis;* to test it, we need to determine whether interest rates and exchange rates are related to one another in the way implied by the preceding equation. The measurement of R, R_J, and E_0 is straightforward, but how can we measure E_1, the *expected* future exchange rate? (Expectations are not directly observable.) We can use today's *forward* exchange rate F_0 as an estimate of investors' current expectations of the future exchange rate. The forward rate is the rate at which people agree today to exchange currencies *in the future,* and it is easily observed (it is published daily in the financial press). It can be shown that today's forward rate is very close to the expected future "spot" rate E_1, so that the parity condition may be rewritten as follows:

$$R - R_J = (E_0 - F_0) / E_0 = 1 - (F_0 / E_0)$$

Actual interest-rate and exchange-rate data are quite consistent with this equation: The difference between domestic and foreign interest rates is approximately equal to the percentage difference between spot and forward exchange rates.

One important practical implication of the interest-rate parity equation is that *increases in the U.S. interest rate cause the dollar to appreciate,* that is, they cause the spot rate E_0 to rise. When R rises and R_J remains unchanged, the left-hand side of the equation increases. For the condition to remain satisfied— for international capital market equilibrium to be maintained—the right-hand side must also increase; an increase in E_0 is one way (in practice, the most important way) for this to happen. Why does the dollar tend to get stronger when

U.S. interest rates rise? When R (and $R - R_J$) rises, American bonds become more attractive investments relative to Japanese bonds, so investors (both American and foreign) wish to exchange foreign currency for dollars in order to purchase U.S. bonds. This increased demand for dollars drives up the exchange rate. Why would anyone be willing to hold Japanese bonds after American interest rates have increased? Because once the dollar has appreciated, investors regard it as "overvalued," and therefore likely to fall in the future. (They subscribe to the view, "what goes up, must come down.") The more the exchange rate goes up today, the faster they expect it to depreciate over the next year. The dollar appreciates today until the resulting increase in future anticipated depreciation just offsets the increase in the interest rate differential.

U.S. macroeconomic experience of the early 1980s provides a graphic (although somewhat painful) illustration of the link between interest rates and exchange rates. The contractionary (anti-inflation) monetary policy pursued by the Federal Reserve under Paul Volker, and the expansionary fiscal policy (tax cuts and increased military expenditure) pursued by the Reagan administration both drove U.S. interest rates to their highest levels in recent history. Consistent with the interest-parity hypothesis, the dollar appreciated by about 40 percent between 1980 and 1985. Such an appreciation is a double-edged sword. The good news is that it reduces the dollar cost to Americans of purchasing foreign goods and services (such as imported oil); this raises our real income, and it also reduces inflationary pressures. The bad news is that it also makes our goods more expensive for foreigners to buy, hence less competitive in global markets. The U.S. trade balance (exports minus imports) declined from $57 billion in 1980 to −$130 billion in 1986; an important part of this decline was due to the appreciation of the dollar induced by soaring domestic interest rates.

The preceding discussion has established that when the exchange rate is *flexible*—can change over time—interest rates may not be equalized across countries, even though capital flows freely across countries. But there are groups of countries today, and there have been others in the past, that attempt to maintain *fixed* (or highly stable) exchange rates. The countries (including Germany, France, and Italy) that belong to the European Monetary System (EMS), which was created in 1979, attempt to maintain fixed exchange rates among themselves. (The central banks of these countries try to achieve this by offering to buy or sell any amounts of foreign currency at the fixed rate.) Under fixed exchange rate regimes, one country usually assumes the role of "lead" country, and the other countries act as "followers." Germany is clearly the lead country of the EMS; the United States was the lead country under the Bretton Woods fixed exchange rate system that many countries throughout the world participated in between 1944 and 1971.

Fixed exchange rate regimes may have both some advantages and some disadvantages vis-à-vis flexible (or floating) exchange rate regimes. Some people have hypothesized that highly volatile exchange rates raise the level of uncertainty in international resource allocation and therefore reduce the volume of international trade and investment. They argue that more trade and investment will occur when exchange-rate risk is reduced or eliminated, but strong evidence to support this claim is lacking.

The ability of two countries to chart their own courses, or to pursue distinct (possibly even contradictory) macroeconomic goals, is much lower when those countries attempt to maintain a fixed exchange rate. This may be a blessing or a curse. If the lead country has historically behaved more "responsibly" than the follower, then the fixed exchange rate may impose useful discipline on the follower. Italy has experienced less inflation since 1979 than it did before it joined the EMS because it has had to follow Germany's strongly antiinflation lead. But the lead country cannot always be trusted to behave responsibly: the Bretton Woods system broke down in part because of accelerating U.S. inflation related to Vietnam military spending.

When exchange rates are fixed (and investors expect them to remain so), $E_1 = E_0$, and the interest parity condition reduces to $R = R_J$, interest rates must be equal in the two countries. The central bank of the follower country relinquishes its ability to control interest rates and thereby achieve macroeconomic objectives such as reducing unemployment. When the objectives of policymakers in the two countries diverge (e.g., reduce inflation vs. reduce unemployment), the fixed-exchange-rate regime may have to be abandoned. The recent departure of Britain from the EMS is a case in point. Germany was committed to high interest rates to keep inflation in check. Britain wanted to lower interest rates as a means of stimulating investment and output; to do this, it had to leave the EMS.

FOR FURTHER READING

Baily, Martin, and Arthur Okun (eds.), *The Battle Against Unemployment and Inflation,* 3rd ed. (New York: Norton, 1982).

Feldstein, Martin (ed.), *The American Economy in Transition* (Chicago: University of Chicago Press, 1980).

Hall, Robert, and John Taylor, *Macroeconomics: Theory, Performance, and Policy,* ed. (New York: Norton, 1993).

Hirshleifer, Jack, *Price Theory and Applications,* 4th ed. (Englewood Cliffs, NJ: Prentice-Hall, 1988).

Lichtenberg, Frank, *Corporate Takeovers and Productivity* (Cambridge, MA: The MIT Press, 1992).

Okun, Arthur, *Equality and Efficiency: The Big Tradeoff* (Washington, DC: Brookings, 1975).

Young, Philip K. Y., and John McAuley, *The Portable MBA in Economics* (New York: John Wiley, 1994).

PART TWO

THE FUNCTIONS OF A BUSINESS

Traditionally, a company is organized around different functions and purposes. Each function performs a distinct activity: One makes products, one keeps track of the money, one recruits and rewards the staff, one researches the market, one services the product in the market, one manages the information that all the others produce and need, and one decides how all these other functions should direct their efforts. Like the company as a whole, each function is organized in a hierarchy, with control at the top. Like a body, where the function of each limb and organ is controlled by the brain, a company's different parts pull together under the control of top management, which keeps it operating effectively in the marketplace.

This metaphor would make sense to most people in organizations today. It's a metaphor we grew up with. The metaphor is, however, based on some assumptions about how things work. It operates out of a mechanistic view of the world. The use of word "how" in "how things work" betrays the bias. When most organizations were designed, the "why" of the design was so implicit, so understood, so bedrock that no one questioned it. The "why" was to reflect the wishes and authority of the people at the top of the organization, who were—if not the owners themselves—the owners' representatives. Companies organized this way worked in stable environments when companies could afford both to follow top management's dictums and to endure squabbles among functions for top management's attention and resources.

Few people would argue that today many organizations are still designed to facilitate the control of the people at the top. And with this locus of attention, the functional organization is truly the servant of powerful controlling brains in the head office. Nonetheless, a few farsighted companies have processes that implicitly recognize another view of who's boss.

The Jewel companies, for instance, have a management philosophy in which the CEO works for the people under him or her and so on down the line. This philosophy is built on the idea that the person closest to the customer has the most important job, and that person needs the support and resources his or her superior can offer. It is no accident that with its recognition of the importance of the customer, Jewel had its beginnings as a door-to-door sales company. It is also, however, a sign of how strong the hierarchical culture is, that many companies as forethoughtful as Jewel, are still organized essentially with the control at the head.

In the years to come, companies will increasingly drop this orientation. Mary Anne Devanna's boundaryless company discussed in Chapter 8 has one sure route to profitability, namely, as Frederick Webster points out in Chapter 6, delivering value to customers. And, with that, more and more companies will design their organizations according to processes that serve the customer. Nothing else matters.

Similarly, N. Venkatraman makes clear in Chapter 7 that increasingly the competitive organizing principle will not be the improvement of existing processes, based on old concepts of purpose and scope, but the logic of a business network that exploits the full capabilities of the technology. Boundaries will be crossed and new ventures and relationships will form regularly. In an IT (information technology)-intensive world, control ultimately goes to the person in the company who works with the customer.

Why then, with the importance of customer-facing processes so firmly in place do we organize this part of the book according to the traditional functions of the business? Two reasons. First, because every business is different, it would be nearly impossible to organize a book around processes with enough specificity to be helpful. Rather, in this section, each chapter author indicates how that function or operation will be affected by process organization and how the management of processes will be affected overall by the developments in that area.

Second, the functions of the business are the building blocks of the processes. For a manager to run effectively the "get the right product to the right customer when he or she wants it" department, it will be necessary to understand finance, marketing, strategic planning analytics, methods for motivating people, manufacturing, and accounting; and some people in the company need to be expert in these areas. Without the expertise, companies would be like ships with entire crews who knew where the ship should go and the route to take but no one knew how to sail. Managers need not to dispense with functional expertise—they need to blend it, synthesize it, and apply their knowledge to a greater vision than that produced by their own opinion and functional and departmental battles for supremacy.

The great challenge for managers in tomorrow's organizations will be to integrate functional knowledge and to communicate the new whole to the people who need the knowledge. Leaders inside the company will be integrators organizing their processes according to the value that is created for the customer. They will be translators and interpreters. The leader will be the customer.

MARKETING MANAGEMENT: PROVIDING VALUE TO CUSTOMERS

6

Frederick L. Webster

The founder and chief executive officer of a major computer company was quoted a few years ago as saying, "You only need marketing if your products aren't good enough to sell themselves." This statement is unfortunate for several reasons:

- It shows a fundamental misunderstanding of marketing as a management function.
- It confuses marketing with selling.
- It reveals an important business leader who did not grasp the significance of marketing to his own company.
- It identifies a major reason this company has encountered significant problems and explains why this CEO is no longer involved in the management of the company he founded.

Prior to the development of the "marketing concept" as a management philosophy in the 1950s, marketing *was* defined essentially as selling. The traditional view of marketing up to that time was that marketing was responsible for creating demand for what farms, factories, forests, fishing, and mines could produce. Profit was correlated with sales volume; the more the company could sell, the more profitable it would be. Thus, marketing took the product as a given and selling was the essence of the marketing function.

The field of marketing developed out of economics at the major land-grant universities of the midwestern United States beginning around 1910, with a particular emphasis on markets for agricultural commodities, the processes by which they were brought to market, and the methods for determining their prices. From this early emphasis on commodities themselves, marketing then evolved into consideration of the functions that had to be performed in bringing them to market (e.g., assorting, buying, selling, storage, risk taking, transporting) and the institutions that performed those functions, including marketing channels and resellers of all kinds.

A gradual redefinition of marketing as management decisions and functions to be performed within a business occurred in the 1940s and represented a significant shift away from thinking about marketing as an economic and societal process. This management view was captured in the "official" definition of marketing by the American Marketing Association in 1948 as "the performance of business activities directed toward, and incident to, the flow of goods and services from producer to consumer or user."

In the so-called marketing concept that emerged in the 1950s, the focus shifted to marketing as the process of creating a satisfied customer. Profit was seen as a reward for satisfying customer needs, not for generating sales volume. The product was not a "given" but variable, to be tailored to the customer's needs and wants. Marketing was more than selling; marketing management was responsible for an integrated mix of products, prices, communications, and distribution, each element consistent with and supporting the others.

The managerial approach represented a significant shift in viewpoint away from theoretical description and toward relevance and realism in the study of marketing, with a focus on managerial problem solving, planning, and implementation of marketing decisions. Marketing was defined as the function responsible for creating a satisfied customer and for keeping the entire organization focused on the customer, beginning at the earliest stages of product development through production and distribution to the end user.

A VALUE-DELIVERY CONCEPT OF MARKETING

Even this view of marketing is now increasingly outdated. Instead of focusing on marketing simply as satisfying customer needs, managers need to consider how their companies can match up their particular strengths and capabilities with a precisely defined set of customer needs and wants so that they can deliver superior value to their chosen customers in the hypercompetitive global marketplace. For companies that compete successfully in today's markets, marketing is *the process of defining, developing, and delivering value to customers.*

The new view of marketing is focused on a value-delivery concept of strategy that recognizes any business can aspire to achieve world-class excellence only in a limited range along the chain of activities necessary to convert raw materials, information, and labor into customer-satisfying goods and services. To create a total product offering that delivers superior value to customers, a single company will almost certainly need other companies as partners in performing many necessary functions and processes. The role of the marketing function in such "network organizations" (which are increasingly characteristic of global markets) is to keep the whole alliance of strategic partners informed about the target customer's ever-changing definition of value. Instead of focusing simply on customers, the new value-delivery concept of marketing strategy also considers the company's capabilities, and its positioning relative to competitors' product offerings. We can think of this as "the three C's" of marketing strategy development—the analysis of customers, company, and competitors.

Value is created in the marketplace, not in the factory, when customers pay the marketer for the goods and services being provided. If the price paid is greater than the costs incurred by the marketer, then value has been created and is translated into the profit earned by the marketer. If there is no profit, then value has been destroyed, and the losses will be absorbed by the marketer. Under the selling concept, profit was a function of sales volume. Under the old marketing management concept, profit was a reward for creating a satisfied customer. Under the new value-delivery concept of marketing strategy, profit is a measure of the value that has been achieved by establishing a customer relationship that provides an ongoing stream of revenue from a loyal business partner.

MARKETING IN THE BOUNDARYLESS ORGANIZATION

Marketing is one of several functions that must be performed by the management of any enterprise. Among the other management functions are manufacturing, finance, purchasing, human resources, research and development, and accounting or control. Traditionally, each of these management functions was the distinct responsibility of management specialists, organized in a bureaucratic hierarchy of reporting relationships. Today, these traditional functional responsibilities are becoming less distinct as organizations become more flexible and responsive to a changing competitive environment. As companies become more customer focused and market driven, functional boundaries give way to a more coordinated and rapid response to changing customer needs and competitive product offerings. In the words of John F. Welch, Chairman and Chief Executive Officer of the General Electric Company:

> In a boundaryless company . . . customers are seen for what they are—the lifeblood of a company. Customers' vision of their needs and the company's view become identical and every effort of every man and woman in the company is focused on satisfying those needs.
>
> In a boundaryless company, internal functions begin to blur. Engineering doesn't design a product and then "hand it off" to manufacturing. They form a team, along with marketing and sales, finance, and the rest. Customer service? It's not somebody's job. It's everybody's job.[1]

MARKETING AS CORPORATE CULTURE

In the boundaryless company, marketing is a shared responsibility, part of the corporate culture. This notion of shared responsibility for creating a satisfied customer was at the heart of the original "marketing concept," a management philosophy expressed first by the management writer Peter F. Drucker:

> If we want to know what a business is we have to start with its *purpose*. . . . There is only one valid definition of business purpose: *to create a customer.*
>
> It is the customer who determines what a business is. For it is the customer, and he alone, who through being willing to pay for a good or service, converts economic resources into wealth, things into goods. What the business thinks it produces is not of first importance—especially not to the future of the business and to its success. What the customer thinks he is buying, and what he considers "value," is decisive. . . .
>
> Because it is its purpose to create a customer, any business enterprise has two—and only these two—basic functions: marketing and innovation.[2]

In a company committed to the marketing concept, a basic set of values and beliefs puts the customer's interests first, always, in every decision made throughout the organization. The company strives, through market information, to have the best possible understanding of the customer's needs, wants, preferences, and buying patterns and uses that information to guide all decision making. Everyone in the company is committed to providing the best value to the customer. Marketing as a separate business function is responsible for providing the organizational actors with information about the customer's definition of value. This is a real challenge, because the customer's definition of value keeps changing in response to competitive product offerings and as his or her own buying situation changes.

MARKETING AS STRATEGY

There is more to marketing than corporate culture, however. Marketing is also strategy. A strategy can be defined simply as a plan for allocating scarce resources in the pursuit of business objectives. In a market economy, it is usually asserted that the ultimate objective of the company is to maximize long-run return to the owners. However, given the difficulty of defining and measuring the "long run," long-term business objectives are typically translated into rather short-term goals such as quarterly or annual measures of sales volume, sales growth, profit margins, return on assets, and so on. This often leads to an implicit and dangerous assumption that the satisfaction of the short-term interests of investors, not the long-term interests of customers, ultimately determines the performance and survival of the business. While investors must earn a fair return, it is customers who ultimately determine the survival and profitability of the company, through their willingness to buy the goods and services offered.

Under the marketing concept, the company is managed for profitability, not sales volume. It should be clear that there is no disagreement with the fundamental proposition that long-run profitability is the overriding objective. The problem comes when management puts the short-term interests of the shareholder-owners ahead of the immediate interests of the customers. Delivering superior value to customers is the only way to ensure the long-term profitability and survival of the business. The value-delivery concept of strategy thus calls for customer-, competitor-, and profit-orientation. Customer-orientation means putting the customer first, always. Competitor-orientation means that the business must be completely informed about competitors' product offerings, capabilities, and strategy to develop a superior value proposition for the customer. Profit-orientation means managing all efforts so that all costs are strictly controlled and superior value is created for the customer at reasonable and competitive prices. The customer's willingness to pay is the ultimate test of the value that has been created.

As strategy, marketing is concerned with helping the company position its product offering in the competitive marketplace. To understand this process, it is useful to think of three types of strategy: corporate, business, and functional.

Corporate Strategy

Corporate strategy is concerned with the fundamental questions "What businesses are we in?" and "What businesses do we want to be in?" A business can be defined as a product/market combination—the offering of a related range of products in a clearly defined market. Most companies are in more than one "business," each defined as a distinct combination of products and markets. For example, Procter & Gamble is in many paper businesses (bathroom tissue, facial tissue, diapers, etc.), food businesses (peanut butter, cooking oil, etc.), toiletries businesses (toothpaste, mouthwash, etc.), soaps and detergents businesses (for laundry, kitchen, face, body, etc.), and many more. Each business faces a unique set of competitors and deals with a different set of customers. The concept of a "portfolio" of businesses has been a common element of strategic planning as the company evaluates each present or potential business in terms of its growth rate and other measures of market attractiveness, and the company's market share or position relative to competition.

Corporate strategy is often stated in the form of a corporate mission or vision. In a customer-focused, market-driven company, the mission statement is centered around satisfying customer needs. To illustrate, one New England manufacturer of electrical specialty products has defined its mission as:

> To satisfy the needs and expectations of our customers for retractile cords and cord assemblies by delivering high quality products at the time promised, while providing customer service and technical support that will enable our customers to produce a superior product and compete more effectively.

Likewise, Samuel Cabot, Inc., a manufacturer of premium-quality wood stains and one of the oldest companies in the United States, addresses the specific question of "Who is our customer?" in its mission statement:

> Our mission is to provide a full range system of premium quality stains and related products that beautify and protect all exterior wood and wood-related building materials used in the construction industry—combining our products, our expertise, and our service in order for Cabot Stains to be acknowledged as The Wood Care Specialist.
>
> Although the ultimate end-user/purchaser and controller of our brand strategy is the consumer, purchase decisions are greatly influenced by retailers, contractors, builders, and architects. Due to our limited resources, and the competitive environment, the independent dealer is the focus of our selling efforts.

Business Strategy and the Value Proposition

Corporate strategy is implemented through *business strategy*, which can be thought of simply as the answer to the question "How do we want to compete in the businesses we have chosen to be in?" Some authors use the terms business strategy and competitive strategy interchangeably. At the business strategy level, the problem is to define the *value proposition* of the business, the way it proposes to deliver superior value to its chosen customers by capitalizing on its unique strengths, skills, and resources.

The Cabot mission statement, an expression of corporate strategy, also implies its business strategy—to be known as "The Wood Care Specialist" for its products (limited to stains, not paints), its expertise in wood treatment, and its service. The value proposition is superior protection and preservation of the natural beauty of wood.

Market Segmentation, Targeting, and Positioning

The essential activities in developing a business strategy are *market segmentation, targeting,* and *positioning.* Market segmentation is the process of analysis leading to the identification of distinct subgroupings of customers, in terms of how they respond to product offerings and communications. Market targeting is the selection of one or more segments, or "niches," on which to focus marketing effort. Positioning is the process of conceptualizing the product offering (as distinct from developing the product itself) and related communications to achieve distinct competitive advantage in the chosen segments. We will return to this topic shortly and discuss in detail the nature of this critical process.

The heart of business strategy development is the matching of a set of customer needs, wants, preferences, and buying patterns with the capabilities of the company. These capabilities are based on the skills and resources available to the business. They lead to the development of what has been called *core* or *distinctive competence.* A core competence is something that the company does at least as well as, and preferably better than, any other company in the market. Given that most markets today are global markets, a core competence should be something that the company does better than any other competitor in the world. To be a true core competence, a capability should meet four criteria:

1. It must be valued by customers.
2. It must be relevant for multiple markets, thus providing a vector of growth opportunities.
3. It should be knowledge based, as in the case of proprietary technology and scientific knowledge or engineering skill.
4. It probably should not be based on a physical capability, such as geographic location or access to a raw material, that can potentially be duplicated by competitors.[3]

The identification of the company's distinctive or core competences, and the development of a product and service offering based on them, is the critical activity in defining the company's value proposition in each target market. It is a difficult management challenge, however, to turn resources and skills that are the potential source of distinctive competence into a value proposition and a business strategy. The strategic planning process requires a high level of management skill and creativity, and marketing management has a critical role to play in that process. The central element in that responsibility is for marketing management to be an *expert on the customer,* providing managers throughout the business with the information they need to understand the customer's ever-changing definition of value in the context of competitors' value propositions.

Functional Marketing Strategy

Business strategies are implemented through strategies in each of the functional areas of management including marketing, manufacturing, finance, and so on. Marketing strategy at this functional level has traditionally been defined, under the marketing management concept, by "the 4 P's"—product, price, promotion, and place. While this is a somewhat dated view of marketing management activities, it is useful for thinking about the multilevel nature of marketing strategy and for distinguishing functional strategy from the other levels.

At the corporate strategy level, marketing is responsible for focusing the company on defining the customer needs it is committed to serving and satisfying and for assessing market attractiveness, as part of the critical process of defining the businesses in which the company elects to compete. Marketing management is also responsible for being an advocate on behalf of the customer throughout the organization, creating a customer-oriented culture that puts the customers' interests first.

At the business strategy level, marketing is responsible for market segmentation, targeting, and positioning, and for the development of the value proposition, as the essential requirements for defining how the company is going to compete in its chosen businesses.

Now, at the level of functional strategy, marketing managers must develop product strategies, pricing strategies, promotional (advertising, selling, and sales promotion) strategies, and distribution channel ("place") strategies that implement the business strategy and the value proposition. Specific actions in each of these areas, such as the innovation of a product line extension, the development of a schedule of list prices and discounts, the creation and execution of an advertising campaign, or the expansion of a set of distributors, can be thought of as "marketing tactics," although at this stage it is difficult to make a meaningful distinction between tactics and strategy. From the marketing manager's point of view, these are "strategic" decisions. From the point of view of business strategy, these are "tactics" for implementing that strategy.

The foregoing discussion may help to explain why there is so much confusion about the meaning of "marketing strategy." There are at least three levels of marketing strategy—corporate, business, and functional—and marketing management has a different role to play at each level. No one level is sufficient. All three must be carefully developed, beginning with corporate level and proceeding through business and functional strategies. To attempt to create effective functional marketing strategy without clear guidance from business and corporate strategy is a futile exercise. In the total scheme of things, it is the market segmentation, targeting, and positioning process that is the most critical to the performance of the company. The reason is that customers define the business in a fundamental sense.

CUSTOMERS DEFINE THE BUSINESS

Customers define the business by placing a set of demands on it. The company must be careful to select those customers that it has the capability of satisfying and servicing profitably. Once the company has chosen the customers it wishes to do business with, it must adjust and tailor its operations to deliver the goods and services required and desired by those customers, and to do so as efficiently as possible. This means that it must also acquire, develop, and nurture particular resources, skills, and knowledge relevant to the production of those goods and services. All its activities—research and product development; hiring, training, and supervising personnel; purchasing raw materials, components, supplies, and subassemblies; acquiring financing and creating a financial structure for the company; manufacturing and operations management; distribution; and accounting and control systems—must be organized with the objective of delivering superior value to customers. Because different customers have differing needs, preferences, buying habits, and ability and willingness to pay for the company's products, they make differing demands on the company. No company can be all things to all customers. All companies have limits on their skills and resources and must be careful about the ways in which they commit them. The choice of markets must be made to maximize the attractiveness of the company's product offering to a particular set of customers.

Customer selection is at the core of marketing strategy, at both the business and functional levels. There are good and bad customers. Good customers ask the company to do things that it can do well and challenge it to continue to develop the knowledge, skills, and resources that are at the heart of its distinctive competence. Good customers value the things the company can do for it and are willing to pay for the resources that the company commits to those tasks. Good customers will take the company in directions consistent with its business and corporate strategies. The corollary to this statement is that the company can't define the difference between a good and a bad customer if it doesn't have a strategy. As the well-known phrase puts it, "If you don't know where you are going, any road will take you there."

Bad customers are just the opposite. They ask the company to do things it cannot do well or efficiently and they are unwilling to pay for the resources the company will have to commit to try to satisfy them. They take the company in directions inconsistent with its strategy and detract from rather than add to its knowledge, resources, and skills. Such customers are likely to remain dissatisfied with the company's products and performance. A sales-oriented view of marketing fails to understand this basic fact; there are some customers and some orders that the company is better off without, given the low probability of being able to satisfy these customers at a profit. To quote another well-known phrase, "If we aren't careful, we will end up where we are headed" when the company tries to satisfy bad customers.

Bad customers leave the company worse off. A company with a value-oriented concept of marketing and a sense of its own distinctive competence recognizes this important truth. The marketing vice president of a large multinational chemical company recently illustrated this wisdom when he commented about an Asian-based competitor with virtually no sales or service organization who sells strictly on price, using a fax machine to deliver quotations. In his words, "We want this guy to be successful because we don't want anything to do with his customers!"

MARKET SEGMENTATION

Market segmentation is the process of defining distinct groupings of customers who are alike in the sense that they will have a common response to the marketing effort that the company aims at them, especially its product offering and its communications, because they share similar needs, wants, preferences, buying habits, and definitions of value. Most markets have many segments and subsegments. The analytical process required is one of breaking down the overall market, within which customers have many different definitions of value, into a set of distinct segments that are different from one another but within each of which the customers share a large degree of similarity.

Market segmentation is both an analytical and a creative process. The manager must gather data on customer characteristics, usage patterns, needs and wants, attitudes and preferences, buying patterns, and more. This information may be obtained from library and other secondary sources, survey research, sales reps and their call reports, trade association studies, small group interviews, customer visits, and other sources. With a focus on understanding how different customers define value, each segment would ideally consist of customers with a common definition of value, that is, who seek a common set of benefits. For example, a manufacturer of an industrial product might find three distinct segments:

1. *Price-sensitive* customers, who buy based strictly on lowest price.
2. *Service-sensitive* customers, who value easy ordering, applications assistance, and quick delivery.
3. *Technology-sensitive* customers, who want the latest technical solutions in the form of new products that they can use to improve their products and processes.

These buyers each put different value and priority on the different characteristics of the product offering—price, availability, and technical service.

In the area of consumer products, an excellent example of market segmentation is provided by "athletic" shoes, most of which are probably not purchased for athletic use but for reasons of fashion. They are distinguished by a variety of designs, shapes, heights, different materials and construction methods, unique cushioning and support features, *each* intended for a distinct market segment. A particular model or line may be promoted as best suited for walking or jogging or basketball or tennis or squash or hiking or sailing or "cross training," which means multiple purpose in the athletic shoe lexicon. Each type of shoe is aimed at a distinct market segment in terms of its perceived need for traction, support, comfort, style, bounce, and other dimensions of shoe performance.

At the core of the market segmentation exercise is a matching of customer needs and product benefits. Ideally, each market segment would have a distinct set of needs and would be interested in a distinct set of benefits. Even if the customer is clear about what is most important to him or her, such as price or availability or technical support, this does not mean that the other characteristics of the product offering are unimportant. The shoe customer who needs superior traction on the squash court may still be very interested in styling and price.

There is also another important problem in market segmentation: *finding observable and measurable characteristics* that are correlated with needs, wants, preferences, buying habits, benefits desired, and definitions of value. Customer needs and benefits are seldom observable directly, but must be inferred based on other variables that can be observed and measured. How can the marketer identify those customers who are most price sensitive or service sensitive? What kinds of communication methods and media are most likely to reach one market segment or the other? Consumer marketers tend to rely on population demographics and psychographics to segment markets. Demographics, consisting of variables such as age, income, and occupation, are much easier to measure than the psychographics, which include variables such as lifestyle, self-concept, and attitudes. Industrial marketers typically segment their markets in terms of the "demographics" of geographic location, size, and industry classification. Instead of consumer-type psychographics, the industrial marketer is likely to use variables related to the nature of the buying process for more precise, microsegmentation.[4]

The problem is to determine if segments based on needs and benefits have common demographics that will make the need or benefit segmentation operational. This may be very difficult. Price-sensitive customers may be found in all size classifications, industries, and geographic locations. The price-sensitive segment may not be a distinct segment at all as far as the ability of the marketer to identify such customers and to direct specific communications and product offerings to them. The segmentation process is only complete when observable and measurable customer characteristics can be found that are closely related to definitions of value and buying habits. Thus, the industrial marketer may learn that the three segments have the demographics and buying behavior shown in Table 6-1.

This table shows that the marketing manager has an indication of what types of product variables and selling messages to stress with these customers, as well as which members of the organization to focus attention on.

Having defined the market segments, the company must then decide which of those segments it wishes to serve. This is the market targeting decision.

TABLE 6-1   The segmentation process

Technology-Sensitive	Technology-Sensitive Demographics	Technology-Sensitive Buying Behavior
Price-Sensitive	Large companies	Use closed bidding
	Steel, brick, and glass industries	Purchasing managers dominate process
		Very knowledgeable about market prices
Service-Sensitive	Small- to medium-size companies	Marketing and operations managers heavily involved
	Nonurban areas	
	Service companies	Buy on annual purchase contract, negotiate price
Technology-Sensitive	Large- to medium-size manufacturing companies	R&D and operations managers most involved, along with purchasing
	High-tech industries	
	Small start-ups	Negotiate cost-plus contracts

MARKET TARGETING

Market targeting is the process of deciding in which segments to compete. As noted earlier, it is the critical strategic choice that the company makes, the choice of customers. Each market segment chosen as a target will require a somewhat different marketing strategy, tailored to its unique characteristics. Understanding competitors' product offerings and their strengths and weaknesses in each market segment is critical to deciding whether and how to compete in the chosen segment. The company is seeking opportunities for delivering superior value to customers based on its unique strengths and resources relative to those of competitors. Customers will make the final determination of value by comparing the company's product offerings with those of its competitors.

The chosen market targets should be in a sense "underserved," that is, not entirely satisfied with competitive product offerings, especially when they learn about the company's improved product offering. It is important to understand the concept of the product offering in its full meaning—not just as the physical product but including all the service variables that are added to complete the product offering. If the company has an enhanced product offering relative to competition, it may be able to define new market segments—to segment the market in new ways—that will define unique market targets. For example, to enter the motorcycle market in the United States, the Japanese manufacturers offered smaller machines that were less expensive to purchase and operate and targeted consumers of both sexes who were more "mainstream," fun-loving, and somewhat older, compared with the traditional "macho" motorcycles that had been targeted at young men. This created whole new market segments for motorcycles and enlarged the total market significantly. Over time, the Japanese manufacturers added larger machines and began to compete aggressively for the traditional segments as well.

The selection of customers, the market targeting decision, becomes the basis for all strategic thinking, and for most of the measurements of business performance. Market targeting becomes part of the fundamental definition of the business. The objective of the business is to satisfy customer needs, but that becomes a meaningful objective only after it has identified its target customers. To illustrate, "quality" is now understood to have meaning as a concept only in terms of meeting customer expectations. The company must define its target customers before it can assess the business's quality—relative to those customers' expectations. Likewise, market share can only be measured after the company has defined its served market. Defining the target market is the necessary first step.

We will soon be developing the concept of relationship marketing, a fundamental dimension of the new marketing concept. The company must carefully choose its customers before it can intelligently commit to building a relationship. Customer loyalty is increasingly seen to be a key strategic resource. This assumes that the company has correctly chosen its customers, its target markets. It makes no sense to invest resources in trying to retain customers if the company has incorrectly or unwisely defined its target market. Money is doubly wasted when it is spent trying to retain bad customers.

To complete the argument about the importance of the market targeting decision, it must be noted that the concept of "distinctive competence" is based on the fundamental notion that a competence must be valued by customers. So a manager can only define the company's distinctive competence in the context of its customers' definition of value.

POSITIONING—DEVELOPING THE VALUE PROPOSITION

The last step in the segmentation-targeting-positioning sequence is the development of the value proposition. Once again, we must define our terms. Positioning is the process of identifying the important dimensions that customers use to evaluate competitive product offerings and communicating the company's product offering on those dimensions relative to competition. The emphasis in positioning is on communication, not on the development of the product itself. This is an important distinction. In the words of Al Ries and Jack Trout, the authors who developed the concept of positioning:

> Positioning starts with a product. A piece of merchandise, a service, a company, an institution, or even a person. Perhaps yourself.
> But positioning is not what you do to a product. Positioning is what you do to the mind of the prospect. That is, you position the product in the mind of the prospect.
> So it's incorrect to call the concept "product positioning." You're not really doing something to the product itself.[5]

Some authors will use the phrase "the value proposition" to mean the same thing as "positioning" or "the positioning statement." But the value proposition is a much broader strategic concept. The value proposition is the total promise that the company makes to its customers in a given market segment. It is an articulation of the precise intersection of the customer's needs and wants with the company's distinctive competences. Positioning is one-way communication to the customer. The value proposition is just as important in communicating a sense of strategic direction within the company as it is in communicating the promise of superior performance to the customer. The value proposition focuses the energy of every person within the organization on the fundamental purpose of all organizational activity. It is the essence of what it means to be customer oriented in a competitive business environment.

We can illustrate the concept of the value proposition by going back to our earlier example of the company that identified three segments that it wished to target: Price-sensitive; service-sensitive; and technology-sensitive. That company might develop the following value propositions:

- *For price-sensitive customers.* We provide basic products that will allow you to have consistent quality and an uninterrupted production process at the lowest available cost.

- *For service-sensitive customers.* We provide products and services that enable us to work with you as a partner who helps you identify opportunities for continuous improvement in the use of our products in your production processes, to improve your quality and reduce your costs, with a focus on technical applications assistance and efficient ordering and delivery.

- *For technology-sensitive customers.* We are your strategic partner in the development of new technologies and applications that significantly enhance the attraction of your products for your customers, helping you to meet the challenges of your changing markets, while also providing excellent products and services to support your ongoing production requirements.

The best value propositions are usually more succinct than these examples and capture the essence of the company's commitment to its customers. It is always a question whether the company can manage more than a few value propositions, just as it is a question whether the company can develop distinct product and service offerings for multiple segments and keep them distinct over time.

Segmentation, targeting, and positioning are concepts that are relevant for a given business, not for the total company. Large corporations, such as Procter & Gamble or General Electric, are in many businesses, each obviously requiring a different definition of value for customers. Each of those businesses may serve multiple market segments. The question is whether a given business can maintain distinct segmentation and positioning for each of more than, say, three or four target markets. It is easy for people within the organization to become confused about what they should be doing for a given order or customer. Sales, service, and operating personnel may not be able to tailor their efforts precisely, as required by the value proposition, to customers who value service more than price and then turn around and serve equally well (and at the proper cost and commitment) those who value price more than service. This is an argument in favor of parsimony in the segmentation, targeting, and positioning exercise. What may appear to be a good idea in terms of strategy formulation may as a practical matter be hard to implement—especially if customers in one segment become aware of the benefits being offered to those in another segment.

CREATING LOYAL CUSTOMERS, NOT MAKING SALES

It should now be very clear that the purpose of marketing effort, under the new marketing concept is to create a customer, not simply to make a sale. We have seen that a focus on sales volume can be expensive in terms of attracting customers who cannot be satisfied by the company, given its limited resources, or who cannot be served profitably. This point has been underscored by our discussion of the strategic importance of customer selection and of the market segmentation, targeting, and positioning process.

Under the new marketing concept, the primary strategic resources of a company are its customers, its knowledge of them, and its understanding of how they define value. Knowledge of customers becomes a key distinctive competence of management, and a major source of influence for the company in keeping its alliance partners, including suppliers, resellers, and providers of technology, focused on the customer and contributing to the fulfillment of the value proposition.

There is convincing evidence that a loyal customer is a much more valuable customer than a new customer. Established customers offer the opportunity for repeat sales and for sales of related additional products and services at a fraction of the selling costs required to attract new customers. Also, it is likely to be much easier to satisfy existing customers than new customers, especially if the new customer has been attracted by a low price or other sales promotion inducement. Established customers are better atuned to the marketer's value proposition and have found the relationship of the product offering to their needs and preferences. The current trend toward leasing of automobiles is based on this fact. Auto makers see the opportunity to increase customer satisfaction by avoiding product performance and service problems since the new leased car is fully covered by warranty and less subject to the problems associated with aging. The leasing customer will be a very good prospect for a new car when the lease expires. The company will not have to use rebates and other price inducements to the same extent with the leasing customer. The leasing customer is a more valuable customer for these reasons. The auto maker has created a customer, not simply made a sale.

RELATIONSHIP MARKETING

Under the new marketing concept, ongoing customer relationships become the preferred basis for doing business as opposed to the one-time transaction or sale emphasis of the old marketing concept. The sale is not the end of the marketing process; it is the beginning of a mutually rewarding relationship with a customer. The relationship becomes the basis for a series of transactions over time. In some instances, the relationship becomes a true strategic partnership or alliance between the buyer and the seller. In these strategic partnerships, each party becomes highly dependent on the other and the relationship requires carefully planned management attention. There are many ways to characterize this range of buyer-seller relationships. We will look briefly at three distinct concepts—transactions, relationships, and strategic alliances—although the buyer-seller relationship is best thought of as a continuum from pure transactions to complete strategic alliances with an infinite number of relational possibilities in the middle.

Transactions

Transactions are one-time events. For many years, the study of marketing, and marketing theory, focused on transactions, reflecting the roots of marketing in microeconomic, or "price," theory. In the simple economic paradigm, the central elements are companies, consumers, products, and prices. Companies sell undifferentiated products and consumers have homogeneous preferences. Thus, price contains all the information necessary for both buyer and seller to decide whether to engage in a transaction. Each party is motivated by the desire to maximize personal utility and assumes that the other party will conduct the transaction motivated purely by self-interest, resorting to guile to the extent possible to achieve personal advantage.

   In their pure form (almost never found), transactions involve no prior knowledge on the part of either the buyer or the seller and they have no consequences for future transactions. Buyer and seller do not know one another. The product is undifferentiated and price is the only variable that the buyer and the seller need to know in order to complete the transaction. The sale and purchase of future contracts for agricultural commodities may meet the criteria of a pure transaction, but even here the contracting parties probably have an ongoing relationship with a broker and the transaction is based on a high degree of trust, something that is not present in a pure transaction. Another example of a pure transaction might be the purchase of unbranded gasoline by a traveler in a strange town, using cash and with no communication between the buyer and the retailer. Add a familiar brand, previous transactions, the use of a credit card, a friendly exchange of greetings, the availability of a cup of coffee and a restroom, and the possibility of future transactions, and you no longer have a pure transaction.

In less pure form, transactions are very common in both consumer and business-to-business marketing. In common usage, marketers think of "transactions" as those sales that are consummated largely on the basis of price. Thus, the purchases of most consumer packaged goods are probably best thought of as transactions, although products are differentiated and brand name is usually important. Such transactions are far from "pure," however, as there are usually multiple purchases of the same product over a period of time, price is only one of several variables considered by the consumer, and the brand name inspires trust in the product and its consistent quality. Repeated transactions with familiar brands and company names are undoubtedly the norm in most consumer goods marketing. The presence of trust means that the transaction is moving toward being a relationship, but it is not there yet.

In industrial marketing, many commodity-type products or those with little or no differentiation tend to be at the transactions end of the spectrum of buying-selling situations. Chemicals, wood products, paper, and steel are some good examples of products that are sold largely based on product availability and price, as opposed to strongly differentiated product features and service levels. Industrial buyers "shop around" for the best available price from multiple vendors whose products are more or less interchangeable in the customer's production process. While there may be a long history of transactions and a high level of knowledge of the other company's operations, both the buyer and seller focus on price. It is a "zero-sum" game; what one party wins the other party loses in the price negotiation or competitive bidding situation. The key to profitability for marketers engaged in transaction-based selling is knowing and controlling its costs to serve the price-oriented customer.

Relationships

Relational marketing exists when the buyer and seller are known to one another, when there is a series of transactions between them over a period of time, when the seller can target specific communications to the buyer, and when the buyer can communicate directly with the seller. Relational product offerings are very likely to be differentiated by an enhanced service component, and both parties are, at least in some minimum sense, dependent on the other.

The distinction between transactions and relationships is probably easier to make in consumer goods marketing than in business-to-business marketing. The basis for making this distinction in consumer marketing is the presence or absence of *addressability*.[6] If the consumer is known to the marketer by name and address, and the marketer can therefore send specific communications to that consumer, there is the basis for establishing an ongoing relationship. (This is virtually always the case in business-to-business marketing.) Without knowing the identity of the consumer, and something about their purchasing habits, demographics, media exposure, tastes, and preferences, there is no basis for a relationship. Similarly, the consumer must know the company and its products and be able to communicate with the company directly before it makes sense to think about the buying-selling situation as a relationship.

Relational marketing is becoming increasingly common in consumer marketing because of the availability of information technology to make possible the interactive communications and database management that are at the core of relationship marketing. Catalog retailers such as L.L. Bean and Lands' End are good examples of relationship marketers as are the credit card companies like American Express and Visa, the airlines, and marketers of financial services such as insurance and mutual funds. However, relationship marketing is becoming more common even in consumer packaged goods. Tobacco companies have established extensive databases on smokers, to whom they can direct special promotions and merchandise offers as well as information deemed important to combat the strong antismoking lobby. Makers of household products advertise "800" telephone numbers, allowing customers to contact them directly for product information. These callers are entered into a computer database and become addressable customers for the marketer.

Virtually all industrial marketing has a relational aspect to it because it meets all the criteria for a relationship, even when the actual transaction is primarily price oriented. Even in that instance, the customer is known, addressable, and dependent on the seller to a significant degree. The product, even if it is a commodity-type material, is usually enhanced by a service offering including order-processing, delivery, credit, and postsale service such as applications assistance, and assistance with product recovery and disposal when necessary. For such relationships, however, there is no question that a large segment of the market may consist of price buyers, who shift their purchases among vendors depending on current prices. Thus, transactions and relationships are not neatly distinguishable in most industrial markets.

Strategic Alliances

Strategic alliances are exclusively found in business-to-business buyer-seller relationships. The concept cannot be extended to consumer packaged goods. However, it may be appropriate to think of some consumer buying situations, such as the leasing of a new car or the purchase of a recreation vehicle, as a form of relationship that goes beyond the norm and approaches a form of partnering. The purchase of a home computer, for example, becomes the basis for a relationship between buyer and seller in terms of the provision of new products and services such as applications software, product upgrades, and repair services. On-line computer services such as Prodigy and Compuserve and residential telephone services are other examples of relationships that tend toward partnering. The marketer's product offering isn't simply "consumed"; rather it becomes part of a kind of production system within the household, with multiple users and multiple outputs. These buyer-seller partnerships, while increasingly important in today's hypercompetitive marketplace, do not meet the criteria of a true strategic alliance.

A strategic alliance is a cooperative effort by two businesses in pursuit of their separate strategic objectives. A strategic alliance involves the commitment and sharing of resources including money, technology, and people. In some instances, such as a joint venture, a new entity is actually created that has its own financial and organizational structure. Thus Dow-Corning is a joint venture between Dow Chemical and Corning, Inc., in which each is an equal partner, sharing risks and rewards. Each could have purchased the necessary goods and services from the other to produce the products of Dow-Corning but they elected to accomplish their strategic objectives through a strategic alliance.

In industrial marketing, strategic alliances are commonly seen in the form of "just-in-time" (JIT) supply relationships, as pioneered in the automobile industry, especially in Japan. They typically involve a sole-source procurement relationship in which the seller agrees to provide specified quantities of defect-free merchandise on a tightly planned delivery schedule into the customer's assembly facility. The fundamental concept here is to make the supplier's production and logistics system an extension of the customer's plant. Inventories are reduced to minimum levels, lowering significantly the financial costs of carrying inventory as well as the risk of product deterioration, loss, and obsolescence. The marketer and the buyer both become highly dependent on one another; they substitute "bureaucratic control" for "market control" as a method for achieving efficiency and reducing risk. The relationship moves from "win/lose" to "win/win" as the parties cooperate to achieve mutually agreed on goals.

The loss of market control in strategic buyer-seller alliances is a serious issue. As companies gain more experience with such partnerships, there is growing evidence to suggest that the absence of market forces can be a source of instability over time as the buyer begins to question whether the seller is devoting best efforts in terms of cost reduction and innovation to address the buyer's problems. The buyer questions whether the absence of a competitive threat hasn't led to the seller's complacency. "What have you done for me lately?" becomes a real concern. Similarly, the seller may question whether the buyer hasn't negotiated a better deal in terms of service provided than the original agreement stipulated, leading to excessive costs for the marketer that are not fully compensated by the price.

For these reasons, some industrial marketers have moved toward a position of preferring to be one of two suppliers rather than the sole supplier. In such cases, the objective might be to have 75 percent of the customer's business, with another vendor having 25 percent. This may make the partnership more stable over the long run while retaining most of the benefits of strategic partnering including sharing of technology, predictable long-term sales growth, and the incentives for continuous improvement that come from dealing with strategic customers who will force the company to continue to develop its distinctive competences. These partnerships can be the epitome of the "good customer."

SEGMENTING BY TYPE OF RELATIONSHIP

Sophisticated marketers are often able to define distinct market segments based on the type of buyer-seller relationship. In simple terms, there might be three segments consisting of transactions-oriented customers, relationship customers, and strategic partners. Especially for industrial marketers, this may be a useful exercise in tailoring the product offering to the customer's definition of value. We will illustrate this idea with a simple three-way segmentation, although the details and the extent of the segmentation would obviously need to be tailored to each marketer's unique situation.

Transactions customers value price and product availability and are not willing to pay for a great deal of related service. However, they will probably not refuse the additional service if it is offered, and they might even request service but not be willing to pay for it. This creates a problem for the marketer, who must carefully manage the costs of serving each customer to maintain reasonable profit margins.

Transactions-oriented customers are likely to maintain relationships with several vendors, allocating more or less purchase volume among them depending on relative prices and the vendor's performance on matters such as delivery and quality. In many instances, these customers can be served through low-cost methods of selling and distribution, using telephone ordering, for example, or even computer electronic data interchange to transfer ordering information. The marketer should not commit substantial management attention to the account or do significant product and service innovation for these customers unless they agree in advance to reward the marketer's efforts with additional volume or improved pricing. The marketer's innovations on behalf of these customers should be concentrated on reducing the costs to serve them, through continued process redesign and improvement.

Relationship customers view the marketer as a source of solutions to their problems in a particular area. They value the marketer's capabilities to a higher degree than transactions customers, and they want to maintain an ongoing relationship in order to take advantage of those capabilities. They focus more on the service bundle that the marketer can offer, in addition to the unique features of its products. Relationship customers view price in the context of the total product offering, usually putting availability and product quality ahead of price in their purchasing criteria. They may still demand significant price adjustments from their suppliers and work with them to keep prices and costs trending downward. Relationship customers may also maintain several suppliers for a given product, although they will use them differently than transactions customers. Relationship customers are more interested in using vendors for their unique capabilities—say product innovation in one case, additional production capacity backup in another, low-cost production capability in a third—rather than simply playing one against the other to obtain lowest price. These customers need more attention from several areas of the business, including sales, service, engineering, and production planning, and more management-level attention as well. They value these services and, to a degree, are willing to pay for them in terms of somewhat better prices and long-term volume commitments. If the relationship customer has multiple purchasing and using locations, it may be necessary to coordinate efforts at these locations through a national account management system.

Strategic customer partners are likely to be among the company's largest customers and innovative leaders in their own industries. They are looking for supplier partners who can assist them with their own business strategies. They often depend heavily on the supplier's research and development capabilities, involving the vendor in the design and development of new products. Strategic partners fit our definition of good customers—they ask the company to do the things it does well and they reward its accomplishments. They take the company in directions consistent with its strategy, and they force it to continue to develop its distinctive competence. They value the supplier as an asset in their own business.

The only problem with strategic partners is that they are very expensive to service; they are demanding of management time and other organizational resources. Such partnerships must be managed with great care. Astute marketers have learned how to work with strategic customers by identifying specific issues that the customer wishes to have the vendor address, establishing benchmarks for measuring progress, and determining the rewards that will be earned for achieving the goals that have been established for the cooperative relationship.

Goal-setting and performance review can be done on a quarterly basis, with team members rewarded according to their accomplishments. It is vitally important to understand what the customer values and what it does not. The marketer must be careful to avoid incurring expense for activities that are not tied to issues that the customer regards as important.

In general, most marketers would prefer to have more relationship-type customers and fewer transactions-type customers. Marketing effort is frequently aimed at trying to move customers in this direction, by offering them better products and services at somewhat higher prices with improved profit margins. Likewise, there is probably a growing recognition of the tendency for customers who are strategic partners, especially those in sole-source situations, to make price more important over time and to move away from strategic partnering toward a more common "relationship" orientation. Thus, very broadly speaking, there may be a tendency for customers to migrate toward relationship status, especially in industrial markets.

The marketer must exercise careful judgment, based on analysis of each customer situation, before deciding to commit resources to trying to change a transaction-oriented customer into a relationship customer. The price buyer may be quite willing to accept the enhanced services and value of an improved product offering but still be unwilling to pay for it. However, if the marketer has a good understanding of customers and their needs and wants and can develop product offerings that meet the customer's definition of value, then there is the opportunity to move out of price-, transaction-, and commodity- or undifferentiated-product-orientation and into a more profitable relationship with the customer by delivering super value. That is the ultimate goal of marketing effort—to increase customer satisfaction by delivering superior value, profitably.

SEGMENT MIGRATION—ONE VIEW OF THE MARKET LIFE CYCLE

A basic issue in market segmentation is that customers may not stay in the segments to which they have been "assigned." The driving force here is the customer's changing definition of value. This process can be thought of in the context of the market life cycle, often called the "product" life cycle. (The life cycle concept really describes evolution in a market over time, not the product itself.) Stages in the market life cycle have typically been labeled Introduction, Growth, Maturity, Saturation, and Decline. Profit margins tend to be highest at the end of the growth stage and the beginning of the mature stage. As the market matures, competitors continue to enter the market, prices erode, the costs of marketing and continued product development increase, and the market becomes increasingly segmented and fragmented as new niches are created by the efforts of marketers. In the saturation and decline stages, companies begin to leave the market, segments are combined and reduced, prices continue to decline but more slowly, and the costs of marketing and R&D can be reduced as the surviving companies focus on maintaining margins by controlling costs.

Another way to view the market life cycle is to look at what is happening to the market segments. As products mature, the average customer is becoming somewhat more sophisticated and knowledgeable about product use and market conditions. The customer needs less of the support offered by the marketer and becomes more aware of alternative product offerings. The customer becomes more confident in evaluating alternatives, in using the product in new or different ways, in extending the product use system, and in shopping for better prices and service.

For example, the new purchaser of a personal computer may need substantial assistance from a nearby retailer as she learns to use the product and becomes familiar with its operation. She may want advice on the purchase of additional software. When she encounters a problem, she likes being able to use the telephone to call for immediate assistance. After several months, she becomes a confident user of the computer and begins to explore new applications. She is comfortable ordering software and accessories from catalogs at reduced prices. Price becomes much more important relative to service. She has moved out of the relationship segment and into the transaction segment.

Over time, customers tend to migrate toward lower-price, lower-service segments. Competition is a major force driving this process. Competitors may be willing to offer similar service at reduced prices, as a way of gaining market entry. The market pioneer may be stuck with a higher cost to serve, in terms of both product costs and the cost of the service bundle, than later market entrants. Newer competitors may also simply offer less service, thus reducing their costs and prices, which may be of little concern to the increasingly confident, sophisticated, and independent customer.

As market prices decline, the company that entered the market early is under pressure to reduce its price and its costs to compete and remain profitable. Of course, it may be reluctant to reduce prices hoping, instead, to rely on more aggressive selling effort and continued improvement in the product offering to maintain the loyalty of existing customers, especially those in relationship and partnership segments. This strategy will be successful only if the customer remains interested in the high levels of service and product differentiation. The risk is that the customer's definition of value has changed to one emphasizing low price and minimum service. It is obviously inefficient to offer these customers both low price and high service if they do not value the service.

THE CONCEPT OF THE AUGMENTED PRODUCT— ANOTHER VIEW OF THE MARKET LIFE CYCLE

Yet another way of thinking about this process is provided by Theodore Levitt's concept of the "augmented" product.[7] At the center is the *core* product, the basic set of product performance characteristics that define the product itself. This might be the physical product—"the thing you can drop on your foot," such as a standard grinding wheel, or the basic service offering, such as a seat on an airplane going from Boston to New York. Nobody buys only the core product. They buy the *expected* product.

The expected product includes all of the supporting product attributes and services that the customer routinely expects to receive as part of the product offering. The grinding wheel customer expects overnight delivery and guaranteed replacement in the event of product failure. The air traveler expects to be able to purchase a reserved seat by dialing an 800-number, to use a credit card, and to receive a snack on board the aircraft. The expected product is what Levitt calls "the table stakes," the minimum required to play in the game. The marketer *must* offer at least the expected product to have any hope of creating a satisfied customer.

The *augmented* product has features and services that are not expected by the customer and that differentiate it from competitive product offerings. It is the marketer's attempt to deliver superior value to customers, not just to meet their expectations but to exceed them, to "delight" the customer. The grinding wheel customer is delighted to learn that the grinding wheel sales rep has some excellent ideas about how to improve productivity and can offer a safety stock of wheels for the customer's inventory on a consignment basis. The air traveler is delighted to find that the aircraft assigned to this flight is a modern, wide-body jet, and that there is cocktail service and a brief in-flight video entertainment.

So far, so good. The augmented product is a way of achieving unique competitive advantage and delivering superior value to customers by exceeding their expectations. The marketer has succeeded in insulating itself, at least to a degree, from pure price competition. This should provide some opportunity for improved profit margins. And it may, in the short term.

The problem is a familiar one: The customer's definition of value keeps changing. In terms of this view of the market life cycle, *the augmented product becomes the expected product.* The grinding wheel customer now expects technical advice on a regular basis along with consignment stocks, and demands this from other vendors as well. The airline customer expects better in-flight service and entertainment and competitors respond by offering it at reduced prices. The augmented product moves toward becoming a commodity and loses its differentiation in the eyes of the customer.

The solution to the marketer's problem lies in the *potential* product, all the opportunities for innovation and improvement, in terms of both product features and supporting services, that are available to the marketer in both its products and in the processes that provide them to customers. The alternative to continued efforts to offer a newly augmented product is to resort to pure price competition, hoping to improve productivity in order to become the low-cost producer and to win the competitive battle based strictly on price. While continued cost improvement is a necessity for every marketer, pure price competition is seldom the best strategic alternative for the leading companies in an industry. Continuous improvement in products and services must be the dominant part of the value proposition.

DEFINING THE BUSINESS AS A SERVICE BUSINESS

Even in the world of high-technology products, marketers increasingly realize that it is the service bundle accompanying the product offering that provides the major opportunities for product differentiation and unique competitive advantage. Excellent performance and quality in the physical product is absolutely essential and is simply assumed to be there by the customer. The service bundle becomes not only the principal area for exceeding the customer's expectations but also potentially the source of the most serious *dissatisfiers*. The grinding wheel customer may switch vendors because he is not able to easily telephone in orders for replacement inventories or because of frequent errors in billing. The airline customer gets fed up with frequent flight delays, dirty airplanes, and surly cabin attendants and consciously avoids flying on the carrier that has the biggest airplanes.

Every business can be redefined as a service business by focusing on customer needs and how the company attempts to satisfy them. Each product with its services provides a bundle of benefits for the customer. By concentrating on the benefits rather than the product features themselves, the marketer comes much closer to the customer's definition of value. Simply but powerfully stated: "The product is what it does for the customer." The corollary to this simple proposition is that different customers may buy the same product for different reasons, thus defining distinct market segments. Producers of industrial gases, for example, sell molecules of nitrogen, oxygen, and argon. The nitrogen customers, however, buy many different things. Some are buying cooling and freezing for products such as hamburger patties. Others are buying freshness preservation, such as snack food packagers. Still others are buying an inert environment for processes such as cleansing piping and tubing. The product is not what is made in the factory; it is how the product is used by the customer.

Redefining a business as a service business opens up major opportunities for improvement and augmentation of the product offering. The producer of industrial gases may learn that its major customer satisfiers are its reliable truck delivery system, its routine maintenance of storage tanks at the customer's site, and its state-of-the-art technology for pumping gases between truck and tank and into the customer's production process. It may also learn that its major dissatisfiers are its billing system and its slow-to-respond technical service. The purity and quality of its gases are excellent, as are those of all its competitors. Quality is defined as meeting or exceeding customer expectations. It is the service bundle, not the physical product, that is the focus of those expectations.

As a general proposition, enhancing the service bundle may be a way of moving customers out of transactions-oriented segments and into more profitable service-oriented segments. This assumes that the company can develop a service offering that is truly responsive to customer needs and wants.

CONTINUOUS IMPROVEMENT AND INNOVATION

Redefining the business as a service business underscores the importance of continuous improvement and innovation on behalf of customers. Because the customers' definition of value keeps changing in response to changing problem-use situations and competitive product offerings; because the augmented product becomes the expected product; because new competitors enter the market with better offerings at reduced prices; because customers migrate out of high-service segments into low-price segments—for all these reasons, the company that survives in the hypercompetitive marketplace must be committed to continuous improvement and innovation. In the phrase often heard from advocates of total quality management, "Good enough is not."

Continuous improvement, sometimes identified with the concept of "reengineering," typically concentrates on the processes by which the company delivers value, including most importantly all elements of its service package. It should also be defined to include specific improvements in the product itself.

Continuous improvement and innovation are essential to fulfillment of the concept of customer orientation, and of a commitment to a customer-oriented definition of quality. Continuous improvement should also lead to lower costs and a more responsive organization. When the benefits of lower costs and greater efficiency and responsiveness can be shared with the customer, then this demonstrates the value to the customer of developing and maintaining a long-term relationship. To maximize the value of the relationship to both parties over time, and to build customer loyalty, the company must be able to create new products and service enhancements. New products also provide the opportunity to attract new customers and expand the base of loyal customers.

FROM MASS MARKETING TO MASS CUSTOMIZATION

The old marketing concept evolved in the 1950s in a market environment of postwar consumerism and pent-up consumer demand. Mass markets were being created, to be served by mass production systems of superior efficiency. The dominant marketing model was one of standard products to be manufactured and sold in large quantities through mass marketing methods, depending especially on magazines, newspapers, radio, and the new medium of television. Based on the results of large-scale market research, the mass media offered standard products to the average consumer. This system generated the heavy sales volume necessary to support the large factories required to generate the economies of scale in production essential for serving the mass market at low cost. Mass production and mass marketing depended heavily on highly standardized products and standardized messages that would appeal to the maximum number of potential customers.

The market conditions of the 1950s and the old marketing concept provide a marked contrast to the consumers, competitors, and company capabilities of the 1990s and the new marketing concept. Informed, sophisticated, and affluent consumers can demand much more precise response by marketers of goods and services to their evolving needs and wants. Competitors from around the world stand ready to attempt to offer superior value at lower prices. Mass markets have disintegrated into specialized and fragmented market niches where particular marketers concentrate their attention on carefully defined customers, increasingly known as individuals rather than as data points in a mass market. Consumers can demand and receive a precise response to their needs and preferences for everything from a pizza to a Porsche. For most financial services, customers can use home-based telecommunications to access global markets for virtually any combination of product characteristics. Automobile companies have the capability to produce a unique combination of product features for every single customer among the millions who buy cars each year, beginning with over 600 basic models offered on the American market. Information technology is a major facilitator of the increasing ability of marketers to meet consumer demands with a precise tailoring of the product offering.

In the days of mass marketing, the process began with an innovative product idea that was then transformed into a standard product that could be manufactured by mass production methods. The classic example was Henry Ford's Model T, available in "any color as long as it's black!" The key to profitability was long runs of standard products to achieve low cost, using mass marketing techniques to create homogeneous consumer preferences for the standard product. Of course, most markets were not that homogeneous, and the standard product usually became a "sitting duck" for a niche marketer who could do a more precise job of market segmentation, targeting, and positioning. As markets mature, fragmentation of mass markets becomes the norm.

Mass markets also have fragmented under the development of new communication media, especially cable television and the advent of thousands of special interest magazines. Computer networking services offer the potential for users to tailor news and entertainment in a magazine format that fits unique interests. Such developments have generally decimated the mass audiences once offered by the major television networks and the large-circulation consumer magazines. Mass markets are disintegrating as the costs of trying to serve them through available media options escalate.

Finally, the competitive pressures of the 1970s and 1980s led to the recent emphasis on total quality management and its related concept of continuous improvement. Companies in consumer, industrial, and services industries have all learned that they must do a much better job of responding to the needs of individual customers, not to the "average customer" or the "mass market." From this commitment to customer orientation and continuous improvement, the next step is to "mass customization" as a management concept, increasingly relevant and realistic in the markets, and with the information technology, of the 1990s.[8]

Mass customization is simply a process of designing, developing, and delivering a unique product offering, a unique combination of value, for each customer. It is sobering to realize how many products and services that at first appear to be the results of "mass production" are in fact produced to the order of an individual customer. For example, virtually every paper mill today produces only to individual orders rather than for inventory. Each roll of paper is produced with a particular customer's name on it and a specific set of product characteristics. Airline reservations systems contain millions of "orders," for a given seat on a given flight on a given day for a specific customer, identified by name, address, telephone number, and a record of the person's travel history and service preferences. Every automobile going down the assembly line is being produced for a specific dealer and perhaps for a specific retail customer, with a set of specifications ordered by that individual.

With mass customization, the product truly becomes a variable, as called for by the new marketing concept. This is the ultimate fulfillment of the marketing concept!

SUMMARY

In this chapter, we have developed a new marketing concept, focused on a value-delivery concept of strategy. The old marketing concept emphasized customer orientation and innovation as the two essential business activities. It replaced a sales-oriented view of the marketing function. But the original marketing concept was incomplete as a strategic framework because it did not address the question of *how* the company was to satisfy customer needs and achieve unique competitive advantage. The new marketing concept considers more carefully how the company can match up its distinctive competences with a relatively underserved set of customer needs and offer superior value to those customers.

The new marketing concept highlights the critical strategic importance of customer selection in defining the business. Market segmentation, market targeting, and positioning, ideas that were developed as part of the original marketing concept, become even more important strategically under the new concept. The value proposition, matching up customer needs and wants with company capabilities, becomes the central communication device both for customers and for all members of the organization, focusing their attention on the company's strategy for delivery of superior value to customers.

If this chapter had been written a few years ago and had followed the old marketing concept, it would have been organized around what were believed to be the four primary decision areas for a marketing manager—product, price, promotion, and distribution. It would have implicitly concentrated on marketing as the function responsible for generating sales volume, for finding the next customer, and for allocating resources to earn a maximum return on marketing investment. It would have had a transactions orientation.

The new marketing concept shifts the focus from making the sale to creating a customer, a business partner providing a stream of revenues and profits over a long time period. Customer loyalty is the objective, not making the next sale. Relationships and buyer-seller partnerships replace one-time transactions to a significant degree, although the company may also have to develop the skills necessary to satisfy the price-oriented transactions buyer as a distinct market segment. Under the new marketing concept, a broader concept of the product offering, looking at the core product plus its related service offering, replaces the focus on products per se. The redefinition of the business as a service business draws attention to the importance of constant improvement not only of the product itself but of all the processes involved in providing superior value to customers. The distinction between marketing and the other business functions has become blurred under the new marketing concept, and the boundaryless organization becomes more focused on the customer, less focused on internal organizational requirements.

Superior marketing, defined as customer-focused problem solving and the delivery of superior value to customers, is a more sustainable source of competitive advantage than product technology per se in the global markets of the 1990s. The new marketing concept is much broader than the old, more pervasive throughout the organization. Marketing is not a separate management function. Rather, it is the process of focusing every company activity on the overriding objective of delivering superior value to customers. It is more than a philosophy. It is a way of doing business. It is a fundamental set of values and beliefs that dominates the organization, putting the customer's interests first—always! It provides expert information to all decision makers throughout the company about the customer's changing definition of value. It informs strategy development at the corporate, business, and functional levels. It is the whole business seen and directed from the customer's point of view. In the final analysis, only the customer can decide whether the company has created value and whether it will survive in the hypercompetitive global marketplace.

FOR FURTHER READING

Pine, Joseph B., II, *Mass Customization: The New Frontier in Business Competition* (Boston, MA: Harvard Business School Press, 1993).

Quinn, James Brian, *Intelligent Enterprise* (New York: Free Press, 1992).

Ries, Al, and Jack Trout, *Positioning: The Battle for Your Mind,* 1st ed.-rev. (New York: Warner Books, 1986).

Schewe, Charles, and Alexander Hiam, *The Portable MBA in Marketing* (New York: John Wiley, 1992).

Webster, Frederick E., Jr., *Market-Driven Management: Using the New Marketing Concept to Create a Customer Driven Company* (New York: John Wiley, 1994).

Zeithaml, Valarie A., A. Parasuraman, and Leonard A. Berry, *Delivering Quality Service: Balancing Customer Perceptions and Expectations* (New York: Free Press, 1990).

INFORMATION TECHNOLOGY: THE CHALLENGE OF STRATEGIC TRANSFORMATION

7

N. Venkatraman

During the past decade, the general view of the role of information technology in business has shifted significantly from its traditional back office functional focus toward one that fundamentally pervades and influences the core business of an organization. Information technology not only affects our vision of how a business is managed but also the way in which resources are spent. By the year 2000, according to *Fortune* magazine, total spending by business on information technology (hardware, software, and communication technology) will surpass total capital spending on other capital goods.

THE EVOLUTION OF INFORMATION TECHNOLOGY

Managers have been besieged with articles and books on the virtues and potential of information technology (IT) and information systems (IS) to provide new sources of advantage for business operations.[1] Indeed, the operative phrase today is "IT changes the way we do business." These publications have either developed intuitively appealing prescriptive frameworks that provide alternative approaches to leveraging IT competences or have described cases

Acknowledgments. This chapter builds on and extends my work reported in "IT-induced Reconfiguration," in *The Corporation of the 1990s,* Michael Scott-Morton, Editor (New York: Oxford University Press, 1991) and "IT-Enabled Business Transformation: From Automation to Business Scope Redefinition," *Sloan Management Review* (Winter 1994).

160

of successful exploitation of IT for obtaining firm-specific benefits as a way of encouraging managers in other companies and industries to consider IT as a strategic weapon.

Figure 7-1 highlights that the role of information technology can be viewed in terms of two major eras: the first one involved leveraging and exploiting information technology capabilities for accounting and operations; the second has leveraged the powerful capabilities for information and knowledge to deliver superior value to customers. The first era (circa 1900 to 1980) focused on using structured data for periodic review and management control to improve administrative and operational efficiency of organizations. In contrast, as Figure 7-1 highlights, the second era (1980 onward) has exploited "real-time" information to analyze and act (faster and better than competitors) in ways that improve the overall process of value-delivery to customers and enhance effectiveness in business operations.

However, many managers entered the 1990s with a high level of skepticism regarding the actual benefits from IT. The productivity gains from IT investments have been disappointing. An article in *ComputerWorld*, a leading industry publication, observed, "Despite years of impressive technological improvements and investment, there is not yet any evidence that information technology is improving productivity or other measures of business performance."[2] Max Hopper of American Airlines—whose SABRE Computer Reservation System (CRS) is often invoked to illustrate the competitive potential of IT—recently remarked that the era of competitive benefits from proprietary systems is over since computers have become as ubiquitous as the telephone and that any travel agency could replace its CRS within 30 days.[3] Further, looking beyond a single case at the macroeconomy, we see essentially no correlation between levels of investments in information technology and such business performance indexes as: sales growth, profit per employee, or share-

FIGURE 7-1   Changing role and impact of information technology on business operations

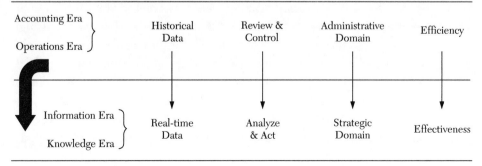

holder value.[4] Regardless of the benefits, or lack of them, in a related development, many companies have handed over the management of their IT and IS operations to external vendors or systems integrators, such as Electronic Data Systems (EDS), IBM, CSC Index, and Andersen Consulting[5] and the stock market seems to respond favorably to such moves.[6]

Against this backdrop, managers are confronted with such questions as:

- Is the logical requirement of aligning business and IT and IS strategies, so compelling just a few years back, now obsolete?
- Has IT (and IS) become a common utility that is best managed for efficiency alone?
- Is the role of IT fundamentally different in my business today than in the past decade?
- Does IT still play a role in shaping new business strategies, or does it simply play a supporting role in executing my current business strategy?
- Is the source of IT competence inside my organization or outside through partnerships and alliances?

These are valid questions as we are at the threshold of fundamentally reassessing the logic for organizing business activities as well as reevaluating the potential role for IT within business operations. Indeed, these questions indicate that the management of IT resources has increased so in importance that it is no longer an administrative support but instead reflects the strategic competence of modern organizations.

To address these questions systematically, we need to understand the shifts in the logic of alignment between business and IT competences. Figure 7-2 shows the evolving alignment between business and IT competences over time. Around 1975, when businesses competed primarily on the basis of their relative cost levels with strategy analyses rooted in "experience curve analyses" and "market share dominance due to low costs," the IT function was primarily expected to enhance operational efficiency (blue-collar productivity) and/or administrative efficiency (white-collar productivity). Subsequently, in the 1980s, businesses adopted a two-pronged strategy: low cost combined with high quality—as opposed to the erstwhile business assumption that low cost and high quality were opposite ends of the continuum. The additional focus on high relative quality compelled business managers to leverage IT functionality to redesign their business operations. The importance of business process redesign can be seen in the growing popularity of approaches such as total quality management (TQM) and reengineering. More recently, the dominant business competence appears to be business flexibility (faster response to market needs,

FIGURE 7-2   Evolving alignment between business and IT competences

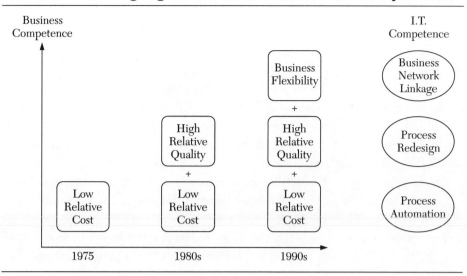

customized products and services, and continuous innovation and adaptation) with significant competences brought together within a flexible business network of interorganizational arrangements—joint ventures, alliances and partnerships, long-term contracts, technology licensing, and marketing agreements. In such situations, the role of IT goes beyond automation and redesign toward becoming a fundamental enabler of new business competences.

Wal-Mart provides a classic example of exploiting IT functionality to create new business competences. For the year ended January 1994, Wal-Mart posted sales of US$ 67.3 billion with net profit of $2.3 billion and return on equity of 21.7 percent. One of the several characteristics of Wal-Mart's strategy that has been consistently admired is the company's ability to leverage the data from their network of stores to infer critical emerging patterns and take actions consistently sharper than those of their competitors. This is best highlighted by the words of Jack Welch, Chairman of General Electric, an organization that is trying to develop this competence: "Quick Market Intelligence is GE's term for the magnificent boundary-busting technique pioneered by Wal-Mart that allows the entire company to understand, to touch the changing desires of the customer and act on them in almost real-time. . . . The rhythm of the Wal-Mart intelligence-action cycle encourages experimentation, because whatever doesn't work is never in place for more than a week. The secret of Wal-Mart is that it keeps its small company speed and behavior as it grows bigger. QMI is a change for us to get bigger—by acting smaller."[7]

THE TRANSFORMATIONAL TRAJECTORY

In this chapter, I present a framework of IT-enabled business transformation, illustrate it with a wide array of examples, and derive a set of management implications and guidelines. This framework is based on two basic dimensions: the *degree of organizational transformation,* incremental to radical; and the *range of potential benefits from IT*—efficiency to effectiveness. The central thesis underlying this framework is that the benefits from IT deployment are marginal if only superimposed on existing organizational conditions (especially strategies, structures, processes, and culture). Thus, the benefits accrue in those cases where investments in IT functionality accompany the corresponding changes in organizational characteristics. A related thesis is that the range of potential benefits shifts from efficiency, at the first level of localized exploitation, to an effectiveness, at the final level, that involves redefining the business scope itself.

Figure 7-3 is a schematic representation of this framework, which proposes a *hierarchy of five levels of IT-enabled business transformations.* It is important to underscore that these levels are not conceptualized as stages of evolution since I believe that effective strategies do not (and should not) follow any one prescribed evolutionary stage model. I describe the distinctive characteristics for each level as well as offer a set of management guidelines. While the higher levels of transformation indicate potentially greater benefits, they also require a correspondingly higher degree of changes in organizational routines such as the logic of structuring, reporting relationships, performance assessment criteria,

FIGURE 7-3   Five levels of IT-enabled business transformation

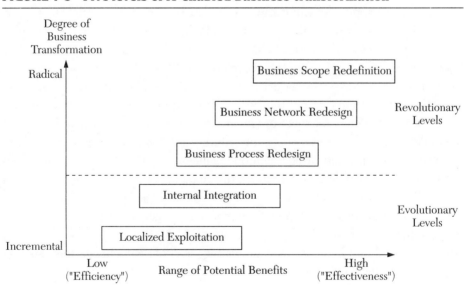

and informational flow. Thus, each organization should first identify the transformational level where the benefits are in line with the potential costs (efforts) associated with the needed organizational changes. Over time, however, higher levels may be necessary depending on competitive pressures and the need to deliver greater value than others in the marketplace.

LEVEL 1: LOCALIZED EXPLOITATION

This represents the basic level for leveraging IT functionality within a business. The term *localized exploitation* indicates that, in many cases, decisions to deploy isolated systems (e.g., a customer order-entry system, toll-free customer service system, inventory control system, internal electronic mail system) are decentralized to the appropriate functional, operational managers. The result is minimal intraorganizational learning of benefits and limitations from such initiatives. Typically, these systems are initiated and deployed by managers to respond to operational problems or challenges; for example, a 24-hour, toll-free support system to enhance customer service; the use of CAD/CAM capability to reduce the cycle time for manufacturing; systems by Hertz, Avis, and others to streamline car rentals at major airports; or decision support systems to help insurance underwriters evaluate the risk levels of new policies. Indeed, this level should be familiar to every manager.

My research indicates that this level of exploitation of IT functionality is best viewed as the deployment of standard IT applications with *minimal* changes to the business processes. This use underleverages the potential capabilities of an IT application and fails to provide the organizations with advantages it might have gained had attempts been made to change the business processes to leverage the technical functionality. The main weakness is that standard technical applications with minimal changes to the underlying business processes can be easily imitated by competitors, which neutralizes sources of strategic advantages.

Hence, in assessing the strategic impacts of an IT application, each manager should pose two questions:

1. By what criteria is this application considered a success?
2. What changes in performance criteria have been instituted since the deployment of this application?

During the past decade, some managers have found it useful to create a new category termed "strategic information systems" which they describe as a "success" based on criteria that I call "past practice." These managers often indicate that their chosen IT application either *reduced* the cost of a certain process (e.g., use of bar codes, order-entry systems) or increased speed of their response to customer requests (e.g., 24-hour, toll-free unattended, fax reply), measured against past levels of performance. A typical response would be, "The installation of a toll-free telephone system has allowed us to process twice the number of customer requests." When I evaluated such success stories (and corresponding improvements relative to past practice) against the best practice in the marketplace, they were *no different* from standard business practice in the marketplace at that time. This is because most applications at this level are designed using standard, off-the-shelf functionality (with minimal changes in the organizational routines to use them). As vendors flock to sell similar applications to others within the same vertical market, competitors are able to easily imitate such practices.

This does not mean that small, focused IT applications should not be used within corporations. On the contrary, these applications, when accompanied by corresponding changes in internal business processes, could result in significant sources of advantage. Let us consider the case of a retail establishment. Here, it is a rather straightforward decision to install an 800-number. Indeed, such a capability has become a basic necessity for carrying out business today, and this system per se does not confer any competitive benefits. However, when such a standard application is enhanced by using call-identification features to direct each call to the most appropriate service center with corresponding supporting information displayed on the service representative's screen, the result is enhanced customer service rather than an efficient call-answering system. Thus, the decision to install an 800-number should be motivated by a focus on differentiation (say: superior customer service) rather than efficiency alone.

A powerful example here is the use by the Whirlpool Corporation—a leading name in the consumer appliances market. Their new customer service center in Knoxville, Tennessee, is designed such that the toll-free call from the customer is routed to a service agent along with the call identification signal to an IBM host that is able to download the relevant customer information to the agent's screen. The agent is also supported by an image server on the local area network (LAN) in retrieving routine product and service information as well as by an expert system that helps in diagnosing and solving more complex problems faced by the customers.

The second question reflects the reality that the ultimate driver of behavior is the performance system. Thus the appropriateness of the performance criteria needs to be evaluated subsequent to the deployment of the IT application (and the corresponding organizational changes). The realizable benefits from every IT application can be considerably enhanced, beyond efficiency, when the performance criteria are realigned to reflect the new IT-enabled business process. In one setting, I found that the company had redesigned the telemarketing activity into a customer service support activity with appropriate telecommunication and database capability but had not changed the criteria used to assess the service center representatives. At the end of one year, it was not surprising that the service quality measures (customer surveys) did not show any improvement as the representatives continued to be evaluated on such traditional criteria as number of calls serviced and average calltime. No attempt was made to learn from the *content* of these calls and improve the overall process of customer service.

In contrast, Jones Truck Lines, Inc., which competes in what is known as the less-than-truckload movement of cargo, installed an integrated database and freight-handling application to increase operating efficiency as well as customer service. This was accompanied by a fundamental shift in the logic of performance assessment. Bonuses are now based on improvements in customer satisfaction reflected in an annual survey dealing with on-time performance, condition of freight, billing accuracy, and so on, as well as technical capabilities.[8]

Within the level of the localized exploitation, it is important to recognize that no single IT application—however powerful—is *strategic* in its generic form. Information systems, per se, are *not* strategic; it is what an organization does with the information (translated into knowledge and action, with corresponding changes in performance appraisal criteria to differentiate their product-service offering) that is strategic. Not all order-entry systems are strategic, although some could provide critical sources of competitive advantage if accompanied by appropriate business process changes. Similarly, not all airline reservation systems are strategic, although there are strong reasons to believe that American Airlines and United Airlines have leveraged them more effectively than their competitors. The reasons lie in their ability to use the information content for more detailed analyses as well as insightful pricing and promotional decisions than their competitors.

LEVEL 2: INTERNAL INTEGRATION

This level is a logical extension of the first, reflecting a more systematic attempt to leverage IT capabilities throughout the entire business process. This level is best viewed as involving two types of integration: *technical interconnectivity*—dealing with the interconnectivity and interoperability of the different systems and application through a common IT platform; and *business process interdependence*—dealing with the interdependence of organizational roles and responsibilities across distinct functional lines of operations. *Neither alone is sufficient; both types are important.*

During the past few years, managers have paid more attention and effort to technical interconnectivity than to business process interdependence. Efforts at technical interconnectivity have been enhanced by significant developments in connectivity capabilities over the past decade: increased availability of integrated technological solutions and favorable cost-performance trends. Nearly every company that I know or studied had a technical committee (varying in their degree of formality) responsible for ensuring technical interconnectivity, while only in a few cases did parallel, cross-functional teams exist to address the challenge of business process interdependence. This is disappointing. External technical vendors and systems integrators could very capably ensure technical interoperability, while the responsibility for business process interdependence lies squarely within the company. The important question that few managers ask is, "Even if we have achieved a seamless technical platform, will our managers operate as a coherent organization rather than as functional stovepipes?" When business processes (with supporting performance assessment system) are not interdependent, the organization's ability to leverage a seamless, and interoperable technical platform, is weakened.

Let's consider some examples. Baxter International's success in the highly competitive pharmaceutical distribution marketplace is not due merely to the deployment of its now-famous *Analytic Systems Automated Purchasing* (ASAP) system, but to the organization's ability to leverage the IT infrastructure to deliver high-value products and services through the *ValueLink* Just-in-Time business offering that is consistent with market needs.[9] USAA—a leading company in the insurance industry and well known for its customer service—has balanced business process interdependence with technical integration to achieve its business vision: "All customers calling the insurance company should be able to accomplish their task with a single call." Similarly, Frito-Lay, a division of PepsiCo, has been able to leverage its integrated technical platform such that its marketing managers can respond with enhanced effectiveness to diverse competitive moves in the various regional markets; and this has been attributed to have a direct impact on their product-line profitability of snack foods.

In a similar vein, while Max Hopper of American Airlines remarked that the age of ownership of proprietary systems (or "screen bias") may be over, he stressed the value of analyzing the distinct data elements for better decisions throughout the business operations.

Ingersoll Mining Machine Company,[10] an emergent leader in heavy machinery lines, competes on its ability to offer customized products at competitive prices. Ingersoll executes this strategy through a computer-integrated manufacturing (CIM) platform capable of delivering the required products at optimum speeds with minimal waste or inventory. The internal business process is driven by a Hitachi Data Systems (HDS) mainframe, which links over 200 CAD/CAM terminals and diverse functions such as purchasing, billing, order handling, payroll, and shop floor—all supported by an integrated database. The key advantages of internal integration include the ability of the system to place purchase orders for necessary parts based on an engineer's drawings on a CAD/CAM software and a computerized "nesting" system that determines the most efficient way to carve raw plates of steel and reduce the manpower requirement by 90 percent while increasing reliability and quality manyfold. More important, this system is linked to the bill-of-material, routing, payroll, cost, and master scheduling, thus minimizing the finished goods inventory to one of the lowest level in the industry.

Similarly, Otis Elevators[11] has leveraged its information systems— *Otisline*—as the basis for streamlining its internal operations to design and implement state-of-the-art elevators capable of providing the highest level of service operations. Otisline—primarily a centralized dispatching service that handles about 9000 calls per day—services as the central conduit for crucial information exchange among field service mechanics, salespeople, design and manufacturing engineers, and managers. Recent enhancements include remote elevator monitoring (using a microprocessor to report malfunctioning elevators to the central dispatching office via modem), direct communication with passengers trapped inside the car, and monthly reports on each elevator for subsequent analysis of performance patterns. Beyond dispatching service mechanics to rectify problems and obtaining feedback data on elevator performance as inputs for the consolidated database, the internal integration characteristic of Otisline is seen in its support for the sales function. Salespeople use Otisline to access NES (new equipment sales), an integrated database management system capable of providing immediate quotes for prospective clients. Thus, the logic of internal integration is to support the business vision; according to George David, Chief Executive of Otis: "Any salesperson in the organization should be able to order an elevator within a single day."

Recent entries in the luxury automobile market offer another powerful example of internal integration: the makers of *Lexus* and *Infiniti,* for instance, collect important data on automobile performance during service visits and have linked such data to their design and manufacturing databases. Such an integrated system allows them to analyze the performance of their cars on a systematic and comprehensive basis and detect possible problems earlier than otherwise possible. Such early-warning systems have allowed them to perform preventive maintenance and thereby raise their level of customer satisfaction to new heights. This system has alarmed the Japanese automakers in their efforts to create and maintain their reputation as serious contenders in the luxury car market with high levels of reliability and customer service. In a similar vein, to keep track of order status and for early-warning, the Saturn Corporation[12] has deployed an information system capable of 2-way data and 1-way video information exchanges. This system enabled Saturn to recall 1800 cars that had been shipped with a defective cooling liquid within 3 days of its initial occurrence in the field. Normally, this defect would have been discovered through warranty claims and may not have been communicated to the manufacturing plant for several months.

Internal integration offers both efficiency and effectiveness benefits. As managers embark on this journey, they should address the following two questions:

1. What is the rationale for internal integration—improved efficiency? superior customer service? coordinated decision making? other factors?

2. How does the resultant business process compare with the "best-in-class" in the marketplace?

The first question emphasizes the view that each company should develop its own vision for internal integration after assessing the benefits of integrating the set of current business processes. As Michael Hammer[13] has observed: "Instead of imbedding outdated processes in silicon and software, we should obliterate them and start over." If the current processes are deemed to be effective, then it is important to articulate the specific objectives of internal integration; for instance, some managers may seek to create cross-functional, horizontal business process that parallel the traditional organization's vertical functional lines. Alternatively, the logic for internal integration may reflect a transition toward a fundamental redesign of business processes.

The second question highlights the need to ensure that the internal integration efforts are guided by external, market-focused referents. Simply fine-tuning existing outmoded processes through current technological capabilities does not create the required organizational capabilities. In the words of a frustrated manager struggling with internal integration: "The best way out for us is to scrap our existing DL/1 database systems on an IBM 4381 system in favor of a new database based on Natural2 fourth-generation language running on an IBM 3090. But, we have not been given resources to support such a major migration and so we have been tinkering at the margin and falling behind our competitors every day. We don't assess the *real costs of not migrating* to the new system and that's our weakness." Internal integration should not be the result of automating inefficient business processes.

These two levels are termed "evolutionary" since they require minimal changes to the business processes relative to the three levels that follow. These also represent the current "state-of-the-art in practice." Managers are able to achieve these two levels because of both the favorable cost-performance trends in technological capabilities as well as the increased availability and affordability of technologies that interoperate across different platforms, time zones, and geographic boundaries. At the same time, it is important to recognize that the phenomenon is not technology-driven but technology-enabled. The organizational enablers that have contributed to these two levels are the managerial awareness of the costs and benefits associated with localized exploitation and internal integration, and the competitive pressures to enhance both operational efficiency and relative quality of product-service offerings.

LEVEL 3: BUSINESS PROCESS REDESIGN

However integrated current business processes and IT functionality may be, as seen in level two, their benefits are not fully realized if the technology has been superimposed. The reason for this is that current business processes are the result of organizational principles which developed from the particular circumstances of the Industrial Revolution. Organizational and management concepts such as centralization versus decentralization, span-of-control, line versus staff, functional specialization, authority-responsibility balance, and administrative mechanisms for coordination and control are derived from this general set of principles. Although these concepts are generally valid even today, it appears that IT functionality could significantly alter some of these "first principles." The implication is that some modes of organizing may be rendered relatively inefficient. The professional and academic community holds some strong and consistent views that the new logic of organization should be predicated on the capabilities offered by current and emerging IT and IS.[14]

Research conducted as part of the *MIT Management in the 1990s* program[15] strongly indicated that IT functionality should not be simply overlaid on the existing business processes but should be used as a lever for designing the new organization and the associated business processes. Rank-Xerox of the United Kingdom, widely viewed as an exemplar of this level of transformation, is a good example of the organizations that are exploiting a new logic of business process redesign—a "new industrial engineering" with IT capabilities playing a central role.

Table 7-1 is a summary of the reasons business process redesign is an important management issue of the 1990s. It also identifies the central role played

TABLE 7-1   The emergence of business process as the central management focus

Distinguishing Characteristics	Traditional	Emergent
Expertise	Functional knowledge	Cross-functional knowledge
Decision making	Centralization or Decentralization	Coordinated across multiple experts
Workunit	Individual	Teams
Role of information	"Supporting"	"Enabling"

by IT functionality. Business process redesign "focuses on a well-structured set of activities designed to produce a specified output for a particular customer or market."[16]

One manager inquired during my research: "I sense a high level of frenzy regarding business process redesign these days. Do you believe that every business process should be redesigned?" The answer is emphatically *No*. What is important, however, is to understand the rationale of the current business process—especially its strengths and limitations. Such an understanding will allow managers to approach business process redesign more rationally and systematically than emotionally. I found very few cases where, given their business strategy, the managers had systematically assessed their organizational logic before embarking on efforts to redesign their business processes.

In my view, business process redesign should be initiated after ascertaining the significant changes occurring in the business processes of key competitors—especially the new entrants—so that appropriate responses can be formulated beforehand. In the late 1980s, a proactive credit card provider could have asked "what do AT&T's and GM's entries into the credit card market mean for my business? What responses—business process changes as well as others—are required to counter these competitive moves?" Asking such questions before competitors actually launch their products gives managers more lead time for effective responses.

Several successful cases of business process redesign have been provided by various observers, particularly Tom Davenport, Michael Hammer, and James Champy. Davenport discusses the cases of Rank-Xerox and Digital Equipment Corporation while Hammer and Champy in *Reengineering the Corporation* offer insightful analyses of Bell Atlantic, Hallmark Cards, Ford Motor Company, Taco Bell, Capital Holding, and IBM Credit Company. In these different examples, managers sought to achieve significant improvements in the performance of their processes, such as decreased costs, improved customer response, and customer service delivery. Readers interested in this theme would find these to be useful sources.

Business process redesign is not "zero or one" but reflects several variants. A careful analysis of the costs and benefits of current design against a feasible set of options allows an organization to execute a coordinated plan of business process redesign. Most business process redesign attempts that I observed during my research could only be termed as "quick-and-dirty responses" to a crisis. These are inefficient as well as ineffective in countering competitive actions.

Benefits from business process redesign are limited in scope if the processes are not extended outside the focal organizational boundary to identify options for redesigning the nature of relationships with the other organizations that participate in the task of delivering value to the ultimate customer.

LEVEL 4: BUSINESS NETWORK RECONFIGURATION

The three levels discussed thus far have focused on IT-enabled business transformation within a single organization. These levels, either implicitly or explicitly, assumed that the boundary of the focal organization is fixed or given. Even where interconnections exist with external businesses such as suppliers, buyers and other intermediaries, the distribution of business activities across the different firms was not altered. In contrast, this level represents the redesign of the nature of exchange among multiple participants in a business network through effective deployment of IT capabilities.

Key Characteristics of Business Network Reconfiguration and the Enabling Role of Information Technology

Business Network Redesign Is More Than Electronic Data Interchange

Table 7-2 distinguishes business network redesign from electronic data interchange (EDI) because there is a strong—and mistaken—tendency to equate the two. I suggest that an EDI platform is best viewed as a means to redesign the business network rather than as an end in itself.

TABLE 7-2   Distinguishing business network reconfiguration from electronic data interchange

Distinctive Characteristics	Electronic Data Interchange (EDI)	Business Network Reconfiguration
Dominant objective	Efficient data interchange	Process interdependencies across organizations
Primary focus	Technical domain; data elements	Business domain; business partners
Responsibility	II (and IS) managers	Business managers
Management focus	Operational; tangible	Strategic; intangible
Orientation	Collaborative advantage	Competitive advantage
Performance assessment	Efficiency of technical standards	Effectiveness of business arrangements
Action steps	Standard (common procedures)	Unique (firm-specific)

Business Network Reconfiguration Is More Than the Choice between Common versus Proprietary Interfaces

The second issue, a major area of controversy, focuses on whether a company should choose a proprietary and common interface for dealing with external partners (such as suppliers, buyers, or other intermediaries). The popular examples of IT-based competitive advantage—American Airlines' *SABRE* system, Baxter's *ASAP* system, McKesson's *Economost,* and Otis Elevators' *Otisline*—are based on company-specific proprietary systems. Although these systems were deployed in the 1970s under a very different set of competitive characteristics and interorganizational relationships, the dominant view is still that IT-based advantage accrues if (and only if) the company deploys its own version of interorganizational systems (IOS).[17]

There is, however, absolutely no evidence that deploying proprietary interorganizational systems *per se* provides any competitive advantage. During the 1980s, the role of proprietary systems as a source of competitive advantage had been glorified through some overused examples with no systematic, quantitative evidence. During 1988 and 1989, I carried out a systematic research study to assess the benefits of proprietary IOS in the property and casualty segments of the U.S. insurance industry.[18] I selected a set of 80 independent insurance agents who were electronically interfaced with one focal insurance carrier, who had deployed the proprietary IOS. For the purpose of systematic experimental assessment, I also selected a matched set of 80 agents (similar in size and geography) as my control group. Based on performance data over a one-year period (from 6 months prior to the system installation to 6 months after), I could not statistically demonstrate that the agents electronically interfaced through proprietary IOS performed any better than the control group. Subsequent analysis within the same study revealed that the agents who had redesigned their business processes to exploit the interfacing functionality performed significantly better than those agents who simply automated their inefficient business process[19] through this system.

This does not mean that companies should not adopt proprietary interfacing systems. Indeed, I expect that we will continue to see the deployment of such systems in markets where there may not be sufficient forces to create common protocols from the beginning. To be truly beneficial, however, these systems must serve as a means to achieve differential advantage rather than as ends in themselves. While IOS is an efficient *conduit* to exchange important information between trading partners, it is only the organization's capability to leverage these systems to create interdependent processes (as in the case of my insurance study) or enhance decisionmaking (as with the link between American's SABRE and its revenue management systems) or provide distinctive value-added services (as in the case of Baxter's ValueLink) that leads to effectiveness.

Scope and Benefits of Business Network Redesign Are Broader Than Efficient Transaction Processing

It is commonly held that IT functionality allows efficient information-exchange (eliminates multiple data-entry and enables faster response). Whereas this is one of the benefits, the potential, as highlighted in Table 7-3, is much broader.

Transaction processing is the exchange of structured data on transactions—purchase orders, invoices, material schedules, electronic payments—in a machine-readable standard format using computers and communication capabilities across independent organizations. This is facilitated by using standard EDI protocols (e.g., ANSI X12 standards). The main benefit of computerized transaction processing is increased administrative efficiency (data entry costs, mailing costs, paperwork, etc.). During the 1980s, the use of EDI for structured transaction processing increased significantly and the forecast is that by the end of this decade, over 75 percent of interbusiness transactions will be over EDI networks. Thus, this becomes the basic level of interdependency among businesses as long as they accept the prespecified standards.

Inventory movement is the moving of inventory from one organization to another through efficient transaction processing without the intervention of

TABLE 7-3   Scope and benefits of business network redesign

Scope/ Functions	Description	Participation Conditions	Potential Benefits
Transaction-Processing	Seamless interconnection for exchanging structured data on transactions	Potentially unlimited under conditions of acceptance of standards and security requirements	Administrative efficiency enhancements
Inventory Movements	Trigger inventory movements across organizations based on predefined conditions without human intervention	Governed by standard contracts between the participating organizations	Operational efficiency enhancements
Process Linkages	Interdependent process linkages for unstructured tasks (example: design and manufacturing)	Governed by specialized contracts or strategic alliances based on mutual benefits	Potential for differentiation in the marketplace through greater coverage of sources of competences
Knowledge Leverage	Creation of a network for leveraging skills and expertise	Governed by professional norms rather than contractual conditions	Enhanced learning—potentially valuable under high uncertainty situations

the relevant organizations' managers. For example, interconnected information systems trigger the movement of materials from one manufacturing stage to another—although these stages of manufacturing may be in different organizations. The participation conditions for this function are stricter, however, than those for transaction processing. As noted in Table 7-3, inventory shifts across organizations are governed by standard business contracts among the relevant participating businesses, whereas transaction processing may not require such a contract. Similarly, in the airline industry, the reservation systems make the "inventory of seats" visible and available—but differentially to the different travel agents based on their preferred carrier status and CRS ownership. Finally, the potential benefits are not only in administrative efficiency (as before) but also in operational efficiency (streamlined inventory levels throughout the supply chain).

Process linkage expands the scope of business network redesign in very important ways. For instance, the design stage of one organization linked to the manufacturing stage of another in a vertical chain through a common CAD/CAM/CIE platform represents a very different type of network redesign than the previous two functions. Navistar International has a process linkage with Dana Corporation with a common quality assurance system that eliminates duplicate tests since Navistar has the ability to monitor the quality when needed. Similarly, Ford Motor Company has process links with Goodyear Tire Company that allow it to exploit concurrent engineering and reduce the time of new product introduction. Toyota has instituted its own proprietary Value Added Network (VAN) to crate seamless processes with suppliers within its *keritsu*. This type of business network redesign does not lend itself to participation by all potential organizations. Such business arrangements are governed by the use of specialized contracts or strategic alliances, where each party agrees to the relationship on a mutually beneficial basis. The potential benefits are that each partner could leverage the competences in the extended network without resorting to costly options of vertical integration.

Bose Corporation—a leader in providing high-end audio products—provides an exemplary case of process linkages that leverage IT capabilities to restructure business relationships. Over the past five years, Bose has been pioneering an advanced version of a just-in-time (JIT) manufacturing system with a patented name: JIT II®. The distinctive aspect of the process linkage is that seven major suppliers have in-plant representatives at the facilities owned and operated by Bose. They have replaced the traditional roles of suppliers' salespersons and buyer's purchasing staff. The representatives are empowered to use Bose's purchasing orders and place orders on the suppliers. They are additionally allowed to practice concurrent engineering attending any and all design engineering meetings involving their company's products, with full access to Bose's facilities, personnel, and data. Both Bose and the seven suppliers that have been involved in the program over the past four years claim that this has been mutually successful. For Bose Corporation, the benefits include (1) liberation of purchasing staff from low-value administrative tasks to more high-value areas; (2) the cost of supplies has been reduced including inventory charges; and (3) EDI capabilities have been exploited to link with critical suppliers for enhanced learning. For the suppliers, the benefits have included (1) elimination of sales efforts (offset by full-time in-plant representatives); (2) evergreen contract with no end date and no rebidding activities; (3) streamlined supply; (4) efficient invoicing and payments as well as higher probability of growth in sales than otherwise.[20] Lance Dixon of Bose who originated the concept of JIT II®, had the following distinction in describing the traditional JIT and JIT II: "JIT eliminates *inventory* while JIT II eliminates the *salesman and the buyer.*"[21]

Knowledge leverage is the expertise that can be sourced from network through IT-based linkages. In contrast to structured EDI Platforms, the platform here is capable of richer, unstructured information-exchange within a virtual intellectual network that cuts across physical, organizational, and geographic boundaries. For example, the University of Pittsburgh Medical Center has a multimedia network that allows neurophysiologists from remote locations to assist neurotechnicians in performing complex operations.[22] Unexpected complications can be solved by pooling different experts who may not be present in the operating room. In a similar vein, networks are evolving in such specialized areas as law, finance, taxation, and geology. Participation in such knowledge networks is not open to everyone, however, but is restricted based on levels of skills and expertise. In the case of the neurophysicians, the participation is based on academic credentials and prior achievements within the profession. The potential benefits lie in the ability of one partner to leverage critical sources of knowledge and expertise in a broader domain than is possible without the functionality offered by the technology.

Effective Business Network Redesign Calls for Coordinating Distinct Functional Strands of Relationships through a Common IS Platform

Managers need to formulate and implement the strategy for business network redesign in a coordinated way. Over the past decade, managers have devoted increased attention to restructuring external relationships: purchasing departments have devised their own approach to streamlining the supply process (reducing the number of suppliers, increasing the length of contracts, shifting performance criteria to reflect nonprice factors, enhancing the use of EDI, etc.); marketing departments have attempted to reconfigure the product delivery and customer service process (vertical channels, cooperative advertising, micromarketing, product and service customization, etc.); and finance and insurance departments have restructured their relationships through such activities as self-insurance and risk sharing. In most companies that I studied, the redesign of business relationships in these "functional domains" has occurred independently (akin to localized exploitation). Such independent efforts have increased operational efficiency but have fallen short of exploiting the full potential of business network redesign through a seamless IT platform exploiting a wide array of functions ranging from transaction processing to knowledge leverage.

Based on the preceding four considerations, managers seeking to exploit the potential of business network redesign should address the following four questions:

1. What is the rationale for the current approach to business network redesign? and what are the strengths and limitations?

2. Does it make sense to invest in proprietary interfaces to define the new rules of network interrelationships or does it make sense to pursue "common standards"?

3. What are the opportunities for restructuring the business network? What is (could be) the potential functionality for information technology applications, from transaction processing to knowledge leverage?

4. Does the firm have a coherent strategy for redesigning the business network, or does it simply have isolated functional strands of relationships?

I strongly believe that the real power of IT for any company lies not in streamlining internal operations (efficiency enhancements) but in restructuring the relationships in the extended business networks to leverage a broader array of competences that will deliver superior products and services. Any systematic attempt to reposition a company has implications for the company's business scope—which is the fifth level of the transformation.

LEVEL 5: BUSINESS SCOPE REDEFINITION

Strategy analysis typically starts with the question—"What business(es) are we in—and why?" The fifth level of transformation directly addresses this question but with an important variant: "what role—if any—does IT play in influencing business scope and the logic of business relationships within the extended business network?"

Strategy concepts such as economies of scale (within the hierarchy), product-line extension through vertical integration as well as mergers and acquisition that led to increased emphasis on vertical integration are being replaced by newer concepts such as joint ventures, alliances and partnerships, and virtual business networks with a marked emphasis toward a more flexible and fluid corporate scope.[23] My interest here is to focus on the specific enabling role of information technology in this movement. My argument is that the redesign of business networks (Level 4) from transaction processing to knowledge networks has direct implications for the logic of business scope and the consequent redistribution of revenue and profit (margin) streams in a given market. Some tasks may be eliminated (such as repetitive quality control steps, billing invoices, preparing delivery slips, etc.), some tasks may be restructured optimally across organizational boundaries (joint design or collaborative manufacturing), and some tasks may be expanded (value-added services that are rooted in IT functionality).

We have witnessed some powerful illustrations of IT-enabled business scope redefinition over the past decade. American Airlines has leveraged SABRE beyond the traditional marketing support role to derive a significant proportion of its total revenue from SABRE-related fees: by one estimate, the profit level from SABRE is higher than flying the airplanes.[24] Similarly, Otis Elevators has leveraged IT-enabled features such as remote elevator monitoring as an additional source of revenue (fee of $50 per elevator per month with high profit margins).[25] With the advent of electronic filing of individual tax returns in the United States, innovative tax-return preparation firms have expanded their business scope to include refund-anticipation loans and other financial and tax-related services.[26] Baxter has evolved from distribution of hospital products to managing inventory within hospitals on a stockless basis[27] and Federal Express has been leveraging its reliable IT platform to handle customer service processes for noncompetitors as well as to manage time-sensitive inventory of spare parts for companies such as IBM and Boeing.

Beyond these examples, which highlight expansion of business scope, this level of transformation also fundamentally restructures activities within a value chain. Thus, business scope should not be articulated in terms of historical considerations ("we have always done this process inside and we can never think of getting it done outside"). Managers should increasingly demonstrate that using IT applications for enhanced coordination and control is both efficient and effective for carrying out the set of business processes inside as well as coordinating with the business processes outside ("we leverage the 'best-in-class' expertise within our extended business network").[28]

The current strategic thrusts around *core competence* and *outsourcing* should be accompanied by a systematic approach to *combine* the critical competences in a form acceptable to the customer. Such attempts at combining the required competences on a flexible basis are greatly enhanced and facilitated by IT capabilities. I fully agree with James Brian Quinn's observations that "companies are outsourcing integral and key elements of their value chains, because outsiders can perform them at lower cost and higher value-added than the buying company"[29] and that "strategy concepts need to focus internally more on developing 'best in world' capabilities around a few key activities . . . and externally more on managing a rapidly changing network of 'best in world' suppliers for its other needs."[30] However, I extend Quinn's logic further by emphasizing that the flexible combination of different fragments of activities to provide customers the required products and services is fundamentally enabled by the superior information-processing capability. We cannot effectively talk about network-based coordination to deliver flexible products and services if we do not have inherent IT infrastructure for efficient coordination and control.

Hence, for strategists, IT is not simply a utility like power or telephone, but a fundamental source of business scope reconfiguration to redefine the "rules of the game" through restructured business networks (Level 4) as well as redesigned business processes (Level 3). Thus, the core logic of organizational strategy involves the three higher levels of the transformational framework with business processes designed (Level 3) to support the logic of business scope definition (Level 5) and the specific positions in the reconfigured business network (Level 4).

THE STRATEGIC MANAGEMENT CHALLENGE: EXPLOITING THE IT CAPABILITIES

Which Level of Transformation Is Right for You Now? In the Future?

One of the most common questions about this framework is "Which level of transformation is appropriate for my company?" There is no one best level for all companies as each level in Figure 7-3 indicates a set of potential benefits (horizontal axis) that is consistent with the organization's exploitative capability (vertical axis). The evolutionary levels (1 and 2)—in my opinion—are to be viewed as transitions toward creating the new strategic logic that reflects and exploits the potential offered by the higher "revolutionary" levels. The pace of transformation, however, is dictated by several factors, both internal and competitive.

Opportunity or Threat?

My framework is based on a strong premise that the potential benefits from IT are directly related to the degree of changes made in organizational routines (strategies, structure, processes, and skills). Thus, a critical issue in deciding about the desired transformational level is to evaluate whether the managers view IT capabilities as a source of opportunity to redefine their strategies or as a threat to the status quo. In some companies, I have encountered situations where flimsy and unsubstantiated excuses—"We tried something like this before and it didn't work" (the past failure may not necessarily imply failure in the future) or "We can't afford to make such changes now" (what's the cost of not changing?)—would be invoked to prevent initiation of the higher levels of transformation.

Assessing where the leading competitors are positioned within this framework is very useful not only to create awareness of the limitations of the status quo but also to gain commitment: if, for instance, Federal Express has developed a logic for its business processes that is derived from its articulation of business scope (Level 5) and its unique set of interorganizational business arrangements in the business network (Level 4), then it does not make too much sense for its competitor (say, United Parcel Service) to aim for internal integration as the ultimate goal. Similarly, if you are competing against Otis Elevators, which is redefining its business scope using IT capabilities, simply being at Level 1 or 2 may be inadequate unless you have other distinctive sources of advantage.

What Is the Raison d'être for Business Process Redesign: Rectifying Current Deficiencies or Creating Future Capabilities?

The transformational framework highlights that IT-enabled business process redesign can be approached from two different (and sometimes contradictory) perspectives. Figure 7-4 shows these two avenues: One, which I term "efficiency-enhancing" (lower left arrow), focuses predominantly on rectifying current weaknesses; and the other, which I term "capability-creating" (top right arrow), aims to create strategic capabilities for competing in the future. Both are valid but the context favoring one over the other should be understood before embarking on the business redesign activities.

When efficiency-enhancing business process redesign is pursued, the boundary conditions specified by the current strategy (business network and business scope, reflecting Levels 4 and 5 in the framework) are considered fixed and given. Thus, the main objectives of redesign are to achieve operational excellence within this boundary condition. Even if the business process redesign efforts extend outside the focal organizational boundary, no attempt is made to shift the scope of the business from within the firm to outside and vice versa (except for streamlining administrative efficiency). Much of the current writings in business process redesign embrace this view of administrative and operational efficiency improvement through business process redesign.[31] For

FIGURE 7-4   Alternative avenues for business process redesign

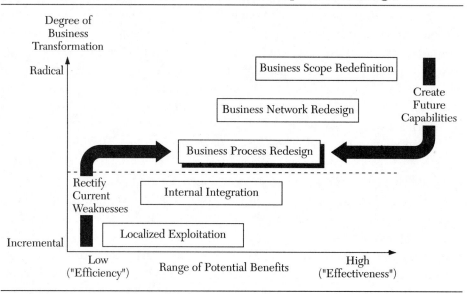

instance, Hammer and Champy define reengineering (their term for redesign) as "the fundamental rethinking and radical redesign of business processes to achieve dramatic improvements in critical . . . measures of performance."[32] They use examples of redesign of business processes for IBM Credit Corporation, Ford Motor Company, and others that involved minimal changes to business network and business scope, yet achieved significant improvements in operational measures of performance. Such an approach is perfectly valid under conditions where we do not expect a radical redefinition of business scope through fundamental realignment of business processes within the business network.

On the other hand, capability-creating, the other avenue to business process redesign, starts with the articulation of business scope and the corresponding logic for business network reconfiguration to specify which business processes need to be redesigned and under what guiding conditions. This approach starts with a careful and focused analyses of how the organization is likely to be positioned in the business network before deriving the objectives and requirements for business process redesign.

I illustrate the importance of this distinction with an example from the college textbook publishing marketplace. The traditional business processes for manufacturing and distributing standard textbooks are acquisition, editing, printing and binding, selling, distributing, and adoption by the universities and colleges. It can be seen as a linear, sequential set of processes involved in converting the ideas in the mind of an author into a form that is usable by the educators in a mass market. If one adopted the efficiency-enhancing avenue to redesigning these business processes, it would be possible to leverage the current and emerging IT capability to improve operational performance of cost and quality. However, the key capability for competing in the market appears to be shifting away from efficient distribution of standard textbooks to effective provisioning of custom textbooks to suit the individual requirements of the educators. McGraw-Hill has pioneered the custom textbook offering, *Primis*, through a set of business processes that begin with user specification of the requirements, invariably involving reconfiguration of chapters and articles from various diverse sources, and end with the availability of a custom textbook in lot sizes as small as 25 within a week. The result is a radically different set of business processes that cut across multiple partners with a diverse set of business competences (scanning, selective binding, information sources, electronic printing as opposed to traditional offset printing, etc.). In this case, redesign for operational efficiency alone might not have yielded the desired impact on the marketplace.

CONCLUDING REMARKS: A JOURNEY, NOT AN EVENT

Undoubtedly, IT functionality will have a more profound impact on businesses than its effect thus far. Nevertheless, successful businesses will not treat IT as either the *driver* or the *magic bullet* for providing distinctive strategic advantage. Successful companies will be differentiated by their ability to visualize the logic of the new business world (Level 5 of the transformation model) and leverage IT to create an appropriate organizational arrangement—internal and external (Levels 3 and 4)—to support the business logic. In this regard, the trajectory of transformation is a moving target shaped by the fundamental changes in the competitive business world. The management challenge is to continually adapt the organizational and technological capabilities to be in dynamic alignment with the chosen business vision.

FOR FURTHER READING

Davenport, Thomas H., *Process Innovation: Reengineering Work Through Information Technology* (Boston, MA: Harvard Business School Press, 1991).

Hammer, Michael and James Champy, *Reengineering the Corporation* (New York: HarperCollins, 1993).

Keen, Peter G. W., *Shaping the Future: Business Design through Information Technology* (Boston, MA: Harvard Business School Press, 1991).

Scott-Morton, Michael S., *The Corporation for the 1990s* (New York: Oxford University Press, 1991).

8 HUMAN RESOURCE MANAGEMENT: COMPETITIVE ADVANTAGE THROUGH PEOPLE

Mary Anne Devanna

As we emerged from the 1980s, most sophisticated, cutting-edge organizations realized that they had reaped most of the competitive advantage available to them through downsizing and financial restructuring. Looking for new ways to increase productivity and market position in the 1990s, these organizations increasingly turned to a statement that had been given mostly lip service in the past—"People are our most important asset"—as a source of competitive advantage for the next decade.

As a consequence, managers began to pay increased attention to the processes that always held the promise of leveraging employee behavior and began to depend on selection, appraisal, reward, and development to change the way in which the organization accomplishes its goals and objectives.

In this chapter, we will first discuss the human resource cycle as a process, examining each of the functions in detail. Then we will look at the way that these functions are being used by organizations undergoing fundamental change to provide the necessary skills to manage more participative, flatter organizations in which individual learning and growth are paramount. Finally, we will deal with the organizations within which the managers operate. What is it about the underlying philosophy in organizations that can help or hinder the manager's success in accomplishing the changes demanded by the marketplace?

THE HUMAN RESOURCE CYCLE

Figure 8-1 shows how the four generic human resource functions—selection, performance appraisal, rewards, and development—impact organizational performance. The dependent variable in this model is behavior. This series of managerial tasks will impact performance at both the individual and organizational levels.

Historically, the unit of analysis in the human resource cycle was the individual. In today's interdependent organization it is the team. This has ramifications for every facet of human resource management. As we talk about the cycle, we must try to be self-conscious about these differences. A person is selected for a job in the organization with the idea that he or she will be able to carry out the responsibilities of the position. To ensure that this objective is met, the organization monitors the individual's performance in the position and evaluates his or her ability to meet its responsibilities. Based on this appraisal, the organization rewards the individual who is able to meet or exceed the standards for performance in that position, thus reinforcing the desired behavior while simultaneously providing developmental help to correct weaknesses in the individual's performance. Over time, the reinforcement of the positive behavior and the correction of weaknesses results in increased performance levels for the individual and the organization.

It is simple to change the unit of analysis on the printed page so that we think in terms of hiring people to fit into a team whose performance will be monitored to reinforce the desired behavior while providing developmental help to correct weaknesses in the team's performance. However, the changes are far from simple to accomplish. We will discuss the difficulties involved in this transformational process after we have completed a discussion of the cycle.

FIGURE 8-1   The human resource cycle

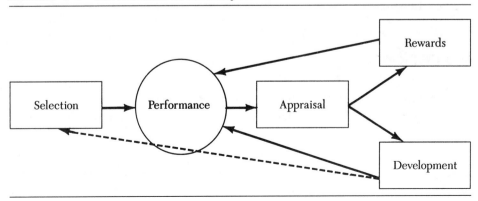

The activities described in the model seem relatively simple to explain and understand, but they are difficult to execute, because as Allan Cohen explained in Chapter 3, people behave in unpredictable ways and group dynamics can lead to negative as well as positive results. Individuals come to the organization with different levels of training and capacities for learning new skills and different rewards that they seek to obtain from the organization, as well as a set of life experiences that determine both how they give feedback and how they take it. They also have different capacities to tolerate change and this issue has become critical in times of rapid changes in the outside environment.

Historically, the organization's challenge was to provide an environment that enhanced the positive inclinations of its employees and provided links between the personal goals of individuals and organizational objectives. This challenge has grown in importance and difficulty in an era of downsizing and competitive pressures that require fundamental change in the way that people in organizations relate to one another across hierarchical and functional barriers.

An indication of the extent of this challenge is provided by a recent American Society for Training and Development study of self-managed work teams at U.S. organizations with more than 100 employees. A majority of such teams set their own work schedules and production quotas, determine their own training needs, and deal directly with external customers. In addition, a growing minority of them write their own performance appraisals and handle budgeting, hiring, and firing for their team. Such radical departures from the norms of management might seem to be a rarity. But the same study concludes that 35 percent of all U.S. businesses with more than 100 employees now have at least one self-directed work team and that, on average, 32 percent of employees at these firms are members of self-directed work teams. From these two statistics, we can infer that about a sixth of all employees of midsize and large firms are now part of a self-directed work team.

The following sections look at the human resource processes as they relate to the model and more importantly as they can be used by managers to increase organizational performance.

SELECTION

Selection includes not only hiring but also moving people across positions internally. In hierarchically controlled organizations or organizations controlled by one strong function, the time and resources that an organization or its managers devoted to this task often revealed whether they truly believed that all people in the organization were their most important asset. Traditional human resource practices related to selection devoted 90 percent of resources to five percent of the population. Today, this narrow focus will not support organizations because ever-widening spans of control put a premium on filling each and every job with the best possible candidate available. Each employee must be able to initiate actions consistent with corporate goals.

Honda provides an example of a company that has long believed that the ability to fit into the company is as important as the technical skills a person brings to the job. When managers hire workers for their assembly-line operations in Marysville, Ohio, they believe that each job candidate must be carefully screened if the organization is to realize the advantage of putting the best people in each position. A worker who applies for a job at Honda will be asked to write an essay about life goals and how working at Honda will help to achieve them. Ninety percent of all applicants are screened out when the managers who read these essays find no link between the applicant's desire to work at Honda and his or her personal objectives. The remaining 10 percent now pass to the next stage of the process, where they are interviewed to determine how well they will fit in with the Honda way of doing things. Those who are selected undergo three weeks of intensive training before they are placed on the assembly line. Their initial placement on the line will be next to the most experienced workers so they will learn good habits.

One of the benefits of devoting the time and resources required by a hiring system like Honda's is the belief of the workers that their performance on the job is important to the success of the organization. It is easy to see that a firm that devotes significant resources to the hiring and training of all workers will convey this message better than one that simply gives lip service to the idea.

By hiring the best, the organization also provides itself with a better pool of candidates to fill vacancies that may occur. And, it ensures that a balanced business debate is more likely to occur when competitive circumstances force the organization into a major reassessment of its corporate strategy.

PERFORMANCE APPRAISAL

If you spend time in organizations, you will soon come to the conclusion that the most despised and avoided of all managerial tasks is that of performance appraisal. Billions of dollars have been spent on appraisal systems in an attempt to encourage managers to give their subordinates feedback on how they are performing. The problem, however, is not in the form but in the process.

In most organizations, performance appraisal is an annual ritual in which the manager evaluates the subordinate's performance and the evaluation is then used to determine how much of a merit increase the subordinate will receive. The manager is concerned that negative feedback will be demotivating and that subsequent interaction with the subordinate will be difficult. The subordinate knows that valued organizational rewards are riding on the outcome of the appraisal and tends to focus on the bottom line rather than the reasons behind it.

This ritual has little to do with a manager's primary responsibility to coach and counsel subordinates. This role includes frequent doses of praise for the things that are done well and instruction either on the job or in a more formal training program to correct deficiencies in performance. Appraisal should be an ongoing process of open and honest exchanges between manager and subordinates—individuals or teams—with an eye to continuous improvement.

Historically, organizations attempted to deal with the mixed feelings of employees about the evaluation process by providing increasingly greater structure. Thus, we saw them install forced distribution systems which maintain that a manager's appraisal of his or her subordinates will be normally distributed. This assumption probably never fit reality but it certainly is of little use in an organization that does a superior job of selection and development. Assuming the purpose of a performance appraisal system is appraisal of current performance and not of potential for higher level positions, we should not see a wide disparity in the spread of performance evaluations in high-performing companies.

In today's flatter, more team-oriented companies, the performance appraisal system provides an opportunity to fix the employees' attention on the things that really matter. If employees are informed of the organization's goals and how their jobs fit those objectives, they have the ability to determine for themselves what is important and to set priorities among tasks of differing value to the organization's success.

Again, this sounds simple. However, in looking at the results of many studies conducted by the Management Institute at Columbia Business School, more than 60 percent of the middle managers and professionals working in successful companies complain about lack of goal clarity. Few were able to tell us what the organization's strategic goals were. These intelligent and well-educated people had few clues that would have enabled them to manage themselves—they had to be told what to do! Many of the efforts launched by cutting-edge firms such as General Electric, Allied Signal, and Hewlett Packard in the past five years have as their objective correcting this situation. They are training managers to coach and communicate with subordinates rather than telling them what to do today. They are encouraging subordinates to become problem solvers instead of order takers, and they are putting appraisal systems in place that permit subordinates to evaluate a manager's effectiveness, that encourage teams to monitor their own performance, and that break down the barriers hampering effective communication in the organization.

REWARDS

Two important issues are of interest in the area of rewards. The first is to analyze the reward system and ascertain what is being rewarded: membership or performance. The second is to identify the full range of rewards the organization has at its disposal to motivate its employees.

Analyzing the Reward System

Some reward categories go to employees for membership. For example, all employees at certain levels of the organization receive the same benefits regardless of performance, while most organizations say that pay is based on merit. Historically, most organizations on merit pay systems did not use the system to leverage performance. There was usually little play in the range of pay increases that differentiated the superior performers from the average performers, and in most cases, increases were not made public so people did not know if a real difference based on performance existed.

As organizations have become less hierarchical, they have been forced to become more creative with pay since promotions occur less often, with substantial time lapses between moves. Companies like General Electric have in recent years been using lump-sum bonuses to reward long-service middle managers and professionals for superior performance. These bonuses are tied to overall company performance and do not become part of the base nor do they increase pension or other salary-related benefits.

In the long run, we would not expect a true merit pay system in a high-performing company to be marked by large differences in merit increases within a group. Performers who are not delivering superior performance should be developed so they approach the ideal. If they have difficulty meeting the criteria for a particular position, they should be transferred to jobs that better match their abilities.

Identifying Organizational Rewards

The second important issue in reflecting on organizational rewards is to think beyond pay and promotion. Not only is the list too limiting, but it is also not very useful at a time when organizations are restructuring by eliminating hierarchical layers and when low rates of inflation limit the size of merit pools. The following list shows the variety of rewards that research has shown employees value:

1. Career opportunities—a long-term chance for growth and development. In today's organization many of these opportunities will not come from upward mobility but through job enrichment or lateral moves that represent

new challenges for individuals while enhancing their value in the labor market.

2. Pay in its many forms, such as salary, bonuses, stock options; and benefits, such as health insurance.

3. Responsibility, in the form of meaningful work that is important to the organization's success.

4. Autonomy in deciding how to best get the work done, including improving the process.

5. Managerial praise and recognition.

6. Job security, especially important in tight economic times.

7. The opportunity to interact with and receive feedback from customers and suppliers.

8. A work environment marked by mutual respect among all employees.

Most of these rewards are underutilized by organizations and the way that rewards systems are administered deserves special attention in the current competitive environment. The simplest way to insure rewards are modernized is to give employees a voice in their design.

The Definition of Success

Organizations have an enormous ability to define success for their members. Indeed, many of the human resource problems that managers wrestle with today emanate from an attempt to maintain a reward system that is at odds with the economic realities that their organizations are facing.

The reward system was designed to meet the human resource problems American companies faced in the post-World War II era. There were significant shortages of qualified managers during a period of vibrant economic expansion. Most companies dealt with these shortages by adopting the crash training methods used to develop officers during the war when newly minted lieutenants, ensigns, and pilots were known as "90-day wonders." If they showed a flair for leadership, they were quickly rewarded with battlefield commissions or promotions to higher rank. Similarly, organizations relied heavily on on-the-job training, and those who showed any aptitude for management were quickly promoted to more responsible positions. Driven by necessity, organizations experienced little harm in the practice since their growth hid a multitude of sins, and the greatest danger that companies faced was not a lack of experienced managers but a failure to take advantage of the enormous opportunities generated in the postwar economy.

Since the organization wanted to encourage employees to take on the challenge of new positions, often before they had mastered the skills needed to do their present job, they created pay systems where the largest pay differentials were not accessed by mastering the present position but by moving to another organizational level.

In this environment, managers learned to avoid big mistakes in any assignment since they would soon be promoted if they avoided serious gaffes in their current jobs. Also the beginnings of a short-term orientation emerged. A manager who would be in a job for only one to two years did not have to worry about the long term, but only had to make the short-term results appealing. If there were long-term pitfalls in the strategy employed, some successor would pay the price.

Thus, the definition of success was one of rapid promotion from one job to another, always on a upward trajectory.

The problems engendered by this definition of success became more evident as organizations faced a less forgiving environment where growth was not available to hide mistakes and mistakes became ever more costly.

Despite the almost universal acknowledgment that the world has changed dramatically, most organizations still try to struggle along with the old definition of success. Indeed, the problem has been exacerbated since the pace of advancement for those who would be stars has accelerated, and the differences in pay and other forms of recognition between those who succeed and those who are left behind has widened.

This career system also had implications for the way jobs were designed. Jobs had to be narrow enough that someone could move into a position and perform adequately in a short period. Many people rose to high levels of the organization without a clear picture of the work of the whole organization. Furthermore, they became the victims of the skill that brought them to the top: analysis, breaking an item down to its component parts. They tended to lack the skill of synthesis that would have enabled them to better understand the impact of the component parts on one another and on the goals of the organization.

It is changing the definition of success and providing the skills needed to operate in a flatter organization that has preoccupied most organizations looking to revitalize their workforce for the challenge of an increasingly competitive environment.

DEVELOPMENT

There are many approaches to the development task, but they have in common two things that pose new challenges to managers today. First, they recognize that development is an increasingly critical issue that has ramifications for near-term productivity and competitiveness. And second, they recognize that there is a complex interaction between individual and group development, which means that the learning rate of the individual can regulate the learning rate of the organization as a whole and vice versa. For instance, Peter Senge concludes in *The Fifth Discipline* that five new disciplines are essential to a fast-learning, creative, flexible organization. These disciplines create a challenging agenda for individual development, and they illustrate the implications of individual development for organizational growth and development as well.

The disciplines include personal mastery, which is most clearly a matter of individual development. Training, goals and rewards, and appropriate work assignments can be used to help employees achieve personal mastery. But the other four disciplines are group oriented, requiring interactive management of team and organizational development along with the development of the individual. They are:

1. Achieving systems thinking, the ability to see the woods for the trees and understand how particular actions affect the entire business system and are affected by it.
2. Managing mental models, the shared assumptions that often limit an organization's ability to grow and develop.
3. Building shared vision, the common values and direction that unify the newly decentralized modern organization.
4. Creating team learning, in which teams of employees develop together through a facilitated team process.

These four new development challenges make it impossible to achieve a fast-learning organization through the traditional human resources focus on individual development. They require a more integrated and systematic approach, in which the organization's development is considered hand in hand with the individual's development. Human resource management is increasingly thrust into the role of change agent, responsible not only for the creation of a cadre of well-prepared future managers, but also for the reinvention of the organization through the systematic development of new capabilities in its entire workforce.

The need for a more systematic development process poses a significant challenge to many organizations today. The problem is that most of the development that occurs in organizations takes the form of on-the-job training coupled with an informal mentoring system. Thus, both blue-collar workers and managers tend to be insufficiently trained to meet corporate objectives.

In organizations that are meeting the global challenge for improved quality and productivity, the successful shop floor revolution depends on heavy doses of training for both workers and supervisors. In a growing number of cutting-edge companies, the revolution goes beyond the shop floor to include all levels of management including the office of the chairman.

Historically, as noted above, most training, even for managers, consisted of on-the-job training and informal mentoring. The effectiveness of this approach depends on a number of conditions.

First, the organization must think about job rotation as a developmental sequence aimed at producing people to fill key positions in the company. In the past, the typical managerial career progression involved movement from first-line supervisor through middle-management ranks and on to top management. Among the skills stressed in this progression were interpersonal or leadership skills. As organizations are restructured to make them more competitive and responsive to environmental pressures, layers of management are being removed, and many positions that provided developmental opportunities for general managers are being eliminated. Middle managers frequently find themselves managing information or resources rather than people. As a consequence, managerial career progression is less of a continuous flow in which leadership skills become ever more critical. Rather, it is increasingly a discontinuous process where the opportunity to develop leadership skills is constrained. To the extent that the skills needed at different levels of the organization are not part of a continuum, it will be necessary to supplement job experiences with more formal development opportunities.

The second condition needed for on-the-job training and informal mentoring processes to be effective tools for developing key successors is that the management processes and leadership characteristics currently composing the corporate culture must be the ones that the organization wishes to perpetuate in support of its future strategic direction.

Few organizations have been satisfied that their succession systems provided an adequate supply of corporate talent in relatively stable environments. Most are confounded by today's challenge—developing people whose skills are significantly different from those of its current executives. Yet, we frequently hear of the need for more risk taking, more entrepreneurial behavior, more willingness to make decisions.

The major issue is how to develop a new generation of leaders whose characteristics differ from those who have gone before. The growing consensus is that this cannot be accomplished solely through on-the-job training and informal mentoring activities.

Our aim is not the development of a small cadre of heroic figures to keep the organization safe from the threats of a hostile environment. Rather, the goal is to develop broad leadership capabilities that enable the company to survive. This brand of leadership is a behavioral process capable of being learned and managed. It is supported by systems that push accountability and responsibility down in the organization.

In *The Transformational Leader*, [1] Noel Tichy and I used the metaphor of drama to describe the challenges facing today's managers. In Act I, the leader must find a way to make the organization aware of the challenges it faces; in Act II, leaders must create new visions for the organization and mobilize commitment to those visions; and, in Act III, leaders must find a way to institutionalize organizational changes by designing management systems to support the new organizational reality.

The framework is useful in identifying the skills that managers need to operate in today's competitive environment and to consider how these skills can be developed. In the final chapter of *The Transformational Leader*, we describe some of the tools that can be used to accomplish the organizational transformations facing many companies today.

THE CORPORATE GOVERNANCE SYSTEM

The organization is a social system and like all social systems, there are "laws" or "mores" that tell the members what behavior will be rewarded and what behavior will be punished. In some functional areas, such as accounting, the organization is specific about the rules and carefully monitors the control systems that guarantee their enforcement. As discussed in Chapter 10, many controls are in place to ensure that managers meet their fiduciary obligations to external constituencies. In addition, most organizations have carefully monitored internal controls to ensure that managers are using one of the organization's important assets—capital—in a way that best serves the organization and its shareholders. The laws are spelled out and enforced through a variety of control systems so that individuals are not tempted to use organizational assets for personal gain at the expense of the organization.

Over the years, the government has also placed a number of constraints on organizations in terms of the way they use another organizational asset—people. Starting with a societal concern centered on health and safety, the government passed a number of laws regulating the use of child labor and safety standards in mines and factories. In consideration of economic justice, laws set a minimum wage. In the 1960s, recognizing the role that organizations played in distributing wealth and opportunity in the society, the government transferred its concern to the area of social justice: Did all citizens have equal access to the job in large organizations that offered the best opportunities for economic mobility? These laws were meant to guarantee that workers would have access to the organizational opportunity structure and advancement through it on the basis of merit.

These laws initiated a change in the way organizations viewed the management of human resources and the function that served as its internal watchdog—the personnel or human resource function. Increasingly complex regulations from the Equal Employment Opportunity Commission (EEOC) and the Occupational Safety and Health Administration (OSHA) triggered organizational efforts to staff the personnel function with more sophisticated managers. Despite the neglect in the decade of the 1980s by government agencies charged with the enforcement of the equal opportunity legislation, the focus on the management of human resources continued to intensify as organizations faced increased global competition. Books appeared attributing the stunning success of the Japanese as global competitors to their methods of management. The major difference between Japanese and American management was in the way people were managed.

The pressures of global competition also made the job of corporate governance more difficult since a significant percentage of American companies found their labor costs out of line with those of their international competitors. Many resorted to massive layoffs to bring these costs into line, and in the process, they lost the faith and trust of many of the governed.

Organizations have paid a price for their lack of clarity about the corporate governance system. In most organizations, it is difficult to find written "laws" that govern. Yet, in the absence of a clear message, employees infer—sometimes correctly and sometimes incorrectly—those laws by observing what happens to people in the organization. Every organization has made a decision either explicitly or implicitly to answer two basic questions that play a vital role in determining commitment to and effort for accomplishment of corporate goals. The first of these questions is, What is the nature of the psychological contract that we hold with our employees?

In the United States, organizations have had a broader range of alternatives in specifying the nature of the employment contract than European or Japanese firms enjoy. In Europe, government legislation complicates the process of employee termination. In Japan, tradition plays a strong role in determining practice. And, while the recent recession in Japan has begun to erode the traditional lifetime employment contract, most workers still will spend their entire career with one employer.

American companies that had espoused this "Japanese" concept of lifetime employment, such as IBM, General Motors, and General Electric, have largely abandoned this position in the face of competitive pressures. This leaves institutions such as university faculties and professional partnerships in accounting and law firms among the few organizations that continue to grant the promise of lifetime employment to at least some of their employees.

Unfortunately, companies where the nature of the psychological contract has been made explicit are in the minority. Most organizations never define the nature of the contract, and employees are left to deduce it by observing what has happened to people in the organization over time.

If we observed the practices of most American companies, we would discover two psychological contracts operating—one for "high potential" people, often referred to as corporate property, whom management go to extraordinary lengths to bind to the organization—and another for all other employees. At many of these companies, managers whose early careers had been marked by rapid advancement found that in midlife their own opportunity structures had contracted along with the organization's growth rate. Other smaller companies could have provided new challenges but these managers found that the financial sacrifice involved in leaving the organization would be high. Golden handcuffs in the form of back-loaded compensation systems kept them tied to the organization long after the promise of increasingly challenging assignments could be kept.

The short-term fallout of this bimodal system was that a significant number of workers were perceived as being cared for—not critical to the organization's success, but guaranteed job security if they performed adequately. When the economic pressures hit, they became the scapegoats for the organization's woes; first blue-collar workers were deemed to be lazy and indifferent to quality, and then middle managers were characterized as less committed to their organizations than their foreign counterparts.

In the previous edition of *The Portable MBA*, we wrote, "The traditional bimodal American human resource system designed to worry about the few rather than the many will become obsolete. The companies that persist in that old pattern will be at a competitive disadvantage with those companies who understand that strength at every position is critical to success."

So the organizations that we believe are most likely to succeed in the 1990s are referred to as "new way" organizations in Figure 8-2. The transition from the "old way" to the "new way" organization and the maintenance of the new way organization place a heavy emphasis on managing people in new and innovative ways.

THE SECOND QUESTION IS HOW AND BY WHOM WILL DECISIONS BE MADE IN THIS ORGANIZATION?

Companies tend to reflect one of two images—authoritarian or participative. This dimension reflects the extent to which employees are involved in the decision-making process. If we know which option an organization has chosen, we usually can predict the direction information flows as well. Authoritarian firms tend to centralize information, while participative ones would distribute information widely through the organization. Participation does not mean that all employees are involved in all decisions—it more closely approaches business

FIGURE 8-2   Transformation leadership in the 1990s

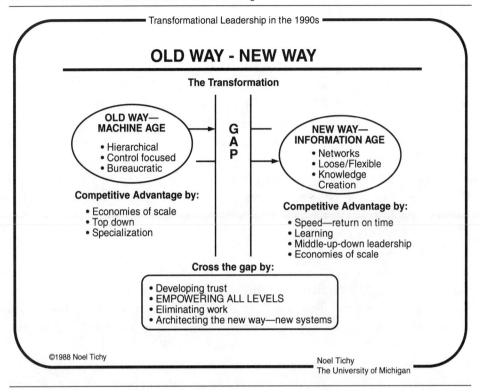

philosopher Russell Ackoff's concept[2] of representative democracy in which all have a voice in deciding matters that affect them. Most companies, whether they be American, European, or Japanese, tend to be more authoritarian than democratic in practice if not in theory. The exceptions are the organizations that have moved closer to the goal of self-directed workforces. This group of organizations includes companies such as Honda and SAS. Therefore, they are not "Japanese," "American," or "Scandinavian," but rather companies whose management style and systems can be characterized as information age rather than machine age. The benefits they derive from their management process are speed in adapting to shifts in the marketplace, the ability to attract more entrepreneurial people, and a higher level of commitment from their workforces.

One can argue that this fundamental shift in corporate governance enables some firms to take on and outperform established competitors. Furthermore, this belief pushes us to a normative rather than a contingency view of how organizations should be structured. It enables better understanding of how a company like Honda can enter a mature auto industry in 1965, and not only survive by taking market share away from the giants, but also set the standard against which others are being measured.

This trend toward flatter organizations staffed with self-directed workforces continues to confound many organizations. They are discovering the difficulty of matching the competitive advantage of organizations who have spent their time developing superior management processes with the goal of achieving strength at every position. The difficulty in moving organizations to this ideal is one of the great paradoxes of economic activity in the West. The paradox arises from the two strong beliefs in the industrialized world: (1) free markets are more efficient than centralized planning because they minimize the cost of information. (2) Democratic social systems are inherently more stable than authoritarian ones, yet the organizations that serve as the producers in the marketplace historically have constructed systems of corporate governance that violate both of these principles.

The pressure in organizations today is toward more democratic systems, because they can respond more rapidly in the marketplace. The battle will be won by the organization that can transform itself from a machine age to an information age company designed to deal with environmental uncertainty and staffed by a self-directed workforce. It will have mastered the modern paradox by becoming an organization of entrepreneurs! It will succeed because its leadership understands that the primary mission of organizations is not profit but development, and that in highly developed organizations, profit is the byproduct of superior performance.

HUMAN RESOURCE MANAGEMENT IN THE "NEW WAY" ORGANIZATION

When we look at the generic human resource functions: selection, appraisal, rewards, and development, major shifts are required in the characteristics of the people and the processes needed to sustain this new form of organization.

Selection

The organization will still need people with the appropriate technical skill mix to carry out its mission and strategy. While this will be a necessary condition for success, it will not be sufficient. The following skills will be required to maintain the "new way" organization:

- Facilitation skills to create and maintain the social networks that support process-based new way organizations.

- Problem-solving skills to identify issues critical to the organization's success and organize task forces with the appropriate technical skill mix to resolve problems.
- Ability to motivate with the use of influence rather than power.
- Knowledge of the business equation so that individuals can set priorities and make the required decisions in an organic control system.
- Ability of managers to teach others what they have learned.

Appraisal

The appraisal system will provide managers with an effective way to focus attention on the revised goals and strategies of the organization. The organization must come to grips with the potential problems it creates when it focuses its measurement and control system on the search for high-potential entrepreneurs whose skills tend toward achieving short-term results.

The legacy of defining career success as upward mobility is that it encouraged people to spend more time on their own advancement than on the accomplishment of organizational goals. This implicit belief is reflected in the career development literature, particularly the literature focused on mentoring or the development of subordinates in the organization. Most articles maintained that managers who were still on a steep upward trajectory could not be expected to play the role of mentor to others in the organization. The role of teaching others was reserved for those who had plateaued! The measurement system that accepts this reality cannot support a learning organization. If the organization is to learn, then its leaders must be skilled at teaching.

Organizations will have to move away from measurements based only on bottom-line results and provide teeth for the often espoused belief that the processes by which the results are obtained are also important. General Electric has publicly wrestled with this problem and its letter to GE shareholders in the years 1991–1993 catalogs the efforts the organization made to shift the focus in the organization. Jack Welch said there were four types of managers: Those who don't make the numbers and don't embrace the values of the company; those who make the numbers and embrace the values; those who embrace the values but do not make the numbers; and, those who make the numbers but do not embrace the values.

In the first case, those who neither make the numbers nor live the values, the decision is easy. They will be severed from the organization in a humane way. The second case also is easy—these managers have a bright future with GE. The third case, those who live the values but do not make the numbers, is seen as an opportunity for a second chance because they were possibly put into the wrong job. The final case is the most difficult. Historically, when confronted with a manager who made the numbers but did not live the values, Welch claims the organization tended to wink at the shortcoming. But, no more. Welch told the shareholders that of the five officers who left the company in the past years only one left because he did not make the numbers.

Organizations must move away from admiring the bold decisive move and rewarding it with rapid movement to new positions since it tempts the ambitious into recommending short-term strategies that may have a negative impact on the long-term viability of the project of business.

Rewards

In the past decade, the wage gap between the top and the bottom of most American companies has widened. If the many count, then the pay system should reflect that reality. In addition to fostering a sense of fair play in middle managers and blue-collar workers who are being asked to shoulder a greater share of the decision-making responsibility in organizations, it also plays a role in determining who will be attracted to work in the organization. Are they more likely to find satisfaction in developing a high-performance organization or in the prospects for a fast-track career? The cooperative behavior needed to maintain a new way organization is more dependent on the former than the latter.

The modern organization believes that vigilance will permit it to avoid the unwanted consequences of extreme pay systems, but there is little evidence to support this contention. When experienced middle managers realize that they are not going to make the jump to senior management, where more and more of the benefits of organizational membership can be found, they are more likely to leave the organization since there is a heightened sense of relative deprivation. When they leave, they take with them the accumulated knowledge of 15 or 20 years' experience in the company and leave a hole in the network needed to maintain a new way organization.

Senior managers also understand that while their discretionary pay may depend on the overall performance of the organization, their careers depend on their performance in a small part of the organization for which they bear direct responsibility; and it is here that the short-term tradeoffs are likely to be made. It also provides an enormous temptation to use corporate assets for personal career advancement.

Development

The role of development is critical to the new way organization. Running a process-based organization requires managers to know a great deal more than their own job or function.

These heavy developmental demands come at a time when resources of both managerial time and money are frequently stretched to the limit. The challenge is to move from the development of a few to run the organization to organizational development, from investments in high-potential human resources to investment in high-leverage human resources.

How can the available resources be leveraged? By educating teams devoted to critical projects and by making investments in those employees who are willing to share what they learn with others in the organization.

Finally, two issues that new way organizations must be able to manage if they are to succeed: diversity and stability.

Diversity

We are all aware that organizations are placing emphasis on diversity because the implications of the changing demographics. If fewer than 50 percent of the new hires are white males, then the organization that does not find a way to fairly develop and utilize the talents of the majority will find themselves in the position of drawing from an ever smaller pool of candidates to solve the organization's problems and evolve its strategies.

But, perhaps even more important than racial, ethnic, and gender equality is the notion that organizations successful at integrating people of different backgrounds and experiences will also be more successful at incorporating divergent opinions into their decision-making processes. Theses challenges to conventional thinking may well hold the key to survival in a globally competitive world.

Stability

New way organizations require greater levels of stability than traditional hierarchically controlled organizations. New way organizations depend on effective team performance rather than individual effort. This requires an investment in team development. It is the difference between preparing a baseball team and a basketball team. Baseball players can practice alone while honing their batting, pitching, or fielding skills. Basketball players, on the other hand, must practice together if they are to achieve excellence.

CONCLUDING REMARKS

Human resource management in the 1990s will play a significant role in creating value-added resources in organizations and provide those who successfully make the transition from the old way to the new way of managing people with a significant competitive advantage. It is an advantage that is difficult to achieve but also difficult to duplicate by competitors and thus can provide a long-term edge in today's difficult environment.

FOR FURTHER READING

Beer, Michael, et al., *Managing Human Assets: The Groundbreaking Harvard Business School Program* (New York: Free Press, 1985).

Fombrun, Charles, Noel M. Tichy, and Mary Anne Devanna, *Strategic Human Resource Management* (New York: John Wiley, 1984).

Fortune, "So What Is the Best Way to Pay," June 5, 1989.

Galbraith, Jay, *Organizational Design* (Reading, MA: Addison-Wesley, 1977).

Kanter, Rosabeth Moss, *The Change Masters* (New York: Simon and Schuster, 1983).

Mirvis, Phillip, *Building The Competitive Workforce: Investing in Human Capital for Corporate Success* (New York: John Wiley, 1993).

Pasmore, William A., *Creating Strategic Change: Designing the Flexible High-Performing Organization* (New York: John Wiley, 1994).

Pfeffer, Jeffrey, *Competitive Advantage Through People: Unleashing the Power of the Workforce* (Boston: Harvard Business School Press, 1994).

Tichy, Noel, and Mary Anne Devanna, *The Transformational Leader* (New York: John Wiley, 1986).

OPERATIONS MANAGEMENT: PRODUCTIVITY AND QUALITY PERFORMANCE

9

Linda G. Sprague

Severe competition in world markets has focused attention on productivity and quality performance, particularly within U.S. companies but also companies in Canada, Europe, Asia, and Australia. The operations function within an organization bears ultimate responsibility for output and, hence, for quality and productivity, as well as for cost and delivery performance. The result has been a heightened awareness of the operations function and its contribution to the effectiveness of the organization and, ultimately, for the success of its strategic plans and marketing strategies.

In well-managed organizations, this awareness leads to the development of effective operations functions that become key parts of the competitive arsenal. In too many organizations, this awareness comes too late—when the marketing campaign is strangled by lack of product, when market share slips because the competition is offering superior service, or when a financial crisis looms.

Operations management constitutes the fundamental action of an organization—the provision of goods and services. This chapter reviews a number of the concepts, techniques, and methodologies used in the design, development, analysis, and management of operations, and relates them to the strategic mission of the firm. The basic concepts of capacity, standards, inventory, scheduling, and control will provide a basic framework for the analysis of strategic options available to an organization. The underlying theme behind this framework is a presumption of pervasive quality in all that the organization does.

203

OPERATIONS FOR PRODUCT AND SERVICE ORGANIZATIONS

The United States is the first economy in history dominated by service delivery instead of manufacturing or agricultural activity. Fewer than 25 percent of the American workforce are employed in the manufacturing sector. While the United States is first, the major industrial powers are rapidly catching up:

Percentage of Workers in the Service Industry in 1990[1]

United States	74%
Britain	67%
Japan	65%
France	56%
Germany	55%

The old rule of thumb was that productivity growth was almost impossible in service operations, thereby offering some explanation for the slowdown in productivity growth in the United States during the 1980s. So much for the old rules: The recent surge in the U.S. economy's productivity has been powered by productivity growth in *both* manufacturing and services.

The concepts that influenced the development of management based in manufacturing industry are being adapted for application to service operations. At the same time, manufacturing organizations are learning that market success requires integration of customer service with the product itself. Success also requires identification of the myriad service activities that surround the actual manufacturing process making it equally effective and productive. Successful management of operations therefore requires effective management of a physical product's manufacture as well as of its full complement of presale, postsale, and manufacturing support services.

While it is commonplace to characterize an entire business or industry as either "manufacturing" or "service," this distinction is not useful for operations analysis. For example, IBM and Digital Equipment Corporation are categorized as *manufacturing* firms. Yet less than 10 percent of their workforces are directly engaged in manufacturing activities—and there is considerable effort to reduce this further through outsourcing and productivity improvement. Even within a manufacturing facility, the service functions that support the actual manufacture of product often dominate the direct manufacturing workforce. Production control, quality assurance, data processing, maintenance, manufacturing engineering, and methods—functions that serve the manufacturing core—are service operations that demand excellence if the central mission of the firm is to be achieved.

Therefore, the focus here is on operations whether within a manufacturing firm or a service organization. Indeed, at the product planning stage, the combination of product and service that will be delivered to the customer should be designed as an entity. The marketing phrase *bundle of benefits* is a good description of the complete package that is being offered for sale. This more comprehensive definition of the "product" makes it possible to better design and develop the set of operations required to carry out the marketing mission.

Examples of the product/service package being offered to the customer are common in industrial sales. Large-scale computer systems and custom-designed machine tools required substantial presale design and development, and considerable engineering development of both hardware and software. After-sale service and maintenance can be more profitable than the original sale, and excellence in after-sale support can help sell the product.

The potential involvement of the customer in the production process sets the stage for some of the critical differences between service and manufacturing operations. In general, the less direct contact the customer has with the mechanisms for delivery of the product or service, the greater the opportunity to employ factory methods emphasizing high productivity and efficiency. When the customer becomes part of the process, efficiency has traditionally been traded off against the customer's perception of quality. Extreme examples of this dichotomy include automatic tellers versus a personal banking service, a fast-food restaurant versus a chef-owned and operated small restaurant, or a high-volume furniture manufacturer versus a cabinetmaker.

A FRAMEWORK FOR THE ANALYSIS OF OPERATIONS

The abundance of techniques and methodologies employed in operations analyses can sometimes make it seem that the central problem—the provision of goods and services to the customer—is a secondary issue. Five basic concepts, interconnected, provide a framework for understanding the basic management task, as well as for selecting and exploiting the many analytic techniques and methodologies available today. These concepts also describe the key managerial activities that compose an organization's operations functions.

These concepts drive and support the methodologies and permeate the fundamental vocabulary of the field:

- Capacity.
- Standards.
- Scheduling.

- Inventory.
- Control.

The most powerful insights for management derive from understanding these basic concepts, and then their interrelationships. Just-in-time (JIT) systems are good examples: These are often described as methods for driving inventories down, yet no explicit attention is given to inventory in the development and implementation of a JIT system. The focus is on improved control over capacity and its arrangement, on careful attention to the design of standard methods and procedures, on elimination of schedule variability—on everything except inventory itself. Successful JIT programs result in dramatically reduced inventories through concerted and sustained attack on all four of the other basic notions. The relationship among the fundamental concepts provides an organization with a framework for the design and constant development of effective operations.

Capacity and Its Management

Capacity is the ability to yield output. It is a measure of capability, a statement about the load limits of an operational system. Capacity is determined from a complex mix of the organization's resources relative to the demands of those resources, but essentially capacity is a description of the system's limitations.

In most organizations, the operations function is uniquely charged with the responsibility for developing and maintaining capacity. Since productivity is, in its simplest form, a ratio or outputs to inputs, management of capacity—the denominator in the productivity equation must be the source of any substantial and sustained productivity improvement.

Whereas capacity is often viewed as a relatively straightforward notion—"We can turn out 15,000 units a week" or "We can handle 350 customers an hour"—it is, in fact, a complex concept. For example, these statements about two organizations' capabilities are simple shorthand measures that can effectively mask important operational and customer service issues. Such brief statements about capacity are acceptable only as quick sketches: the process of definition and establishment of the organization's ability to achieve its objectives must be a continual effort. Business process engineering (or *re*engineering) is the most recent attempt to focus attention on the never-ending problem of most effectively matching resources and their configurations to the ever-changing needs of customers.

Defining an organization's capacity requires identification of those inputs and resources that place limitations on the ability to produce—to yield product and/or service. Such an analysis of capacity can be broken down into analyses of the common components of capacity—the *determinants of capacity*. The four determinants of capacity are *manpower, machinery, materials, and money*—sometimes called the "4 Ms of Manufacturing."

The idea is straightforward: The ability to yield output depends on the right mix of these elements, and whichever is in shortest supply—the key determinant—determines the capacity of the organization. Ensuring the right mix of these determinants over time is the fundamental task of capacity management. As such, capacity management is a key element in the marketing program, particularly where service is being provided.

The mix of manpower, machinery, and materials is critical for effective operation of an organization. To make matters more difficult, however, the mix within each of the elements is crucial. For example, hospital manpower must include the appropriate mix of physicians (and the specialty mix within that set), nursing personnel, technicians, housekeeping, maintenance, and so on.

As automation increases, the mix of required personnel changes dramatically. With relatively low levels of automation, the skill-level profile for a manufacturing operation approximates a bell-shaped curve: most work requires semiskilled labor, there are relatively few highly skilled workers, and there are comparatively few low-skilled jobs. The skill-level profile required to support an increasingly automated environment changes radically: It becomes bimodal, with most work requiring either high skill levels or very low levels that promise little growth potential for the incumbents. There are relatively fewer jobs at the semiskilled level.

Examples of unskilled jobs in automated manufacturing would be general lugging and toting, opening boxes that are not ready for introduction onto an automated line when delivered and, perhaps, housekeeping and cleaning; in the service arena, such jobs would include data entry tasks, mail opening and sorting, and other routine physical handling of paperwork to bring it into form for automatic processing. The highly skilled jobs at the other end of the bimodal distribution could easily include electronic, electrical, mechanical, and computer hardware and software skills—all in one person.

Where service is being provided, the customer's direct experience with the process of service provision becomes a major factor in the design of capacity. As extreme examples, contrast a dirty, noisy, smelly manufacturing plant staffed by surly employees with a spacious, nicely decorated, air-conditioned, modern branch bank staffed by friendly people. Ignoring for the moment that the plant is probably not meeting its productivity potential, both environments could preclude "high quality" as perceived by customers. The perceived "quality" at the bank would drop dramatically if any one of its capacity elements were to change. If you have ever dealt with a bank or restaurant during an air-conditioning breakdown in August, you are familiar with the customer service implications of a capacity determinant failure in a service operation.

Technology in Terms of Manpower and Machinery

Manufacturing firms tend to describe their capacity in terms of physical technology, whether or not this is strictly true. A machine shop, for example, might be described as having "1,000 machine hours of capacity per week" or a stamping operation as being capable of "100 smacks per minute." These statements are tacitly understood to be true only if the machines are appropriately staffed. Another common statement about capacity focuses on the output rate in terms of finished product—65 cars per hour, 100,000 gallons per day, and so on. The immediate image is of physical technology—machinery, hardware, capital equipment.

This emphasis on physical technology carries over into service operations where hotels are described by their number of rooms, hospitals by their number of beds, and banks by their dollar assets. Such simplified capacity descriptions that focus on a single aspect of the physical technology are in common use because people in these businesses can quickly envision their implications. An experienced hospital administrator, for instance, can almost instinctively recite the detailed personnel implications of change from 275 to 350 beds. Similarly, a plant manager is able to quickly provide rough estimates of the labor impact of a growth in output from 10,000 to 14,000 boards per day. These mangers understand intimately the relationships between single process or output definitions of capacity and the rest of the capacity determinants.

Whether in a manufacturing or service operation, however, the physical technology alone does not constitute the capacity to provide goods and services. From an operations perspective, "technology" means humans and their machines. The physical technology must be matched with the appropriate labor-embodied technology—people with their skills, training, and talents. This is "manpower" in the list of capacity determinants. It is the mix of physical technology and labor-embodied technology that establishes an organization's capacity.

It is commonplace to associate physical technology with manufacturing operations, and labor-embodied technology with service operations. This association has some merit, particularly if we view extremes: The steel industry's capacity seems dominated by the massive scale of its physical equipment, and the hospital's operating expenses are dominated by personnel costs. Yet, steel industry capacity and productivity are equally determined by its steelworkers, as has become increasingly clear with the recent successes of steel minimills that have embraced new approaches to workforce management. And, when a power failure occurs in a hospital, its ability to provide care can quickly drop to a life-threatening level.

The *mix* of physical and labor-embodied technology determines productive capacity for an organization. How much and what kind of each of the forms of technology are required to meet customers' needs is an increasingly complex question. This is the arena in which the economists' concept of "substitution of capital for labor" becomes the issue of the appropriate level of automation. As information technology becomes increasingly accessible, a wholly new dimension is added to the capacity mix equation.

This description of technology, consisting of both machinery (and today including computer hardware and software) and people, is not the popular definition. To many people, "technology" implies inhuman (and likely inhumane) machinery working with a "mind" of its own. Managers who deal with the most sophisticated machinery available know only too well that an effective operational technology is possible only if appropriate physical technology is matched with the right labor-embodied technology.

Information technology has evolved rapidly from an exotic machine attended by highly trained specialists to ubiquitous gear used throughout organizations by everyone from sales clerks to senior executives. The highly trained computer specialists—in hardware, software (and now "firmware")—remain, but now reside largely at the suppliers. Still, it is worth remembering that the technical power likely sitting on your desk or in your briefcase was not available at any price and in any size only 25 years ago. Software development has shifted the balance, absorbing substantial labor-embodied technology, thereby permitting widespread use of what was quite recently astounding analytic and transaction capability. It should be no surprise that the full exploitation of this technological miracle is barely underway. The potential is just beginning to be realized, resulting in some dramatic restructuring of enterprises to take advantage of opportunities that continue to expand. A distinctive feature of some "business process reengineering" examples is the full exploitation of modern information technology.

The mix of physical and labor-embodied technology is generally the key determinant of capacity for an organization. While capacity can mean simply the raw ability to generate output, it more correctly means the ability of the organization to yield quality, variety, and delivery performance. The design of an organization's capacity is indeed a critical competitive tool.

Materials

Material resources are vital to effective operations. By its nature, a manufacturing operation is visibly dependent on material availability. A service operation is generally not thought to be critically dependent on material resources. The result, however, is often vast oversupply of nonessential materials that are loosely managed (and overstocked) because of their perceived low priority. This peculiar logic results in such phenomena as a $6 million inventory of pharmaceuticals and supplies at a large teaching hospital: this figure translates into $6,000 worth of linens, disposable supplies, drugs, and so forth, per patient available at all times. As you will see in the later discussion of inventory, too much material on hand can be as bad as too little.

It is a rare organization that has not had to cope with the results of a material shortage. The business press focuses regularly on the extreme shortage of one type of computer chip or another, and its impact on manufacturers of products ranging from personal computers through cars, toys, and kitchen appliances. The threat of fuel shortages causes headlines because of the potential effects on medical service delivery as well as on manufacturing capability.

These dramatic shortages of raw materials critical to a particular industry make good press. Yet, on a daily basis, small crises caused by material shortages occur that do not make the evening news: shortage of a particular blood type can halt critical surgery; delay in the delivery of the right forms has brought governmental agencies and some insurance companies to a standstill.

A vital segment of operations management focuses directly on maintaining a consistent supply of all materials necessary to achieve productive capacity, ensuring that materials will *not* become the key determinant of capacity.

Ensuring material supplies to operations (while part of the capacity determination) involves both the inventory and scheduling functions in an organization. Whatever the organizational structure and relationships, these functions must be carried out:

1. *Materials acquisition* tasks range from the establishment and maintenance of effective vendor relationships through product and process evaluations in light of material availabilities.

2. *Materials storage* generates the large inventory numbers shown on many balance sheets. The minimum necessary "storage" inventory is that being actively worked on in the production process. Yet, in many organizations more than 90 percent of this "work in process" inventory is in fact idle—waiting for something to happen.

3. *Materials logistics* has three basic aspects: distribution from the supplier to the firm, internal movement, and physical distribution to the customer. Distribution of finished product in a manufacturing organization is often a responsibility shared between operations and marketing. This latter function, which is a critical part of the marketing plan, often requires special expertise in transportation, routes and rates, distribution channels, and so on.

Money

The scale and form of an organization's capacity is substantially constrained by the availability of capital. This is dramatically apparent in small, relatively new companies where a corporate form of Catch-22 is at work: To lure a large order, the firm must have substantial new equipment, but to finance this capital expenditure the firm is required to show that the order is already in hand.

Larger, more mature organizations are more likely to have access to the funds necessary for expansion and/or replacement of physical technology through combinations of retained earning and external funds sources. In recent years, it has become apparent that some of the techniques for justification of new technology are wanting: Justifying modern technology through labor savings alone does not allow for the incorporation of such critical market needs as product flexibility, improved quality, and delivery performance. Capital budgeting, nominally a part of the organization's financial function, can play an important role in capacity determination. If the capacity determination activity is executed effectively, the result will be improved productivity and profit performance, which in turn can make money available for future capacity changes.

Aggregate capacity planning is the first phase in the process of capacity planning. At this stage, decisions are made about the overall scale of operations. It is therefore carried out for the longer range: The common planning horizon for aggregate capacity planning is beyond the maximum lead time of the elements of capacity. Given the long-term nature of aggregate planning, and the high cost usually associated with changes in the amount or kind of capacity, it is no surprise to find this activity as part of the strategic planning process at high level in the organization.

Since aggregate capacity planning is a crucial part of the organization's long-range strategy development, it cannot be carried out in isolation. Market forecasts and marketing strategies, in particular, must be developed concurrently with operations plans and strategies. The operations function is dependent on the marketing function for sound information about the competitive situation and alternatives for responding to the market. Similarly, the marketing function is dependent on accurate capacity planning if products and services are to be delivered in a manner consistent with the market strategy.

One of the most difficult aspects of long-range capacity planning is the matter of technological forecasting. Typically, considerable enthusiasm for such forecasting is applied to new product development. Equal attention should be given to the impact of technological development on processes for manufacturing and for service delivery.

Capacity Configuration

Capacity configuration encompasses the philosophy of operations reflected in the spatial arrangement of physical space and equipment. This design is often embedded in architecture, where it can become an overwhelming force preventing needed change in an organization. If poorly understood, physical arrangements can be the source of serious material and information flow problems and, as a result, the source of major productivity loss.

Capacity configuration, scale of operation, and effectiveness are closely linked. As Figure 9-1 shows, two combinations of scale and configuration type are not productive—the northeast and southwest corners of the Hayes/Wheelwright product/process matrix. Maintenance of the proper balance between volume and configuration is a constant management challenge. Drifting off the diagonal in this matrix without understanding the implications of the situation often causes major output and efficiency crises.

The extremes of philosophies of operation are shown as the end points of the "process structure" axis in Figure 9-1. Pure end-point cases are relatively rare in practice: Mixed mode or middle ground configurations are much more common.

In a *job shop,* the operational processes themselves set the dominant theme for the organization. This *process-dominated* capacity configuration results in groupings of like process capabilities. Traipsing through an outpatient clinic in an older hospital—from admitting (in the old building) to X-ray (in the basement of the new surgical building) to the lab (on the second floor of the annex), you personally experience the implications of a job-shop configuration. Similar equipment and specialized personnel cluster in a single place, with substantial advantages: All related expertise is together, permitting more effective professional supervision, training, and control. Specialized equipment is physically concentrated, increasing the potential for higher utilization and easier maintenance. Customer service is not a primary issue.

An important characteristic of such an arrangement is the flexibility provided by the process-dominated capacity configuration. In theory, such a structure can accept any product request: Since there is no standard flow pattern, any sequence can be developed and implemented. The phrase "jumbled flow" describes the result—each "product" has its own route through and around the available capacity. For example, while you went from admitting to the lab to an examining room because of your unique treatment requirements, I went directly to X-ray, then to the lab, back to X-ray, and then to the orthopedic clinic. In a manufacturing environment with this configuration theme, departments are focused on manufacturing technologies—milling, drilling, turning, inspection, grinding, and so on. Any part can be manufactured in any sequence. Products requiring a sequence of milling, drilling, and grinding can as easily be accommodated as those requiring grinding, then drilling and turning, followed by finish grinding.

FIGURE 9-1 Product structure: Product life-cycle stage

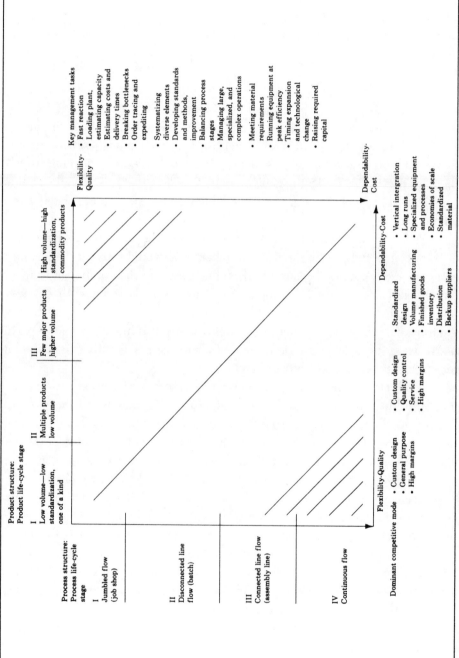

From: "Link Manufacturing Process and Product Life Cycles," R.H. Hayes and S.C. Wheelwright, *Harvard Business Review,* January-February 1979.

Capacity planning and management are extremely difficult in a job shop. Material handling and control is a constant problem, as is management of the work-in-process inventory level. Because of the diversity of tasks facing each process-focused department, high skill levels are generally required of the workforce. The other side of this coin is the flexibility to do anything within the skills of the workforce and within the capabilities of the general-purpose equipment.

Batch flow is what happens to a job shop that begins to produce more than one of a kind. In theory, a job shop never makes the same thing twice. However, in practice the "one-off" is quite rare. The manufacture of a single unique machine tool, for example, will require multiples of many parts—sets of identical shafts, support brackets, special-purpose bolts and screws, and so on. And, although a particular product may be unique, it is likely that it is actually a unique combination of several standard subassemblies with a small percentage of truly unique parts.

The result is the requirement for numbers of the same part, subassembly, or even completed product, but not numbers that would warrant dedication of equipment and people. Because it takes time to set up the equipment to manufacture each part, there is a logic that suggests making more than one—a "batch"—of the required parts. While modest capacity savings result through grouping parts to take advantage of setups, the result is higher inventory particularly when the batches are determined by forecast needs rather than absolute requirements based on orders in hand.

Batch flow shops are a compromise when there is repetition in parts manufacture. Much of the research in manufacturing operations is focused on the batch flow shop because it is so difficult to manage. While the hope is realization of the flexibility advantages of the job shop coupled with some of the efficiency of the assembly line, the reality is often the worst case—the awkward material flows of the job shop with the inflexibility of the assembly line.

In an *assembly line,* the product requirements dominate and form the process structure. This *product-dominated* capacity configuration results in regular movement of the product past the capacity requirements, arranged in proper sequence. A physical examination at a "multiphasic screening center" or at a military induction center provides personal experience with the important characteristics of this arrangement of physical and labor capacity. All incoming clients go through the same sequence.

The phrase *assembly line* carries a quite specific meaning in manufacturing. The essential characteristics of an assembly line are (1) continuous uniform movement of work, (2) a fixed sequence of balanced operations, and (3) simultaneous performance. If any of these features is missing, the work is not being accomplished by a true assembly-line method.

In a product-dominated structure, the physical facilities are arranged in the sequence required by the product. So, if a manufactured product requires milling, then drilling, then milling again, milling capacity will be split to accommodate the product's requirements.

The automobile assembly line is probably the most widely known—and least understood—example of this form of capacity configuration. Its advantages include smooth, logical, and efficient flow of product, leading to reduced in-process inventory needs and relatively limited material handling. Since the assembly line is dedicated to the production of a high volume of the same product, and since the work is typically broken down into very small tasks, relatively unskilled labor can be used.

On the other hand, an assembly-line style of operation has severe limitations, the most serious of which is the line's lack of flexibility. Once a line is designed and established for one product, it is difficult for that line to produce any other product: change in the product means change in the design of the line. A further, and often more serious, lack of flexibility is the insensitivity of the line to volume changes. The classic response to a drop in volume requirements is a shutdown of the line in order to balance supply with demand; when demand increases, so does overtime, second shift work and, ultimately, third shift.

As product volumes increase, most organizations attempt to gain the efficiencies of the product-dominated capacity configuration without losing the flexibility of the process-dominated structure. In manufacturing, modern equipment technologies have pushed the range of the effective beyond the narrow band suggested in Figure 9-1. Programmable machinery, for example, can provide flexibility along with the premium efficiencies associated with higher volumes: Computer-controlled machines can often shift from one product to another with little physical change required.

A fundamental notion in the design of an assembly line is the concept of balance—ensuring that each station on the line has exactly the same amount of work to do in order to maintain the steady and productive flow of output. In a perfectly balanced assembly line, each worker contributes the same amount of work to the product resulting in smooth flow and complete productivity for each person. This basic notion can also be applied at a more global level in the analysis of, for example, the movement of product through all steps from the generation of raw material to distribution to the ultimate customer.

Whether the analyses are carried out at the micro or macro level, the same rule applies: The capacity of the entire system is determined by the element with the least capacity availability, or the largest amount of work to be done. The work for this point is also the most descriptive—the bottleneck.

Continuous flow is the objective of the assembly line: yet continuous flow is not truly realized until the material itself is fluid. Continuous flow is seen in oil refineries, milk-processing plants, continuous flow bread-making machines—literally pipelines. Capacity is physically limited by the bottleneck, the narrowest section of the pipe, and work-in-process inventory is specified by the length and diameter of the pipe. Flexibility is limited to variants within the inputs such as crude oil from different sources with different natural characteristics.

Although the horizontal axis of the Hayes/Wheelwright framework is called "product structure," meaning the product's place on the product life cycle, in fact it is a measure of volume. From the point of view of the producer, the number of similar (ideally identical) products required is the critical issue. At the extremes, if every product is to be truly unique, the job shop is the appropriate process choice; if 500 cars are being sold every day, the assembly line is the answer to the process choice question.

The question becomes complex when, as is almost inevitably the case, "a few" of the same products are being sold while other "uniquely configured" products are also needed; or when the 500 cars sold each day are not exactly the same. A common problem for small start-up manufacturers is movement across the top of the Hayes/Wheelwright framework as "success" set in and more and more "unique" products must be produced in the job shop environment that was appropriate in the firm's early days. Moving down the process structure axis requires more than just different equipment: It requires different job skills, especially on the part of the management.

An important insight that becomes clear through the Hayes/Wheelwright framework is the critical importance of *focus*—preventing the operations function from trying to do everything at once. The classic example is the difficulty of getting a single prototype through a dedicated assembly-line style environment; for example, trying to squeeze this year's models for the annual furniture show onto the schedule for regular high-volume runs of current styles. While it can be done (and too often is), the disruption to the basic operation shows up in reduced productivity and, ultimately, effectiveness. The other side of this is inserting a steady high-volume job into a job shop: Here the talents and skills of the highly versatile workforce are wasted on repetitious unskilled tasks.

A well-known method for getting around the problem—basically trying to design for all advantages of both end points while avoiding the disadvantages of each—is the manufacturing cell. In its classic form, the cell is developed after a *group technology* analysis. In its original form, this analysis is carried out within a job shop that is manufacturing thousands of different parts. The analysis consists of examining the sequence of operations of each manufactured part, seeking groups of parts that share roughly the same technological sequence. When the groups are identified, machines are moved together into cells that permit the parts to move smoothly through the sequence of machines.

The rules governing the operation of a manufacturing cell are quite straightforward:

1. A part made in a cell is made *only* in that cell.
2. A cell makes *only* the parts assigned to it.
3. Parts go through the cell in one direction only, skipping a machine if required.
4. All prints, jigs, fixtures, and tools required for the machining of the parts assigned to a cell are kept at that cell.

Even with no additional analysis of the parts involved, dramatic improvements result immediately when job shop manufacture is shifted to cell manufacturing *provided* that the analyses have been done thoroughly and that the simple rules are followed. Material handling drops from days or weeks to minutes, thus radically reducing the manufacturing cycle time for the affected parts and therefore cutting work-in-process inventory levels for these parts. Since a major fraction of setup time for a manufactured part consists of tracking down prints, tools, and so on, setup times are normally cut in half even without any attention to the details of the setup itself.

Since the parts assigned to a manufacturing cell tend to be roughly the same physical size, further setup time reductions occur naturally since no allowance need be made for serious changes in the size of parts going onto a machine. If the group technology analysis is followed by an intensive setup time reduction program, it is common to see setup times drop from hours to minutes, thereby permitting economic manufacture of very small lot sizes, further contributing to cycle time and WIP inventory level reductions.

All of this supposes that the workforce staffing the cell is prepared for a work pattern very different from that of either a job shop or assembly-line environment. A job shop places a premium on high levels of specialized skills—master machinists specializing in a type of machine. The assembly line places a premium on exact repetition of short-cycle tasks. The cell worker must master a variety of types of machinery, yet there will be repetition because of the limitation on the number of parts going through the cell.

A manufacturing cell offers improved efficiencies as well as the considerable flexibility that derives from manufacturing cycle time reduction. However, once established, the cell requires vigilance to ensure that its potential is met and maintained. As new products are developed and old ones dropped from the line, there will be changes in the parts required. Maintaining the integrity of a successful manufacturing cell over a period of years requires sustaining the level of analysis that created it.

When this form of analysis is applied to the business as a whole—particularly when service support operations are the basis of the business—the result is now being called *business process reengineering*. There are a number of variations on the theme of reengineering, but they share some characteristic steps:

1. Specify the customers' objectives.
2. Describe and analyze the existing processes, identifying those that add value.
3. Reengineer (redesign) the processes to most effectively meet customers' objectives.

The scope of process engineering can vary from pieces of the operation (e.g., improving the paperwork flow surrounding the ordering/receiving/inspecting/paying cycle) through the business as a whole. Some proponents champion only the latter, insisting on "radical" rethinking and redesign of the entire business. Others are more modest, urging that various functions be reengineered to better meet customer needs. An important aspect of the reengineering activity is exploitation of modern information technology in the redesign of processes to meet customers' needs.

To take a very simple example, a utility examined its purchasing-receiving-payment cycle and found that as many as seven organizational groups were involved with all incoming materials and supplies: the originating department, the purchasing department, the receiving room, the quality control department, inventory control, accounts payable, and the using department (not necessarily the originating department).

Within these groups, more than a dozen people handled every purchase, regardless of size. After determining that more than 80 percent of purchases were less than $100 in value—and in the spirit of radical reform—the firm thoroughly reengineered the process for these orders. Originating departments requiring "ordinary" (more in a minute) purchases for less than $100 call the "authorized supplier," place the order, receive the goods, and write the check for acceptable goods. Actual lead time experienced by originating/using departments dropped through dramatic contraction of time taken up with ordering/receiving/inspecting. Speedup in payment to suppliers resulted in improved supply reliability. Quality problems identified by using departments were transmitted directly to suppliers, permitting faster and more appropriate response to problems.

The implications of this simplification are easy to see: Purchased items must be identified as ordinary by the purchasing department, single-source "authorized suppliers" must be identified by the purchasing department, receiving capability must be set up within originating (now also using) departments, and these departments must be given a set of blank checks (with a $100 limit). Consider, though, the ramifications:

*   The *originating/using department* now deals directly with the supplier, receives and approves incoming materials and supplies, and pays the bills.

- The *purchasing department* must identify ordinary materials and supplies, qualify sole-source suppliers, track supplier performance to maintain qualification; no longer places orders for purchases less than $100.
- The *receiving room* may physically handle incoming materials and supplies but no longer handles associated paperwork including transfer to quality control.
- *Quality control department* is no longer directly involved through receiving inspection; must help establish incoming inspection procedures to be carried out by the using department.
- *Inventory control* is no longer involved in receipt of some incoming materials and supplies.
- *Accounts payable* is no longer involved in actually paying bills for purchases less than $100; must establish control procedures based on paperwork coming from using departments.

The follow-on effects of a partial process reengineering make implementation difficult since so many segments of the organization are likely to be affected. The impact on jobs throughout affected organizational groups can be severe.

A serious concern where process reengineering is underway is a program for sustaining the successes that may result. The preceding example was done through a "systems and procedures" (S&P) analysis in the early 1960s, with dramatic effect on productivity and cost. The improvement for the "customer," in this instance the using department, was noted at the time although it was not the centerpiece of these S&P analyses. The success lasted only about three years. It is not difficult to see how the improvement collapsed: the logic of this process within the organization interfered with the "normal" operation of the affected departments and was based on trusting the using departments to carry out a number of previously specialized tasks. The decay began with concerns about accountability since using department forepersons were writing company checks, carrying out inspections, and placing orders directly with suppliers. It was a short step to a return of the original process—in order to maintain control, provide proper technical expertise, and so on.

The potential within a process *re*engineering is as large as the difficulty of sustaining it once accomplished. The most successful approach for the long term is to focus on the work process—which is by definition continuous. As customer needs shift, the processes required to support those requirements must evolve. Freezing any process assumes the unlikely situation of no change in what must be done. An organization's capacity is a function of the processes that it has in place to satisfy customer requirements.

Regardless of the capacity configuration, two essential issues affect the management of capacity—capacity mix and capacity balance. The dynamic nature of demand makes maintaining the most effective mix and balance a constant struggle. It is commonplace to find an organization with its capacity perfectly mixed for the previous year's demand. In the determination of the organization's capacity, theoretical concepts such as economies and diseconomies of scale or learning and experience curves become the realities of brick and mortar, and of people with their talents, skills, education, and training.

Standards

The language of companies is generally taken to be that of accounting, measuring activity in dollars or other currencies. For the operations function, time is the essence of the matter—the time it takes to make something, to do some task, to provide some service. Standards are the detailed time estimates that permit planning of capacity requirements for labor and equipment. They are also the yardsticks by which the amount and quality of output are measured.

At its heart, the establishment of standards for performance can, and often does, involve time-and-motion study. When properly performed, such a study encompasses job design as well as work, operations, and process analysis. These techniques, often associated in the public mind with exploitation of labor and the struggles of the union movement, are widely misunderstood. Until recently, they were downplayed in most organizations. The corporate enthusiasm for so-called Japanese methods brought a number of these techniques for the analysis of work back into favor during the 1980s. The present focus on process reengineering brings some of these analytic techniques squarely into the center of the action.

Process flowcharts and material process charts are the basis of the analyses underlying process engineering. The symbols used for process analysis were introduced by the Gilbreths in the late 1920s, and were later approved by the American Society of Mechanical Engineers (ASME):

Activity	Description	Symbol
Operation	Adds value	■
Transport	Movement	●
Inspection	Assures quality	▼
Delay/storage	Interruption in the process	●

A process flowchart shows each activity by its symbol. Only "operation" contributes directly to the product or service: The objective is to develop a new process flow that is dominated by value-adding operations, with all other activities minimized.

The process flowchart appears simple, but developing one is rarely a straightforward activity. Typically, disagreements abound about exactly how certain operations are done, which sequences can be altered, under which circumstances, and how often, even what does and does not add value. Once the current process "map" is drawn, the question "WHY?" is the foundation of the next step in the analysis:

- Why is this step done?
- Why is this done at this point?
- Why is this done in this department?
- Why is this done by this person?

There are two objectives: achieving customer satisfaction, and using the minimum non-value-added activity. A handbook[2] prepared in 1958 for the Work Simplification Conference recommends the following steps for moving from analysis of an existing process to development of the improved (reengineered) process:

1. *Work with facts—not opinions.* Opinions are difficult to work with and cause many arguments. Facts, on the other hand, are easy to work with and tend to produce definite conclusions. A fact does not vanish when we ask *Why?*

2. *Work on causes—not effects.* A bucket under the drip is not the cure for a leaky roof. If a fountain pen leaks, the user does not put on a rubber glove but instead attempts to get the pen repaired. Get at the causes of the difficulty in order to make the best improvements.

3. *Work with reasons—not excuses.* Excuses dodge the question and often cover up the facts. Find out why every detail is handled the way it is. Teamwork in a green-light atmosphere usually minimizes excuses. ("Green-light atmosphere" means an environment that welcomes new ideas and avoids "red-light statements" such as "We tried that once and it didn't work," "That's a dumb idea," "Never work—too complicated." Work simplification's ideal environment was characterized by this slogan: "The mind is like a parachute: it only works when it's open.")

The techniques that underlay the setting of standards are the same as those at the foundation of process engineering, since sound process and job design depend on analyses of flow, balance, speed, repeatability and, ultimately, doing just what needs to be done to satisfy customers.

The use of standards for planning and estimating costs, delivery, and service promises is difficult and sometimes exasperating. When done routinely, it is rarely a source of profound organizational distress. However, when analyses of processes and work are ignored until crises occur, major upheavals are likely to result. The use of standards for evaluation and control, on the other hand, is at the heart of the majority of labor disputes.

Scheduling

Essentially the act of detailed planning, scheduling is generally understood to mean the designating of work to be done, either from incoming orders or from forecasts of future demand. It is the function of coordination of resources, of their allocation and arrangement, of their organization by time and place. Scheduling is the task of appointing or designating in advance a particular arrangement of manpower and physical resources to ensure that the demands of customers are effectively fulfilled.

An important first element of this activity is the conversion of incoming information about demand into the impact of that demand on the available capacity. In one sense, the operations function in an organization is less concerned about the demand itself than in the load that the demand imposes on the capacity. This focus on the processes for yielding output rather than the output itself can get out of hand: Operations managers sometimes forget that effective operations management depends on keeping the customer, the product *and* the process in perspective. Customer service, productivity and, ultimately, profitability depend on the matching up of supply and demand. If capacity management can be characterized as the generation of supply, scheduling can be viewed as the linking of supply with that demand.

There are three levels at which scheduling is carried out:

1. *Aggregate scheduling.* Generally done concurrently with the development of the aggregate capacity plan, this establishes the overall capability of the organization for the longer term—typically one to three years.
2. *Master scheduling.* Assignment of work to specific time periods, using a combination of real orders and forecasts, with a shorter time horizon—typically three to nine months.
3. *Dispatching.* Decision making at the point of service provision or product manufacture to match up supply and demand at execution.

This hierarchy of scheduling sets constraints that limit the possibilities available to the short-range activity, particularly evident when the organization links scheduling activity with capacity planning. At the moment of execution—when dispatching occurs—the dispatcher can react only within the limits set by the capacity availability, which is linked to the previously developed master schedule.

Service operations add several complications to this already difficult management task. In many situations, the "job" being scheduled is a person who will perceive the schedule, and may even resist it. The schedule itself then becomes a critical factor in the customer's perception of the service delivered and of its quality. Queue management in a manufacturing operation is the essence of work-in-process inventory control: In a service operation, it is as important to customer satisfaction as is the delivery of the service itself.

Material requirements planning (MRP) systems are the most widely used scheduling tools in manufacturing organizations. These computer-based information systems merge data about the structure of manufactured product, availability of its subassemblies and parts, and lead times with the requirements imposed by customer orders and forecasts. The result is information about when parts orders must be placed, and when work on parts manufacture and assembly must begin, in order to satisfy customers' demands.

The straightforward logic of an MRP system looks simple enough:

1. What does the customer want?
2. What do I have?
3. What do I need?

The "MRP Logic" in the center of Figure 9-2 is these three questions. This sketch appears simple enough; however, this simplicity masks fundamental decisions that will significantly affect the organization's ability to compete effectively.

Each segment of the MRP flow diagram is a set of management decisions, often regarding the nature of the available capacity, which must continually evolve to provide complete customer satisfaction. Overall inventory positions as well as customer service performance are essentially determined by the decisions implied in the MRP system flow diagram.

More recently, manufacturing resource planning (MRPII) has become popular. MRPII is the evolution and extension of a manufacturing-focused MRP system to encompass the entire organization. The complete diagram in Figure 9-2 shows the important difference between MRP and MRPII: In the latter case, the business plan drives the financial, marketing, and production plans. In practice, this means that the information from financial, marketing, and production functions is integrated within a single system.

Manpower Scheduling

Most commonly, scheduling means job scheduling—routing an order through the production process, thereby generating work-in-process inventory. Difficult

FIGURE 9-2 Manufacturing resource planning (MRPII)

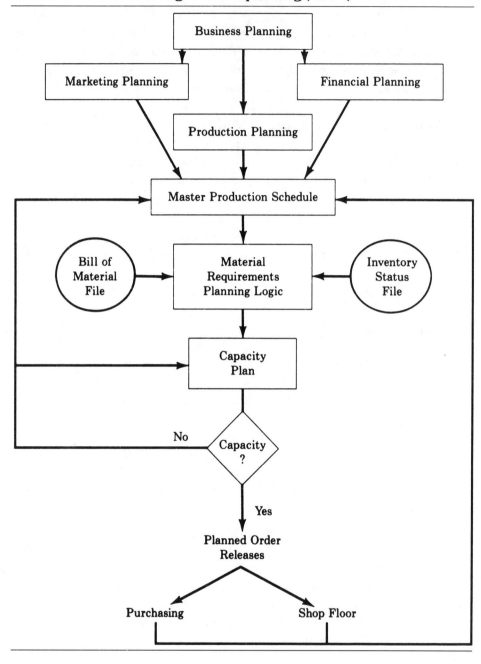

as this task is, it pales by comparison with the less publicized task of scheduling customers and personnel. In job scheduling, the item being scheduled—whether a steel shaft or a circuit board—is inert and insensible to its own schedule. While any number of people may become agitated about the route, or more likely the amount of time it takes, the item itself remains mute.

When people are the "items" being scheduled, however, the entire picture changes. If it is customers whose schedules are being planned—through a set of medical clinics, for instance—these *people* will experience the routing and any travel or delays, as well as the service being directly rendered. The customer's perception of service quality will be affected by the schedule itself. Further, the customer may not remain content with the schedule: rather than waiting patiently in a queue as would a metal part, the customer may demand to be moved to the head of the queue or may resent not being so moved; the customer may not follow instructions and may arrive early or late. In general, the customer may not willingly participate in execution of the planned schedule, thus having an impact on the effectiveness, efficiency, and productivity of the service operation.

Any operation that does not work a regular eight-hour day, five days a week, finds itself involved in the complexities of manpower scheduling as part of capacity determination. This then involves the operations function in such complexities as the impact of shift work on worker effectiveness (e.g., a particular concern when scheduling airline pilots), the development of equitable procedures for assigning workers to needed work schedules (the constant headache for a hospital's nursing department), and establishment of appropriate planning horizons for publication of staffing schedules (of great concern to all workers as holidays approach).

Inventory

Inventory is, after plant and equipment, a manufacturing firm's major asset. In certain analyses, it is treated as a "liquid" asset although, in fact, it has no cash value to speak of if the firm is badly in need of cash. The dominant view about inventory within the financial arm of an organization is that it is money tied up—money that has been converted into an asset that should be generating returns, that could be put to more productive use, and that has been transformed into an apparently uncontrollable form. Given this perception, it is no surprise to find that the financial arm of the organization has a simple attitude toward inventory—there is always too much of it.

On the other hand, inventory can permit immediate sale of goods that would take considerable time to produce. In this way, the customer is not directly exposed to the true manufacturing cycle time. If a customer can order a customized product for delivery within three weeks although the actual time to manufacture such a product is closer to three months, it means that inventories are providing improved customer service in the form of rapid delivery. Those closest to the customer in an organization—typically sales and marketing—will argue forcefully, therefore, for more inventory to better support the customer base.

These competing views—both of which have validity—help explain why inventory is so often an organizational "hot potato." One part of the organization sees inventory as a questionable use of the firm's money; another views it as a major contributor to the marketing strategy. Inventory management—as distinct from inventory control—involves the resolution of this dilemma to provide the best inventory system to support the organization's strategic and profit objectives.

Another view of inventory deserving mention is that of the people responsible for the physical stock itself. Inventory is composed of real items that must be picked up, put down, found, retrieved, moved, handled, assembled, air-conditioned, disassembled, cut, glued, stacked, and shipped. These items get misplaced and lost, they deteriorate and go out of style, rust and rot. The physical care of stock is a nightmare that feeds directly into the enormous work-in-process and finished goods inventory positions in many firms.

Those responsible for the physical stock have ambivalent feelings about it. On the one hand, the less physical stuff there is, the easier it is to control. On the other hand, the less there is, the more likely that whatever someone else needs will not be there. When that lapse occurs, considerable grief is usually poured onto the heads of those in charge of physical stock. The result is not surprising: From the point of view of the person well below the level of the balance sheet, more is better.

Classical theory formed the basis of U.S. inventory management systems and practice for decades. About 20 years ago, this theory began to take a considerable beating. Classical inventory theory was the original target at the beginning of the MRP crusade in the early 1970s. In the 1980s, it was blamed for the magnitude of manufacturing's work-in-process stock positions in many firms, in contrast with remarkably low levels at some highly publicized Japanese manufacturers.

These experiences make it worth asking if the basic rules of the game have changed. Have the earlier successes of the MRP crusade and some more recent results from Japanese-style systems confounded theory and established new rules for the management of that most pervasive and inconvenient of assets—the inventory?

Our review of inventory fundamentals will begin with what we have "always known" about inventory (the classical model) and evaluate that against its decades of testing in manufacturing firms here and abroad. This discussion will describe what we now know about both the theory and practice of inventory management. It will also show what is and is not unique about the currently popular JIT (Just in Time) approach.

The Classical (Old-Fashioned) Model

Classical inventory theory, which has been the underpinning for most production and inventory control systems for more than 50 years, holds that an organization's inventory is primarily a cost generator. The profit potential of inventory has received virtually no attention, and that almost exclusively by those in distribution management. The focus has been on the use of inventory to serve a number of basic organizational functions. To put this theory another way, inventory has been viewed as the appropriate solution to certain difficult manufacturing and distribution problems. Within this context, the basic theme of inventory management and control has traditionally been to seek the lowest combination of all associated costs while solving these inevitable problems.

Cost, in this regard, has come to mean those costs captured by the company's accounting system. Some costs and benefits associated with inventory are not captured or recorded in the normal cost accounting system, but these are typically ignored in favor of those readily available. Introduction of the profit implications of inventory is ordinarily accomplished through invocation of the concept of customer service with procedures for attempting to discover the costs of service failure.

The newer approach makes a fundamental shift: It states that inventory is so powerful a cost generator that it is to be avoided. Whether any benefit can or cannot be properly recognized and ascribed is not at issue, since the basic presumption is that total associated costs of inventory will inevitably dominate these benefits.

The effect of this primary assertion is to focus attention on the problems that must be attacked directly to prevent the creation of "problem-solving" inventories. The following examples demonstrate this approach when applied to the basic functions of inventory or, more specifically, to some problems of manufacturing and distribution that can indeed be ameliorated or solved through the use of inventories.

Variability

Variability is anathema to production processes. Whether the variability is the result of forecast error, human variety, "acts of God," or Murphy's Law, the result is the same: lowered efficiency, disruption of workflow, deterioration in customer service and, in the end, higher cost.

The variability comes in two forms—the predictable and the uncertain. Management responses to the problems of variability have tended to focus on inventory as the solution. A company with basically smooth production schedules all year in the face of marked seasonal demand is building and draining an inventory to compensate for this predictable form of variability. Wherever safety stocks are set, inventories are being used to protect the firm from uncertainties in demand or in supply.

Most organizations have become so accustomed to these variable inventories that they rarely attack the sources of the variability directly. The variability is viewed as beyond the organization's control, so the resulting inventories are deemed inevitable.

Much of traditional inventory theory is devoted to the proper calculation of these inventory levels. Unquestionably, from this arithmetic, variability is costly: The cost/cost trade-offs that go into the figuring make this expense clear. Moreover, the behavioral implications will lead to even greater inventory positions than those calculated. Crises over stockouts have caused more than one inventory planner to fudge the numbers a bit, adding a "safety lead time" here and there, "just in case."

Variety

The form of variability that deserves special mention in inventory management is variety—product variety in particular. Simple arithmetic, not to mention complex mathematics, clarifies the inventory implications of increased product variety. The more options and variety available in the product line, the greater the geographic availability of the product, the greater the resulting inventory positions. There is no news here: This basic notion has been understood for decades. A central tenet of traditional inventory theory states that product and geographic proliferation causes inventory growth. Bankruptcies caused by cashflow disasters tied to overgrown stock positions—too much in too many places—provide vivid support for this theoretical notion.

This form of variability, which leads inexorably to inventory growth, generally is hidden from view. Decisions to add to the firm's product line or to widen its distribution net are typically made in an environment in which inventory implications are not thoroughly considered.

Permanent decreases in inventory levels require minimization of variability and variety from the product as well as from supply and demand. Aggressive quality improvement and supplier relationship development programs, as well as comprehensive management of product design and conscientious management of bills of material, form the foundation of modern inventory reduction programs, thus attacking the problem at its roots.

Economy

In the realm of economy, classical inventory theory shines. From the working hypothesis that setup, or other one-time charges, are immutable facts of life, scale economies are balanced against the costs of inventorying the resulting overproduction. This is the thrust of the economic lot size (ELS) or economic order quantity (EOQ) calculation.

While considerable hand-wringing transpires over the highly suspect data used for such calculations, elation abounds in the end because of the robustness of the classical EOQ model. The model is, in fact, insensitive to data quality, can (and does) absorb substantial error and fiddling, and still produces usable results. Delight with the model may have helped obscure the merit in attacking data sources, in particular the realities of setup and order costs.

It takes minimal analysis to show that if setup times are directly attacked, the size of lots that can be economically produced drops. So, if inventories are to be avoided, setup and other one-time charges are natural targets.

Decoupling

Using inventories to "decouple" stations on an assembly line is the common solution to the problem of close dependency of one work site on earlier sites. The objective is to prevent the entire line's having to stop if one station on the line stops, and to compensate for individual variability at each workstation.

At a larger organizational level, this phenomenon is replicated to permit better decentralized control of separate operations. Again, the objective is to reduce the dependency of one element on other preceding elements. The overriding concern is the specter of an idle line or entire organization because of upstream supply problems.

If, however, the cost of an idle line may be less than the cost of defects, decoupling is best avoided. The more decoupling, the slower the response to real problems—and the greater the number of defects that will likely be produced before corrective action can be taken.

Pipeline

Geographic spread as a cause of inventory buildup is so well known and understood as to be ignored in practice. Our colleagues in physical distribution and logistics wage the constant battle against this pervasive inventory, the more so as business moves into the international arena. We may therefore expect to find a predilection for proximity to supply embedded in newer inventory management systems.

Manufacturing inventories, however, are only part of the story. Fully developed competitive strategies include all outbound and inbound inventories from raw materials supply through to the final consumer. While U.S. inventories continue to hold at historically low levels, remember that the sheer physical dimension of the United States will limit the drop in overall inventory positions, particularly if compared with geographically small nations.

Summary on Inventory

Two studies, one based on computer simulations and one on a survey of manufacturing firms, have come to a similar conclusion: Overall manufacturing performance is substantially improved through the following procedures:

- Setup and lot size reduction.
- Process yield improvement.
- Capacity smoothing.
- Increased worker flexibility.
- Product structure improvement.

A long-term study of U.S. factories led to several conclusions about what factors lead to improved productivity and overall factory performance. A sustained level of capital investment in physical technology was important, but systematic programs for waste reduction and the removal of work-in-process inventory were as critical. This study also pointed to the reduction of confusion on the factory floor as a key to productivity improvement.

The attitude that inventory is such a powerful cost generator that it is to be avoided has substantial merit where manufacturing inventories are concerned. This viewpoint means that the use of inventories to solve fundamental manufacturing problems is not warranted. This decision, in turn, means that those problems must be attacked directly. Direct attack on such fundamental problems as variety and variability characterizes Japanese production methods.

A classic example of the difference between the traditional approach to inventory control and that of JIT programs is evident in the EOQ model. An organization can respond to the result of an EOG analysis by accepting the calculated (and probably high) order quantity or, if the theme of inventory avoidance is predominant, observe that this high number comes from a high setup and then work on bringing down the high setup time.

In short, the rules of inventory management have not changed. If anything, the successes of "new" systems for inventory control have served to confirm the wisdom and rules that have been around for years. However, this substantiation is not necessarily good news: Management have not been avid adopters of the "older" methods. When it becomes apparent that the present enthusiasm for

JIT methods is masking the same old facts—and the hard work and tough decision making that go with it—the real risk is a return to business as usual. This reversal will signal the return to good old "just in case" inventories.

Control

The basics so far—capacity, standards, scheduling, and inventory—are determined beforehand. Capacity is configured and its scale determined, expectations about output are turned into standards, schedules are developed and posted, and inventory positions are set. The point of all this is execution: making refrigerators, producing cornflakes, serving a party of four hundred, delivering a package in 24 hours, providing emergency service to a heart-attack victim. The real question is: Did it work?

Control is an after-the-fact evaluation and correction if necessary. Was the capacity there and was it properly utilized? Was the objective of avoiding any customer's waiting more than three minutes achieved? Did the shipment arrive at 4:00 P.M. as promised? Was the inventory able to meet the needs of our customers? Without a control system to answer such questions, planning activities make little sense.

There are three steps to control:

1. *Observe.* See what actually happened.
2. *Compare.* Examine what did happen in the context of what was supposed to happen.
3. *Decide.* If the comparison shows that objectives were not met, determine what needs changing, and change it to ensure success next time.

This deceptively simple notion is at the heart of competitive success: The standards for comparison should be closely allied with what the market demands. The most common error organizations make is to measure and evaluate performance against historic or other convenient standards. Reliable delivery 95 percent of the time is not the point if the competition is guaranteeing 100 percent reliability.

The Management of Manufacturing and Service Operations

The five basic concepts described in Figure 9-3 are inextricably interrelated. Capacity utilization is a function of scheduling, scheduling is affected by inventory policy and practice, and inventory control can lead to improved capacity utilization. Indeed, inventory is often defined as "stored capacity," reflecting the close relationship between these two fundamental notions.

**FIGURE 9-3   Framework for operations management
in a product operation**

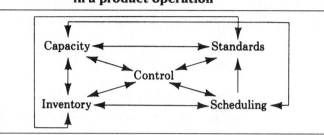

The art of operations management is working with these basics to achieve an organization's goals and objectives over time. The manager can orchestrate the five concepts to meet quality, delivery, and cost performance targets.

The operations manager in a service operation struggles against a profound problem. Since service cannot be stored, the concept of inventory has no meaning. Particularly where labor-embodied technology is involved, nothing can substitute for "production/consumption simultaneity," the economist's term for "producing" at the same time you are "consuming," for something like a successful appendectomy to occur. The manager of a service operation has neither inventory nor any of its relationships with the other four basic notions to work with.

Eliminating inventory from the framework leaves a substantially curtailed set of conceptual relationships, which are necessarily even more tightly interconnected than in a manufacturing environment where inventory is available. Figure 9-4 shows this graphically. Managers of service operations lack an important shock absorber available to their counterparts in manufacturing. This helps explain some of the productivity problems peculiar to service operations.

Effective management of service operations is in many ways more difficult than management of purely manufacturing operations. The most difficult of all is the most prevalent: management of operations comprising both service and manufacturing activities. Managing the design and development of a product—the combination of product and service performance to meet the needs of the market—requires continuous work with the basics; the work continues with the management of the processes for yielding and delivering the product/service combination that will satisfy customers over time. This work is the "blocking and

**FIGURE 9-4   Framework for operations management
in a service operation**

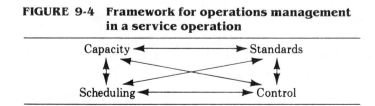

tackling" mentioned so often in news reports of efforts to maintain the United States' position as the most productive nation in the world.

THE QUALITY IMPERATIVE

The operations function has traditionally been charged with responsibility for quality. For many years, this was interpreted by most organizations to mean that *only* the operations function had this responsibility. The result was barely adequate quality performance, which became a serious problem in the marketplace when the competition began showing what quality could mean to the customer.

Most U.S. firms today are engaged in some sort of quality program, usually under the general guidelines of one of the dozens of quality gurus who have responded to the critical need for quality improvement. The quality of most products available in the United States today—whether produced domestically, overseas, or (most likely) in some combination of the two—has improved dramatically in the past decade.

A wide variety of quality programs are available to firms today. Each claims to offer a unique approach to the quality issue, but all have a few themes in common:

1. *Pervasive responsibility.* There is enough evidence now to prove that sustained high quality as perceived by the customer cannot be achieved if the responsibility is left to a single group within the organization. Whether phrased as "top management commitment/support," "full organizational involvement," "everyone's job," or "Job 1," the lesson is the same: Every person, function, level, aspect of the organization must understand that quality performance ultimately rests with them.

2. *Prevention not detection.* Decades of experience with "inspecting the quality in" has proven the case: It doesn't work. The organization's focus must be on doing it right the first time, heading off problems before they start, and anticipating what might go wrong so it can be prevented.

3. *Analysis not blame.* Prevention is only possible when the underlying causes of problems are understood. Therefore, the emphasis must be on the collection and analysis of data. The first rule—that quality is everyone's business—means that data gathering and analysis are also everyone's business. The result is a focus on training and education of the entire organization to make prevention effective.

A long-term study of manufacturing firms in Europe, North America, and Japan shows the importance of quality. After analyzing the performance of these firms over a decade, and also studying the programs underway at each site, the conclusion was clear: Only with a primary focus on quality are other programs likely to be effective. In particular, cost improvements do not succeed unless they are preceded by fully developed quality programs, supported by programs to improve process dependability and cycle speed.

There is an interesting link between process design and quality programs. The ISO9000 standard developed by the International Standards Organization is part of the program of qualification for selling within the European Community. Members have developed a voluntary standard for certifying manufacturing and service operations, based on strict documentation of actions and verification that the documentation is an accurate depiction of reality.

The ISO9000 certification is essentially a process that manufacturing and service operations can use to set a standard for quality management *systems*. It is an official assurance to customers that there is conformity to requirements throughout the entire design to service process. Many organizations are now engaged in process engineering before attempting ISO9000 certification. This is sensible since it is easier to certify a rationalized process focused on customer requirements than on the awkward and complex processes that have evolved over the years and that likely have lost any customer emphasis they might once have had. U.S. firms with serious interests in developing business within the European Community are enthusiastically involved in ISO9000 certification.

FOR FURTHER READING

Crosby, P. B., *Quality Is Free* (New York: Mentor Books, 1979).

Hammer, M., and J. Champy, *Reengineering the Corporation: A Manifesto for Business Revolution* (New York: Harper Business, 1993).

Hayes, R. H., and S. C. Wheelwright, *Restoring Our Competitive Edge: Competing through Manufacturing* (New York: John Wiley, 1984).

Ishikawa, K., *Guide to Quality Control* (Tokyo: Asian Productivity Organization, 1976).

Juran, J. M., *Juran on Planning for Quality* (New York: Free Press, 1988).

Miller, J. G., A. DeMeyer, and J. Nakane, *Benchmarking Global Manufacturing: Understanding International Suppliers, Customers and Competitors* (Homewood, IL: Business One Irwin, 1992).

Niebel, B. W., *Motion and Time Study* (eighth edition) (Homewood, IL: Irwin, 1988).

Rothery, B., *ISO9000*, 2nd ed. (Hampshire England: Gower Publishing and Brookfield, VT: Gower Press, 1993).

Skinner, W., *Manufacturing: The Formidable Competitive Weapon* (New York: John Wiley, 1985).

Vollmann, T. E., W. L. Berry, and D. C. Whybark, *Manufacturing Planning and Control Systems*, 3rd ed. (Homewood, IL: Business One Irwin, 1992).

10 ACCOUNTING AND MANAGEMENT DECISION MAKING

John Leslie Livingstone

THE ROLE OF ACCOUNTING IN ORGANIZATIONS

Accounting for Management Control Purposes

Seluk was the Keeper of Pharaoh's goats. His position was one of great honor, and also of great responsibility. It was to Seluk that Pharaoh looked for goats' milk for the royal table and for the beauty baths of his many wives. Pharaoh looked also to Seluk for goat meat to feed his army, for goat wool to make rugs, and for goat leather to fashion whips, camel reins, and sandals. In modern words, Seluk was manager of the Goat Division of Pharaoh, Inc.

Seluk had charge of some 2,000 goats. At the time of each full moon, he met with Ebis, the High Priest. To Ebis he gave a report of how many billy goats, nanny goats, and kids there were in the flock at latest count. To Ebis he reported also how many ewers of milk had been delivered this period to the palace, how many carcasses to the army, how many skeins of wool to Pharaoh's rug weavers, and how many goatskins to the royal leather workshop. All of this Ebis set down on his papyrus, asking questions of Seluk as he wrote:

My faculty colleagues at Babson College offered many helpful comments on earlier drafts of this chapter. For their warm interest and generous assistance, I would like to thank Professors Allan Cohen, Michael Fetters, Carolyn Hotchkiss, William Lawler, Clinton Petersen, and Srinivasan Umapathy.

235

Seluk, how is it that your flock is now larger than before, but the ewers of milk have become fewer? Seluk, at the rising of this moon, the goats numbered 1,991, and there were 2,013 at the setting of this moon. Kids born this moon were 240, and 98 carcasses were delivered to the army. Should not your ending goats be 2,133 rather than the 2,013 which you reported unto me? Where are the remaining 120 goats?

Seluk, you claim that you delivered to the army this moon 98 carcasses. But the army reports to me that only 87 carcasses were indeed received. Explain to me where are the 11 missing carcasses.

What Seluk was recounting to Ebis each moon were the monthly financial statements for Pharaoh's flock of goats. Ebis, by his questioning, was performing an audit of these financial statements. Why were they doing these things?

Seluk was entrusted by Pharaoh with the royal flock of goats. His responsibility as a manager made him *accountable* to Pharaoh for the goats, for their natural increase, for their yield in milk, wool, meat, and hides. This accountability required Seluk to report monthly on how well he had carried out his duties to his king. His report was the scorecard on his administration. It also served to direct attention to matters requiring explanation or decision.

Ebis was a highly educated bureaucrat, able to read, write, and count. These rare abilities made him Pharaoh's business manager, and the auditor of Pharaoh's enterprises. His audit was designed to ensure that Seluk was competent and diligent in his duties, and also honest—resisting any temptation to steal goats, milk, wool, meat, or leather.

If Seluk became incompetent, Pharaoh would want to know, in order to remind Seluk of his duty, or to coach him, or to rebuke him, or to replace him. If Seluk were found to lack in diligence or in honesty, Pharaoh would certainly wish to find out in order to punish his disloyal lieutenant and to set an example for any other of his followers who might be slacking off or perhaps even stealing royal property.

Is it surprising to hear that audits were performed as far back in history as ancient Egypt? Actually, auditing goes back a long way. Primitive audits are referred to in the Bible. As early as the thirteenth century, the city of London was audited, and in 1492 an auditor sailed to the Americas with Christopher Columbus.

In this story, we see one essential role of accounting in organizations: to make those placed in authority and given the responsibility over resources accountable to the people they serve. Managers are held accountable for being competent, diligent, and honest. Accounting provides the scorecard, and auditing is designed to ensure that the scorecard is correct.

Since accounting provides the scorecard, it is important to understand that what is reported on the scorecard will have a powerful effect on behavior. For example, there is abundant evidence that managers of large public corporations exert strenuous efforts for their corporate financial statements to reflect earnings with a smoothly increasing trend from year to year. This kind of trend, they believe, will keep the stockholders contented and thereby improve job security and the pay of the management. Remember: What counts is what is counted.

The natural tendency of management to put their best foot forward in the financial statements is yet stronger when the rewards of management (such as bonuses) are specifically linked to financial statement results. Such incentives are healthy, provided they do not go to extremes. But if there is extreme pressure to meet difficult financial targets regardless of circumstances, then management may be tempted to cheat. In that event, either sham transactions will be entered into to enhance the reported earnings, or the financial statements may be rigged to convey false results.

For example, consider the true story of a company to which I will give the name of Smith and Associates, an organization providing investigative and security services. Under its founder, "John Smith," the company grew to 100 offices nationwide and 12,000 employees. Its blue chip clients included AT&T, Delta Airlines, Allstate Insurance, State Farm Insurance, Dow Chemical, and IBM. In the 1980s, "Smith and Associates" provided security at political conventions, and also guarded construction projects at U.S. embassies around the world.

But the company was not expanding fast enough to satisfy Mr. Smith. When sales figures fell short of targets, he coerced subordinates to create phony sales invoices, supported by phony investigative reports based upon bogus files. By 1989, false sales of $45 million had been recorded. The deception was discovered, however, and by 1994 Mr. Smith had pleaded guilty to 29 counts of fraud in federal court.

The activities discussed thus far refer to the *control* function of accounting. Now we turn to the *planning* function of accounting.

Accounting for Business Planning Purposes

Pat Jacobs (PJ) was applying for a loan to start her new business, McSoft. She described her concept to the bank loan officer (LO): a store selling computer software to small businesses.

LO: How much money will you need to get started?

PJ: I estimate $40,000 for the beginning inventory; $18,000 for store signs, shelving, a cash register, and a counter; and $12,000 working capital to cover operating expenses for about two months. That's a total of $70,000 for the start-up.

LO: How are you planning to finance the investment of $70,000?

PJ: I can put in $50,000 of my savings, and I'd like to borrow the remaining $20,000 from the bank.

LO: Suppose that the bank lends you $20,000 on a one-year note, at 15 percent interest, secured by a lien on the inventory. Let's put together *pro forma,* or projected, financial statements by rearranging the figures you gave me. Your beginning balance sheet would look like this:

McSoft: Balance Sheet as of 1/1/1994

Assets		Liabilities and Equity	
Cash	$12,000	Note payable	
Inventory	40,000	(bank loan)	$20,000
Current assets	52,000	Current liabilities	20,000
Fixed asset: equipment	18,000	Owner capital	50,000
		Total liabilities and	
Total assets	$70,000	owner equity	$70,000

The left side shows McSoft's investment in assets. It splits the assets into current (turning into cash within a year) and noncurrent, or fixed (not liquid within a year). The right side shows how the assets will be financed—the note to the bank (payable in a year) and your equity as the owner.

PJ: Now I see why it's called a balance sheet. The financing on the one hand must be equal to the assets on the other hand. It's like both sides of the same coin. I also see why a distinction is made between current and non-current assets and liabilities: The bank wants to see whether assets turning into cash in a year will provide sufficient funds to repay the loan. Well, will you approve my loan?

LO: I don't know yet. We need more information. First, how much do you think your operating expenses will be?

Here's what I estimate for year 1:

Store rent	$18,000	
Utilities and phone	7,200	
Assistant's salary	20,000	
Interest on bank loan	3,000	(15% on $20,000)
Depreciation	1,800	(10% of $18,000 equipment)
	$50,000	

PJ: My understanding is that the store equipment will last 10 years. Therefore, the depreciation for wear and tear is 10 percent each year.

LO: Good. Now how much do you expect your year's sales to be? And your gross profit?

PJ: I'm confident that we can reach sales of $360,000. The cost of the software from suppliers will be $240,000. That will give us gross profit of $120,000 using the customary markup in the industry. Add this gross profit onto the cost of $240,000 and we get back to the sales figure of $360,000.

LO: Excellent. Let's organize this information into a pro forma income statement. We start with the sales, then deduct the expenses, and end up with the famous bottom line: net income. [The loan officer began to write on her yellow tablet. She put down the following figures:]

McSoft:
Income Statement for the Year Ending 12/31/94

Sales		$360,000
Less cost of goods sold		240,000
Gross profit		$120,000
Less expenses:		
Salaries	20,000	
Rent	18,000	
Utilities & phone	7,200	
Depreciation	1,800	
Interest	3,000	$ 50,000
Income before taxes		70,000
Income tax expense (40%)		28,000
Net income		$ 42,000

Pat, this looks fine for your first year in business. Many new businesses find it difficult to make a profit at all in their first year. They do well just to break even and stay in business. Of course, I'll need to go over all your sales and expense projections with you, to make sure that I agree they are realistic. But so far, so good. Now we are ready to do the year-end pro forma balance sheet. I need to ask you how much cash you are planning to draw out of the business in the first year for living expenses.

PJ: Well, my present job pays $38,000 and I plan to keep to this same standard of living with McSoft for year 1.

LO: Let's see how that works out after we complete the pro forma financial statements. Now for the year-end balance sheet. [Again, the loan officer wrote on the yellow tablet and this is what she put on the paper:]

McSoft:
Balance Sheet as of 12/31/1994

Assets		Liabilities and Equity	
Cash	$17,800	Note payable	$20,000
Inventory	40,000	(bank loan)	
Current assets	57,800	Current liabilities	20,000
Fixed asset:			
Equipment	18,000	Owner capital 1/1	50,000
Less depreciation	(1,800)	Add net income	42,000
		Less drawings	(38,000)
Net equipment	16,200	Owner capital 12/31	54,000
		Total liabilities	
Total assets	$74,000	and owner equity	$74,000

LO: Pat, let's go over this balance sheet together. You'll see that the asset side has changed, compared with the beginning balance sheet. Leave cash aside for the moment. I just put in a *plug number* that kept the balance sheet in balance for now. We'll come back to it later. The equipment has the depreciation deducted, to write it down to $16,200. On the other side, your equity is increased by the net income, and reduced by what you drew out to live on. Getting back to cash, here's a problem. Cash is only $17,800 but the bank note of $20,000 is due for payment. We have hit a snag.

PJ: I realize that McSoft will need cash to repay the $20,000 on the loan, and I'll still need to keep $12,000 cash on hand for about two months' operating expenses. That's a total of $20,000 plus $12,000, which adds up to $32,000. With only $17,800 cash on the balance sheet, it seems I'm about $14,000 or $15,000 short on cash. Do you think I'll have to cut my drawings down from $38,000 to $23,000 to come up with the difference? Here I am, opening my own business, and it looks as if I'm going back to what I earned five years ago!

LO: That's one way to do it. But here's an alternative that you may find easier. After your suppliers get to know you, and do a few months' business with you, you could ask them to open credit accounts for McSoft. If you pay on the usual 30-day basis, then your suppliers would be financing one month's inventory. That would be $1/12$ of annual cost of goods sold, which is $1/12$ of $240,000 or $20,000. In essence, accounts payable of $20,000 would replace the bank loan of $20,000 on your balance sheet. The cash payment of $20,000 that you would normally make to suppliers in December 1994 would be used to pay off your loan instead of your suppliers.

PJ: That sounds like a perfect solution. But could we first see how the balance sheet would look with your suggestion?

LO: Good idea. Also, we still need to work through the cash flow statement. First, let's tackle the revised balance sheet. [Once more, the pen moved over the yellow tablet as the loan officer wrote:]

McSoft:
Balance Sheet as of 12/31/1994

Assets		Liabilities and Equity	
Cash	$17,800	Note payable, bank	$ 0
Inventory	40,000	Accounts payable	20,000
Current assets	57,800	Current liabilities	20,000
Fixed asset:			
Equipment	18,000	Owner capital 1/1	50,000
Less depreciation	(1,800)	Add net income	42,000
		Less drawings	(38,000)
Net equipment	16,200	Owner capital 12/31	54,000
		Total liabilities	
Total assets	$74,000	and other equity	$74,000

When you pay off the note to the bank, it disappears from the balance sheet, and accounts payable of $20,000 appears in its place. Cash remains at $17,800 and is enough to cover a couple of months of operating expenses. Now we move on to the cash flow statement.

McSoft:
Cash Flow Statement for the Year Ending 12/31/94

Sources of Cash	
From operations: Net income	$42,000
Add depreciation	1,800
Add increase in accounts payable	20,000
Total cash from operations	63,800
Less: Withdrawn by owner	38,000
Cash reinvested to grow the business	25,800
From financing: Bank loan repaid	(20,000)
Total sources of cash	5,800
Uses of Cash	
Invested in equipment	0
Total sources less uses (increase in cash)	5,800
Add cash at beginning of year	12,000
Cash at end of year	$17,800

Pat, do you have any questions about the cash flow statement or the balance sheet we have just put together?

PJ: Actually, the cash flow statement makes sense to me. I guess in the last analysis there are only two places where a business can get cash: from the *inside,* by making a profit, and from the *outside,* by external financing like bank loans or owner's capital. In this case, the outside financing is negative because it is a repayment of a loan.

I also see that the use of cash is to invest in equipment to grow the business, even though this happens to be zero for McSoft in 1994 because no further new equipment is acquired. But the part of the cash flow statement that I find a little unfamiliar is the cash from operations section. Can we talk about that some more?

LO: Sure. As you said, profit is the source of internal cash generation and so we begin with net income. But we have to convert it to a cash basis. First, we add back depreciation to net income. Remember that we deducted depreciation as one of the expenses in order to arrive at net income. Adding back depreciation just backs it out of net income. In short, we ignore it in figuring cash flow. Why do this?

Here's why. Since the depreciation is just a portion of the total cost of the equipment, the total cost of equipment is a cash outflow that should not be counted twice: once when the equipment is purchased and again when we write off part of it as expense, for depreciation. We don't write a check for depreciation, so it should not be treated as a cash outflow.

We also add back the increase in accounts payable for this same reason. In arriving at net income, we deducted all the cost of goods sold, even the part we have not yet paid for: Remember the $20,000 we talked about before? We add back the $20,000 because that amount of cash has not yet been paid out.

With these adjustments, cash from operations is $63,800. The business has generated $63,800 of cash and can invest it for future growth. But your withdrawal of $38,000 reduces the amount available for reinvestment of $25,800 as the statement shows.

Also, notice that the statement ties in with our balance sheet cash figure: It reflects how the beginning cash amount changed into the ending cash amount.

PJ: Thanks. Now I understand. Am I right that you want to review my projections, and that you will then let me know about the loan?

LO: Yes. I'll be back to you before the end of the week. By the way, would you like me to make you a photocopy of the pro forma financial statements to take with you?

PJ: Yes, please, I'd appreciate that. They certainly do put the finances of the business into clear focus. I am grateful to you for putting them together with me.

As Pat walked out of the bank, she reflected that she had a good interview with the loan officer. She had also learned some accounting skills that would be valuable to her as an entrepreneur.

Points to Remember about Financial Statements

When Pat got home, she sat down and summarized on paper what she had learned about balance sheets:

1. The basic form is Assets = Liabilities + Owner equity.
2. Assets are the investments, such as inventory and equipment, made by the firm to operate its business. The liabilities and owner equity reflect how the assets are financed.
3. Balance sheets summarize financial position at a given moment in time and change as each transaction is recorded.
4. Every transaction is an exchange, and both sides of the transaction are always reflected. For example, when the bank loan is paid off with cash, the loan vanishes from the balance sheet and cash decreases by the same amount.
5. Only transactions measurable in money are recorded: We cannot put a transaction onto the balance sheet if it does not have a definite monetary amount. For example, if McSoft gains favorable publicity through a TV news interview, nothing is reflected on the balance sheet, since no definite money value can be assigned to this event.
6. Profits increase owner equity, and cash withdrawals by the owner decrease equity.

These simple rules and the example of McSoft, provide you with a beginning of understanding of the basic structure of an actual balance sheet for a major corporation.

Next, Pat noted what she had learned about income statements:

1. The basic form is Revenues − Expenses = Net income
2. Net income is not the same as cash from operations.
3. Some expenses are never cash outflows (depreciation, for example), and some expenses may be partly paid in cash this period and partly in the next period (cost of goods sold, for example).
4. Owner withdrawals are not an operating expense, but are a distribution out of net income.
5. Profit, after being adjusted to a cash basis, is how cash is internally generated.

While Pat was summarizing what she had learned about balance sheets and income statements, the loan officer was preparing for her next day. She knew that she would be analyzing the cash flow for a well-established large company, so she reviewed some guidelines that the bank had given out on reading cash flow statements.

In reading a cash flow statement, be alert to the following indicators:

1. Is cash from operations positive? Is it growing from one period to the next? Is the increase in working capital growing faster than sales, and if so, why?

2. Are cash withdrawals by owners (or dividends) only a small fraction of cash from operations? If cash withdrawals are too large a share of cash generated from operations, then the business is being milked of cash and will not be able to finance its future growth.

3. Of the total sources of cash, how much is generated inside the business through operations, and how much is obtained from outside financing? There are exceptions, but it is normally wise for businesses to rely more on internal cash generation than on outside financing to fund their future growth.

4. Of the outside financing, how much is equity and how much is borrowed money? While there are exceptions, it is wise to use more equity than debt funds for growth.

5. How much of its total sources of cash is the company using to invest for growth, and how much to increase its cash resources, or liquidity? Is it overinvesting (total uses greater than total sources of cash) or underinvesting (total sources greater than total uses) by too wide a margin?

6. Just what is the company investing in? Is it likely that these investments will be profitable? How long will it take for these investments to repay their cost, and then to earn a return?

These sample questions reminded the loan officer that the cash flow statement supplies valuable information that goes to the core of the company's business strategy and to the effectiveness of its management. She felt ready for tomorrow and decided to end her business day.

The Auditor's Report

In our opening story, Ebis received the account of Seluk's management of Pharaoh's goats. Ebis checked Seluk's report by asking important questions. Ebis served Pharaoh as a true watchdog, by verifying that Seluk had made a full and fair report. This valuable watchdog function remains alive and well in our times.

It is performed today for the investors in the company by the outside independent auditor, whose report must accompany all annual financial statements published by companies with publicly traded securities.

The auditor's report follows a standard format. The first paragraph says *what the auditor did,* namely, that the auditor has examined the financial statements by following generally accepted auditing standards, which include tests (rather than 100% examination) of the accounting records. The second paragraph gives the *auditor's opinion,* based on the audit examination performed.

The key words in the opinion paragraph are *present fairly* and *in conformity with generally accepted accounting principles applied on a consistent basis.* This opinion provides comfort to users of the financial statements that the information is fairly and consistently presented. If this were not the case, the auditor would say so in the auditor's report. Phrases such as "subject to" or "except for" are often used in such situations. In other words, this phrasing indicates that the watchdog is barking.

Companies with publicly traded securities must publish annual audited financial statements. Other firms are not required by law to do so. However, they may still need to provide audited financial statements in order to borrow from banks and other lenders, or to satisfy large investors, major suppliers, or major customers. Unaudited financial statements are not as reliable as audited statements.

Before you review any set of audited financial statements, first read the auditor's report to see if the auditor has flagged anything in the examination. Do not remain asleep when the watchdog is barking!

We now have obtained a basic understanding of the three main financial statements and the auditor's report. It is time to put our knowledge to work in making decisions as managers.

USING FINANCIAL STATEMENTS IN MAKING BUSINESS DECISIONS

The following is a short list of some of the *users* and *uses* of financial statements. This list is by no means complete:

1. Equity and debt investors, to monitor the performance of management.
2. Prospective investors, to decide in which companies to invest.
3. Banks and other lenders, to decide whether to make new loans, or continue existing loans.
4. Investment analysts, money managers, and stockbrokers, to make investment recommendations or decisions for their clients.

5. Rating agencies (such as Standard & Poor's, Moody's, and Dun & Bradstreet), to assign credit ratings.

6. Major suppliers and customers, to evaluate the strength and financial staying power of the company as a long-term resource for their business.

7. Labor unions and employee associations, to assess what the company may be able to afford to pay in upcoming labor negotiations.

8. Management, to assess the company's standing with the present and potential investors, bankers, the financial community, customers, suppliers, and workers.

9. Management, to review their effectiveness in running the business, and to plan the future of the company.

10. Corporate raiders, seeking hidden value in companies with underpriced stock.

11. Competitors, to benchmark their own progress in the industry against what the company has achieved.

12. Potential competitors, to assess how profitable it may be to enter the industry, and how strong a competitor the company would be.

13. Government agencies who are responsible for taxing, regulating, or investigating the company.

14. Politicians, consumer advocates, single issue groups, lobbyists, environmental activists, foundations, and other parties who are either promoting or fighting a particular cause.

15. Joint venture partners, trade associations, franchisors or franchisees, and other present or potential business associates who have an interest in the company and its financial position.

This brief list shows how important and useful the roles are that financial statements play in the business world. It also shows how essential it is for managers to master the understanding, analysis, and use of financial statements for making business decisions.

How to Analyze Financial Statements

Imagine that you are a physician, working in the emergency room of a large hospital. Some patients arrive with serious injury or illness, some barely alive or even dead, some with minor problems, and some with only imagined ailments. Your training and experience have taught you to make a careful diagnosis, based on certain tests. In a case that appears serious, you check the vital signs: pulse, blood pressure, respiration, temperature, and EKG.

We check the financial health of a company in much the same way, using the financial statements for our examination. The tests that business doctors use are mostly based on *financial ratios.* It is convenient to classify these tests and ratios into three categories:

1. Short-term solvency
2. Long-term solvency
3. Profitability

We will describe each of these categories next.

Short-Term Solvency

We must emphasize the importance of sufficient cash resources or liquidity, which enables a company to pay its bills and to stay in business. Liquidity means survival, and insufficient liquidity means bankruptcy to a business. The essential nature of liquidity is why current assets (which turn into cash within a year) and current liabilities (which require cash payment within a year) are shown separately on balance sheets. In the short-term solvency test, liquidity is measured with the following financial ratios.

The *current ratio* is total current assets divided by total current liabilities. It indicates the company's ability to meet current obligations out of its current resources. It is expressed as "2.5 to 1," or "2.5:1," or just "2.5." A current ratio that is greater than one is needed to provide some margin of safety.

Bear in mind that the current ratio is not a precise measure. There is no point in calculating it to more than one decimal place. It is open to "window dressing," quite legitimately, as firms attempt to put their best foot forward in their financial statements (which they are tempted to do to present their management performance in the best possible light).

For example, suppose that current assets are hypothetically $200, and current liabilities are $100. Then the current ratio is 2.0. The financial year ends in one week. The firm decides to make early payment on $50 of accounts payable. The current assets are now $150 (cash decreased by $50), and current liabilities are $50 (accounts payable decreased by $50). The current ratio becomes 150/50, or 3.0 rather than 2.0: a great improvement on paper! Regard *all* financial ratios as rough figures and not as precise measures.

In some cases, inventories are not liquid in a crisis situation (except at "fire sale" prices). This condition is especially likely in a trendy or high-fashion business, or where technological obsolescence is probable, or where the market is saturated. In these cases, the current ratio is modified by including only the more liquid items in current assets and excluding inventories and prepaid items.

This variation is called the *quick ratio,* or *acid test ratio.* It, too, is expected to be greater than one by some margin of safety.

Next, we consider turnover in relation to liquidity. Faster turnover of assets allows us to do more business without an equivalent increase in assets. Speedier asset turnover means that we tie up less cash in assets, which in turn helps liquidity. By the same token, slower turnover of liabilities assists liquidity. However, too slow a liability turnover may reflect lack of enough cash to pay the bills. Three ratios are commonly used to measure turnover of accounts receivable, inventories, and accounts payable, respectively.

- *Accounts receivable* is:

$$\frac{\text{Accounts receivable}}{\text{turnover}} = \frac{\text{Credit sales}}{\text{Accounts receivable}}$$

Suppose that credit sales for the year are $120,000, and accounts receivable are $30,000. Then the receivables turnover is 120,000/30,000, or 4, which shows that receivables are "turning over" on average four times a year. It can also be expressed as *days' sales*, by dividing 365 days (in a year) by 4 to get an average of 91 days. This expression says we are carrying receivables averaging 91 days sales. That is fine if our credit terms call for payment 90 days from invoice. It is not fine if our terms are 60 days, and it is alarming if terms are 30 days. Unlike vintage wine or great works of art, receivables do not improve with age! Slow receivables turnover signals danger to liquidity.

- *Inventory turn* is *cost of goods sold* divided by *inventories*. Unlike receivables, the numerator here is cost of goods sold rather than sales. The reason is that inventories are carried on the balance sheet at *cost* (not selling price: Check back to the McSoft balance sheets to verify this fact). So, to have a consistent "apples to apples" ratio, both numerator (cost of goods sold) and denominator (inventory) must be in the same terms, namely cost.

  In this example, cost of goods sold this year is $100,000, and inventory is $33,333. Then, inventory turn is 100,000/33,333, or 3 times per year. This figure can be expressed as 365/3 = 122 days supply of inventory on hand. In the auto manufacturing business, 60 days supply of cars is about normal, and 122 days would be regarded an unacceptable. That oversupply would trigger a vigorous rebate campaign to clear out the excess vehicles. Slow inventory turnover is a serious red flag for liquidity.

- *Accounts payable turnover* indicates the extent to which a firm is keeping current in paying its suppliers. This ratio is:

$$\frac{\text{Accounts payable}}{\text{turnover}} = \frac{\text{Cost of goods sold}}{\text{Accounts payable}}$$

Cost is used in the numerator for the same reason as in inventory turn: The accounts payable are owed to suppliers of goods for resale and are recorded at cost. To illustrate, cost of goods sold this year is $100,000, and accounts payable is $20,000. Accounts payable turnover is 100,000/20,000 = 5 times a year. It can also be translated into 365/5 = 73 days average. This average should be compared to a relevant yardstick (we shall discuss relevant yardsticks later).

We have now concluded all the ratios indicating short-term solvency. If your analysis of a company reveals poor liquidity ratios, you may have finished your work. This patient is almost dead, and only desperate measures can save the day. On the other hand, if your patient passes the liquidity tests, the business doctor is ready to make the next set of tests: long-term solvency.

Long-Term Solvency

The two tests of long-term solvency focus on a firm's ability to meet its obligations to pay interest and principal on the long-term debt. One test is for interest and one for principal.

The test of ability to pay interest on the long-term debt is based on a statistic known as *times interest earned.* This statistic is the ratio of earnings before interest and taxes (EBIT) to the interest on long-term debt. The numerator represents profit available to meet interest expense. Bear in mind that business interest is tax deductible so that income taxes are calculated on income after interest expense.

For example, assume that McSoft had a long-term loan payable of $30,000. Suppose that interest is 12 percent per year or $3,600. Also suppose that McSoft had EBIT of $10,800 this year. Then, times interest earned is 10,800/3,600 = 3.0. This ratio indicates that McSoft could meet its interest expense three times over, thus providing a safety cushion for the lender. However, if the ratio had been 1.0, there would be no cushion at all, a serious red flag.

The ratio to test the safety of principal on long-term debt involves the proportion of long-term debt in the total long-term capital structure of the firm. The long-term capital structure means long-term liabilities plus owner equity on the balance sheet. This ratio shows how the fixed assets plus the working capital (current assets less current liabilities) are financed out of long-term funds.

Returning to McSoft, suppose that the latest balance sheet showed the long-term capital structure as follows:

Long-term debt		$30,000
Owner equity: Owner capital	$20,000	
Retained earnings	9,000	29,000
Total long-term capital structure		$59,000

The item of concern may be measured as the *debt-to-equity ratio,* 30,000:29,000 which is approximately one. Alternatively, it may be measured as the proportion of long-term debt in the total capital structure, the *debt to debt-plus-equity ratio* of 30,000:59,000, which is approximately 50 percent. Either approach is commonly used. This option makes it important to clarify which method is being applied in a particular case to avoid any possible misunderstanding.

An acceptable level of this ratio causes little worry, but too high a level is grounds for concern. When it exceeds the comfort level, the larger this ratio (whichever way it is measured), the riskier the enterprise. This increased risk results because the debt is senior to the equity (meaning that interest must be paid before dividends can be paid). In liquidation, the principal and interest of the debt must first be paid in full before any cash remaining can be paid to the equity holders.

The comfort level of the debt-to-equity ratio varies from one industry to another and depends on the stability or volatility of the industry, and the value of the collateral (if any) securing the debt. So-called "junk bonds" are regarded as "junk" because their issuers often have poor debt-to-equity ratios. This discussion concludes the long-term solvency tests.

The third and final group of tests examines profitability.

Profitability Ratios

There are two categories of profitability ratios. The first category is *percentage of sales.* Consider the following income statements:

	1993	1994
Sales revenues	$8,976	$9,864
Cost of goods sold	5,296	6,017
Gross profit	3,680	3,847
Operating expenses	2,441	2,792
Selling, general, and administrative expenses	637	750
Operating profit	602	305
Interest expense	201	201
Income before taxes	401	104
Income taxes	160	41
Net income	$ 241	$ 63

What do these income statements reveal about the financial results for 1994 versus 1993? The good news is that sales *increased* by about $900; the bad news is that net income *decreased* by about $180. How did this frustrating situation develop where sales are up but profits are down? The reason is hard to see from the income statements. Is it due to increased expenses? The income statements do show that most expenses rose in 1994. However, sales were up too, so we would reasonably expect expenses to increase with the higher level of business activity. Why we gained sales but lost profits in 1994 is still vague.

Now, consider the same income statements again, but with added columns for percentages:

	1993	Percent	1994	Percent
Sales revenue	$8,976	100.0	$9,864	100.0
Cost of goods sold	5,296	59.0	6,017	61.0
Gross profit	3,680	41.0	3,847	39.0
Operating expenses	2,441	27.2	2,792	28.3
Selling, general, and administrative expenses	637	7.1	750	7.6
Operating profit	602	6.7	305	3.1
Interest expense	201	2.2	201	2.0
Income before taxes	401	4.5	104	1.1
Income taxes	160	1.8	41	0.4
Net income	$ 241	2.7	$ 63	0.6

The percentage columns show sales each year as 100 percent, and each line item on the income statement is shown as a percent of sales. In other words, out of every sales dollar we can see how much went to each type of expense and why we ended up with a net income per sales dollar of 2.7 cents in 1993, but with only 0.6 cents in 1994.

Now it becomes clear why we had disappointing results in 1994 and how they happened. Mainly, the gross profit ratio to sales fell by 2 percent (39% vs. 41.0%), while the operating expenses ratio to sales rose 1.1 percent (28.3% vs. 27.2%), and SG&A expenses increased by 0.5 percent (7.6% vs. 7.1%). The combined impact of these effects was a 3.6 percent drop in operating profit, from 6.7 to 3.1 percent. This 3.6 percent drop was partially offset by decreases in interest expense (0.2%) and income taxes (1.4%), resulting in an overall fall of 2.1 percent in net income.

With the percentage columns, we have a clear picture of what happened. We can also calculate the dollar impact of events:

	Percent	Dollars
Sales revenue for 1994	100.0	9,864
Expected net income for 1994	2.7	266
Less deterioration: Gross profit	(2.0)	(197)
Operating expenses	(1.1)	(109)
SG&A expenses	(0.5)	(49)
Add improvement: Interest expense	0.2	20
Income taxes	1.4	138
Actual net income for 1994	0.6	63

The use of *percent of sales* ratios is a simple but powerful technique for examining the behavior of gross profit and the various types of expenses. The main ratios of this kind are:

1. Gross profit percent.
2. Operating expense percent.
3. SG&A expense percent.
4. Operating profit percent.
5. Income before tax percent.
6. Net income percent.

The second category of profitability ratios is the return on investment type. This category takes into account the amount of capital invested and indicates the profit earned on the investment as a percentage yield. It is a most important and widely used type of profitability measure. We explain it by using the following summary balance sheet, together with the example income statements that we discussed in dealing with the *percent of sales* ratios.

Summary Balance Sheet 12/31/93

Current assets	$1,200	Current liabilities	$ 700
Fixed assets	2,500	Long-term debt	1,600
		Owner equity	1,400
Total assets	$3,700	Total equities	$3,700

Summary Income Statements for the Years Ended 12/31/93 and 12/31/94

	1993	1994
Operating profit	$602	$305
Less interest expense	201	201
Income before taxes	401	104
Income taxes	160	41
Net income	$241	$ 63

The first ratio we consider is *return on total assets before taxes* (ROTABT), which is *operating profit* divided by *total assets.* In 1990, this ratio was 602/3000 = 20.1 percent. There are several points to keep in mind with ROTABT. Note that it measures the basic earning power of the assets of the firm, regardless of whether these assets are financed by equity or by long-term debt. It focuses directly on the assets that are financed by equity and long-term debt, by calculating total assets as *fixed assets plus working capital* (which is current assets less current liabilities). This formulation makes the total assets consistent with, and equal in amount to, the long-term capital structure when calculating the return on investment-type ratios. The current assets, in relation to current liabilities and liquidity, have already been taken into consideration in the tests of short-term solvency. We do not need to duplicate those tests by again taking into account current liabilities when we test long-term solvency. The summary balance sheet for this purpose is rearranged as follows:

Rearranged Summary Balance Sheet 12/31/93

Current assets	$1,200	Long-term debt	$1,600
Less current liabilities	700	Owner equity	1,400
Working capital	500		
Fixed assets	2,500		
Assets	$3,000	Long-term funds	$3,000

Note that the numerator in ROTABT is EBIT. This formulation excludes any effect from the ratio of how assets are financed, by leaving out interest on debt and the tax impact of interest. Excluding the effects of financing enables us to compare ratios for more than one firm, regardless of how any particular firm finances its assets. Remember, the aim is to measure the basic earning power of assets, unaffected by methods of long-term financing. This same point is true for the next ratio also.

Return on total assets after taxes (ROTAAT) is:

$$\frac{\text{Net income} + \text{Interest expense net of income tax deduction}}{\text{Total assets}}$$

This ratio allows for the fact that interest is deductible for income tax purposes. Therefore, the cost of debt to the firm, after tax, is the interest less the related tax saving. This tax saving is the tax rate (40 percent) times the interest of $201, which is $80. So, interest net of the tax deduction is $121 ($201 − 80). Then, our ratio is $241 (net income) + $121 (net interest after tax) divided by $3,000 (total assets) = 12.1 percent.

Long-term debt is usually a less expensive form of financing than equity for two reasons. First, the interest on debt is deductible for tax purposes. However, dividends on the equity capital (stock) are not tax deductible. The

254 The Functions of a Business

advantage of tax deductibility makes debt interest relatively less expensive to the firm. Second, debt is senior to equity and is thus less risky to the investor. Investors are able to demand a higher return for riskier investment securities. This ability makes the required rate of return on a firm's equity securities higher than on its debt securities. For these reasons, debt is usually less costly to a firm than equity.

The example financial statements reflect such a tendency. Note that interest after tax is $121 on the long-term debt of $1,600 or 7.6 percent, but recall that ROTAAT was 12.1 percent. Therefore, the firm earns 12.1 percent, and after paying the holders of long-term debt their 7.6 percent, the firm benefits by the difference between the 12.1 percent earned and the 7.6 percent paid on debt financing. How much is this benefit? We measure it by the next ratio—*return on equity*.

Note that there are two kinds of equity. Preferred stock usually has a fixed rate of dividend, like a fixed rate of interest on long-term debt, and it is senior to the other kind of equity: common stock. Common stock has no fixed rate of dividend, and it is always the most junior form of long-term capital. Some companies do not have preferred stock, but all companies have common stock. When people use *return on equity*, they usually mean return on the *common equity*.

Return on equity (ROE) is probably the most important ratio to the common stockholders. It indicates the return on their equity investment in the company. *Return on equity* is the *net income* (less preferred dividends) divided by *common equity*, which in our example is 241/1,400 = 17.2 percent. We recall that ROTAAT is 12.1 percent. Therefore, if there were no long-term debt, then ROE would also be 12.1 percent. However, the long-term debt, costing only 7.6 percent after tax, enables ROE to be boosted to 17.2 percent. The benefit to the owners is their higher ROE of 17.2 percent versus the 12.1 percent that they would have earned without the debt. This tactic is known as *leverage*.

Leverage is regarded by some investors as a turbobooster to earnings. Therefore, it is no wonder that debt financing is in vogue and that junk bonds have become so popular. Also popular are leveraged buyouts—purchases of businesses financed heavily by debt and with abnormally low equity. Leverage gives a higher return on equity so long as profits are large. On the other hand, if profits shrink, leverage has the opposite effect.

Recall in our sample income statement that net income fell from $241 in 1993 to $63 in 1994. The 1994 ROE is 63/1,600 = 3.9 percent, compared with 17.2 percent in 1993. This is reverse leverage! 1994 ROTAAT is 6.1 percent, calculated as follows:

$$\frac{\text{Net income (\$63)} + \text{Interest after tax (\$201} - \$80 = \$121)}{\text{Total assets (\$3,000)}}$$

Without debt, the ROE would have been 6.1 percent, but the cost of the debt after tax was 7.6 percent, leaving only 3.9 percent return to the equity owners. The *negative benefit* is −2.2 percent (3.9% − 6.1%) to the equity owners. This calculation illustrates the downside risk of excessive leverage. In summary, high leverage will make the good years better and the bad years worse for equity owners.

The financial markets reflect this relationship by demanding larger rates of return on both debt and equity as leverage increases beyond the comfort level. Investors willing to take greater risks ask for greater returns. However, once past a certain point, further increase of a firm's leverage is no longer economic because the rising cost of financing will outpace any further gain from leverage.

The next profitability measure is the well-known *earnings per share* (EPS). EPS is *net income* less *preferred stock dividends* divided by the *number of common shares outstanding* (excluding treasury stock, which is stock repurchased from stockholders by the company). If a company has issued convertible debt securities (where holders have the option of converting their debt securities into common stock), there are two versions of EPS—*primary* (or *undiluted,* as previously described) and *fully diluted* (assuming that all of the conversion options have been exercised).

Stockholders are wary of dilution because when more stock is issued, the earnings per share must perforce go down. EPS reveals dilution by stating earnings in relation to a single share of common stock.

The next ratio is also on a single share basis. It is known as the *price/ earnings* (PE) *ratio.* It, too, applies only to common stock and is the ratio of the *market price* of the stock to *earnings per share.* The PE ratio is a return on investment-type measure, but (unlike REO) it uses the market price per share as the investment base.

Two points are worth noting. First, the EPS used may be for the past year (actual), the present year (estimated), or the next year (projected). Past EPS is sometimes referred to as a "trailing" EPS. The PE ratio is an upside-down return on investment concept: The usual *return on investment* is the *return* divided by the *investment.* But the *PE ratio* is the reverse: *Investment* divided by *return.* Why is it done upside down? Who knows: It is simply a time-honored tradition!

All the ratios discussed reflect the actual results of the *past.* But the PE ratio is by its very nature a *prospective* ratio, because the stock market builds future prospects into present stock prices. The same is true of all ratios based on market prices or projections, which includes our final ratio.

The final ratio is also a per share of common stock ratio. It is the ratio of the market price per share to the book value per share of common stock. Sometimes it is called the *market-to-book ratio. Book value per common share* is the *common equity* (total owner equity excluding preferred stock) divided by the *number of common shares outstanding*. It simply translates common equity into a per share basis. The ratio indicates whether a company is worth more in market value than the cost it paid for its assets (less its liabilities).

A ratio greater than one means that market value exceeds the book value. This excess may be taken as a sign that management (and possibly good fortune) have created stockholder value over and above the acquisition cost of the assets. Many experts in business strategy say that the ultimate goal of management is to maximize stockholder value. The market-to-book ratio is one indicator of success in achieving this objective.

For some regulated companies, regulation is based on a fair rate of return. Then, the market-to-book ratio indicates the extent to which regulation is indeed fair. A market-to-book ratio of approximately one indicates 100 percent fairness. (The regulator is allowing the company to earn the market rate of return.) A market-to-book ratio significantly above one suggests overgenerosity by the regulator (allowing an excessive return), and a ratio substantially below one is a sign of a regulator allowing an inferior rate of return.

We have now discussed all the main financial ratios, and they are summarized in Table 10-1.

Practical Use of Financial Ratios

Keep in mind a number of important points for the effective use of ratios. First, the ratios can never be more reliable than the data on which they are based. Therefore, it is essential to check the reliability of the basic data. Remember: Garbage in, garbage out! Beware of: Garbage in, gospel out!

Remember that our discussion of financial statements has dealt with fundamentals; some of the highly technical aspects can challenge even the experts. For example, financial statements include footnotes that can contain important information affecting the interpretation of those statements. Some of these footnotes are complex, and you should seek professional advice if you come across anything that you do not fully understand.

Be aware of areas where the accounting treatment of certain items is not cut and dried. Two ways of accounting may be equally acceptable methods of treating the same item but give very different results. These diverse results can, in turn, affect the financial ratios and make them better or worse than they might otherwise be.

Often, the ratios will not provide a decisive answer. Do not be surprised if this happens. Uncertainty is a signal to investigate further by gathering more facts and by using other suitable techniques.

Ratios can be affected by seasonal factors. For instance, retailers commonly end their financial years on January 31, when business is slack and the

TABLE 10-1   Summary of financial ratios

Ratio	Numerator	Denominator
Short-Term Solvency		
Current ratio	Current assets	Current liabilities
Quick ratio (acid test)	Highly liquid current assets	Current liabilities
Receivables turn days' receivables	Credit sales 365 days	Accounts receivable receivables turn
Inventory turn days' inventory	Cost of sales 365 days	Inventories inventory turn
Payables turn days' payables	Cost of sales 365 days	Accounts payable payables turn
Long-Term Solvency		
Times interest earned	Operating income (EBIT)	Interest on long-term debt
Debt-to-equity ratio	Long-term debt	Owner equity
Debt ratio	Long-term debt	Total financial structure
Profitability: Profit-to-Sales Ratios		
Gross profit	Gross profit	Sales
Operating expense	Operating expense	Sales
SG&A ratio	SG&A expense	Sales
Pretax income	Pretax income	Sales
Net income	Net income	Sales
Profitability: Return on Investment Ratios		
Return on Total Assets:		
Before taxes	Operating income (EBIT)	Total assets (working capital + fixed assets)
After taxes	Net income + Interest after tax	Total assets (working capital + fixed assets)
Return on equity	Net income − Preferred dividends	Common equity
Earnings per share (undiluted or primary)	Net income − Preferred dividends	Number of common shares outstanding
Earnings per share (fully diluted)	Net income − Preferred dividends	Number of common shares outstanding (all conversion options exercised)
Price-to-earnings ratio	Market price per common share	Earnings per share of common stock
Market-to-book ratio	Market price per common share	Book value per common share

inventories are low. Since inventories are at their seasonal low, the inventory turnover ratios look faster than they normally are. Remember to keep seasonal effects on ratios in mind.

Few financial ratios are meaningful when considered in a vacuum. They need to be measured in relation to a standard or appropriate yardstick. The simplest yardstick is to compare ratios for a firm against its ratios for previous periods. One firm may be compared with another firm in the same industry, or against composite ratios for the industry as a whole. The industry ratios are often available from firms specializing in financial statistics, such as Dun & Bradstreet, Standard & Poor's, and Moody's, among others.

Keep in mind that the trend over time is critical in considering ratios. For example, a current ratio of 1.5 may seem barely satisfactory. However, if it was only 1.0 last year, then this year's 1.5 may be a substantial improvement. On the other hand, if the ratio last year was 2.5, this year's 1.5 is not good news.

Some companies helpfully include ratios with their financial statements. Table 10-2 shows such an example from an annual report of Sega Enterprises, a Japanese maker of video games.

FINANCIAL ANALYSIS AND BUSINESS STRATEGY

Financial ratios can be combined into a DuPont chart. The DuPont method was originally developed at the DuPont Company for financial planning and control purposes. It shows how the key financial ratios are logically interrelated. Also, it reflects how the ratios interact to determine profitability measured as return on equity. The brief form of the DuPont formula is:

Profit Margin		Asset Turnover		Return on Assets
$\dfrac{\text{Net income}}{\text{Sales}}$	$\times$	$\dfrac{\text{Sales}}{\text{Total assets}}$	$=$	$\dfrac{\text{Net income}}{\text{Total assets}}$

Return on Assets (ROA)		Financial Leverage		Return on Equity (ROE)
$\dfrac{\text{Net income}}{\text{Total assets}}$	$\times$	$\dfrac{\text{Total assets}}{\text{Common equity}}$	$=$	$\dfrac{\text{Net income}}{\text{Common equity}}$

In turn, these ratios can be broken down again into their component ratio parts for further analysis, as we shall see.

The DuPont formula is a financial X-ray of the business that reveals how the key ratios link with each other to govern total business profitability. As an

TABLE 10-2   Six-year financial summary, SEGA Enterprises, Ltd.*

	Millions of Yen					
	1988	1989	1990	1991	1992	1993
Net sales:						
Consumer products	¥18,037	¥25,008	¥39,153	¥ 58,277	¥135,124	**¥229,270**
Amusement center operations	11,265	12,240	17,325	24,627	41,410	**58,914**
Amusement machine sales	19,467	17,268	21,606	23,290	36,427	**57,558**
Royalties on game software	347	710	550	386	356	**1,195**
Total	49,116	55,226	78,634	106,580	213,317	**346,937**
Cost of sales	32,819	38,190	54,594	73,162	150,873	**251,834**
Gross profit	16,297	17,036	24,040	33,418	62,444	**95,103**
Selling, general and administrative expenses	9,501	9,762	11,854	15,548	23,153	**32,563**
Operating income	6,796	7,274	12,186	17,870	39,291	**62,540**
Net income	2,302	2,855	4,845	8,244	14,014	**28,017**
Depreciation and amortization	2,562	2,998	3,715	5,579	9,067	**15,591**
Total assets	44,622	65,956	98,450	115,512	226,065	**295,153**
Total shareholders' equity	29,769	45,640	69,090	77,075	90,318	**116,511**
Financial ratios:						
Return on average assets	6.3%	5.2%	5.9%	7.7%	8.2%	**10.8%**
Return on average equity	10.2	7.6	8.4	11.3	16.7	**27.1**
Payout ratio	7.7	4.6	4.2	6.5	8.9	**8.7**

illustration, Table 10-3 shows summarized financial statements for American Stores, a well-known chain of supermarkets.

Figure 10-1 shows the financial information for American Stores in a Du-Pont format.

The DuPont formula is even more valuable than an X ray. It also enables us to ask "what if" kinds of strategic questions. For instance, it can deal with issues such as:

1. If inventory turnover improves 10 percent, how much will ROE increase?

2. If price is cut by 4 percent, and volume increases by 12 percent, what will be the effect on ROA?

3. What would net income be if leverage is reduced by 25 percent?

TABLE 10-3   DuPont chart for American Stores

Summarized Balance Sheet

Average 19XX	$ Million	% to Sales
Accts receivable	140	1.0
Inventory	1235	8.9
Other current assets	107	0.8
Total current assets	1482	10.6
Less current liabilities	(1256)	(9.0)
Equals working capital	226	1.6
Net fixed assets	2017	14.5
Total assets	2243	16.1
LT liabilities	1266	9.1
Preferred stock	255	1.8
Common equity	722	5.2
Total liabilities plus equity	2243	16.1

Summarized Income Statement

19XX	$ Million	% to Sales
Net sales	13,890	100.0
Gross margin	3,343	24.1
Operating expenses	2,920	21.0
Operating profit	423	3.0
Interest	129	0.9
Other income	16	0.1
Income before tax	310	2.2
Income taxes	155	1.1
Net income	155	1.1
Preferred dividends	25	0.2
Net income: Common	130	0.9

These capabilities make the DuPont formula a useful technique for strategic analysis. With the added power of a computer spreadsheet, the DuPont formula can rapidly calculate the answers to a large array of "what if" questions.

Accordingly, to assess the effects on ROE of changes in the key ratios, we perform a "what if" analysis on American Stores as shown in Table 10-4.

"What If" Analysis

The "what if" analysis asks how much ROE will increase if certain financial ratios could be improved. The following possibilities are considered:

1. Test the change in ROE for a 2 percent relative improvement in the ratios of gross margin and operating expenses to sales.

FIGURE 10-1   DuPont chart

American Stores

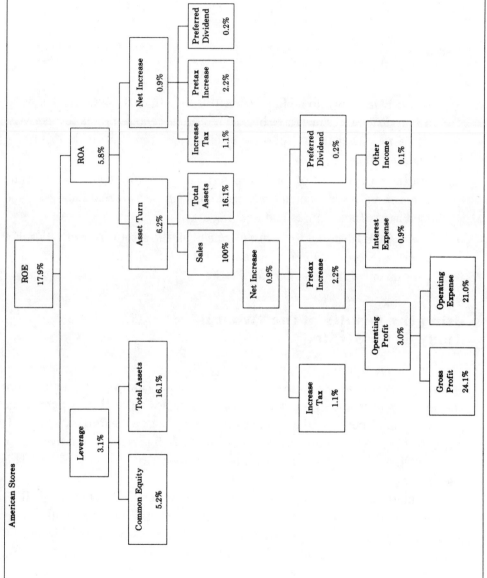

TABLE 10-4 "What if" analysis for American Stores

% to Sales	Present Value (%)	Improve by (%)	To (%)	ROE Grows from 17.9% to (%)
Gross profit	24.1	2	24.5	27.2
Operating expenses	21.0	2	20.6	26.0
Accounts receivable	1.0	5	1.0	17.9
Inventory	8.9	5	8.4	18.0
Current liabilities	9.0	5	9.5	18.0
Fixed assets	14.5	5	13.6	18.1

Result: ROE proves to be highly *sensitive* to both of these ratios. The ROE of American Stores increases by 9.3 and 8.1 percentage points respectively, with a relative gain of 2 percent in either gross margin or the operating expense ratio.

2. Test the change in ROE for 5 percent relative improvement in each of the turnover ratios for accounts receivable, inventories, current liabilities, and fixed assets (net fixtures and equipment).

Result: ROE turns out to be *insensitive* to all the asset turnover ratios. For American Stores, ROE goes up only by 0.1 or 0.2 with a 5 percent improvement in any of the asset turnover ratios.

Using the Results of the "What If" Analysis for Strategy

These results are most surprising. The ROE increases as the gross margin and operating expense ratios improve. This is predictable. However, the high degree of improvement is not so predictable: ROE increases more than 4 percentage points for each 1 percent relative improvement in the gross margin ratio. Specifically, with a gross margin increase from 24.1 to 24.5 percent (a relative rise of 1.7%), ROE goes up from 17.9 to 27.2 percent (a relative increase of 52%). This rise is an extremely strong response.

Similarly, the operating expense ratio has a powerful effect on ROE. ROE goes up by 4 percentage points for each 1 percent relative decrease in the operating expense ratio. In precise terms, if operating expense is reduced from 21.0 to 20.6 percent (a relative fall of 2%), ROE increases from 17.9 to 26.0 percent. The response is strong, although not as dramatic as the response of ROE to a change in gross margin.

These results demonstrate that the *spread* between the gross margin ratio and the operating expense ratio is crucial in determining ROE. This spread is operating profit; operating profit is the main driver of ROE for supermarkets.

Also surprising is the lack of ROE response to asset turnover improvement. This absence is especially interesting because one of the main rules of thumb in retailing is to improve the asset turnover, most importantly for inventories. Then, why does a 5 percent asset turnover improvement for American Stores not result in a higher ROE?

Keep in mind that asset turnover is usually rapid for supermarkets. Therefore, additional improvement in the asset turnover is added onto already fast-turning assets. The small extra gain in the asset turn adds nothing to ROE, given the already rapid turnover of assets.

Does this mean that asset turnover is unimportant for ROE? Certainly not. It means only that a small improvement in the presently rapid asset turnover does not continue to increase ROE.

The "what if" analysis shows that the key to improved ROE for American Stores is higher operating profit margin, rather than accelerated asset turnover. Thus, the "what if" analysis draws attention to the two highest profit strategies on which to concentrate: first, those that increase the percentage of gross profit to sales, and second, those which decrease the percentage of operating expenses to sales.

Examples of strategies for a supermarket to raise its gross profit percentage are to offer more high-profit items such as fresh produce, refrigerated cooked gourmet meals, hot and cold deli, and high quality fresh-baked goods. Note that use of the DuPont chart leads directly to important business strategy issues, and note also how it points out and prioritizes the most effective methods for raising ROE. This is a simple example of the benefits a DuPont analysis can provide in dealing with business strategy. Financial ratios are useful in examining past performance, as discussed earlier. Now we see that they are also valuable for the design and the implementation of business strategy for the future.

In fact, the DuPont formula can be expanded to encompass the overall strategic objective of maximizing the market value of the company's common stock. Previously, the basic DuPont formula as presented as:

$$\text{Profit margin} \times \text{asset turnover} \times \text{leverage} = \text{Return on equity}$$

Return on equity consists of net income/common equity, where common equity is based on the cost (book value) of assets and not market value. The expansion in the DuPont formula is to multiply return on equity by the price/earnings (PE) ratio, which is the ratio of the market price per common share to the earnings per common share. The resulting product is the market-to-book ratio, as shown algebraically in the following equation:

$$\frac{\text{Net income}}{\text{Common equity}} \times \frac{\text{Price per share}}{\text{Earnings per share}} = \frac{\text{Market price}}{\text{Book value}}$$

It is generally agreed that the overall strategic objective is to maximize the market value of the company's common stock. This is equivalent to maximizing the market-to-book ratio. From a practical point of view, maximizing the market-to-book ratio is achieved by focusing on the four component ratios in the DuPont formula that result in the market-to-book ratio. These four component ratios are as follows:

$$\frac{\text{Profit}}{\text{margin}} \times \frac{\text{Asset}}{\text{turnover}} \times \frac{\text{Financial}}{\text{leverage}} \times \frac{\text{Price}}{\text{earnings}} = \frac{\text{Market-to-book}}{\text{ratio}}$$

This shows the four component ratios in the DuPont formula that are the drivers of overall business strategy.

FOR FURTHER READING

Anthony, Robert N., and James S. Reece, *Accounting: Text and Cases,* 7th ed. (Homewood, IL: Irwin, 1983).

Carmichael, D. R., Steven B. Lilien, and Martin Mellman, (eds.). *Accountants' Handbook,* 7th ed. (New York: John Wiley, 1991; supplements annually, since 1992).

Davidson, Sidney, Clyde P. Stickney, and Roman L. Weil, *Financial Accounting.* 4th ed. (Hinsdale, IL: Dryden Press, 1985).

Davidson, Sidney, and Roman L. Weil, (eds.). *Handbook of Modern Accounting,* 3rd ed. (New York: McGraw-Hill, 1983).

Horngren, Charles, and Gary L. Sundem, *Introduction to Management Accounting,* 7th ed. (Englewood Cliffs, NJ: Prentice Hall, 1987).

Livingstone, J. L., *The Portable MBA in Finance and Accounting* (New York: John Wiley, 1992).

Logue, Dennis E. (ed.), *Handbook of Modern Finance* (Boston: Warren, Gorham, Lamont, 1994).

Needles, Belverd E., Henry R. Anderson, and James C. Caldwell, *Financial & Managerial Accounting* (Burlington, MA: Houghton Mifflin, 1988).

Tracy, John, *How to Read a Financial Report,* 4th ed. (New York: John Wiley & Sons, 1993).

11 FINANCIAL MANAGEMENT: OPTIMIZING THE VALUE OF THE FIRM

John Leslie Livingstone

James E. Walter

THE FINANCE FUNCTION

The Board of Directors of Colossal Computer Corporation was holding its quarterly meeting in the handsomely paneled conference room. Dale Douglas, Colossal's Chief Financial Officer (CFO), was answering questions from directors. "Dale," asked Tiffany Bowes, "The Federal Reserve has just raised short-term interest rates by half a point. What impact will that have on our borrowing costs and on our earnings?"

Dennis Greenberg, another director, wanted to know how the fall of the U.S. dollar against the Swiss franc would affect Colossal's sales in European markets. Next, Judy Jackson asked, "Do you think we are a merger target, and who might make a run at acquiring us?" Another question came from Kenneth Chong: "Our sales this quarter were up by 10 percent, but our inventories rose by 40 percent. Did we overestimate the demand for our products?" Finally, Alison Aikman wanted to know what the prospects were for making sales to the Peoples' Republic of China, and how the company could ensure that it would receive payment for the products sold. She also asked if increased autonomy by the Palestinians in Gaza and Jericho offered any potential business opportunities for Colossal.

These questions give some flavor of the role of the financial function in a large corporation. The CFO is a key member of the top management team, is the architect of the company's financial policies, and is called on to analyze the impact of economic changes and major business decisions. The CFO plays a major part in the development of corporate strategy and business plans, and evaluates the financial performance of the various divisions and operating units of the company. The CFO builds and maintains important relationships for the company with members of the financial community, such as commercial banks, investment bankers, insurance companies, brokerage firms, stock exchanges, government regulators at the federal, state, and local levels, bond and credit rating agencies, and the financial press.

An essential financial function is to ensure that funds are available when required by the company to expand operations, and that funds generated by the firm's business are invested profitably. For example, consider the cash flow statements reproduced in Table 11-1 for Sega Enterprises, Inc. (a Japanese video game company).

Table 11-1 shows that Sega generated 14,544 million yen from operating activities in 1992. Also in that year, Sega invested 37,877 million yen, primarily for additional property and equipment, as well as increased investment in subsidiary companies, fixed leasehold deposits, deferred charges and intangible assets. The internally generated 14,544 million yen was not sufficient to finance the total investments of 37,877 million yen. Therefore Sega had to obtain substantial outside funds, and as Table 11-1 shows, increased its long-term debt by the large sum of 66,178 million yen. Part of this long-term debt helped

TABLE 11-1   Non-consolidated statements of cash flows, SEGA Enterprises, Ltd. For the year ended April 30, 1990, for the 11-month period ended March 31, 1991, and for the year ended March 31, 1992

	Millions of Yen			Thousands of U.S. Dollars (Note 3)
	1990	1991	1992	1992
Cash Flows from Operating Activities:				
Net income	¥ 4,845	¥ 8,244	¥14,014	$105,487
Adjustments to reconcile net income to net cash provided by operating activities:				
Depreciation	3,622	5,466	8,695	65,450
Amortization	93	113	372	2,800
Provision for severance indemnities	129	8	—	—
Provision for retirement benefits for directors and statutory auditors	12	23	32	241
Loss on sale or disposal of property and equipment	106	89	254	1,912

TABLE 11-1   *(Continued)*

	Millions of Yen			Thousands of U.S. Dollars (Note 3)
	1990	1991	1992	1992
Changes in assets and liabilities:				
(Increase)/decrease in notes and				
accounts receivable	(3,829)	(4,929)	**(28,677)**	**(215,860)**
(Increase)/decrease in inventories	(2,951)	(3,853)	**(9,670)**	**(72,789)**
(Increase)/decrease in prepaid expenses				
and other current assets	176	(54)	**(1,611)**	**(12,126)**
Increase/(decrease) in notes and				
accounts payable	5,287	7,324	**22,336**	**168,129**
Increase/(decrease) in income taxes				
payable	3,418	934	**7,588**	**57,117**
Increase/(decrease) in accrued expenses				
and other current liabilities	609	294	**2,844**	**21,408**
Other payments	2,014	912	**(1,633)**	**(12,293)**
Net cash provided by operating				
activities	13,531	14,571	**14,544**	**109,476**
Cash Flows from Investing Activities:				
Acquisition of property and equipment	(7,395)	(15,786)	**(21,684)**	**(163,221)**
Proceeds from sale of property and				
equipment	290	220	**427**	**3,214**
Decrease/(increase) in investments in				
securities	(953)	(535)	**133**	**1,001**
Decrease/(increase) in investments in				
subsidiaries	(707)	(1,600)	**(6,622)**	**(49,846)**
Decrease/(increase) in other investments	(451)	(857)	**(224)**	**(1,686)**
Decrease/(increase) in fixed leasehold				
deposits	(1,165)	(4,093)	**(4,760)**	**(35,830)**
Additions to deferred charges and				
intangible assets	(128)	(504)	**(5,147)**	**(38,743)**
Net cash used by investing activities	(10,509)	(23,155)	**(37,877)**	**(285,111)**
Cash Flows from Financing Activities:				
Proceeds from new share issue	18,915	—	**—**	**—**
Proceeds from issuances of long-term debt	—	—	**66,178**	**498,141**
Increase/(decrease) in short-term bank loans	(339)	(475)	**(334)**	**(2,514)**
Cash dividends	(275)	(202)	**(844)**	**(6,353)**
Net cash provided by financing				
activities	18,301	(677)	**65,000**	**489,274**
Changes in Cash and Cash Equivalents	21,323	(9,261)	**41,667**	**313,639**
Cash and Cash Equivalents at Beginning of Year	27,903	49,226	**39,965**	**300,828**
Cash and Cash Equivalents at End of Year	¥49,226	¥39,965	**¥81,632**	**$614,467**

The accompanying notes are an integral part of these statements.

to finance the total investments, and the remainder was reflected in the increase of 41,667 million yen in cash and cash equivalents shown in Table 11-1.

Note that the financial picture was radically different from one year to the next; for instance, no long-term borrowing took place in 1991 or 1990. In fact, there was no outside financing at all in 1991, but in 1990 there was a substantial new share issue. Total cash invested was vastly dissimilar from year to year, but the net cash provided by operating activities varied only by relatively little in each year. These large changes demonstrate that financial management is neither routine nor repetitive.

Management of Sega's cash inflows and outflows was a major responsibility of the company's finance function. Each section of this chapter will deal with a different aspect of the finance function, but all sections will include cash flow management in one way or another.

To facilitate discussion of the financial function, we have organized the subject matter along the lines of (1) guidelines for investing company funds, (2) adjustment for the time factor, (3) elements of asset management, and (4) financing decisions. The section dealing with guidelines for investing company funds deals with company objectives, management incentives, and limitations imposed by the environment. The section relating to the time factor pertains to the valuation now of cash flows to be received or paid out in future years. The third section concerning asset management deals with financial planning and plan implementation, otherwise known as capital budgeting. The fourth section pertaining to financing decisions concerns itself with internal and external sources of funds and the appropriate mix of debt and equity.

GUIDELINES FOR INVESTING COMPANY FUNDS

The ultimate financial objective of most firms is to maximize common share value. The shareholder has claim to whatever remains after creditors have been paid off, and is the principal risk taker. As the contributor of risk capital, his or her point of view should prevail.

It follows that the *basic guideline* for investing corporate funds is that the anticipated rate of return on any given investment proposal must be sufficient at least to cover interest charges on borrowed funds and compensate shareholders for the risks associated with the commitment of equity funds or capital. Otherwise, the value of the firm is adversely affected. The stockholder, being last in line, bears the brunt of the loss when the realized return on any investment project falls short of the composite cost of the funds committed to that project. Conversely, the shareowner receives the extra gain on a project when the return on investment surpasses the cost of funds employed.

The cost of any source of funds—whether debt or equity—is the rate of return that investors require for taking on the particular risk associated with the source of funds in question. The cost of debt varies with its location in the *pecking order* of priority and is typically lower than that for equity in the same firm. Interest on debt is also deductible for tax purposes, while the return to stockholders (dividends and appreciation in stock value) is not deductible as a company tax expense. Composite or overall cost of capital is simply the cost of each source of funds, weighted by the ratio of the respective source to total capital or funds employed, and tax adjusted where relevant.

Suppose company policy is to finance investment projects partly by debt to the tune of 30 percent of the funds needed and the remainder by equity. Assume further that the respective costs or required rates of return for debt and equity are 10 and 14 percent, and that the corporate tax rate is 37 percent. The composite cost of capital becomes:

Source of Capital	Weight		Cost		Composite
Debt	.30	×	$.10 \times (1 - .37)$	=	.0189
Equity	.70	×	.14	=	.0980
Combined	1.00				.1169

As the preceding example shows, the weighted average or blended cost of capital is 11.69 percent, comprising the 1.89 percent element for the after-tax debt cost, plus the 9.8 percent element for the cost of common equity.

Now, imagine a one-year investment of $1 million expected to return 20 percent before taxes ($200,000), over and above repayment of the original investment, and suppose that the investment is financed in the manner and at the costs previously assumed. With the corporate tax rate at .37 and debt at 30 percent of the capital needed, the lender would receive repayment of the principal amount loaned ($300,000) plus 10 percent interest ($30,000) for a total of $330,000. The equity investor would also get his money back ($700,000) and expect to receive his required 14 percent return ($98,000) plus, in this case, a bonus of $9,100. The latter represents the base investment of $1 million multiplied by the difference between the after-tax return on investment, with interest excluded, of $.20 \times (1 - .37)$ or .126 and the combined cost of debt and equity of .1169. If less than the expected return is realized, the lender will continue to receive his $330,000 as long as the investment generates at least that amount of cash value, while the equity investor gets whatever remains.

The basic guideline stipulating that anticipated rates of return on prospective investments should at least equal the composite cost of capital depends on management's ability to make unbiased revenue projections and to assess accurately the cost of capital. Strict adherence to the guideline, in turn, may run counter to the personal goals of management. Its application is also constrained by government regulation and other factors.

In the treatment that follows, attention is directed first to the theory that underlies the estimation of the cost of capital and to a critical assumption (market efficiency) on which it is based. Questions relating to (1) the motivation of management to act in the best interest of shareholders, and (2) the limitations imposed by accounting conventions, government regulation, prior commitments, and the like, are then considered. Matters pertaining to the unbiased forecast of revenues are deferred until later.

Cost Estimation

The costs of debt and equity that enter into the calculation of composite cost are not arbitrary. Interest costs can be objectively determined from the explicit costs of the various bond issues and other borrowings that make up the debt component in the total capital structure. The cost of equity, in contrast, cannot be directly measured since it reflects investors' unspecified expectations of dividends and capital appreciation in the future; it must be estimated on the basis of some underlying plausible model of investor behavior.

The *Capital Asset Pricing Model* (CAPM) is an accepted and sensible way of rationalizing the manner in which assets in general and common stock in particular are priced, and thereby assessing the minimum rates of return needed to compensate investors for choosing risky assets. Under the CAPM, investors are presumed to be rational, risk averse, and willing to accept expected rate of return and standard deviation (a measure of variability) of rate of return as measures of prospective reward and risk. Risk aversion implies that investors must be rewarded for bearing risk and will be motivated to minimize risk for any level of expected return through diversification.

In the CAPM model, the market in which assets are bought and sold is assumed to be highly competitive. Buyers and sellers are numerous, operate independently, and individually are unable to affect asset prices. New information is disseminated rapidly and cheaply, taxes are uniform, and transactions costs are minimal. Investors can lend and borrow at a riskless rate of interest, and the investment horizon is uniformly a single period (usually one year) in duration.

Investors have the choice of investing in a riskless asset, a risky portfolio, or a combination of the two. The expected return on the composite portfolio selected is the riskless interest rate *plus* the premium investors generally demand for investing in the risky market portfolio, weighted by the proportion of the investor's own wealth invested in the risky portfolio. If the riskless rate as approximated by, for instance, Treasury bills is on the order of 8 percent, and the risk premium or added return for investing in risky common stocks is 5 percent, the investor with half of his wealth at risk can expect to earn 10.5 percent; that is:

$$8 \text{ percent} \times \tfrac{1}{2} + 13 \text{ percent} \times \tfrac{1}{2}$$

The standard deviation measures the prospective variation of the actual from the expected return and, subject to some debate, is commonly regarded as an acceptable measure of portfolio risk. The standard deviation of any portfolio or package of securities is defined as the square root of the weighted sum of the individual variances and covariances.

Since riskfree assets have—by definition—zero variances and covariances with risky assets, the composite portfolio's standard deviation boils down to the standard deviation of the risky portfolio times the percentage of the investor's resources allocated to it. Substitution into the expected return equation gives rise to the capital market line that states that the expected return on any portfolio equals the riskfree rate plus the *market price* of risk multiplied by the portfolio's standard deviation. The market price of risk is the risk premium associated with common stock in general divided by the standard deviation of the risky market portfolio.

Risk-averse investors are motivated to be diversified to the degree that risks uncorrelated with the return on the market portfolio are washed out for the most part. The expected return or required rate of return on any security or package of securities, and, *by inference, the cost of equity for any given firm,* thus reduces in equilibrium to the return on the riskfree asset plus the market risk premium times the sensitivity of the individual security or portfolio to the market portfolio. The sensitivity measure is known as *Beta.* Beta is the regression coefficient that relates the return on the individual security or portfolio to the return on the market portfolio. In effect, Beta measures—in a relative sense—that part of asset risk that cannot be diversified away. It establishes a straightforward basis for assessing the required rate of return on any asset to the degree that the underlying assumptions hold.

A practical example will illustrate the preceding concepts. Say that we are estimating the cost of common equity for a particular company, which we call Mongo Corporation. As a starting point, we need to know the riskfree interest rate, which is generally taken as the U.S. Treasury bill rate. Say this is presently 4 percent. Next, we need to know the return for the market of common stocks as a whole. History shows that this averages about 12 percent. Finally, we also need an estimate of *Beta* for Mongo Corporation.

Betas can be calculated or can be obtained from investment services such as Value Line. A Beta of 1 indicates that a particular common stock has tended to fluctuate in tune with the market as a whole. Since it has displayed little or no variability relative to stocks as a whole, it would be seen as a stock of average volatility. Stocks of this type often include companies in the food-processing business, which is usually quite stable, such as Campbell Soup and Archer Daniels (a large processor of corn products). A stock of less than average volatility would have a Beta less than 1, indicating that it fluctuated less than stocks as a whole. Stocks of this type are relatively steady, and defensive in nature, and they typically include electric utility companies such as Boston Edison and Carolina Power, with Betas typically in the 0.6 to 0.7 range. Stocks with Betas exceeding 1 fluctuate more than the market, and therefore are regarded as more volatile. Examples include airlines such as Continental, and metal producers such as Phelps Dodge (copper) and Reynolds Metals (aluminum), with Betas in the 1.3 to 1.5 range.

Say that Mongo has a Beta of 1.3. Then the CAPM calculation for Mongo's cost of common equity would be:

$$\underset{4\%}{\text{Riskfree rate}} + \underset{1.3}{\text{Beta}} \times (\underset{12\%}{\text{Market rate}} - \underset{4\%}{\text{Riskfree rate}}) = \underset{14.4\%}{\text{Mongo cost of equity}}$$

If Mongo's Beta had been 0.8, then its cost of equity would be 10.4 percent (4% + 0.8 {12% − 4%}), and if Mongo's Beta had been 1.6, then its cost of equity would be 16.8 percent (4% + 1.6 {12% − 4%}). Note that low Betas give low costs of equity, and high Betas result in high costs of equity, revealing the classic pattern that investors demand increased rates of return as volatility becomes greater.

In a nutshell, the CAPM is a layered approach to estimating the cost of equity. The first layer is the riskfree rate, the next layer is the rate of return premium (over and above the riskfree rate) for the stock market as a whole (because stocks have more volatile returns than Treasury bills), and the final layer is an adjustment up or down depending on the Beta for the particular stock in question. Stocks with a Beta less than one will have a cost of capital below the rate of return for the market as a whole, while stocks with a Beta greater than one will have a cost of capital above the market rate of return.

Market Efficiency

Competition in the marketplace is essential to the process of asset pricing and cost determination in the CAPM just described, as is rational behavior. Competition among investors helps to keep the rates at which money is offered in line with comparable investments and reduces the likelihood of discrimination.

Competition also pressures management and employees to be efficient. Otherwise, the competitor lures the business away since he can offer the product at a lower price.

To the degree that the conditions necessary for competitive behavior prevail, funds flow and resources move from low return to high return areas. Barriers to entry and exit of any consequence are precluded. Values in the marketplace adjust to the point that, in the absence of further shifts, expected returns are uniform for each level of risk.

The financial markets in the United States are judged to be among the most efficient in the world. Sophisticated financial institutions pool the funds of individual investors. Secondary markets exist for all classes of securities and provide the basis for pricing new issues. Information sources and professional help abound for both the financial manager and the investor.

The financial markets are, however, less than 100 percent efficient as evidenced by the October 1987 market crash. Institutions individually and collectively do have the power to affect security prices. Taxation lacks uniformity. Access to information varies directly with the size and character of the company. Spreads may be substantial for small, infrequently traded securities. Market-makers lack the capital to maintain liquid markets under all circumstances.

Since the market-efficiency assumptions that underlie the CAPM are not completely satisfied, estimates of the cost of equity are somewhat tentative. The numbers derived are, however, generally believed to be acceptable and usable as ballpark estimates.

Whose Viewpoint?

On the surface, the shareholder appears to stand atop the corporate hierarchy. Holders of the corporation's common stock, along with any other parties entitled to vote, elect company directors. Directors, acting as agents of the shareholders, set policy and hire and fire chief executive officers (CEOs). The CEO, in turn, operating within policy guidelines has the power to hire and fire other members of management.

In practice, however, shareholders rarely exercise their right to "throw the rascals out." Management may nominate "friendly" persons to be members of the board; management may arrange for staggered boards, to preclude rapid change of control; shareholders may side with management or register disappointment by not submitting their proxies. Proxy battles are both expensive and difficult to win, as several corporate raiders have discovered to their chagrin.

Management, as personified by the CEO, frequently has de facto control of the firm and can—within broad limits—substitute its objectives for those of shareholders. For instance, management may emphasize growth at the expense of rate of return; management may choose to diversify even though shareholders can do it more effectively; management may choose not to borrow optimally despite tax advantages. In potential conflict with shareholder interests, management may opt for a management-leveraged buyout when stock prices are depressed.

Efforts within the corporation to equate the objectives of management with those of shareholders revolve around compensation schemes. Top executives of major firms now receive a base salary plus (1) annual cash bonuses and (2) long-term performance compensation made up of stock options, stock appreciation rights, restricted stock, and performance awards. The underlying idea is to relate an increasing part of compensation to company earnings and to stock price behavior.

Help has also come from the outside, so to speak. Companies that underachieve in stock value open themselves to attack by corporate raiders. The latter create added-value through leverage and sale of underperforming assets and, in so doing, have pressured managements to restructure on their own.

Management has partly countered the threat of takeover by changes in corporate charters and bylaws, adoption of poison pills, lobbying for restrictive state legislation, and management buyouts. The implied argument is that the raider's short-term focus is antisocial and that those who speculate in takeovers are somehow less worthy than long-term investors.

Conflicts are certain to ensue no matter what is done. The fact is that numerous parties have stakes in the corporation. What is good for one may be at the expense of another. The upshot is that, while the basic guideline for investing remains more or less intact, management has—by virtue of its strategic position in the corporation—some leeway to substitute its values for those of the shareholder and to take account of the interests of other parties.

Conditioning Factors

Management is further constrained in its effort to apply the basic guidelines by accounting conventions, tax considerations, government regulation, and contractual agreements. Management may also be sensitive to public opinion, the need to maintain the corporate image, and other factors as well.

Accounting Conventions

Accounting conventions play an important role since they establish the basis on which income is measured. Income or earnings per share and its period-by-period change may directly influence stock value. Investors rely on the independent auditor to affirm the fairness of the accounting numbers.

Accounting numbers are not as precise as they may at first appear to be, however, and they depend to some extent on future projections (such as the service lives of depreciable assets) and the remaining life of intangible assets such as goodwill, which are inherently imprecise. Furthermore, generally accepted accounting principles (GAAP) allow some discretion in the choice of accounting methods, which in turn can influence the figures reported in the financial statements. Therefore, it is important to understand that accounting figures may be no more precise than other financial and economic statistics.

It is also important to understand that accounting figures are usually based on the historical cost of assets and do not purport to represent current market values. For example, say a company purchased vacant land in 1953 for $2 million, and that it still owns that vacant land today. A real estate broker estimates that the land now is worth $11 million. The land will nevertheless continue to be reported in the balance sheet at its original cost of $2 million. This accounting practice has been severely criticized on many occasions.

But some critics do not appreciate that there are sound reasons for supporting the historic cost approach. First, it is factual and objective: There is no ambiguity about the $2 million figure. However, the $11 million estimated selling price may be merely theoretical and largely speculative. Assets such as land are often sold at prices quite different from their estimated selling prices. Therefore, to base financial statements on speculation and guesswork about projected market prices can be a dubious proposition.

Second, the $2 million original cost is meaningful and useful factual information: It represents the actual market price at the time of purchase. In Chapter 10, it was noted that the primary strategic goal of management is to maximize the common stock market-to-book ratio. To accomplish that task, it is necessary to have a reliable measure of book value, which is based on historic costs. This is provided by the historic cost financial statements when they are accompanied by a "clean" opinion from the independent outside auditors. Therefore, historic cost figures are an important element in measuring the success of a company's strategy.

Tax Considerations

Taxes on income shape behavior in at least two ways: (1) Rules for determining taxable income affect the manner in which income is measured for other purposes as well, and (2) all taxes take cash, have economic effects, and are rarely neutral.

Companies may partly negate tax-imposed procedures by legitimately maintaining two sets of books—the first for reporting to investors and the other for the tax authorities. Note, for example, the deferred income-tax item that appears on many financial statements. This item reflects the difference between the effective tax based on accelerated depreciation and the like, and the tax that would have to be paid if, for example, straight-line depreciation were utilized for tax purposes. Limitations to separate bookkeeping nonetheless exist. The firm must, for instance, employ the same inventory valuation method for financial statement purposes as it does for tax purposes.

Economic effects abound. Ability to deduct research and development as a current tax expense places it in a preferred status relative to expenditures on plant and equipment, which can only be deducted over the many years of service expected from these long-lived assets. Interest deductibility alters the cost of debt and thereby the cost of capital. The list could go on, but the point has been established that cash flows associated with prospective investments need to be valued on an after-tax basis. Capital outlays that appear attractive on a before-tax basis may or may not be acceptable on consideration of tax effects.

Government Regulation

Government is everywhere. The belief exists that business, if left completely unfettered, would ignore social concerns unless the bottom line benefited. Land, water, and air pollution are all legacies of earlier neglect by both business and government. Regulatory agencies now press business to limit further damage to the environment. Government agencies also focus concern on employee and customer safety.

Competition itself, if left unchecked, can be ruthless. The objective is to win, and winning may lead to gobbling up one's competition. Antitrust thus has a role to play.

Furthermore, government aims to ensure that the competitive game is played fairly. Disclosure is the key word of securities legislation, since information is the name of the game in stock and bond valuation.

The intent of government, then, is to ensure that the basic guidelines for investing heed social costs and bypass monopoly income. Some investment projects are rendered less desirable; some may be ruled out altogether. Full and fair disclosure, in turn, contributes to market efficiency and thereby reduces the cost of capital.

Contractual Agreements and Other Commitments

Management's ability to invest in projects whose expected return exceeds the cost of capital hinges, in the final analysis, on the firm's flexibility. Companies that are committed to the hilt, subject to unduly restrictive debt covenants, or threatened with massive litigation have reduced flexibility.

Firms are not short-lived organisms. They must commit themselves to the future to survive. This commitment to the future obliges management to enter into contractual and other less formal (but binding) agreements that limit flexibility and add to risk. Armco, a partner with LTV in a mining venture, was placed in jeopardy when LTV declared bankruptcy, and the venture's debt thereby immediately became due. Armco also worried about the mounting costs of its obligation to provide health benefits for retired employees.

Long-term debt commits the firm to a series of future cash repayments. The same is true with respect to financial or capitalized leases and operating leases to a lesser extent. The penalty for failure to meet such commitments can be severe.

Firms must also live with the unintended consequences of past decisions. Confronted with an unending stream of lawsuits arising from its disastrous Dalkon Shield product, A. H. Robbins declared bankruptcy. Johns Manville suffered a similar fate in connection with asbestos claims, and so did Texaco when it lost a huge lawsuit to Pennzoil relating to the acquisition of Getty Oil.

THE TIME FACTOR

Would you rather receive $100 today or two years from now? Most people would choose today, even if the payment two years from now was guaranteed to be absolutely certain. The reason for preferring immediate payment is that the $100 received now could also be invested now. Two years from today, at 5 percent interest, it would amount to $110 and certainly would be preferable to receiving only $100 after two years. However, by the same token, if you were paying out rather than receiving cash, then you would prefer to pay $100 in two years' time rather than today (because you could hold the $100 and earn interest on it for the two years). The lesson is that monetary amounts due at different dates cannot be directly compared: First, they must be adjusted to allow for the interest that could be earned between the dates involved. This adjustment procedure is often referred to as discounting, or discounted cash flow, or present value.

In a very real sense, the principal function of the financial manager is to buy and sell claims to future cash flow in such a way as to create value *now* for the shareholder. Investments or capital expenditures represent the purchase of such claims, while debt instruments and equity shares constitute the sale of claims to future cash flow. Some investments generate cash quickly, some, over an intermediate term, and some, slowly over an extended period. The same holds true for debt and equity as well.

To make claims that are characterized by different cash flow streams and maturities comparable, we resort to discounting. The basic thrust of discounting is that the value of an asset or claim now (its present value) is that dollar amount which, given the firm's required rate of return, will generate the projected or promised stream of future cash flows. Thus, cash flow of $3.00 materializing one year hence is worth $2.61 today if the required return is 15 percent per annum; conversely, $2.61 put to work for one year at 15 percent will grow to $3.00 by year end.

Present versus Future

The future value of one dollar depends on the yearly rate (i) which that dollar can earn and the length of time (T) that the earnings are expected to continue. Thus, future value of one dollar (FV$1) equals $(1 + i)**T$. Note that "$**$" stands for exponentiation, so that (FV$1) equals $(1 + i)^T$. One dollar invested at 12 percent per annum for five years grows, for example, to $1.76 if the interest (i) is reinvested and compounded annually.

The present value of one dollar (PV$1) to be received T years in the future is simply the reciprocal of the future value equation; that is, $PV\$1 = 1/(1 + i)**T$. Present value is that amount which, if invested now at rate i, will grow to one dollar at the end of T years. Total present (PV) or future (FV) value equals PV$1 or FV$1 multiplied by the number of dollars (A) at stake.

Consider now an investment expected to generate cash flows of $1,000,000 per year for each of the next five years. Assume further that the minimum return required is 15 percent. Total present value is determined by summing the product of the cash flow (A) and the respective PV$1 for each year, as follows:

Year (T)	Cash Flow (A)	×	PV$1	=	Present Value
1	$1,000,000		.870		$ 870,000
2	$1,000,000		.756		756,000
3	$1,000,000		.658		658,000
4	$1,000,000		.572		572,000
5	$1,000,000		.594		497,000
Total present value					$3,353,000

In short, shareholders receive more than their minimum required rate of return from this project as long as the price paid for this investment is less than $3,353,000.

Annuities

In many instances, it is convenient to think in terms of a cash flow stream starting at one dollar per period, either remaining constant or growing at some rate, and continuing for a specified period of time. Should there be no maturity, as in the case of a special British bond or consol, the annuity's present value (PVA$1) equals 1/i. Since the maturity is infinite, the cash flow per period is pure interest or income and there is no principal ever to be repaid. Should there be a finite maturity (T), PVA$1 equals the present value of an annuity of one dollar forever minus the present value of a perpetual annuity of one dollar commencing (T + 1) periods in the future. Thus,

$$PVA\$1 = (1/i) \times [1 - (1 + i)\circ\circ - T]$$

Consider the previous example of yearly cash flows of $1,000,000 continuing for five years and discounted at 15 percent. Viewed as an annuity, its present value equals $1,000,000 × PVA$1 where PVA$1 equals $(1/.15) \times [1 - 1/(1.15)\circ\circ 5]$, or 3.352. The annuity value of $3,352,000 differs slightly from the prior PV solution due to round-off. Unless otherwise specified, cash flows are presumed to occur at the end of each period.

For many valuation purposes, an appropriate assumption is that the annuity grows at some constant rate throughout its life. The present value (PVG$1) of cash flows starting at $1 and growing at rate g for T periods equals $[(1 + g)/(i - g)] \times \{1 - [(1 + g)/(1 + i)]\circ\circ T\}$. If T is infinite, PVG$1 simplifies to $(1 + g)/(i - g)$, provided i > g.

Suppose that the cash flow of $1,000,000 in the preceding illustration grows at 10 percent per annum throughout the five years with the discount rate (i) remaining at 15 percent. Present value now equals $1,000,000 times PVG$1, where PVG$1 equals $[(1.1)/(.15 - .1)] \times [1 - (1.1/1.15)\circ\circ 5]$, or 4.384. Total present value is $4,384,000 and is well above the corresponding present value for the constant, nongrowth annuity.

Future values, where needed for the evaluation of pension programs or other purposes, can readily be derived from present values; the future values of a constant annuity (FVA$1) and an annuity growing at rate g(FVG$1), respectively, equal $PVA\$1 \times (1 + i)\circ\circ(T + 1)$ and $PVG\$1 \times (1 + i)\circ\circ(T + 1)$. The use of $(1 + i)\circ\circ(T + 1)$ assumes that the initial cash flow is received or invested at the start—rather than at the end—of the initial period.

Adjustment for Uncertainty

Future values are not known with certainty. Financial managers are, as a consequence, faced with a choice. Should they (1) discount each of the possible outcomes by the risk-free interest rate in order to obtain a set of risk-free present values for each project, (2) assign a utility index value that represents the trade-off between risk and return to each element of the set, and (3) weight each utility index value by its likelihood of occurrence and sum to derive a composite utility value that can then be used for ranking purposes? Or, should managers form expected values for the cash flows in each future period and discount these expected values at a discount rate that reflects the degree of uncertainty?

The latter method seems preferable. It is more readily understood and allows the user to view risk or uncertainty in a global, companywide respect, as opposed to an individual project sense. Risk-adjusted discount rates will be treated subsequently.

Internal Rate of Return (IRR)

Suppose that the project analyst has projected cash flows for each future period and has also estimated the investment outlay (I) that is required to generate the projected cash flows (CF). The financial manager now wishes to know the "true" rate of return on the project in question for comparison with the cost of capital. As illustrated in Table 11-2, the "true" or internal rate of return is that discount rate (.15238) which equates the positive cash flows with the negative cash flow or investment. The investment, I(0), of $10,000 is presumed in this case to be made in a lump sum at the outset.

Table 11-2 shows how the periodic cash flow of $3,000 is divided between interest or income and retirement of the principal amount. Return on investment is always .15238 times the remaining investment at the end of the previous year. In brief, the return on investment is constant throughout the life of the investment, and the original investment is recovered. IRR thereby meets the test of being a constant rate of return over all periods of project life.

TABLE 11-2   Internal rate of return*

Assume that a $10,000 investment generates a net cash flow (after tax) of $3,000 per year for each of the next 5 years. What does an IRR of 15,238 percent mean?

Year	Remaining Investment	Cash Flow	Interest	Retirement of Principal
0	$10,000			
1	8,523.80	$3,000	$1,523.80	$1,476.20
2	6,822.66	3,000	1,298.86	1,701.14
3	4,862.30	3,000	1,039.64	1,960.36
4	2,603.22	3,000	740.92	2,259.08
5	(.10)	3,000	396.68	2,603.32

*The Internal Rate of Return (IRR) is a true rate of return in that it measures the return on the investment outstanding at each point in time. The 10 cent remainder in year 5 is due to rounding error.

Valuation Models

Bonds are valued in much the same manner as capital expenditures. The typical bond is, for example, characterized by a coupon (c) representing the amount to be paid each period, an amount (M)—normally, $1000—to be paid at maturity, and a maturity (T) representing the life of the bond. The bond thus can be viewed as an annuity of c dollars for T periods plus a payment of M dollars at time T; its value (V) reduces to: $V = c/i + (M - c/i)/(1 + i)^{**}T$. With c, i, M, and T respectively set equal to $120, .10, $1000, and 25, the bond value is equal to $120/.1 + (1000 - 120/.1)/1.1^{**}25$, or $1,181.54. If the coupon rate, that is, 120/1000 or .12, exceeds i, the bond value exceeds par (M), and vice versa.

The value of a share of common stock, in contrast, can be viewed as the summed present value of all future cash dividends. Since companies normally reinvest part of earnings at a positive rate of return, the expected internal growth rate (g) equals the portion of earnings retained times the rate of return. Since common stock has no maturity specified, the value of a share of common stock is the value of an annuity growing at rate g forever (in an expected sense) and is equal to $D(0) \times (1 + g)/(r - g)$, where $D(0)$ is the current dividend per share, r is the investor's required rate of return, and $r > g$.

The foregoing valuation model is especially applicable to mature firms that have attained a steady-state growth rate. The valuation of growth companies that have not yet achieved maturity must be modified to take account of changing growth rates. Two- or three-stage growth models can readily be derived, and are described in more advanced books on finance.

ASSET MANAGEMENT

The three phases of asset management are (1) planning, (2) implementation, and (3) control and feedback. Planning establishes the ground rules for orderly development consistent with corporate aims. Implementation translates the plans into action. Control and feedback operates to correct mistakes, move forward along the learning curve, and assign responsibility.

Planning

Management normally tries to look forward three to five years as part of its capital investment planning process. The goal is to give profit center heads clues as to the availability of funds for capital investment and to assess what needs to be done to achieve corporate goals. Go or no-go decisions regarding capital investment frequently must be made well in advance.

Other planning cycles also exist. The short-term cash flow cycle is watched to ensure that cash is available to pay bills as needed. Product cycles are followed to determine the rate at which new products must be introduced to perpetuate growth.

Key policy variables for the investment planning cycle include: (1) identification of "core" business(es), (2) liquidity, (3) degree of leverage, (4) internal versus external growth, and (5) dividends and stock repurchase. Amoco, for instance, stipulates that its two core businesses are (1) petroleum exploration and refining and (2) petrochemicals. Its financial objectives are long-term earnings growth of 8 to 10 percent annually, return on equity between 13 and 15 percent, a debt to debt-plus-equity ratio falling between 20 and 25 percent, and a dividend payout ratio of 35 to 45 percent. These variables, together with management's ability to attain its specific goals and the market's view of company risk, largely determine stock value.

McKesson Corporation (a major pharmaceutical supplier) in a recent report stated that its objective for the next several years include:

- Annual growth of 10 percent to 12 percent in earnings per share.
- Return on equity of about 19 percent per year.
- A debt-to-capital ratio of 40 percent to 50 percent.

McKesson pointed out that in the past few years return on equity had exceeded 19 percent but was expected to decline since "to maximize shareholder value, the company's hurdle rate for new investments is lower than 19 percent." This indicates that the blended cost of capital for McKesson is less than 19 percent, since it would have to be below the hurdle rate for new investments.

Core Business(es)

The type(s) of business that management elects to emphasize influences the sales per dollar of assets, the profit margin, and the sensitivity of revenues to changes in the economic environment. Sales per dollar of assets multiplied by the profit margin gives rise to return on assets (ROA). Intersegment differences in profitability ratios can be substantial even in the case of strong product intercorrelation, as shown for three AMOCO business segments:

Ratio	Production	Refining	Petrochemical	Overall
Sales/Assets	.470	3.080	1.400	.946
Operating profit/Sales	.261	.056	.193	.124
Operating profit/Assets	.123	.172	.270	.117

Cash flow sensitivity, in turn, depends on such product characteristics as price, durability, and market share, as well as on operating leverage. High product prices imply sensitivity to interest rates; durability indicates ability to defer replacement, while market share and product price inelasticity afford management a degree of control over price. Operating leverage refers to the sensitivity of operating cash flows to the underlying percentage change in sales and has to do with the mix of fixed and variable costs; the formula boils down to:

$$\frac{(\text{Sales} - \text{Variable cost})}{[(\text{Sales} - \text{Variable cost}) - \text{Fixed cash cost} + \text{Tax rate} \times \text{Depreciation}]}$$

Management sometimes attempts to reduce cash flow sensitivity in particular and risk in general by means of diversification. Automobile manufacturers partly offset the volatility of new car sales by producing and selling automotive parts whose sales tend to be negatively correlated with new car sales.

Diversification benefits the company in three ways:

1. Diversification averages across company-specific risks, that is, risks that are uncorrelated with each other.
2. Diversification diminishes correlated risks to the degree that the company diversifies into areas that are less sensitive to the underlying economic environment.
3. Diversification may increase the likelihood of company survival in the long run since some products among a diversified set are likely to be winners.

Diversification at the company level has at least two demerits:

1. Management may be unable to manage effectively a diversified set of businesses.
2. Investors are generally better able to diversify than are companies. The result is that diversification at the company level may be redundant and contribute little to enterprise value.

Liquidity and Degree of Leverage

Liquidity, measured by the ratio of cash items to total assets, and financial leverage, measured by the ratio of debt to debt-plus-equity, go hand in hand since the former could be used to retire the latter. General Mills, among others, thus subtracts cash items from debt in deriving its debt ratio. Exxon has even removed over $700 million of debt from its balance sheet since 1982 by placing sufficient government securities in escrow to cover the debt through a procedure called *defeasance*.

From the standpoint of planning, net leverage, that is, debt adjusted for cash items, affects profitability, growth, and risk. Return on equity (ROE) surpasses return on assets (ROA) by a factor that represents the tax-adjusted difference between ROA and interest:

$$ROE = ROA + [ROA - i(1 - T)] \times (D/E)$$

where i is the interest rate, T is the tax rate, and D and E are respective debt and equity. ROA is the after-tax return on assets. With i, T, ROA, and D/E respectively taken to be .1, .4, .12, and .5, for example, ROE becomes .12 + [.12 − .1(.6)] × .5, or .15.

Dividend Policy

Dividends compete with capital investments for the available cash flow, as do stock repurchases. Companies that reinvest all their earnings can be expected to grow at the rate of their normal return on equity, or ROE; those that reinvest half their earnings grow at half their ROE, and so forth. The formula for internal growth (IGF) is ROE × (1 − p), where p refers to the proportion of earnings paid out in the form of cash dividends. Stock repurchases slow down internal growth in a total company sense, but not on a per-share growth basis since repurchases reduce the number of shares outstanding.

Internal versus External

Based on its financial targets enumerated previously and on assumed interest and tax rates of .1 and .4 respectively, Amoco must realize a before-tax return on assets ranging from 18.4 to 23.7 percent to achieve its growth objective of 8 to 10 percent internally. The alternative is to go outside the firm to achieve the desired growth through merger and acquisition. The latter, as Amoco has found in its acquisition of Dome Petroleum, is easier said than done.

Implementation

Implementation, like Gaul (for those who took Latin), is divisible into three parts. The first is management of working capital; the second, capital budgeting; and the third, merger and acquisition.

Management of Working Capital

Working capital, or more precisely, net working capital, is defined as current assets minus current liabilities. Current assets typically include cash items (cash and near-cash), accounts receivable, inventories at various stages of completion, and prepaid expenses. Current liabilities comprise notes and accounts payable and accrued liabilities. The dividing line between current and noncurrent is 12 months.

Waiving cash items, notes payable, and current maturities on long-term debt for the moment, the requisite investment in working capital depends on customer and supplier credit policies and duration of the production and inventory cycle. Creditworthy companies buy materials, hire workers, and the like on credit, and likewise extend credit to worthy customers.

Working capital ratios in recent years for USG, a building materials company, illustrate the point:

	Ratio[1]	Value
1.	(Accounts receivable/Sales) × 360	41.82 days outstanding
2.	(Inventory/Cost of sales) × 360	34.95 days outstanding
3.	(Current liabilities/Operating expenses) × 360	54.70 days outstanding
4.	(1 + 2)/3	1.40
5.	Current ratio	1.25

The number of days outstanding for receivables and inventories taken together *minus* the number of days outstanding for payables largely determines the investment period for working capital. The current ratio, by its very nature, is closely identified with the ratio of these three variables.

Working capital is a mixed bag. It is, as noted earlier, a part of the permanent investment base due to its ongoing, revolving character. It is also, by virtue of its nearness to cash, a one-time source of funds. Accounts receivable can be used as collateral or sold with or without recourse. The finished goods part of inventories is available for the same purpose.

Decisions to extend more or less credit to customers and to hold larger or smaller inventories require the same assessment as any investment decision. The issue to be resolved is whether the return on the added investment exceeds or falls short of the cost of capital. Decisions to rely on working capital as a one-time source of funds depend, in contrast, on the availability and cost of alternative sources of funds.

Cash items, notes payable, and current maturities on long-term debt warrant separate treatment since they are not a part of the more or less automatic credit-inventory-credit cycle. Apart from so-called transactions cash, the level of cash items depends on management's perceived need for liquidity. Short-term loans from banks and other financial institutions, designated as notes payable, bear interest; must be negotiated by management; and, if used consistently, should be viewed as part of the permanent capital base.

Capital Budgeting

Capital budgeting relates to the execution of the firm's long-term investment strategies. It entails (1) product development and search for feasible projects, (2) cash flow forecasting, (3) project ranking, (4) risk assessment, (5) determination of cutoff point, and (6) process control. The focus here is on items (2), (3), and (4). Item (1), however, is critical. No feasible projects means no company future. Cash resources available and worthy projects are rarely in balance: Usually one exceeds the other.

Profit center managers normally originate new investment proposals and rely on aides to prepare cash flow forecasts and follow company guidelines with respect to the project details, forecast horizon, and ranking criteria employed. The magnitude of the investment outlay determines the level in management hierarchy needed for approval. Major projects are reviewed by the finance staff and require approval by the executive committee.

The cash flow worksheet, together with appendixes, constitutes the basic document. The worksheet provides a year-by-year schedule of projected cash outflows and inflows. Outflows include outlays for both plant and equipment as well as working capital. Inflows consist of (1) forecasted profit before taxes and such noncash charges as depreciation (EBDT), minus (2) the EBDT lost on related business due to the project in question, minus (3) the appropriate tax rate times the net EBDT, plus (4) the tax rate times noncash charges, plus (5) the tax-adjusted terminal value of plant and equipment and residual working capital. The schedule of inflows minus outflows, that is, net cash flows, is given in the final column.

Projects differ notably in the degree of reliability with which cash flows can be projected. The easiest to handle is equipment replacement since its profitability hinges on degree of usage and comparative efficiency of the "old" and "new." The next degree of forecast complexity relates to the expansion of facilities to handle increased demand for existing products. Although benefiting from past experience, the analyst must not only project underlying economic variables on which demand depends but also consider the possibility of competition (especially if profit margins are high). Most difficult to forecast are the results of investing in plant and equipment to house new products. Aside from test marketing, perhaps, there is little past history; everything must be projected.

Forecast errors are to be *expected*. The problem for management is to avoid major mistakes and to work toward unbiased forecasts. Major mistakes include the neglect of factors relevant to the outcome, the failure to check for internal consistency, and the application of flawed methodology. It is, for example, inappropriate to dismiss the possibility of competition when projected profit margins are high and entry into the business is easy; it is improper to have changes in working capital that are out of tune with the anticipated behavior of sales and EBDT, and it is methodologically deficient to deduct overhead expense in deriving EBDT unless cash flows are directly affected. The checklist of factors to be considered is substantial.

Sensitivity analysis is a useful way to sort out forecast items of major concern. The effect of forecasting errors on IRR, shown in Table 11-3, indicates (1) delays in cash generation alone can be devastating since the investment grows by $(1 + r)^{**}T$, where r and T are, respectively, the cost of capital and the period of delay; (2) errors in forecasting the exact duration of long-lived investments need not be crucial; and (3) the effects of project overruns and overstatements of cash flow are about the same for comparable forecast errors. Sensitivity analysis helps to determine where to place the forecast effort.

The worksheet for developing cash flow, given in Table 11-4, is arranged somewhat differently from the breakdown just described, but it leads to the same result. Can you explain the differences? The projections in Table 11-4 also appear to be based on a number of questionable assumptions. What are they?

Unbiased forecasts are difficult to achieve although management—conceptually speaking—should be able to compensate for a persistent tendency to depart from the predicted value. The difficulty lies in inadequate record keeping, the long-lived character of many projects, and the bureaucratic process itself. Projects tend to be evaluated on an IRR or net present value (NPV) basis, while records of performance—if kept—are maintained on a traditional accounting basis. Cash flow forecasts for long-lived projects in turn are commonly truncated at 5 or 10 years. Project review likewise is often deferred until the responsible parties have moved elsewhere in the organization.

Methods of summarizing or ranking investment projects, once their cash flows have been estimated, include (1) payback period, (2) accounting rate of return, (3) internal rate of return (IRR), (4) net present value (NPV), (5) discounted payback period, and (6) profitability index (PI). Payback period, defined as the number of years required to recover the investment from project cash flows, is easy to understand and is used as a secondary criterion in cases where risks and inflation are high, and the firm is short of cash. Payback period does not address profitability, or discounting, and should not stand alone as a criterion for investment.

Accounting rate of return (ROI) relates accounting income (before or after depreciation) to gross or net investment; it may relate to a single year or be averaged. The concept of ROI is simple to comprehend, and the numbers on which it is based are the same as those reported to investors. The shortcomings are that a one-year ROI of 15 percent could turn into an 85 percent loss next year if no future revenues are forthcoming, averaging over project life fails to take the timing of cash flows into account, and expense allocations may be arbitrary.

TABLE 11-3 Effect of forecasting errors on IRR

	Project Forecast	Actual			
		Project Overrun 10%	Cash Inflow Overstated 10% per Year	Useful Life Overstated 20%	Cash Inflow Deferred 2 Years
Investment	$10,000	$11,000	$10,000	$10,000	$10,000
Annual net cash flow	$ 2,000	$ 2,000	$ 1,800	$ 2,000	$ 2,000
Example A:					
Useful life	10 YEARS	10 YEARS	10 YEARS	8 YEARS	10 YEARS
IRR	15.1%	12.7%	12.4%	11.8%	10.4%
Actual IRR variance from forecast	—	16%	18%	22%	31%
Example B:					
Useful life	20 YEARS	20 YEARS	20 YEARS	16 YEARS	20 YEARS
IRR	19.4%	17.5%	17.3%	18.7%	15.6%
Actual IRR variance from forecast	—	10%	11%	4%	20%
Memo: Third year ROI (assuming 10-year straight line depreciation)	10%	9%	8%	10%	10%

TABLE 11-4 Worksheet for developing cash flow (in $millions)

Year	Capitalizable Expenditures*	Working Capital Additions†	Investment Cash Flow	Pre-Tax Earnings Before Deprec.	Book Depreciation‡	Taxable Earnings	Net Earnings	Net Cash Flow from Operations	Net Cash Flow
1986	(4.5)		(4.5)	(2.0)		(2.0)	(1.2)	(1.2)	(5.7)
1987	(6.2)		(6.2)	(2.0)		(2.0)	(1.2)	(1.2)	(7.4)
1988	(5.8)		(5.8)	(2.8)		(2.8)	(1.7)	(1.7)	(7.5)
1989			(3.0)	(.3)	1.7	(2.0)	(1.2)	.5	(2.5)
1990		(3.0)	(1.0)	4.7	1.7	3.0	1.8	3.5	2.5
1991		(1.0)	(2.0)	9.7	1.7	8.0	4.8	6.5	4.5
1992		(2.0)	(2.6)	16.5	1.6	14.9	8.9	10.5	7.9
1993		(2.6)		16.5	1.2	15.3	9.2	10.4	10.4
1994				16.5	1.2	15.3	9.2	10.4	10.4
1995				16.6	1.1	15.5	9.3	10.4	10.4
1996				12.9	1.0	11.9	7.1	8.1	8.1
1997				12.9	.8	12.1	7.3	8.1	8.1
1998				12.9	.8	12.1	7.3	8.1	8.1
1999				12.9	.7	12.2	7.3	8.0	8.0
2000				12.9	.6	12.3	7.4	8.0	8.0
2001	.5	8.6	9.1	12.9	1.9	11.0	6.6	8.5	17.6
Total	(16.0)	8.6	(16.0)	151.7	16.0	135.4	80.9	96.9	80.9

*Working capital by 1992, when operating at 100% of capacity, includes:

Accounts receivable (30 days × sales)	$6.2
Raw materials (10 days × materials cost)	.5
Finished product (30 days × mill cost)	3.4
Cash (8 days × Cost of sales − Depreciation)	1.0
Current liabilities (25% of above items excluding cash)	(2.5)
	$8.6

†Investment includes:

Building	$ 2.0
Equipment	14.0
Land	.5
	$16.5

‡Depreciation accruals commence in year facilities start up operation.

289

The remaining four criteria cited take into account the arrival time of cash flow and, subject to slight qualification, are equally acceptable:

1. *Internal rate of return* was previously defined to be that discount which equates cash inflows with cash outflows. The IRR is solved by trial and error, and there may be as many solutions as there are changes in sign in year-to-year cash flows. The rate at which funds are presumed to be reinvested is IRR.

2. *Net present value* represents the difference between the present value of the cash flow generated and the present value of the investment incurred. The discount factor is taken to be the cost of capital. An NPV of zero implies that the cost of capital equals the IRR. Net present value is deemed to be slightly preferable to IRR as a ranking device since it bypasses the problem of multiple solutions and makes the more realistic assumption that funds can be reinvested at the cost of capital rather than IRR. As a concept, however, IRR is easier to "sell" than NPV, and its difficulties can readily be rectified if necessary.

3. *Discounted payback period* is understood to be the number of years required for cash flows from the project to cover both the investment outlay and the cost of capital. It helps to resolve the question of the minimum forecast period required for a go or no-go investment decision.

4. *The profitability index* differs from NPV in that it equals the ratio of the present value of cash flows generated by the project to the present value of investment outlays. Since it scales projects to NPV per $1 of investment, PI facilitates comparison among projects of different magnitudes.

Allowance for risk differentials among projects tends to be somewhat arbitrary. Management typically bases its judgment on so-called project risk; that is, the range of outcomes associated with each project. Management is prone to assign the lowest cutoff rate or equivalent to replacement of equipment and facilities, the median rate to proposals to expand facilities to meet increased demand for existing products, and the top rate for new product outlays.

Theory holds the cutoff rate or its equivalent should reflect the contribution of each investment proposal to the overall risk of the firm. The critical factor is the degree to which outcomes are intercorrelated, since management and shareholders are both motivated to diversify away noncorrelated or project-specific risks. The risk premium, defined as the minimum expected return net of the riskfree rate, should therefore vary directly with the sensitivity of the project's return to the underlying rate of return for the company as a whole.

Assessment of the appropriate adjustment for risk is complicated by (1) the dependence of project outcomes on several factors, (2) potential legal liability, and (3) just plain bias. Dependence on the behavior of multiple economic or other factors reduces the benefit from diversification since each factor may deviate from its expected value, and the sensitivity to each factor may vary from investment outlay to investment outlay. Product liability experience demonstrates that certain project risks—no matter how small in an expected sense—cannot be fully diversified away. Outlays to settle product liability suits have led such major companies as A.H. Robbins and Johns Manville to file for bankruptcy. Worse, insurance companies not only charge high fees to insure against such events, but also place caps on the liability assumed, and sometimes refuse even to write insurance.

In the matter of forecast bias, it is tempting simply to add a few points across the board to the cutoff rate, as some firms do. The problem with this approach is that those who prepare unbiased forecasts are penalized, while those who "lie" win acceptance of their proposals. Elimination of bias is not simple or easy.

No comprehensive solution to the problem posed is available as yet, but awareness of the issues is fundamental. In the short run, the process can be measurably improved by stressing group, as distinct from individual, project performance. The end in mind is to assign responsibility in the light of sufficiently accurate measures of performance.

Merger and Acquisition

Firms that fail to achieve growth and performance objectives internally are motivated to enter the merger and acquisition arena. Acquisitions recently surpassed 3,600 and were valued in excess of $240 billion; the number was below the peak of 4,400 in 1986, but the total value was greater than the $206 billion for 1986, possibly due to the tax change starting in 1987, the market crash in October 1987, and the economic recession.

Acquisition procedures parallel those of internal capital investment in certain respects, extend well beyond the internal capital budgeting process in other respects, require the participation of corporate planners, and generally involve *top* management. Search, cash flow forecast, and evaluation have their counterparts in acquisition analysis. Furthermore, there are complicating factors such as negotiation, competition with other would-be acquirers, target management, employee reaction, and unspecified liabilities.

The first step in acquisition analysis is to examine the appropriate fit between the two firms. As a rule, the target firm must contribute something over and above its stand-alone value. The contribution has been underpriced assets relative to replacement costs due to low stock values in the late 1970s. The plus factor in recent acquisition activity appears to be addition to market share, with diversification to spread risk lagging far behind.

The second step is to determine the upper limit for the value of the target firm. Cash flows must be projected; synergy possibilities explored; a terminal value set, and an appropriate discount factor derived. A major risk is that the available record may not tell the whole story.

Assets not needed in the business and particularly coveted by others add value to the target since they can be sold. Costs of integrating the two companies, in turn, subtract from value. Golden parachutes and other attempts to make the acquisition process expensive have become the order of the day.

The third step is to negotiate an acceptable—if not favorable—acquisition price. The price offered must be in line with prevailing premiums over market price and often turns out to be excessive. Fees paid to merger brokers and advisers hinge on successful conclusion and vary directly with the price paid. Tender offers also invite competitive bidding. The party that puts the target in play frequently loses out in the final bidding.

The list of factors that lead to overpricing is long. Chief executives, for example, may tend to involve their egos and then hate to lose. Relevant information is concealed, overlooked, and misinterpreted. Leveraged buyout specialists base price on bust-up value and availability of junk bond financing.

FINANCING DECISIONS

Asset management is but half the battle. The way in which operating cash flows (net of capital expenditures and additions to working capital) are allocated among financial claims, cash dividends, and stock repurchases also affects total enterprise value and thereby the worth of common stock. Management must determine the proper level of prior financial claims (debt and preferred stock) in relation to the firm's expected cash flows, the mix of such claims, strategies for selling and modifying financial claims, and dividend policy.

Prior Financial Claims

Prior financial claims refer to all legally binding commitments to pay cash that have priority over the residual or ownership interest in the business. The bulk of such claims is summarized on the balance sheet under current liabilities and long-term debt. Prior claims not shown on the balance sheet include operating leases, pension benefits, take-or-pay agreements, and so on.

Debt Instruments

Apart from accounts payable and accrued liabilities that arise in the normal course of business, short-term debt or notes payable typically represent draw downs under multiyear revolving credit agreements with banks. Rates may be fixed but are more likely to be floating. Commitment fees of, for example, 25 percent per year are paid on the unused portion of the bank's commitment. Should the firm's creditworthiness be in question, the credit agreement may, for instance, require the borrower to (1) maintain certain minimum levels of tangible net worth and working capital, (2) meet certain ratio requirements, (3) restrict capital expenditures, and (4) collateralize the debt. Failure to meet these and other requirements that may be imposed could result in termination of the bank's commitment.

Debentures, the traditional long-term debt instrument, are characterized by (1) a fixed coupon rate usually payable semiannually; (2) specified maturity dates of 15, 20, or 25 years; (3) a principal amount to be paid at maturity or earlier, if called; (4) a so-called sinking fund provision for periodic retirement of the debt; and (5) a call provision that permits the company to buy back the bond at par for sinking fund purposes and at a declining call premium for other purposes. The bond indenture or agreement may restrict the firm from taking a variety of actions, including the sale of assets and the payment of dividends.

Tradition notwithstanding, the variety of long-term debt instruments is now virtually unlimited. The breakdown of long-term debt given in Table 11-5 for IC Industries points to the international character of the market for debt, reveals the presence of substantial subsidiary—as well as parent—debt, shows a mixture of fixed rate debt, floating rate debt, and even zero coupon debt that reinvests interest until maturity and features differences in maturities, degree of seniority, and other respects as well.

Table 11-5 also helps us to understand that it may not be a simple matter to calculate the cost of debt for IC Industries as part of computing a blended cost of capital. The overall cost of debt for IC Industries would be a dollar-weighted average of all the various debt issues listed in Table 11-5.

Subordination of debt has been given new meaning with the emergence of the high yield, junk bond market. In response to a takeover threat, USG, a building materials company, proposed on May 2, 1988, to recapitalize the firm by exchanging each share of USG stock for $37 in cash, $5 in face amount of redeemable 16 percent junior subordinated debentures due in 2008, and one share of stock in the recapitalized firm. The recapitalization was to be financed by a term loan of $1.6 billion to be repaid over 17 installments, $550 million of senior subordinated debentures and $260 million of junior debentures. Interest on the junior debentures could be paid either in cash or in junior debentures through 1993. The junior debentures are junk bonds with a vengeance, as they are PIK (payment in kind) debt where interest may be paid not in cash but simply in more junior debentures of the same kind. The book value of the stockholders' equity in USG would become a negative $1.57 billion. For USG, the negative equity indicates that leverage exceeds 100 percent. It

TABLE 11-5   Breakdown of long-term debt: I C Industries

Long-term debt at December 31 consisted of the following:

	(in $ millions)	
	19XX	**19XY**
Parent Company:		
Equipment notes due 1993 to 1996, 10.97% to 13¼%	$ 61.3	$ 66.4
Swiss franc bonds due 1988, 7%	—	24.1
Swiss franc bonds due 1994 and 1995, exchanged for U.S. dollar liabilities, 12½% and 12.2%	104.3	104.3
Canadian notes due 1995, exchanged for U.S. dollar liabilities at 12.2%	38.1	38.1
Loans and notes due 1991 and 1995, effective rates 12.2% to 13½%	124.9	124.9
Bank loans due 1988 to 1992, floating rates	989.0	33.0
IC Industries Finance Corporation, N.V.:		
Guaranteed notes due 1990 and 1991, 8¾% to 12%	185.8	268.2
Split currency bonds due 1993 and 1997, 9.9% and 11½%	144.8	139.1
Retractable notes due 1998, 11⅞%	75.0	75.0
Swiss franc bonds due 1992, 6½%	75.2	104.0
Floating rate notes due 1991	36.6	58.7
Zero coupon bonds due 1994, 14¼%	73.9	64.7
Other Subsidiaries:		
Sinking fund debentures due 1992 and 1995, 5⅞% and 10¼%	25.9	32.7
State and local industrial development bonds and mortgages due 1988 to 2014, 7¼% to 12¼%	36.8	37.2
Various, due 1988 to 2002, 4% to 17.2%	30.6	28.4
Obligations for capital leases	16.0	15.9
Notes payable by foreign subsidiaries due 1989 to 2012, 2.67% to 13.25%	47.3	48.0
Subordinated sinking fund debentures due 1995 to 1999, 10.2% and 12%	32.3	52.1
Total	2,097.8	1,314.8
Less: Amount due within one year	201.2	93.5
Unamortized discount	10.5	14.7
Long-term debt	$1,886.1	$1,206.6

would appear from this case, and others like it, that the amount of leverage possible is almost unlimited.

Firms that wish to reduce the interest cost may issue debt that is convertible into common stock or offer warrants to buy stock as inducement to purchase debt. Convertibility and warrants both imply that shareholders are surrendering part of their residual interest in future cash flows in return for lower explicit interest cost now. Collateral may also have to be offered.

Investment bankers have devoted considerable effort to new product development in recent years. Almost any combination of rate schedule, priority, and maturity is possible.

Leasing

Leasing represents one of several alternatives to borrowing. *Financial leases* are capitalized and recorded on the balance sheet as both an asset and a liability. *Operating leases* involving less stringent terms are merely reported in footnotes to the financial statements.

Much could be said about leasing, but the purpose here is to contrast the financial lease with other debt forms. Leasing is somewhat perplexing in that it represents the combination of (1) a sale of assets, and (2) the sale of a prior debt claim. The assets sold include the future value of the underlying equipment of the facility and the privilege of depreciating the asset. The debt claim carries with it the obligation to make certain cash payments. The value of the debt claim is the present value of the payment stream discounted at the appropriate rate for comparable debt claims.

Motivation for Leverage

The incentive to leverage the company derives from interest deductibility for tax purposes, inflation expectations, and market segmentation or inefficiency. Consider first the case of firms X and Y confronted by zero income taxes and an efficient capital market. Suppose that X and Y differ only in the respect that X is leveraged, while Y has no debt. Should the summed market value of debt and equity for X initially surpass the market value of Y, arbitrage activity will bring the values in line. The lower valued Y will be bought financed partly by debt and partly by the short sale of X's equity. The arbitrager gains from the offsetting transactions as long as the differential in values exists. The process terminates when the values are brought in line and no benefit is derived from the use of debt.

Once taxes are introduced and interest is made deductible for tax purposes, the situation changes. The after-tax combination of interest plus net earnings for firm X exceeds the after-tax earnings of the all-equity firm Y by the tax rate times the interest cost. Since the composite risk of holding both debt and equity in X can be no different from holding an equivalent share of equity in Y, the discount rate must be the same for the composite cash flow of both X and Y. It follows that the total value of X will exceed that of Y by the tax rate times the magnitude of the debt incurred.

The motivation to borrow varies directly with the expected rate of inflation. The point is simply that nominal interest contains both "real" interest and an inflation component. The latter measures the anticipated decline in "real" principal value and thereby constitutes a partial repayment of principal. The borrower gains to the extent of the tax rate times the inflation or principal element inherent in nominal interest.

Differential taxation at the investor level may either augment or negate the benefit of tax deductibility at the firm level. Assuming that taxes cannot be shifted or passed along, the investor bears the burden of taxes imposed at the corporate and individual level. Should the shareholder be taxed at a lower rate on his dividends and capital gains than the lender is on her interest income, the differential tax at the investor level may offset, in part or in whole, the reverse differential at the corporate level.

Debt Policy

The optimum mix of debt and equity ultimately hinges on the likelihood of bankruptcy and the costs associated therewith. The direct costs are bankruptcy filing fees together with legal, accounting, and other professional service charges. Indirect costs comprise lost managerial time, lost sales and profits, and lost ability to obtain credit at reasonable rates. Side effects of bankruptcy include records that may be in shambles, assets that turn out to be nonexistent, and fire sales of good assets.

The costs of financial distress can be significant even in the absence of outright bankruptcy. In its efforts to remain solvent, Armco sold its profitable Aerospace and Strategic Materials Segment and its Fabricated Products and Services Segment. It also incurred restructuring charges of $335.6 and $103.6 millions respectively in 1985 and 1986 in scaling back its Carbon Steel, Speciality Steel, and Oilfield Equipment divisions.

Optimality is achieved when further additions to debt no longer add to the value of the firm and when the tax benefit derived from debt is just offset by the incremental costs in an expected sense associated with an additional $1 of debt. The precise location of the optimum point is subject to considerable debate and depends on one's estimate of indirect costs.

Despite the existence—conceptually speaking—of a "best" mix of debt and equity, it appears that degree of leverage actually adopted by the firm hinges on which of three points of view dominates. The vantage points are those of (1) management, (2) lenders, and (3) raiders. Factors taken into consideration include (1) operating cash flow in relation to fixed financial outlays, (2) cash flow sensitivity, (3) asset composition and liquidity, and (4) company size.

Shareholders can diversify, while management (with job continuation, salary, and stock option values, all depending on the successful continuation of the business) cannot. It follows, therefore, that management—unless pressured from outside—will opt for less debt than shareholders might elect.

Lending institutions, in turn—unless stretching for fee income as some are—require at least two ways out of each loan. The strongly preferred way is through free cash generated in the normal course of operations. The secondary way is by means of asset liquidation.

Pressure to leverage the firm in extreme fashion comes from corporate raiders. Corporate raiders combine cash flow and bust-up value to create the leveraged buyout situation. Banks and insurance companies take sizable senior debt positions in LBOs, while junk bond specialists absorb the junior, subordinated debt needed to provide the equivalent of an equity cushion. Segments of the business are sold to reduce the debt quickly; expenses are cut and capital outlays slashed to provide additional cash flow to service the debt.

In the attempt to avoid takeover, potential targets feel obliged to restructure on their own. USG, mentioned earlier, represents an extreme case, since it was confronted with an actual tender offer by Desert Partners. No wonder an array of debt policies exists.

Financial Strategies

Numerous opportunities exist for the astute financial manager to add to profitability by altering the composition of debt in response to changing market conditions. Interest rates can be hedged. Bonds can be refunded by debt of equal rating or different rating. Fixed interest payments can be swapped for variable interest payments, and vice versa. Bond maturities can be lengthened or shortened.

Nothing stands still! Earnings retained in the firm, periodic retirement of debt, and changes in cash items continuously reshape the capital structure. Bond ratings rise and fall as prospects vary.

The manager can move quickly. Large companies typically register with the Securities and Exchange Commission (SEC) their intention to issue debt or equity at some time over, for instance, the next two years. Once this so-called shelf registration is in place, the firm can then take advantage of rate "windows" without the traditional waiting period. Swaps and hedges can be arranged with a phone call. Here, as elsewhere, the decision rule is based on cost versus benefit.

Residual Claims: Equity

Residual claimants to the business include holders of preferred and common stock. Preferred stock has priority over common stock in liquidation and normally receives a fixed or floating dividend rate—in the case of money markets preferreds—irrespective of how well the company fares. Preferred dividend arrears typically must be removed before cash dividends can be declared on common stock. High-quality preferred stock is attractive to corporate investors by virtue of the intercorporate dividend exclusion of 80 percent.

Common stock occupies the bottom rung of the priority ladder, carries with it the right to receive whatever is left after other claimants have been satisfied, and features voting rights. More than one class of common stock may exist, each with differential voting (and sometimes dividend) rights.

Residual interest in the firm is measured—in an accounting sense—by shareholders' equity, whose component parts include preferred stock (if any), common stock, capital received in excess of par, deferred gains and losses from foreign currency translation, and reinvested earnings. Additions to shareholders' equity result from the issuance and sale of stock and the retention of periodic earnings. The outstanding shares of publicly traded companies usually grow in number through time as a result of dividend reinvestment programs and exercise of stock options by management, whether or not public offerings are undertaken. Changes in number of shares outstanding due to splits and stock dividends that do not affect the investors' position must be considered when making interperiod comparisons.

Unless the stock market is deemed to be "high," as it was alleged to be during the first half of 1987 before the crash, management prefers to augment equity through the retention of earnings rather than through public offerings of common stock. For one thing, management tends to believe that its stock is underpriced in the market. For another, management dislikes the initial dilution occasioned by the offering.

Dividend Policy and Share Repurchase

Cash dividends and share repurchase both represent a partial liquidation of the firm in the sense that assets and net worth are concurrently diminished. Most public companies pay cash dividends; the exceptions are firms that are growing rapidly and firms that are losing money. Many public firms also repurchase stock from time to time.

Cash dividends per share typically depend on past dividends per share and current earnings per share. Management hates to reduce dividends unless other firms are doing likewise for fear of investor misinterpretation. Management likes to raise dividends when sustainable earnings rise.

Consistent dividend behavior signals that conditions remain relatively unchanged in the opinion of management. Deviations from past behavior signify that something is awry. The market responds quickly.

Academicians have previously favored share repurchase over cash dividends due to the differential between the tax rate on dividend income and that on capital gains. The differential has been eliminated for the moment at least, but capital gains remain slightly favored since the tax is not imposed until the gain is realized.

Share repurchase serves several purposes. In the 1970s, it reflected management's belief that common shares were undervalued and represented good investments in their own right. In the 1980s, share repurchases pointed to management's efforts to restructure and to increase leverage. Share repurchases offer management notably greater leeway in terms of magnitude and timing than do dividends.

Whether dividends or share repurchase, the ultimate decision rule seems clear cut. Cash can legitimately be retained in the business as long as management can employ the cash as effectively as the shareholder with due allowance for risk and taxes.

Cost of Capital

Cost of capital is understood to refer to the minimum compensation required by investors for assuming a given class of risks. In the context of the corporation, it is the weighted sum of the after-tax costs of the diverse components that make up the capital structure. The weights are the ratios of the market value of each component to the total market values of all elements.

Costs for the publicly traded debt components are simply the effective yields at which the securities are trading in the market. Costs of privately held, nontraded debt can be estimated by reference to publicly traded issues belonging to the same risk class. The cost of preferred stock is the dividend divided by market price where there is no maturity.

The cost of equity cannot be known with certainty since the price per share represents the present value of an uncertain stream of future cash flows. As explained earlier, the cost of equity can be estimated by the CAPM model, which states that the cost or required rate of return associated with any risky asset should be equal to the riskfree rate plus the relevant Beta times the market risk premium. The Beta for any stock measures the sensitivity of that stock's return to the market and is estimated by reference to historical market data. Alternatively, should the market be judged to be efficient, the required rate of return can be estimated by solving the dividend discount model for the discount rate r; that is, r equals the long-term growth rate in dividends plus the ratio of dividends for the coming year to the current stock price.

As an allocator of corporate resources, cost of capital varies with the contribution of each capital investment project to total enterprise risk. The expected return for each project minus the hypothetical riskfree rate should vary in direct proportion to the project's sensitivity to the underlying economic environment relative to that for the firm as a whole.

Cost of capital is not calculated to the tenth decimal place, or to the fifth, or even to the third. The end purpose is to come up with reasonable numbers that make adequate allowance for significant risk differentials.

CONCLUDING REMARKS

The role of the financial manager is to help allocate limited company resources among competing fund uses to optimize the value of the firm. The scarce or limited resource is internally generated cash flow, supplemented by additions to debt and equity from external sources. The alternative uses are capital expenditures, additions to working capital, dividends and share repurchases. The balancing item in any period is change in cash or debt position. The allocating device is cost of capital.

Asset management, the traditional focus of financial management, is only part of the task. Financing decisions also contribute to shareholder value. The idea is to "sell off" portions of anticipated cash flow in such a way as to maximize total company value and to adjust capital structure quickly as windows open. The manager of a creditworthy firm has virtually unlimited choice.

The broad focus of financial management is summarized by the four elements making up the market-to-book ratio in the DuPont formula:

1. Profit margin.
2. Asset turnover.
3. Financial leverage.
4. Price/earnings ratio.

These are the fundamental factors that interact to determine the market-to-book ratio, which top management should be endeavoring to maximize over the long term.

Most decisions are made under uncertainty, and many decisions relate to cash flows several years hence. Uncertainty is partly resolved by diversification at either the firm or investor level, but there remains the tie-in of the firm with the underlying economic environment. Sensitivity to economic conditions cannot be diversified away and is reflected in estimates of cost of capital.

The timing of cash flows is often critical to the decision process. Delays in cash flow generation can affect IRR significantly. Understanding of the discount process is essential to the comprehension of finance.

APPENDIX: DEFINITION AND DERIVATION OF FORMULAS

Expected Return: Sum of individual returns, each value weighted by its relative frequency.

Variance: Sum of squared deviation from group mean for each observation divided by the number (N) of observations, or by $N - 1$.

Covariance: Sum of deviation from the mean for the tth observation in the ith group times the corresponding deviation from the mean for the tth observation in the jth group, divided by N or $N - 1$.

Variance of a Portfolio: Weighted sum of individual variances and covariances.

Present Value.

    a. Annuity of $1 per year: $1/(1 + i) + 1/(1 + i)^{**}2 + ... + 1/(1 + i)^{**}T$ $= 1/i - (1/i)[1/(1 + i)^{**}T] = (1/i)\{1 - [1/(1 + i)]^{**}T\}$, where T is the number of years.

    b. Annuity of $1 growing at rate g: $(1 + g)/(1 + i) + (1 + g)^{**}2/(1 + i)^{**}2 + ... + (1 + g)^{**}T/(1 + i)^{**}T = [(1 + g)/(i - g)]\{1 - [(1 + g)/(1 + r)]^{**}T\}$.

CAPM.

    a. Expected return $E[Rp] = Rf + (E[Rm] - Rf) \times w$, where $E[Rm]$ is the expected return on an efficient set of risky securities, Rf is the risk-free rate, and w is the ratio of the investment in the risky asset to the investor's total equity.

    b. Standard deviation (S.D.) = sq. rt. of $(w[Rf]^{**}2 \times Var[Rf] + w^{**}2 \times Var[Rm] + 2 \times w \times w[Rf] \times Cov[Rf, Rm]$, where w[Rf] is the percentage of net worth allocated to Rf, Var and Cov are variance and covariance respectively. Since $Var[Rf]$ and $Cov[Rf, Rm] = 0$, S.D. of $Rp = w \times$ S.D. of Rm, or $w = SD[Rp]/SD[Rm]$.

    c. By substitution for w into $E[Rp]$, $E[Rp] = Rf + (E[Rm] - Rf) \times SD[Rp]/SD[Rm]$.

    d. For any security i, $E[Ri] = Rf + Beta(i) \times (E[Rm] - Rf)$, where $Beta = Cov[Ri, Rm]/Var[Rm]$ and Rp is fully diversified.

FOR FURTHER READING

Altman, E. I. (ed.), *Handbook of Corporate Finance,* 6th ed. (New York: John Wiley, 1986).

Brealey, R. A., and S. C. Myers, *Principles of Corporate Finance* (New York: McGraw-Hill, 1988).

Livingstone, J. L., *The Portable MBA in Finance and Accounting* (New York: John Wiley, 1992).

Logue, D. E. (ed.), *Handbook of Modern Finance* (Boston: Warren, Gorham, Lamont, 1994).

Ross, S. A., and R. W. Westerfield, *Corporate Finance* (St. Louis, MO: Times Mirror/Mosby College Publishing, 1988).

12 STRATEGIC MANAGEMENT: THE CHALLENGE AND THE OPPORTUNITY

Liam Fahey

Strategic management is the name given to the most important, difficult, and encompassing challenge that confronts any private or public organization: how to lay the foundation for tomorrow's success while competing to win in today's marketplace. Winning today is never enough; unless the seeds of tomorrow's success are planted and cultivated, the organization will not have a future. This challenge is difficult because the choices involved in exploiting the present and building for the future confront managers with complex trade-offs. Managers must resolve conflicting demands from stakeholders; perennial tensions among different groups and levels within the organization must be fairly addressed. It is encompassing because it embraces all the decisions that any organization makes.

The conflict between the demands of the present and the requirements of the future lies at the heart of strategic management for at least three reasons:

1. The environment in which tomorrow's success will be earned is likely to be quite different from the environment that confronts the organization today. Products change as competitors introduce new variations, sometimes radically shifting the nature of the offering made to customers. New models of laptop computers that are smaller, lighter, and more powerful have changed many customers' perceptions of what constitutes a personal computer. New competitors enter long-established markets with new concepts

The author would like to especially thank Robert M. Randall for his many comments on this chapter, and H. Kurt Christensen, Jeffrey Ellis, Samuel Felton, V. K. Narayanan, G. Richard Patten, and Daniel Simpson for their comments on an earlier draft of this chapter.

of how to serve and satisfy customers. For example, Saturn, at the low end of the automobile market, and Lexus, at the high end, have dramatically altered the dynamics of competition within their product categories.[1] Increasingly, the emergence of substitute products causes highly disruptive industry change. Customers' tastes sometimes change in unexpected ways. Technological developments often alter not only the function of products but every facet of how business is conducted: procurement, logistics, manufacturing, marketing, sales, and service. Political, regulatory, social, and economic change often give rise, directly or indirectly, to shifts in industry or competitive conditions.

2. To succeed in the new environment of tomorrow, the organization itself must undergo significant and sometimes radical change. Organizations as large, as diverse, and as historically successful as IBM, General Motors, Sears, Honda, Sony, Philips, and Rolls Royce have learned this painful lesson in the late 1980s and early 1990s. Old ways of thinking have had to be challenged and reconceived: long-held assumptions and beliefs ultimately have become incongruent with the changed environment. New operating processes or ways of doing things must be learned. Organizational structures, systems, and decision processes inherited from outmoded eras need to be redesigned.

3. Adapting to (and, in many cases, driving) change in and around the marketplace during a time of significant *internal* change places an extremely heavy burden on the leaders of any organization. Yet, that is precisely the dual task that confronts strategic managers. They must:

   • Exploit the present while sowing the seeds for a new and very different future and, simultaneously,

   • Build bridges between change in the environment and change within their organizations.[2]

Change is the central concern and focus of strategic management: change in the environment, change inside the organization, and change in how the organization links strategy and the organization. Change means that organizations can never become satisfied with their accomplishments. Unless an organization changes its products over time, it falls behind competitors. Unless the organization changes its own understanding of the environment, it cannot keep abreast of, much less get ahead of, changes in customers, the industry, technology, and governmental policies. The importance and pervasiveness of change is evident in the strategic management principles noted in Table 12-1.

From environmental change springs opportunities. Without change or the potential to affect change, organizations would neither confront nor be able to create opportunities.[3] Without a managed flow of new opportunities,

TABLE 12-1   Some strategic management (SM) principles

Strategic Management

- Involves the management of marketplace strategy, of the organization, and of the relationship between them.
- Has as a core assignment; management of the interface between the organization and its environment.
- Involves anticipating, adapting to, and creating change both in the environment and within the organization.
- Is driven by the relentless pursuit of opportunities.
- Recognizes that opportunities may arise in the external environment or they may be generated within the organization; in either case, they are realized in the marketplace.
- Necessitates risk taking; the organization commits to pursuing opportunities *before* they have fully materialized (in the environment).
- Is as much about inventing or creating the organization's competitive future as it is about adapting to some understanding of that future.
- Sees the marketplace purpose of an organization as residing outside its (legal) boundaries; it must find, serve, and satisfy customers as a prelude to other returns such as profits.
- Is the task of the *whole* organization; it cannot be delegated to any group within the organization.
- Necessitates the integration of the long-distance and short-distance horizons; the future influences current decisions; current decisions are intended to lead toward some future state or goal.

organizations cannot grow and prosper; they are destined to decline and die. Unfortunately, change is also the source of threats to the organization's current and potential strategies. Thus, organizations must commit themselves to grappling with change—understanding it and transforming it into opportunity. Leveraging and/or shaping change in the environment is, as we shall see in the next section, central to designing and executing strategy.

Although organizations cannot control their environment,[4] they are not helpless in the face of persistent and sometimes unpredictable environmental change. By practicing strategic management, managers can lead more effectively. They can effect change in their strategies: They can introduce new products, enhance their existing products, withdraw from particular markets, compete more smartly against their competitors, and offer better value to customers. Managers can also reconfigure their organization: They can get more output out of existing resources, hone existing capabilities or competencies and develop new ones, and energize the organization through their leadership. As we shall see throughout this chapter, managing more effectively and reconfiguring organizations go hand-in-hand.

To cope with change successfully, strategic management must address three interrelated tasks (see Figure 12-1):

FIGURE 12-1 An integrated model of strategic management

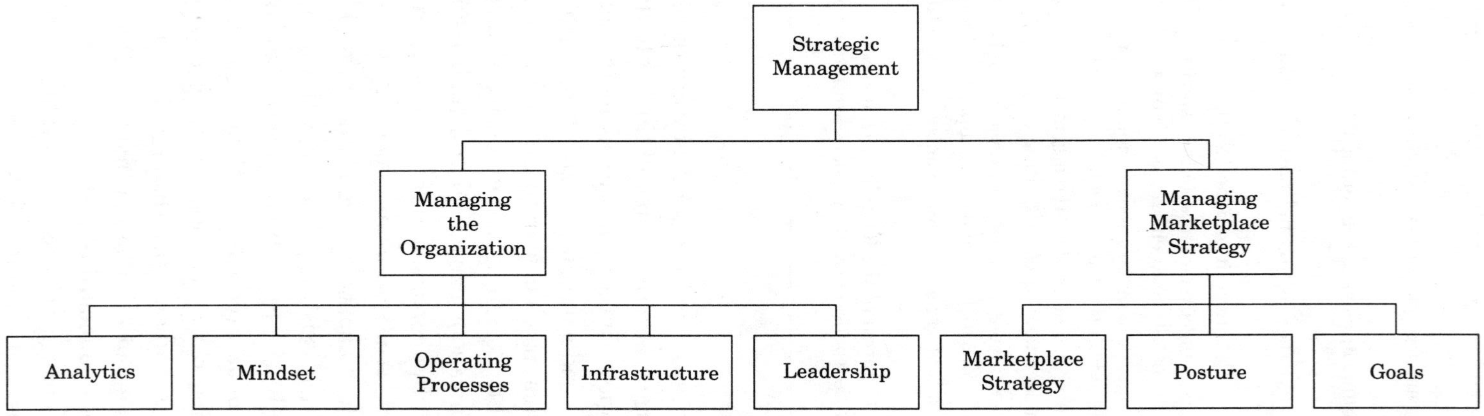

1. *Managing strategy in the marketplace.* Designing, executing, and refining strategies that "win" in a changing marketplace. Strategy is the means by which the organization creates and leverages change in and around the marketplace.

2. *Managing the organization.* Continually reconfiguring the organization—how it thinks, how it operates. Without such internal change, the organization cannot hope to hone its capacity to identify, adapt to, and leverage environmental change.

3. *Practicing strategic management.* Continually enhancing the linkages or "interface" between strategy (what the organization does in the marketplace) and organization (what takes place within the organization). Throughout this book, we have seen that how these linkages are managed determines whether the organization wins today and positions itself for tomorrow.

Each of these three core strategic management tasks will now be discussed in detail.

MANAGING STRATEGY IN THE MARKETPLACE

Few words are as abused in the lexicon of organizations, as ill-defined in the management literature, and as open to multiple meanings as *strategy*.[5] Throughout this book, strategy is a synonym for *choices*. The sum of the choices determines whether the organization has a chance to win in the marketplace—whether it can get and keep customers and outperform competitors. Success in getting and keeping customers allows organizations to achieve their financial, technological, and other stakeholder-related goals. A number of core strategy principles are indicated in Table 12-2.

If a strategy is to successfully create or leverage change, it must manifest an "entrepreneurial content"[6] in the marketplace. Strategies that do not anticipate changes in competitive conditions, such as technological developments, new entrants with distinctly different product offerings, or changes in customers' tastes, will lag behind what is happening in the marketplace and will eventually fail. Strategies that do not create or leverage change to the organization's advantage cannot drive the marketplace; that is, they cannot provide, faster and better than competitors, the offerings that customers want.

How do organizations create or leverage change in the marketplace? What levers can they manipulate to effect changes that are to their advantage? How is change exploited for superior performance? In brief, strategy creates or leverages change in three related ways:

TABLE 12-2   Some strategy principles

Strategy addresses the interface between the organization and its marketplace environment.

Strategy involves three elements: (1) scope, (2) posture, and (3) goals.

Strategy is the means by which the organization creates and/or leverages environmental change.

Strategy is always conditional; the choice of strategy depends on the conditions in the environment and within the organization.

Strategy is in part an intellectual activity; strategies exist in managers' minds.

Strategy is about outwitting and outmaneuvering competitors by anticipating change faster and better and taking actions accordingly.

Strategy's marketplace intent is to be better than competitors at attracting, winning, and training customers.

Strategy is not likely to win unless it possesses some degree of entrepreneurial content: its approach is different from competitors'.

Strategy must be continually renovated; scope, posture, and goals are adjusted to enhance the chances of winning in the marketplace.

Strategy often needs to be (re)invented if it is to achieve "breakthrough" success. A strategy that is new to the marketplace *and* significantly outdistances rivals needs to be created.

1. Through the choice of products the firm offers and the customers it seeks to serve—commonly referred to as the "scope" issue. For example, should Apple Computer Inc. add more powerful computers to its product line? Should General Motors eliminate its Oldsmobile product line or significantly overhaul it by introducing a new set of models?

2. Through how the firm competes in its chosen businesses or product-customer segments to attract, win, and retain customers. We shall refer to this as the "posture" issue. For example, should Apple add functionality—more speed and more features—to its Macintosh line? Should the price on some Cadillac models be lowered to make them more attractive to new customer segments?

3. Through the choice of goals the firm wishes to pursue. Should Apple try to be a major participant in every segment of the personal computer business or aim to be the leader in certain software segments? Should General Motors set out to penetrate the Japanese market?

Scope, posture, and goals are recurring themes throughout this book. Because of their importance to any understanding of strategy, each will now be briefly discussed.

Business Scope

Central to any consideration of strategy are questions concerning business scope. Scope compels choices because it cannot be unlimited. No organization can market an unlimited array of products, and frequently (even with the assistance of partners) it will not be able to reach all potential customers. Indeed, few firms are able to compete or "be a player" in all product-customer segments of their industry.

Scope determination revolves around three general questions:

1. What products (or product groups) does the organization want to provide to the marketplace?

2. What customers—or, more specifically, what customer needs—does it want to serve?

3. What resources, competencies, and technologies does it possess or can it develop to serve its product-customer segments?

These three questions compel an organization to systematically and carefully assess what business it is in, where opportunities exist in the marketplace, and what capacity it has or can create to avail of these opportunities.

Product-Market Scope

The breadth and complexity of the relevant product-market scope questions are distinctly different at the corporate and business-unit levels, as shown in Table 12-3. At the corporate level, a principal challenge is to identify the businesses in which the corporation can generate value-adding opportunities. What businesses can be developed and enhanced over time? The difficulties inherent in this strategic task are well exemplified in the myriad of household-name corporations in the United States (such as, Westinghouse, Kodak, DuPont), in Europe (such as Mercedes-Benz, Siemens, Philips, Rolls Royce), and in Japan (Matsushita, Mitsubishi, Nissan) that, in the past few years, have reported significantly lower performance results than anticipated. Many of these firms have had to sell off what once were described as promising or "can't miss" businesses.

The case of General Electric (GE), a multibusiness conglomerate, illustrates differences in the context and setting of corporate and business-unit scope issues and questions. Viewed from the perspective of the CEO or the board of directors, GE's *corporate* scope is assessed by continually posing the following types of questions with regard to each of its business areas (see Figure 12-2):

- Which business areas confront the greatest opportunities in the form of potential new businesses (that is, new products that would give rise to a new business for GE)?

- What emerging or potential opportunities might *not* be exploited, given the present configuration of business areas? How might the business areas be realigned to pursue these opportunities?

TABLE 12-3 Scope: Some key questions and issues

Corporate Level

Business scope	What businesses is the firm in? What business does the firm want to be in?
Stakeholder scope	What stakeholders can the organization leverage to aid in attaining its goals?
Scope relatedness	How should the businesses in the corporation be related to each other, if at all?
Means of changing scope	Internal development, acquisitions, alliances, divestment; aligning with/opposing stakeholders.
Strategic issues	In which business sectors should the firm invest? Retain the current level of investment? Reduce investment or divest itself entirely?
Strategic challenges	How can the corporation add value to its individual businesses? What might be the basis of synergy between two or more businesses within the corporation?

Business-Unit Level

Product scope	What range of products does the firm want to offer to the marketplace?
Customer scope	What categories of customers does the organization want to serve? What customer needs does the firm want to satisfy?
Geographic scope	Within what geographic terrain does the organization want to offer its products to its chosen customers?
Vertical scope	What linkages does the organization have (and want to have) with suppliers and customers?
Stakeholder scope	What stakeholders can the organization leverage to aid in attaining its goals?
Means of changing scope	Adding/deleting products or customers, moving into/out of geographic regions, aligning with/opposing stakeholders.
Strategic issues	In what products should the organization invest? Retain at current levels? Divest itself? What relationships does the organization wish to develop with stakeholders?
Strategic challenges	How can opportunities be identified and exploited? What is the best strategy to do so?

FIGURE 12-2 The GE Corporation's business sectors

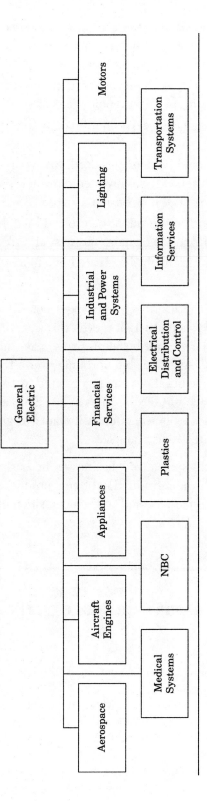

- Which areas should be encouraged to develop new opportunities through the internal development of new products, based on their current knowledge, capabilities, and competencies?
- Which business areas can take existing products to new types of customers or to customers in new geographic regions?
- Which areas should receive minimal, if any, new funds for business development?
- Which areas should be deemphasized, that is, managed with the intent of generating cash that will be invested elsewhere, perhaps in other areas or in the development of new business areas?
- What new opportunities might be created by linking products, skills, and competencies from two or more business areas?
- What opportunities might be created by aligning with one or more other corporations?

Only a few of the major scope changes noted by GE in its 1992 annual report are indicated in Box 12-1. Yet, even this sampling suggests the extensive changes that most large multibusiness firms make in their corporate scope, sometimes within a single year, but certainly over a five-year period.

Some of the same questions can be directed, with considerably more focus and specificity, to each of GE's business areas. Each area must consider which specialized businesses or business units it wants to grow, hold, or divest. The Financial Services area is an example:

- Which of its 22 specialized businesses or business units should be extended through the introduction of new products or services, the pursuit of international markets, and/or the acquisition of businesses?

Box 12-1
SAMPLE GE SCOPE CHANGES*

Aerospace

1. The product-market scope was extended with several major contracts. These included:
   —A Korean Telecom contract for two commercial communications satellites.
   —A U. S. Navy contract for an antisubmarine warfare system.
   —Others from the governments of Italy, Canada, and Turkey, for GE-built solid-state radars.
2. To enhance its position in the engine control and flight control markets, it formed a coventure with GE Aircraft Engines to pursue new opportunities.

(Continued)

Aircraft Engines

1. An ambitious development program is under way to certify the GE90 engine in 1994 and introduce it into active service in 1995.

2. The aviation service business expanded its worldwide reach and capabilities in 1991 with the purchase of an engine overhaul and maintenance facility in Wales from British Airways.

Appliances

1. Expanded its relationships with MABE (a joint venture in Mexico) and other international partners. MABE's breakthrough product, an oven with 30 percent more usable capacity than any other leading manufacturer's gas range, has received a high degree of market acceptance.

2. Signed an agreement in principle to create a joint venture with Godrej & Boyce Manufacturing Co. Ltd., which would provide an opportunity to compete in India's rapidly growing appliance market.

Financial Services

1. Made a number of acquisitions to extend its product-customer scope in specific business areas. For example, Vendor Financial Services purchased Chase Manhattan's technology equipment leasing business, and Retailer Financial Services added the Harrods/House of Fraser credit card business in Great Britain.

2. Corporate Finance developed a special niche in providing lines of credit to bankrupt companies undergoing reorganization.

Industrial and Power Systems

1. In Asia, the business won $350 million of turbine-generator orders outside Japan, and a program to intensify sales coverage in this region was announced.

2. A new agreement with ELIN of Austria is intended to enhance GE's presence in Europe.

Lighting

1. The business is emphasizing new product initiatives for global markets; for example, it accelerated its international momentum with the introduction of a complete line of GE brand lamps for the European commercial and industrial market.

2. New products introduced included the energy-efficient Trimline fluorescent lamp.

Medical Systems

1. Introduced a number of products in magnetic resonance—"literally a renewal of the entire product line."

2. Took a series of steps to increase penetration of the Indian, Russian, and Latin American markets.

° As noted in GE's 1992 annual report.

- Which business units ought to be "pruned" or scaled back?
- Are there business units that should be divested?
- What opportunities can be pursued by combining the products, technologies, and competencies of two or more business units?

Geographic Scope

Increasingly, a geographic dimension is unavoidable in scope determination: Corporate and business-unit strategy must consider the international or global context of business. Even relatively small firms that sell all their output in one country (or even within one region of a country) possess a number of options to gain a toehold in foreign markets—among them, exporting directly or partnering with enterprises in other countries. Indeed, it is not uncommon today to find small firms selling a majority of their output in foreign markets.

Without question, one of the most significant forces that has shaped almost every industry in the past 20 or 30 years has been "globalization." Competitors in any geographic market may have their "home" in any number of countries; raw materials and supplies may be obtained from any region of the world; many customers may be purchasing on a global scale. Dramatic improvements in information technology, telecommunications, and transportation allow information, goods, and services to be shipped around the world at a speed that was unimaginable a mere few decades ago.

Global change affects every organization's portfolio of opportunities. Countries and regions experience different rates of economic growth, demographic shifts affect the size of markets, and political change opens up or restricts access to national marketplaces. In short, as business becomes increasingly globalized, organizations will miss out on extensive opportunities unless they try to penetrate nations and regions beyond their "home" or regional market (their adjacent multicountry market).

Geographic scope thus presents a number of issues and questions:

- What national or regional markets represent opportunities for the firm's current or future products?
- What differences and similarities exist among customers across these national or regional boundaries?
- How can the firm's products be customized or adapted for each customer group?
- How can what is learned about customers, distribution channels, competitors, and the firm's success or failure in one geographic market be leveraged in others?

Stakeholder Scope

Although frequently neglected in the strategic management literature, issues of scope also apply to the "political" arena: the interaction between the organization and its external stakeholders (industry and trade associations, community groups, governmental agencies, the courts, the media, social activist groups, and industry participants such as distributors, end-customers, suppliers, and competitors). Success in dealing with stakeholders is frequently critical to success in the product or economic marketplace. For example, many firms have developed political alliances with some of their product competitors in order to push their preferred technology standard or to obtain favorable treatment from one or more governmental agencies. Scope therefore must include consideration of how the organization wishes to deal with its external stakeholders.

Among the scope issues and questions involving critical stakeholders are the following:

- Which stakeholders can affect attainment of the organization's goals and how can they do so?
- What are the similarities and differences in the "stakes" or interests of these stakeholders?
- Which stakeholders can the organization align itself with to enhance goal attainment and how can it do so?

Scope delineates the businesses or product-customer segments the organization is in or wants to be in. It does not, however, address or provide much guidance as to how to compete in the marketplace in order to attract, win, and retain customers—the substance and focus of competitive posture.

Competitive Posture

Posture embodies how an organization differentiates itself from current and future competitors *as perceived and understood by customers.* Differentiation is the source of the value (compared with the value provided by competitors) that customers obtain when they buy a firm's product or solution. Without some degree of differentiation, customers have no particular reason to purchase an organization's product offerings rather than those of its competitors. For example, unless customers perceive some unique value associated with buying an automobile produced by General Motors, they will have no specific incentive or reason to buy from General Motors rather than from its competitors. In short, a critical purpose of strategy is to create—and to continue to enhance—some degree of differentiation.

TABLE 12-4   Competitive posture: Sample key dimensions

Product line width	Breadth of the product line
Product features	Style
	Design
	"Bells and whistles"
	Size and shape
Product functionality	Performance
	Reliability
	Durability
	Speed
	Taste
Service	Technical assistance
	Product repair
	Hot lines
	Education about product use
Availability	Access via distribution channels
	Ability to purchase in bulk
	How quickly product can be obtained
Image and reputation	Brand name
	Image as "high-end" product
	Reputation for quality of service
Selling and relationships	Sales force that can detail many products
	Close ties with distribution channels
	Historic dealings with large end-users
Price	List price
	Discounted price
	Price performance comparisons
	Price value comparisons

How is differentiation created? What are its principal dimensions? What levers can an organization manipulate to foster and sustain differentiation *as perceived and understood by customers?* Although not intended as an exhaustive listing, Table 12-4 indicates a number of the key dimensions of differentiation employed by organizations in almost all industries. Box 12-2 discusses each of these dimensions.

Box 12-2
KEY DIMENSIONS OF POSTURE

Product Line Width   Providing a full line of products or services is often highly valued by distribution channels and/or end users. Retailers, distributors, and end customers often like to be able to do "one-stop" shopping. Other firms focus on a narrow product line (compared with competitors)

(Continued)

and promote their specialization and expertise in the narrow product line to customers.

Product Features   Products can vary greatly along physical attributes such as design, style, shape, and color.

Product Functionality   All products provide some type of functional benefit(s) to users: newspapers convey information; personal computers allow individuals to better manage their household finances or write articles and books; bread provides sustenance; CDs facilitate listening pleasure. Functionality thus offers organizations myriad means by which they can differentiate their product offerings.

Service   Increasingly, service is a powerful source of differentiation in all types of products. Indeed, customers—both distribution channels and end users—now expect high levels of service. Many industrial product firms offer customers varying levels of technical assistance, education about product use, and aftersale support with application or product-use difficulties.

Availability   Wide or highly select distribution can be a significant source of differentiation. Book publishers strive to get their books marketed through as many different types of distribution channels as possible, including specialist book retailers, institutional (college) bookstores, supermarket chains, direct mail catalogs, and industry and trade shows. Other firms choose select distribution channels as a means of augmenting the image and reputation of their products and services.

Image and Reputation   All organizations and their products develop an image and reputation in the eyes of distributors, customers, suppliers, competitors, and governmental agencies. Recognizing the powerful and persuasive image conveyed to customers via brand names, many firms, such as IBM, Pepsi, Honda, and Levi, invest extensive resources to create and foster the "equity" in their brand name. Some discount stores and distribution channels have successfully created a powerful reputation for quality and low price in the form of generic products. Many firms have successfully differentiated themselves by crafting a well-earned image and reputation for prompt and supportive service.

Selling and Relationships   Many firms have established such tight relationships with their distribution channels and/or end users that rivals have extreme difficulty "getting a hearing."

Price   Customers compare the value provided by competitors against the prices asked for their products.

Posture defines the terms of marketplace rivalry—the battle among firms to create new customers, to lure away each other's customers, and to retain customers once they have been won. Almost any industry (or industry segment) could be used to illustrate the efforts of rivals to distinguish themselves in the eyes of customers along the dimensions noted in Table 12-4 and Box 12-2. Rivalry among firms in the personal computer (PC) business is described in Box 12-3.

The intensity of the pressures to attract, win, and retain customers in almost every industry forces organizations into a never-ending race; they struggle continually to redefine and renew their posture. As detailed in Box 12-3, every firm in the personal computer business continually upgrades its product features; builds greater functionality into the products; adds new service elements; promotes, advertises, and uses every form of customer interaction to advance its image and reputation; broadens the distribution base for its products; works to

---

Box 12-3
RIVALRY IN THE PERSONAL COMPUTER BUSINESS

Rivalry in the personal computer (PC) business is so intense, business journalists describe it as "the PC wars." A large number of firms—well-known, large computer firms such as IBM, Digital Equipment Corporation, Apple, and Hewlett-Packard; smaller and more recent U.S. entrants such as Tandy, AST, and Compaq; Japanese firms such as Toshiba and NEC; direct mail entrants such as Dell Computer, Gateway 2000, and CompuAdd, as well as many others—are all striving to get and keep customers.

The rivalry has multiple dimensions. All competitors are rapidly extending their product lines. New models and line extensions are announced almost daily. Some firms have announced as many as 40 new products within a year. Firms are fighting furiously to stay ahead of each other with the latest notebook, laptop, and desktop models.

Functionality and features are a fierce battleground. Compaq has historically emphasized the performance capability of its products. The so-called "clone" manufacturers have differentiated themselves on comparatively low levels of functionality (yet sufficient for specific customer needs) but at low prices.

Newly introduced products are often aimed directly at rivals' offerings. IBM's low-end Value-Points were positioned to compete directly against some of Compaq's models.

(Continued)

Dell Computer, Gateway 2000, Zeos International, and CompuAdd have used direct distribution (selling directly to the end-customer or user) as an initial primary means of attracting and winning customers. The success of this means of reaching customers has caused IBM to create a new organizational unit, Ambra, specifically intended to compete directly against the mail order providers. Compaq and Digital Equipment Corporation have also announced that they plan to develop direct distribution capabilities.

In efforts to create image and reputation, the rivalry is now direct and intense. For example, one of Dell's advertisements asserts: "The gateway to the hottest PC technology isn't Gateway."

Service is now a primary target of differentiation. Almost all firms offer a package of support services that includes an 800-number, installation, assistance, and technical support. The direct distributors—Dell, Gateway, and others—endeavor to use service features such as rapid response to customer's inquiries as a means of distinguishing the value they provide to customers from that of their more "mainline" rivals such as IBM and Compaq, IBM and Compaq have responded by dramatically upgrading the range and quality of the service they offer.

The extent and intensity of the rivalry has been reflected in continually declining prices.

strengthen its relationships with dealers and users—all with the intent of enhancing the value delivered for the prices charged.

The ultimate power of the modes of differentiation, as illustrated for Dell Computer in Box 12-4, resides in their combination. By providing customers with a continual flow of new models with state-of-the-art functionality, supported by superior service and close working relationships with customers, and prompt delivery at prices that are often below those of many direct competitors, Dell is able to offer customers many reasons for buying its products. Each mode of differentiation contributes to attracting, winning, and retaining customers. Customer-based advantage (why customers buy from one competitor rather than others) always stems from a combination of these modes of differentiation; no one alone is sufficient.

For many products, posture increasingly is tailored to each individual customer—what has become known as mass customization.[7] The modes of differentiation are customized to meet customers' unique needs and wants. Dell Computer is a classic example (see Box 12-4). Dell endeavors to tailor to the needs and demands of each customer the features, power, and capability of each computer as well as the type and level of service offered.

Box 12-4
COMPETITIVE POSTURE: DELL COMPUTER, INC.

Product Line Width   Endeavors to provide a computer configuration to meet the specific needs of each customer.

Features   Varies features to meet customer needs. Uses data about each customer to tailor the feature configuration. Emphasis is on what customers want; technology is not introduced for its own sake.

Functionality   Tries to provide state-of-the-art performance and reliability tailored to how a customer will use the computer.

Service   Has 24-hour customer access via toll-free lines; handles 35,000 service and support calls per day; offers personalized phone numbers for many business customers; provides technical assistance to all customers.

Availability   Distributes directly to customers; uses distribution partners to provide next-day delivery; uses superstore and mass-merchant companies as channels but maintains direct support services to these customers.

Image and Reputation   Working to (1) make a reputation for second-to-none service an integral part of what customers buy when they purchase from Dell and (2) create an image as a firm that will go to any lengths to give customers a computer configuration that meets their needs.

Selling and Relationships   Small field sales force targets business customers; uses direct mail for as many as 15 million catalogs in a quarter. All sales and service calls are aimed at learning about customer needs, wants, and reactions to Dell products.

Price   Historically, has built a reputation for prices lower than those of established computer manufacturers such as IBM and Compaq. Now broadly similar to emerging lookalike rivals such as Gateway 2000 and Northgate Computer. Tries to emphasize price-value relationship, with the price including service and customization.

Goals

The choices made in business scope and competitive posture are to achieve some purposes or goals.[8] It is almost impossible to make sense of an organization's changes in its scope and posture without having some knowledge of its goals. For example, unless one understands that GE's overriding marketplace goal is to be first, second, or third in terms of global market share in each of its businesses, it would be difficult to explain why it divested the television receiver business it had acquired in its takeover of Radio Corporation of America (RCA) even though the RCA brand name was one of the market share leaders in the United States. RCA had a very small share of the global market, and it would have been extremely difficult to increase it significantly in the face of intense Japanese competition.

Consideration of goals inevitably leads to two central questions:

1. What does the organization want to achieve in the marketplace?
2. What returns or rewards does it wish to attain for its various stakeholders—its stockholders, employees, customers, suppliers, and the community at large?

(Specific goals typically considered by organizations are noted in Table 12-5.)

Every organization has an explicit or implicit *hierarchy* of goals that involve some mixture of the marketplace, finance, technology, and other factors. At least four levels of goals need to be considered: (1) strategic intent/marketplace vision, (2) strategic thrusts/investment programs, (3) objectives, and (4) operating goals (see Figure 12-3). We shall discuss each briefly.

Goals at the level of *strategic intent*[9] or *marketplace vision* refer to the long-run concept of what the organization wants to achieve in the marketplace in terms of products, customers, and technologies. For example, a number of firms promulgate an intent or vision somewhat akin to the following: To be the leader in the provision of a specific product class to particular types of customers on a global scale.

For some companies, the intent or vision embodies a goal of reshaping and reconfiguring an industry or some industry segment. In any case, intent or vision is broader in scope and more distant in time perspective than the market share goals (that is, the share of customers for existing or planned products) that are the obsessive and dominant focus in some firms.

Strategic thrusts and investment programs refer to the significant product and other investment commitments that the firm is undertaking or plans to undertake to realize its intent or vision over three- to five-year (and sometimes considerably longer) periods. Examples include investments in alliances, research and development (R&D), product line extensions, new manufacturing facilities,

TABLE 12-5 Goals: Key questions

What does the organization want to achieve in the marketplace?

Vision or intent	In the broad marketplace, where does the organization want to be 5, 10, or 15 years from today?
Businesses	What primary and secondary businesses does it want to get into, stay in, or get out of?
Position	What ranking does it want to attain in each of its businesses in terms of marketplace leadership?
Products	With regard to each product line: —What market share does it want to strive for, over what time period? —What types of new customers does it want to attract? —Which competitors does it want to take share away from?
Differentiation	What type of differentiation does it want to establish?

What returns or rewards does the organization wish to attain for its various stakeholders?

Shareholders/Owners	What level of shareholder wealth creation does it want to strive for? What returns (e.g., ROI) are sought on specific investments?
Employees	What quality of working experience does it want to provide for employees at all levels? What level of remuneration does it want to provide to all levels in the organization?
Government	How can the organization contribute to attainment of the goals of specific governmental agencies? What other contributions can the organization make to good government?
Customers	What degree of customer satisfaction and value does it want to provide its customers? How can the organization help its customers achieve their goals?
Society	In what ways does the organization want to demonstrate that it is a "good citizen"? Are there specific social projects to which it wants to make a monetary or other contribution?

and development of marketing capabilities. The company might have the following representative goals: Build a leading presence in the European marketplace, reorient R&D toward the development of products that are new to the marketplace, and/or fashion a set of alliance partners that brings together two or three types of related technologies.

Objectives refer to goals that transform strategic thrusts into action programs. Objectives tend to specify results that embrace a time horizon of one to

FIGURE 12-3   An organization's hierarchy of goals

three years and represent the broad targets or milestones that the organization strives to attain. For example, a business unit's strategic thrust to penetrate the European marketplace might be guided by objectives such as these: Launch each product line in every major European country within three years, attain 15 percent of the European market within three or four years, achieve average gross margins of 22 percent, and be represented in every major distribution channel in each major country.

Operating goals are short-run targets (usually achievable within one year) that are measurable, specific, and detailed. They can be viewed as accomplishments that contribute to the attainment of objectives. The following are typical operating goals: Attain a particular market share for each product in a specific geographic market or for different specific customer sets, improve margins by a specific amount, and enhance customer satisfaction by some percentage (based on some scale of measurement).

In summary, goals make sense of the organization's actions. The decision by a corporation to divest an entire business often makes sense only when it is known whether its strategic thrust is to refocus on its core business or to raise cash quickly. Goals focus the organization's attention. If the goal is to increase margins, the organization is likely to address those activities that will add to revenues and reduce costs. Goals facilitate coordination of what otherwise might be disparate and conflicting activities. They motivate organizational members and rationalize the organization's actions so that all the stakeholders can contribute to winning.

Linkages among Scope, Posture, and Goals

Strategic management presumes that organizations are goal directed, although seasoned managers recognize that an organization's goals may not be consistent, integrated, widely disseminated, or understood. This is especially so when goals are related to time. Many firms are too busy pursuing today's opportunities to worry about goal consistency. Others are so committed to outdated goals that they don't react quickly enough to critical changes in the marketplace. Thus, in the challenge of strategic management noted at the beginning of this chapter—laying the foundation for success in tomorrow's environment while competing to win in today's marketplace—a central element is management of the conflict between commitment to goals and the need to adapt scope and posture to changing environmental and organizational conditions.

Managing the conflict is a difficult balancing act. A strategic intent or marketplace vision that is out of touch with the environment and with the organization's resources and capabilities can only lead to shattered dreams, intense frustration, and enormous anxiety. On the other hand, if the goals do not push the organization's scope and posture to create or avail of emerging opportunities, they contribute to inferior performance. For example, William Gates III, CEO of Microsoft, has said that one of his greatest regrets is that he did not commit the firm sooner to a vision of "work-group computing" (a means of allowing teams to use networks of interconnected personal computers to share data and information and to cooperate on multiple projects). The intent of being the dominant leader in work-group computing is now reflected in a variety of Microsoft's strategic thrusts and investment programs designed to make a broad-based attack on this marketplace.[10]

In summary, as illustrated for an electronics firm in Box 12-5, scope, posture, and goals are three interrelated elements in marketplace strategy. The electronics firm's long-term goals—its intent and vision—are to establish new technology and customer service standards in a specific domain of industrial applications. These long-term goals create a context for the design and development of scope and posture. The firm's product development thrusts and its search for new customers and new uses or applications refine the firm's marketplace scope over time. Its overall posture of moving toward customizing each "solution" or application for each customer serves as a central plank of its intent to establish a new industry standard for delivering customer-focused value. Its objectives and operating goals furnish milestones and targets to be achieved in the course of executing its strategic thrusts and programs. For example, attainment of the image and reputation objective to become unquestionably the leading brand name is a necessary step on the road to achieving its intent and vision.

Box 12-5
AN ELECTRONICS FIRM'S MARKETPLACE STRATEGY

Broad Goals

Intent and Vision   To become the leading supplier of a range of equipment involving specific technologies for a variety of customer uses. (In so doing, to enhance revenues, profits, margins, market share, and image as product/technology leader.)

Marketplace Scope

Products-Customers   Provides three distinct lines of related products to any type of industrial customer in North America and most European countries. Continues to add variety to its product lines and to search for new applications of its products with both existing and new customers.

Marketplace Posture

Modes of Competing to Achieve Differentiation   Moving toward customizing its solution for each customer by varying product features and performance to meet each customer's specific needs. Also tailoring service agreements to suit customer's requirements and ability to pay. Using own sales force and distributors to reach new customers and build customer relationships through provision of technical assistance and attention to evolving customer needs. Building an image of leading technology developer through promotion and marketing programs and sales force activity. Actual prices tend to be higher than competitors, reflecting superior product functionality, reputation, and added service.

Objectives and Goals

Product Development   To introduce another product line within three years and to add as many variations to the existing lines as customers need.

Market Share   Continue to gain penetration of each major customer class. Attain 25% share of market units within four to five years.

Image and Reputation   To become the recognized leading name for a range of uses of its core product technology (measured by customer surveys).

Distribution Channels   To be preferred product line of each major channel in every geographic region.

Technology   To augment technology capabilities in three specific areas in order to enhance product functionality:

1. Increase revenues by 12 to 14 percent per year.
2. Increase gross margins 8 to 10 percent over three years.
3. Increase net profits 10 to 12 percent over three years.

A final but critical comment on strategy: Strategy provides a sense of marketplace direction that may remain quite stable over time, but substantial parts of its key elements—scope, posture, and goals—may change. Thus, the electronics firm's intent or vision (noted in Box 12-5) may endure for a number of years as a guide to the direction of many of its principal strategic thrusts and investment programs. However, as the firm strives to reach its overarching vision, the strategy may manifest a number of twists and turns as the firm anticipates, responds to, and leverages environmental change. For example, the firm's own technology development may generate unexpected opportunities for new products, extension of one or more of the existing product lines, or new ways to seek differentiation. As the organization reaches for these opportunities, scope and posture are adapted over time.[11]

MANAGING THE ORGANIZATION

Strategies that continue to win in the marketplace don't just happen. Even if an organization stumbles onto a winning strategy, considerable effort and ingenuity are still needed to continually adapt and amend the strategy in order to leverage internal and environmental change. It is no accident that some organizations successfully adapt to an environment and initiate new ventures in a number of related product areas while others never seem able to repeat a single success. In short, what takes place *within* the organization makes a difference.

Winning in the marketplace is heavily influenced by how well the organization makes and executes its choices of where and how to compete. Figure 12-1 sets out five organizational domains that are critical to crafting and sustaining successful marketplace strategies.

Analytics

The determination of scope, posture, and goals involves a plethora of individual decisions: what products to develop and offer, what customers to seek, how best to compete in the marketplace, and what goals to pursue. These decisions require many types of analytical input; especially important are data and insights about multiple facets of the competitive context as well as the organization itself. These data and insights are the products of analysis. *Analytics* here refers to all the analysis conducted by an organization in strategy determination and execution.

Analysis is framed and guided by conceptual frameworks and analytical methodologies. Many different types of frameworks and methodologies are available to capture and assess change in any firm's industry and macro-environment.

The most prevalent industry analysis framework is Michael Porter's "Five Forces" scheme. He suggests that the attractiveness of an industry is a function of five forces: the degree of rivalry among the industry's competitors, the threat of new entrants, the threat of substitutes, the power of buyers (that is, distribution channels and end-customers), and the power of suppliers. Each of these forces contributes to whether an industry is currently profitable, or likely to be at some future time. Thus, each "force" needs to be carefully and critically examined separately and then collectively. Let us briefly consider each one.

The degree of rivalry is strongly influenced by the number and relative sizes of competitors. A large number of similarly sized competitors are likely to engage in rivalry fierce enough to push prices down to the point that nobody earns much profits. A small number of competitors or a single dominant competitor is more likely to lead to a situation in which competitors recognize their mutual interests and interdependencies and thus refrain from initiating rivalrous outbursts such as price wars. Other industry structure attributes such as excess capacity, slow industry sales, and lack of product differentiation contribute to increased rivalry intensity.

The threat of new entrants or the potential for substitute products affect the attractiveness of an industry and the level of profits that can be attained. Unless distinct entry barriers exist such as access to specific raw materials, proprietary product differences, or access to distribution channels, competitors can enter and thus intensify rivalry. The emergence of substitute products can dramatically affect almost every facet of an industry. For example, the fax machine and electronic mail have severely reduced the need for overnight delivery of documents.

Finally, increases in the power of suppliers and buyers may leave rivals with little (short-run) option but to pay more for inputs and reduce their own prices in order to attract and retain customers. The size and distribution of suppliers and customers obviously affect the power vis-a-vis some set of rival manufacturers or service providers. IBM has lost much of its power with respect to its suppliers and customers due to the emergence of many new rivals in the manufacture and sale of computers; its suppliers now have other customers and its customers now have other suppliers.

In summary, these five forces—the intensity of rivalry, the threat of new entrants and substitute products, and the power of buyers and sellers—strongly shape the attractiveness of any industry for current rivals or potential entrants.

The macroenvironment is typically viewed as the environment external to an industry: the political, economic, social, and technological milieu. Each of these milieu can affect the structure of an industry (for example, each of Porter's five forces noted in the previous paragraph) and thus the prospects for industry profitability. It is therefore worth nothing what constitutes each milieu and how it can affect an industry.

The political milieu consists of the formal institutions of government—the executive branch, the legislatures, the judiciary and the regulatory agencies, as well as the electoral process and the informal arenas outside of government in which political activity occurs such as local community settings and the media. It is perhaps the most turbulent of the external milieu. Executive branch decisions such as the imposition of tariffs and quotas or legislative policy changes such as the treatment of R&D investments for tax purposes can quickly change key features of an industry such as the amount of product available in the marketplace (and at what price) and the cost structures of different competitors.

The economic milieu consists of the general set of economic conditions facing all industries. Economic activity is reflected in levels and patterns of industrial output, consumption, income and savings, and productivity. Changes in the overall level of economic activity directly affect supply and demand in almost all industries.

The social milieu consists of demographics, life-styles, and social values. It entails shifts in the age structure and mobility of the population, changes in how people live their lives (for example, where they wish to live, what types of products they choose to purchase, how they spend their leisure time), and changes in social values (for example, whether people consider smoking desirable or harmful). Social changes impact the size of the market for many products and often give rise to or reduce product niches (for example, the importance attached to physical fitness generated substantial markets for many products from running shoes and tennis rackets to nautilus equipment).

The technological milieu is concerned with the level and direction of technological progress and advancements taking place in society. In particular, it addresses the research, development, and application involved in products, processes, and materials. Research and development often generates the new products that become substitutes to existing products. Breakthroughs in process technologies (such as new manufacturing processes) can reshape product quality and industry cost structures.

The outputs of an analysis of an industry and its macroenvironment are threefold:

1. An understanding of the current state of the industry (or industries) and the macroenvironment the firm may enter or in which it currently participates.

2. An identification of likely "alternative futures," that is, potential future states of these industries.

3. An assessment of the implications of the current and potential states of the environment for the organization's existing and potential strategies.

Equally important is analysis of the organization itself. If the organization is unable to take advantage of opportunities or to defend against competitive or environmental threats, there is little benefit in engaging in environmental analysis. Unfortunately, many managers have historically adopted a very narrow purview in analyzing their own organization. Indeed, in some organizations, financial and human resources receive predominant, if not exclusive, attention. Other facets of the organization, such as managers' assumptions about the current and future state of the industry, remain relatively unexamined.

This chapter offers a broad framework for the analysis of any organization. It suggests the need to thoroughly assess the organization's prevailing mindset, operating processes, infrastructure, and leadership—each of which may impede or facilitate the development of strategy. It emphasizes that each of these organizational domains can contribute to the identification and development of marketplace opportunities. The outputs of organization analysis include:

1. An understanding of the state of the organization's mind-set, operating processes, infrastructure, and leadership.

2. An identification of the organization's strengths (such as its capabilities and competencies) and weaknesses (such as its vulnerabilities, constraints, and limitations).

3. An assessment of the implications of the state of the organization for its current and potential strategies.

It is never enough merely to analyze. Analyses of the environment and of the organization must be transformed into strategy alternatives that are then assessed before the organization commits to its existing direction or selects new directions. Strategy alternatives need to be articulated in terms of possible alterations to scope, posture, and goals. Analytics therefore needs to be specifically focused on a crucial, complex, and creative task: turning the knowledge and learning acquired as part of ongoing environmental and organizational analysis into the specification of potential opportunities and threats.

Once strategy alternatives are identified and developed and their implications are understood, they can then be evaluated. The analysis of strategy alternatives requires that each alternative be subjected to searching and demanding questions. This level of analysis should be part of a continuous process to enhance an organization's strategy. In our rapidly changing business environment, the product of this analysis is likely to be a set of strategy recommendations for altering the organization's scope, posture, and goals.

Analytics poses a number of managerial challenges. First, analytics must be strategically focused; that is, the analysis must be aimed at detecting opportunities. It is not sufficient merely to capture and promulgate warnings of environmental and organizational change. Second, an emphasis on opportunities compels continuous consideration of the future. Managers conducting analysis often must dare to break free of the intellectual shackles that the past imposes on anyone who tries to anticipate the future.

Mind-Set

Analysis is conducted by individuals in an organizational setting. It is influenced by the collective state-of-mind or mind-set of the organization. Mind-set is the sum of vision (what managers see the organization striving to attain), values (what they consider important), beliefs (what they consider to be cause-effect relationships), and assumptions (what they take for granted).

An organization's *vision* offers stakeholders a view of the future it wants to achieve. Apple's vision is to change the world by empowering individuals through personal computing technology. Whether a vision is explicit or implicit, it transmits the organization's overarching strategic goals, as discussed earlier, to its members. Vision thus shapes a common theme in the organization's state-of-mind. For example, in the 1960s, Komatsu established the vision of being the world's leading earthmoving equipment manufacturer. At the time, it seemed an unachievable goal, but this aim served as a rallying cry and unifying force as Komatsu set out to overtake Caterpillar's dominant lead in the global marketplace.[12]

Visions are not likely to move organizations to decisive action unless they are reflected in *values*—what organization members consider important. Values connect a vision to decision making; they link the organization's aspirations and goals to day-to-day actions and decisions. For example, organizations that are product- or technology-driven (versus customer- or marketplace-driven) manifest distinctly different values. In technology-focused firms, driving values might be stated as: "If it is technologically feasible, let's do it," or "Each product must incorporate the latest technological capability." Customer-focused firms manifest these values: "What the customer wants is more important than what is technologically possible," or "Each technological development should be tested against customers' needs and perceptions as early as possible."

Most organizations construct value statements that typically address broad items: "a commitment to excellence," "doing what is right," "treating employees with respect and integrity," and "providing value to customers." However, such statements do not provide enough guidance for decision making and action. Excellence at any cost? Doing what is right by what code? Values truly become a core element in an organization's mind-set only when they are localized and internalized by organization members. For example, Komatsu could not have sustained its assault on Caterpillar unless the vision of becoming the world's leading earthmoving equipment manufacturer translated into values such as the need to continually upgrade the quality of the product line, the need to provide superior value to customers, the need to manufacture extremely functional and high-performing machines.

Beliefs are the organization's understanding of cause–effect relationships. Beliefs may address matters that are internal (e.g., improvements in the manufacturing process will lead to higher product quality and lower costs) or external (e.g., competitors' lower prices will not lead to higher market share). In either case, they may be widely shared and embedded in the organization. Beliefs are an important component of mind-set because they strongly influence behaviors. If an organization believes that alliances are the only way to quickly penetrate and sustain a dominant position in a particular industry segment, it will likely forgo other options and craft a series of alliances.

Assumptions are distinct from beliefs. They are "givens" such as information or situations that the organization is willing to consider givens. Organizations make assumptions about many internal and external factors, including customers, competitors, industry evolution, regulation, technology, and the organization's resources, competencies, and cash flows. Assumptions such as "Competitors will not be able to introduce a superior product for the next three years" or "Our own organization will be able to generate all the funds it needs for capital investment from cash flow" become central elements in the organization's mind-set.

An organization's mind-set is the worldview that results from its own members' interacting with each other over time. Eventually, organizational members begin to share with each other and reinforce their vision, values, beliefs, and assumptions. The worldview defines and shapes opportunity and risk. For example, stories about the difficulties of dealing with a particular distribution channel or an end-customer group may become legend within an organization and implicitly lead it to shy away from doing business with these customer segments.

Mind-set is of central importance to strategic management because it can either buttress or inhibit strategy. Its effects on scope, posture, and goals can be dramatic. Visions have frequently transformed the mind-set of organizations so that they could then achieve what earlier might have seemed impossible.

False beliefs and assumptions preordain strategy failure. IBM's recent, well-publicized difficulties can in large measure be traced to false beliefs and assumptions about the future of the mainframe segment of the computer industry. The mainframe segment had catapulted IBM to its position of dominance in the computer industry. IBM believed that its technological prowess could add to the mainframe a level of functionality that customers would appreciate and value. It also assumed that the rate of market decline would not increase and that new customers could be attracted to the mainframe. The combination of these beliefs and assumptions allowed IBM to stumble into disaster. The decline of the mainframe sales and profits led to shareholders' losing billions of dollars and employees' losing tens of thousands of jobs.

The managerial challenge therefore is to ensure that mind-set recognizes environmental change. This recognition is a prerequisite to developing and executing strategies that can win in the marketplace. Ideally, to achieve strategic leadership, an organization should be able to adopt a new mind-set as a way of positioning itself to profit from environmental change. The challenge for managers then becomes one of continually assessing the organization's existing mind-set and questioning whether it is reflecting past or emerging potential environmental change.

Operating Processes

Analytics and mind-set are necessary, but they are not sufficient for an organization to function—to get things done. Operating processes constitute how work gets done in and around any organization. A large number of operating processes exist in every organization. A listing of critical operating processes for most manufacturing firms is shown in Table 12-6. Each operating process represents a task that must be completed in order for an organization to survive. Without operating processes, organizations cannot systematically learn about the marketplace, develop new products, acquire the raw materials and

TABLE 12-6 Typical operating processes in manufacturing firms

Scanning the environment for marketplace opportunities.

Designing products that meet customers' needs.

Acquiring raw materials and components.

Acquiring and training personnel.

Building product prototypes.

Manufacturing products.

Marketing.

Selling and detailing products to customers.

Delivering products to customers.

Receiving and fulfilling customers' orders.

Providing pre- and postsales service to customers.

components to assemble and produce products or services, access capital, acquire and develop human resources, market and distribute products, or provide service to intermediate or end customers. In the execution of these tasks, operating processes are intimately linked to the development and implementation of strategy.

Operating processes are the focus of considerable attention in almost all organizations. The object of continuous improvement and quality management programs is enhancement of operating processes. For example, these programs frequently aim to make the processes noted in Table 12-6 more efficient (that is, to get greater output for the same or less resources) and more effective (for example, to add greater value to customers).

Operating processes have critical import for a strategically managed organization, for many reasons. Among them are:

1. If the organization does not do the right things, then both its thinking and its actions are unlikely to generate competitive success. Each organization must identify its critical or core operating processes—those that are most central to winning in the marketplace.[13]

2. Many core operating processes, such as product development, fulfillment of customers' orders, and learning about marketplace change, transcend organizational boundaries and thus serve to integrate functional groups (such as R&D, manufacturing, and marketing) around common external purposes (such as serving customers better).

3. If operating processes are not well managed, the organization's overall efficiency will be severely hampered. For example, in the 1990s, managers of operating processes in cutting-edge firms have greatly reduced cycle times (such as speed to market or the time it takes to fulfill a customer's order).

Like analytics and mind-set, operating processes can positively or negatively affect each element in strategy: scope, posture, and goals. With regard to scope, many companies, after recognizing the poor returns from their R&D and product commercialization activity, have struggled to redesign and invigorate the new product development process. In particular, in the 1990s, some industrial product companies have established integrated product development teams and radically changed the work flow related to identifying ideas for products, doing basic or applied research, creating product prototypes, and market-testing prototypes in customer facilities. No longer is product development solely the responsibility of the R&D and/or new product development departments. Rather, new product development groups are established with representation from all the affected functional areas or departments—R&D, product design, manufacturing, marketing, sales and service, accounting and finance, and human resources. This integration replaces having one phase of new product development done by one department or group without much consultation with all the others in the development chain, and then "handed-off" to the next department or group.

Operating processes have perhaps a more direct impact on posture than on scope. In company after company, the redesign and enhancement of operating processes are leading to significant improvement in the quality, speed, and responsiveness of these organizations—how they anticipate changing customer needs, acquire and fulfill orders, and ensure that customers are satisfied after they have purchased their products or services.

Managing operating processes presents a number of challenges:

1. Analysis and redesign of operating processes must be guided by their marketplace strategy relevance because their ultimate value resides in how they contribute to getting and keeping customers.

2. Operating processes constitute an integrated organizational system: altering one process often affects many others. Thus, they must be managed at the systemic level, not at the individual level.

3. Because operating processes reside at the heart of an organization's capabilities and competencies, they often are the source of marketplace opportunities.

Infrastructure

Analytics, mind-set, and operating processes exist within an organization's infrastructure: its structure, systems, and decision-making processes. As with the other organizational elements, infrastructure must be managed with an eye to helping the organization cope with and leverage environmental change.

Structure refers to how the organization is organized internally as well as to its relationships with external entities. Internal structure addresses (1) how the organization divides itself into units (such as business sectors, business units, and departments) and (2) the linkages among these subunits[14] (such as reporting relationships). An increasingly critical element in structure is the linkages that an organization effects with other entities (suppliers, distributors, customers, competitors, technology sources, venture partners, and community and public interest groups) through alliances, partnerships, and networks. External linkages help organizations to gain access to critical resources (such as capital, knowledge, and skills) and facilitate the development of key capabilities and competencies.

An organization's structure, however elegant and innovative its design, is merely a shell. *Systems* are required to move information through the structure, oversee and control the flow of resources, reward and motivate organizational members, and facilitate the making of decisions. Information, control, remuneration, and planning systems play critical roles in ensuring that an organization anticipates, copes with, and leverages change.

Decision processes are the organizational procedures and routines that bring organizational members together in the making of decisions. They may be largely formal, as when planning system procedures, committees, task forces, and regularly scheduled meetings, or informal, as when ad hoc meetings or other get-togethers of individuals are charged with making specific decisions. They may range from consensus-generating routines that involve interaction among many individuals at multiple levels of the organization on top-down, authoritarian routines in which decisions are made and announced by one person or a small number of individuals, with all others then expected to fall in line and execute the decisions.[15]

Infrastructure is not incidental to making and executing strategy. Structure can serve to focus and reinforce an organization's efforts to win in the marketplace or it can hobble managers who might otherwise take initiatives. Many business units have found ways to succeed in reshaping and enhancing their product line and to aggressively pursue customers once they have been freed from the infrastructural shackles of a prior corporate parent. Lexmark, almost as soon as it became independent of IBM, began to change its scope and posture in the printer business and achieved dramatic results; it had struggled to do so for many years as an IBM business unit.

Systems can affect scope, posture, and goals in many ways. For example, managers' incentive systems sometimes have an unintended and unanticipated influence on scope decisions. In one well-known leading U.S. corporation, senior executives did not approve any capital investment in new product development, geographic expansion, or potential alliances if it was likely to have a negative impact on short-run earnings. Why? Because they did not receive *any* bonus if earnings dipped below a prespecified level. On the other hand, if managers' incentives are closely tied to increased sales, a common result is that the organization goes to extraordinary lengths to attract new customers.

Decision processes sometimes directly influence goals. The CEO in a large single-business firm was unable to generate a consensus among his top management team as to which of a number of strategic alternatives or opportunities the firm should pursue. In his estimation, part of the difficulty in reaching a consensus stemmed from the inability of the top management team to devote sufficient time, as a group, to considering the alternatives and choosing among them. His solution was to take the management team for a five-day "retreat" at an executive education facility where the team would have the time and commitment needed to seriously consider the options. The team eliminated some opportunities, identified linkages among others that previously had not been noted, and rank-ordered the opportunities in terms of their potential sales and their fit with the organization's resources, capabilities, and competencies. The short list of opportunities then became the focus of further analysis once the executive team returned home.

Managing infrastructure also presents a number of challenges:

1. Structure, systems, and decision processes tend to ossify: they take on a life of their own. For example, once managers and others get used to a particular information system, they become reluctant to change.

2. Structure, systems, and decision processes that were appropriate for one set of environmental conditions may be ineffectual for identifying and adapting to emerging opportunities spawned by change.

3. Structure, systems, and decision processes are interrelated; thus, like operating processes, they must be managed at the systemic level.

Leadership

A dominant presumption underlying strategic management is that managers can make a difference. The organizational elements previously discussed—analytics, mind-set, operating processes, and infrastructure—can never be allowed to go on "automatic pilot." Leaders must continually guide the analytics, modify the mind-set, orient and integrate the operating processes, and adjust the infrastructure. They should do so in anticipation of change in the environment rather than in reaction to it. Effective managers can create change within the organization *before* performance results suggest that it is necessary.[16] Effective managers continually adapt and sometimes radically alter strategy—scope, posture, and goals. These actions are the substance and focus of *strategic* leadership.

Simply stated, the purpose of leadership is to make a difference by:

- Increasing the chances of winning in the marketplace—the strategy difference.
- Building and sustaining an organization that supports and executes marketplace strategy—the organization difference.

Managers must lead if the organization is to outperform its competitors in the marketplace. The strategy-relevant purpose of leadership *within* the organization is the alignment of the other organizational elements—analytics, mind-set, operating processes, and infrastructure—to take maximum advantage of opportunities in the marketplace. In the face of persistent environmental change, organization leaders have little choice but to continually confront and revamp the analytics, mind-set, operating processes, and infrastructure. Leadership is thus the distinguishing contribution of managers; it is their "value-added" to the organization. Broadly viewed, leadership is the capacity of individuals *at all levels* of the organization, from team leaders to the CEO, to inspire, motivate, and energize those around them to do what it takes to win in the marketplace and to excel in what the organization does and what they do as individuals.

The challenges inherent in strategic leadership can be best illustrated by considering a specific organization. Consider the leadership challenges confronting Jack Smith, the CEO of General Motors, and his team of senior executives, as noted in a recent *Business Week* article:[17]

- Extend and revamp the product lines of each product group.
- Upgrade the product lines more frequently.
- Lower the cost per vehicle (which exceeds both Ford and Chrysler).
- Mend the tattered relations with suppliers angered by the draconian practices of a former head of purchasing.
- Reduce the bureaucracy and improve upward, downward, and lateral communication within the organization.
- Streamline the production and procurement of parts and components.

PRACTICING STRATEGIC MANAGEMENT

As we have defined it, strategic management entails managing strategy, organization, and the linkages between them in order to win both today and tomorrow. Managing strategy or the organization alone is not sufficient. Creating and leveraging change requires a simultaneous focus on both the environment and the organization. Managers must lead by persistently challenging the accepted view of the future and its implications, the basis for success of their strategies, and the ability of their organization to identify and avail itself of opportunities.

This section emphasizes the bridges between strategy and organization by addressing the following key tasks that are central to strategic management:

- Delineating the current state of strategic management.
- Assessing the presence of strategic leadership.
- Identifying and developing strategic alternatives.
- Choosing the preferred strategy.
- Implementing the chosen strategy.
- Outperforming competitors and winning customers.
- Renovating strategy.
- Reinventing strategy.

These tasks serve as the focus of linkages between strategy and organization (see Figure 12-4). Each task will be briefly discussed.

FIGURE 12-4   Strategic management: Linking marketplace strategy and the organization

	The Enterprise	
Managing the Organization		Managing Marketplace Strategy
Current Organization Configuration →	Delineating Strategic Management	← Current Marketplace Strategy
Organization Leadership →	Strategic Leadership	← Marketplace Leadership
Organizational Creativity →	Opportunity Development	← Marketplace Capture
Organization Evaluation →	Choosing Opportunities	← Marketplace Assessment
Organization Alignment →	Executing Strategy	← Strategy Coherence
Organizational Competence →	Outperforming Competitors and Winning Customers	← Marketplace Advantage
Organization Revitalization →	Strategic Renovation	← Strategy Renewal
Organization Transformation →	Strategic Reinvention	← Strategy Entrepreneurship

Delineating the Current State of Strategic Management

Delineating the current marketplace strategy (scope, posture, and goals) and the organization's configuration (the state of its analytics, mind-set, operating processes, infrastructure, and leadership) is a task that must be undertaken before the development and assessment of a future strategy direction. An understanding of the current marketplace strategy and organization configuration gives essential input to the identification and assessment of the presence and extent of strategic leadership, relevant marketplace opportunities and threats, and the resources and capabilities that can be leveraged for advantage, as well as to recognition of the organization's vulnerabilities, limitations, and constraints.

An understanding of current marketplace strategy develops when the interrelated dimensions of scope, posture, and goals are mapped and detailed, as summarized for the electronics firm in Box 12-5.

Because analytics, mind-set, operating processes, infrastructure, and leadership are so deeply ingrained in the day-to-day activities and functioning of the organization, it may be difficult for managers to delineate their prevailing state. Yet it must be done.

As emphasized earlier, it is the interplay between strategy and organization that needs thorough scrutiny, especially if it has previously received minimal attention. Consideration of the linkages between strategy and organization often results in significant surprises. Managers are frequently shocked to discover that their strategy is constrained not by environmental change but by their own values, beliefs, and assumptions.[18] Similarly, a successful strategy may be reinforcing the current operating processes and infrastructure but restricting the organization's ability to win if the marketplace changes.

Assessing the Presence of Strategic Leadership

Merely to understand what the marketplace strategy is or how the organization is configured is not enough. A crucial test of strategic management is whether the organization is attaining and sustaining marketplace leadership: Is it outdistancing its current and future competitors? Is it regarded by customers as the most innovative and premier supplier or merely as one of the pack? Marketplace leadership can be denominated and measured in many ways; the typical indicators are noted in Table 12-7. Without some degree of marketplace leadership, it

---

TABLE 12-7   Indicators of marketplace leadership

Is the organization creating new visions of what the industry might look like at some point in the future?

Is the organization the leader in introducing products that are new to the marketplace?

Is the organization the leader in building linkages between products that previously were unrelated?

Is the organization the leader in extending product lines and in modifying existing products?

Is the organization driving change in how customers understand and use products or solutions?

Is the organization serving the most demanding and challenging customers?

Is the organization leading in the creation of new customers?

Is the organization driving technology change that underlies key product changes?

Is the organization seen as the innovator in product functionality?

Is the organization seen as the innovator in new forms of service, distribution, and delivery?

is difficult to argue that organizations can fend off rivals nipping at their heels or generate long-term superior financial performance.

Marketplace leadership is the ultimate test of any organization's capacity not just to anticipate change but to shape and leverage it in the form of products and services that attract, win, and retain customers. An organization committed to strategic leadership wants:

- To have its product offerings or "solutions" rated as the best in the market.
- To be recognized as the leading innovator in products or solutions in its field.
- To provide customers with not just the best value but with some excitement about their purchase.
- To be the organization with which customers strive to do business.
- To create new ways of obtaining and retaining customers.

Marketplace leadership cannot be achieved and sustained in the absence of organizational leadership. Management must first set strategic intent and direction in terms of scope, posture, and goals; it must decide what product domains it wants to be in, what customers it wants to serve, and how it wants to attract, win, and retain customers. In short, management must provide the overarching intent of what the organization wants to achieve in the marketplace and then lead the organization in the pursuit of its broad goals.

Organization leadership contributes to marketplace leadership not just in terms of focusing and inspiring marketplace goals but in choosing, fostering, and extending the specific capabilities and competencies that can be leveraged for marketplace opportunity. In short, operating processes need to be honed and extended so that they contribute to capabilities and competencies that directly or indirectly result in value and benefits for customers. Increasingly, organizations are building capabilities and competencies around "what we do well" and finding best-in-class outside vendors for products and services that are not central to their skill and knowledge base.[19]

Internal infrastructure, in the form of incentive, control, and planning systems, must be focused on fostering the required capabilities and competencies. External infrastructure must be aimed at cultivating relationships with other organizations that are necessary to augment and extend the organization's capability and competency profile. Organizations as diverse as Honda, IBM, and AT&T have recently acknowledged the need to redirect their internal infrastructure toward developing and refining capabilities and competencies as one of the requirements to gaining and solidifying marketplace leadership.

Organization leadership, as noted earlier, facilitates the entrepreneurship and innovation necessary to attain and sustain marketplace leadership by constantly challenging the organization's analytics and mind-set (a challenge to which we return later, in the discussion of strategic renovation and strategic reinvention).

Identifying and Developing Strategic Alternatives

Strategic leadership emanates from the identification, development, and exploitation of marketplace opportunities. Recognized marketplace leaders such as Microsoft, Intel, Merck, Johnson & Johnson, and Proctor & Gamble enhance and extend their marketplace leadership by continually shaping new opportunities. New entrants to every industry or market segment are driven by the presumption that they have detected a market opportunity for their products. Each marketplace participant will ultimately falter before the onslaught of existing competitors and new entrants unless it renovates or reinvents its strategy.[20]

Sustained leadership in the marketplace can only result from an obsessive pursuit of opportunities. Opportunities come in many forms. Some are new not just to the organization but to the marketplace; for example, the introduction of Chrysler's minivan created a new product class or category. More typically, opportunities constitute extensions of the present strategy: They broaden the product line, reach more of the existing customers, and offer the current or slightly augmented product line in new geographic markets. Opportunities range from the very promising to the very restricted in terms of sales, customer reach, and profit potential, and firms must estimate the costs and benefits of pursuing each opportunity.

Irrespective of their scope or scale, opportunities do not fall like manna from heaven. Although they are nurtured, exploited, and realized in the marketplace, opportunities are first identified, developed, and shaped by individuals *within* the organization. Opportunities therefore must be captured: Individuals must see them in terms of emergent, visible, or potential change. The purpose of the industry, macroenvironmental, and technological assessment is to identify key trends and patterns within the organization's environment, the drivers of these environmental changes, and how they might translate into opportunities.

Opportunity identification and development must be continually managed. Detecting, making sense of, and projecting environmental change must be oriented toward the identification and development of opportunities. Opportunities ranging from the obvious to the "unthinkable" need to be surfaced. Detecting and documenting demographic and lifestyle changes are comparatively straightforward activities; the difficulties and rewards lie in isolating what opportunities might exist in such change. For example, the rapid explosion of single-person households has created a corresponding upsurge in the demand for convenience foods, yet many food packagers have been slow to detect how such change could be transformed into opportunity. The increasing cost-consciousness in many corporate, governmental, and not-for-profit organizations has given rise to an array of opportunities for "solutions" that help these organizations to become more cost-efficient.

In the absence of leadership that challenges mind-sets, opportunities will not be developed and evaluated even though they may be identified. In one consumer goods firm, a group of product managers steadfastly refused to give serious consideration to the option of selling products produced by the firm under a brand name other than its own historic brand name or to provide products to private-label distributors. Only after competitors had successfully done so did the firm belatedly decide to go after these opportunities. It takes effective leadership to promote opportunities that do not fit outdated mind-sets.

Infrastructure may help or hinder analytics and mind-set in shaping opportunities. Planning systems that do not support interaction among business units do not foster the detection and development of opportunities that lie outside the domain of any one business unit. Conversely, planning and information systems that transmit data about change in customers, technology, and industry growth and evolution across functional boundaries, within a business unit, or across business units may spark an insight that leads to opportunity detection. For example, in one large telecommunications corporation, a report disseminated to all business units by a senior corporate executive detailed some of the current and emerging technological challenges confronting some business units. One unit realized, from reading the report, that a technology it was attempting to develop possessed considerably more market opportunity than had been previously determined.

Choosing the Preferred Strategy

Ceaseless opportunity detection, development, and assessment are central to strategic management. A true test of leadership is whether it inspires the organization to surface and develop opportunities that will stretch it beyond its current resources.

The greater the strategic change (scope, posture, and goals) embedded in an opportunity, the greater both the potential payback (returns) and the risk. The challenge in assessing opportunities resides in the following dilemma: Strategic success requires organizations to create and leverage change in the marketplace. Unfortunately, their efforts to do so may result in strategies (or adjustments to existing strategies) that are inconsistent with current or future environmental change. For example, IBM's efforts to reshape its strategy in the mainframe computer segment may flop in a world where smaller computers can do the work previously performed by mainframes. If strategic change is too far ahead of or behind environmental change, it is not likely to generate superior marketplace or financial performance.

Thus, potential opportunities must be subjected to extensive and intensive scrutiny to ensure, to the extent it is possible to do so, that they are congruent with current and future environmental change. Opportunities must be subjected to the types of questions noted in Table 12-8. Few tasks so test the strategic management prowess of any organization as its capacity to insightfully subject potential opportunities to thorough scrutiny and yet maintain an entrepreneurial orientation.

The analysis challenge is considerable. Opportunities are framed and interpreted through the organization's preferred analytical tools and techniques. For example, in many firms, the early imposition of financial criteria often prematurely leads to the rejection of valuable alternatives.[21] An emphasis on marketplace criteria such as market share and sales growth often propels organizations to favor scope and posture alternatives such as product line development and product proliferation. In some firms, technology reigns supreme, and any opportunity that builds on the organization's technological prowess or takes the organization in new, "exciting" technological directions is accorded favored status. The risk here is that the firm may select alternatives that are inconsistent with emerging or potential industry change or broader environmental change.

TABLE 12-8 Assessing opportunities: Key questions

What is the nature of the opportunity?
What environmental change underlies the opportunity?
   —What are the specific industry changes?
      Customer change?
      Supplier change?
      Technology change?
      Substitute product change?
   —What is the macroenvironmental change?
      Social change?
      Economic change?
      Technological change?
      Political and regulatory change?
What organizational change supports or is needed to exploit the opportunity?
      Change in mind-set?
      Change in operation processes?
      Change in infrastructure?
      Change in leadership?

Mind-set also shapes opportunity selection. A well-disseminated vision, reinforced by widely shared values, can shape the lens through which the organization views specific opportunities. The risk is that an organization's mind-set will blind it to opportunities that are radically different from those it is experienced at evaluating. One telecommunications firm that saw itself as a future leader in specific types of equipment missed out on a major new business opportunity: It did not give serious consideration to "wireless" opportunities because they fell outside its designated purview.

Infrastructure must be continually assessed for its opportunity assessment implications. Business-unit or product-group structure can dramatically influence opportunity assessment. If the opportunity is not seen as falling directly within the unit's product-market domain, managers may have little incentive to give it a serious appraisal. Decision-making procedures that emphasize rapid and decisive decision making often eliminate alternatives that have "obvious" potential. Too often, alternatives are rejected before they are fully understood.

Implementing the Chosen Strategy

To realize valuable opportunities, products or services must be created and customers must be won and retained. An action agenda is required to translate the potential of opportunities into the reality of results. Action is required on a myriad of fronts—redesign of the current product or "solution" to meet customers' needs; development of new products; delivery of products and services to customers; execution of marketing, promotion, and sales programs; fulfillment of customer orders; provision of customer service; recruitment and training of personnel; and acquisition of capital. Key milestones for action programs must be developed, the sequence and timing of actions must be determined, and control and monitoring of actions must be given proper attention.

As actions are executed, the organization observes the results and learns from them. Product development may lead to unexpected breakthroughs (or bottlenecks); manufacturing may unearth ways of producing at less cost; sales programs may identify superior ways of reaching customers; order fulfillment may generate more efficient ways of reaching customers. The consequent learning should change the intended actions or plans; some opportunities can be reshaped and refined as the strategy is being executed. For example, as products are introduced to the marketplace, firms frequently find that the intended customers respond less positively than expected but other customers adopt the products with enthusiasm.

As strategy is rolled out, managers must execute it coherently in the marketplace; scope, posture, and goals must be consistent and reinforcing. Scope coherence requires distinct differences within and across product lines;

product lines that are tailored or customized to specific customer segments or niches; products that address distinct customer needs (rather than serving the same customer group or needs). Computer and automobile firms, for example, strive to shape multiple product lines that have distinct features and benefits to satisfy different customer needs.

Coherence is especially critical within posture. For example, an upmarket image would be inconsistent with low price; a narrow product line would be inconsistent with an intent to develop a corporate image and reputation as the solution to most customers' needs; availability of a product through all types of distribution channels and retailers, ranging from discount outlets to exclusive, high-end merchandisers, is likely to confuse customers. Yet, posture is not static; for example, Dell Computer (see Box 12-4) is a company with a coherent but constantly changing posture.

Goal coherence is the rock on which strategy execution often founders. Unless the organization's multiple goals support and reinforce each other, the organization is pulled in conflicting directions and sends contradictory messages or signals to its multiple stakeholders: suppliers, distributors, end-customers, competitors, employees, and shareholders. Some classic examples are worth noting. A long-run goal to achieve marketplace leadership in terms of product superiority can be sabotaged by a goal of maximizing short-run financial performance: Investments in research and development and marketing programs intended to build relationships with key customers are postponed. In many firms, manufacturing's pursuit of product standardization and cost minimization conflicts directly with marketing's desire for product and service customization.

Strategy coherence is greatly abetted by organizational alignment—that is, alignment in the form of linkage and integration among analytics, mind-set, operational processes, infrastructure, and leadership, and alignment with the focus, direction, and thrust of the marketplace strategy. Otherwise, the organization is not driving in the direction that is required by marketplace strategy.

To understand the importance of organizational alignment, we need only look at firms striving for rapid sales growth and penetration of many customer segments. In the computer industry, companies such as Microsoft, Compaq, and Dell confront a number of distinct alignment challenges because of the pressures brought about by rapidly expanding sales. In particular:

- Rapid sales growth requires that operational processes and infrastructure be intimately integrated. For example, information and control systems need to be continually adapted to monitor whether such operating processes as order fulfillment and customer service are being over-stretched and thus are detracting from value delivered to customers.

- Leaders need to continually challenge and reinvigorate the analytics and mind-set to ensure that they stay congruent with the needs of many distinct types of customers. Many rapidly growing firms, obsessed with meeting current demand, have neglected to think about future product needs.

In particular, strategy execution places heavy demands on the alignment of operational processes (how the work gets done). If the strategy centers on new product introduction, critical operational processes—product design, product testing, product manufacturing, marketing and promotion, sales, and order fulfillment (how orders are taken, filled, and delivered to customers)—must not only be put in place but aligned. Each process contributes to transforming a dream about a new product into an offering that is available to and satisfactory for customers.

The role of infrastructure in strategy execution often receives primary attention in strategy textbooks. However, infrastructural change is not an end in itself; at a minimum, its implications for operational processes need to be carefully considered. Organizational structures, systems, and decision-making procedures often need to be adapted and modified to facilitate the development or refinement of specific operational processes. For example, departmental structures (and their associated mind-sets) often get in the way of developing and shaping the necessary operating processes. In many companies, the so-called functional "silos" that grow up around departmental boundaries prohibit departments such as research and development, marketing, and manufacturing from working together to create better designed products that customers are eager to buy. Needless to say, such organizations experience considerable difficulties in developing a scope and a posture that attract, win, and retain more customers than do their competitors.

Outperforming Competitors and Winning Customers

Opportunities cannot be realized unless competitors are outmaneuvered and outperformed and customers are attracted, won, and retained. These goals take leadership and good management. Customers are the ultimate arbiters of rivalry among competitors. No matter how well strategy is conceived and executed, unless customers want to do business with an organization rather than with its competitors, any success it achieves will be short-lived.

Strategy therefore must generate some measure of distinctive and sustainable advantage in the marketplace. Marketplace advantage is created when both intermediate customers (distribution channels and retailers) and end customers (those who use the product or service) choose the organization's offerings rather than those of its competitors. Such advantage stems from differentiation.

Marketplace advantage is difficult to sustain. Advantage in product functionality and features is generally easy for competitors to replicate. In automobiles and computers, few product advantages last beyond the next model. The decline in market share of the Honda Accord, for a number of years the number-one-selling model in the U.S. market, attests to the difficulties in sustaining advantage based on functionality and features. American and Japanese manufacturers were able to catch up to the Accord. "Unique" services often can be copied in a matter of months. Advantages in image, reputation, selling, and relationships are typically more enduring. However, the travails of IBM, Digital Equipment Corporation, General Motors, and Ford in the past decade clearly indicate that advantages in these domains can be overcome by aggressive and committed competitors.

Sustaining marketplace advantage thus requires the organization to incessantly enhance its advantage base; it must continue to give customers more reason to do business with it. However, the changes inherent in the dynamics of marketplace rivalry render it difficult to sustain marketplace advantage. Once an advantage (such as superior product functionality, broader distribution, closer relationships with customers or lower price) is attained by one firm, competitors immediately have a long-jump distance not only to be matched but to be surpassed. The competitive rivalry and the consequent need to renovate and reinvent strategy are never-ending.

When marketplace advantage is so difficult to sustain in the face of competitors' moves, can it be created and augmented by anything managers do to (re)configure the organization? The answer is an emphatic *yes!* The key lies in the development and refinement of capabilities and competences that lead, directly or indirectly, to value or benefits that customers appreciate. Thus, the challenge of strategic management is developing and refining capabilities and competences for products, services, and benefits that result in positive differentiation in the eyes of customers.[22]

Capabilities and competences drive marketplace advantage in a number of ways. "Invisible" competences, such as the ability to learn about the marketplace, often give an organization the capacity to detect opportunities before they are manifest to competitors. For example, Dell Computer's intelligence capability enables it to learn very quickly and accurately from customers what they value (and do not value) about new offerings, what they would like Dell to offer, and what they value in competitors' offerings. This capability allows Dell to rapidly and continually refine its product "solutions" to meet specific customers' needs. Technology-based capabilities and competences, such as the ability to design and develop products or flexible manufacturing systems that allow the rapid production of small lots, promote continuous product development and enhancement. At 3M Company, for example, competences in substrates, coatings, and adhesives underlie many of its products. The important point here is that capabilities and competences provide a platform for the development and enhancement of multiple products as well as for how the organization can differentiate these products.

Within the organization, analytics, mind-set, infrastructure, and leadership need to be directed toward enhancing capabilities and competences that increase marketplace advantage. Analytics must be directed toward key questions about existing and desired competences and how they contribute to marketplace advantage. Mind-set suggests that organizations need to think in terms of developing competences and not in terms of short-run product differentiation. Competence development almost always requires that structural barriers, such as the decision-making and information-retaining prerogatives of individual business units or departments, must be demolished. Leadership necessitates a choice of the competences that are to be developed and a commitment of the resources to do so.[23]

Renovating Strategy

Winning customers and outperforming competitors can be achieved in two distinct and quite unrelated ways: (1) strategic renovation or renewal and (2) strategic invention or reinvention.

Strategic renovation takes the existing strategy as its point of departure. The search is for opportunities that can be pursued using the organization's current strategy. Product lines are extended, improved, and adapted, and new customers are actively pursued. Posture along many dimensions is enhanced: Product quality and service are upgraded, image and reputation are augmented, distribution is extended, and considerable effort is expended in embellishing selling and relationships. Goal change tends to be incremental and continuous: gaining more market share, providing greater value at distinct price points, improving margins and profits, and gaining technological advantage over competitors.

The motivation for strategic renovation is clear and specific: If an organization does not continually renew and reinvigorate its strategy—its scope, posture, and goals—it becomes a sitting target for current and potential competitors. Successful computer manufacturers as varied as IBM, Digital, Compaq, and CompuAdd, and automobile firms as diverse as Mercedes-Benz, Honda, and Saab have all learned the hard way that product lines that are not renewed become easy prey for rivals. In short, organizations have little choice but to renovate their marketplace strategy if they want to stay even marginally ahead of their competition.

Strategic renovation is reflected in the dynamics of rivalry in almost all sectors of all industries. Rivals continually extend their product lines; the proliferation of product varieties is most evident in electronics goods such as personal computers, computer accessories, television sets, radios, and stereos. Japanese firms are infamous for continually changing the form, features, and styling of their basic products. Their automobiles undergo hundreds of body modifications from one model year to the next. The features and functionality of many consumer products, such as breakfast cereals, canned food, soft drinks, and frozen meats, often remain significantly unchanged from one year to another, but rivals seek to renew their scope and posture by recrafting their image and reputation through advertising campaigns, augmented relationships within the trade, and experimentation with premiums, minor price changes via discounts and coupons, and other means.

Strategy renewal is mirrored in the need to revitalize the organization: Unless analytics, mind-set, operating processes, infrastructure, and leadership are reinvigorated, strategy renewal is less likely to occur or to be sustained.

Strategy renewal is often sparked by change in analytics and mind-set. For example, analysis that leads to change in assumptions and beliefs can lead directly to change in product development and customer focus. One industrial products firm concluded from a study of its customers' buying behaviors that service, and not price or loyalty to a long-established vendor, was the primary reason for switching from one competitor to another. It then beefed up its levels of service and matched them to customers' needs. In the process, the firm reconstituted the "product" customers had been purchasing; from a physical product, it became a "solution" for a specific set of needs. The result was a rapid increase in market share and in customer satisfaction and retention.

Infrastructure tends to solidify over time, a process that inhibits strategy renewal. The solution is frequent reviews and critiques. For example, information and control systems designed for one product-customer segment may be inappropriate if an organization renews its strategy (e.g., through extending its product line) to win customers in another segment. A leading electronics firm found that its control system, which was designed to have all phone queries answered within five hours, was counterproductive as the firm moved toward high-end customers. The new customers wanted extensive personal service rather than a quick telephone response.

The linkage between infrastructure and operating processes is evident in this telephone answering example. Strategy renewal often requires extensive change in many operating processes. Indeed, in many cases, as illustrated in the previous discussion of the linkage between marketplace advantage and organization competence, the revitalization of operating processes (the building blocks of an organization's capabilities and competences) makes possible extensive strategy renewal.

Reinventing Strategy

Strategic renovation can lead to regaining lost or declining marketplace advantage and rehabilitating or even extending existing competences and capabilities. Unfortunately, strategic renovation often is not sufficient if the organization wishes to catapult itself "out of the pack" or into the position of a "breakthrough" leader. Initiatives to create or redefine an industry or market segment require real strategy entrepreneurship. This entails the management of fundamental—and often radical—shifts in scope, posture, and goals. The combination of all three elements of strategy characterizes strategy entrepreneurship. In short, the organization must invent a strategy—new products or solutions that serve distinct customer needs, offer a unique way of competing, and lead to distinctive goals.

Unlike strategy renewal, strategic reinvention necessarily entails radical redirection of scope and posture. The choice is either the creation of products new to the marketplace or the reinvention of existing products and services to set new standards or norms in the marketplace. Such strategy entrepreneurship is likely to be based on the reconceptualization of customer needs. Almost by definition, such strategies lead to the creation of new industries or new industry segments. Apple's creation of the user-friendly computer, Nike's popularization of the running shoe, and Nucor's new specialty steel products are all examples of strategy entrepreneurship.

Indeed, any industry, over time, may witness a series of entrepreneurial strategies. The computer industry has seen IBM's development of the mainframe, Digital Equipment's launch of the minicomputer, Cray's design of the supercomputer, Apple's introduction of the personal computer, and Compaq's pioneering of laptop computers.

Posture reinvention almost always is closely associated with scope reinvention. It entails the creation of new ways of attracting, winning, and retaining customers. Significant deviations from conventional practice in key posture dimensions such as functionality, service, image, reputation, selling, and relationships create new grounds for fostering and sustaining competitive advantage. For example, Apple promulgated "user-friendly" as the means to win customers; it represented a radical departure from how computer firms had previously approached the challenge of making computers attractive to users. Dell's use of direct marketing invented a new way of reaching both commercial and consumer users of personal computers.

Associated with scope and posture reinvention are major shifts in goals. The creation or invention of a new market sector or even a new industry is often the distinguishing feature of organizations' strategic intent and marketplace vision. For example, Apple was driven in its early years by the goal of putting a computer in every home. The Saturn division of General Motors has been driven by the aim of creating an automobile that will be superior in quality to its predominately Japanese rivals—in short, reinventing the low end of the automobile market.

It is not a coincidence that many of the preceding strategic invention examples cite firms that started from scratch. In going concerns, strategic reinvention necessitates dismembering and reconstructing the organization's historic analytics, mind-set, operating processes, and infrastructure. The historic molds of thinking and doing must be broken if reinvention is to occur. Nothing less than *reinventing how the organization does business* is required.

Organizational leadership incurs its most severe challenges in effecting and sustaining strategic entrepreneurship. The weight of the old ways of doing things squashes fragile potential product and operating breakthroughs. The current obsession with business process reengineering[24] reflects a desire to transform how the organization works as a means not just to attain operating efficiencies (e.g., lower costs and shorter cycles) but also to facilitate radical product development and posture shifts.[25] For example, radical redesign of how a number of functional departments interrelate in making decisions can lead to dramatic breakthroughs in the design and development of new products as well as in posture dimensions such as product functionality (e.g., higher reliability), faster and more effective service levels (e.g., providing new types of technical assistance to customers), and closer working relationships with customers (e.g., joint development of products or joint debugging of prototype products).

A central challenge in strategic reinvention is the management of analytics and mind-set. Strategic entrepreneurship is a product of thinking differently; old ways of thinking cannot suffice. The past offers little guidance to the future. Old paradigms or recipes for industry success or competitive differentiation inhibit the detection, visualization, and development of emerging and potential marketplace opportunities. It is not an overstatement to assert that organizational reinvention presumes that individuals can unlearn their own past as well as that of others.

Leaders committed to strategic reinvention must translate what is to be invented into a vision (including a set of aspirations and motivating targets) and values (a set of principles that guide individuals' behaviors) that are meaningful, tangible, and invigorating for the organization's members. Motorola is an example of a company whose leaders have established visions entailing new product directions (betting the firm on new products long before the opportunity is apparent to others) that inspired the organization to achieve results that few could have expected.

CONCLUDING REMARKS

Strategic management involves the management of marketplace strategy, the organization, and the linkages between them. It represents the central challenge of management. The extensiveness and intensity of change make it a never-ending challenge. Moreover, there are no simple recipes or algorithms; the fun and the excitement of strategic management lie in the creation of new ways to win in the marketplace and new ways to configure the organization to facilitate doing so.

FOR FURTHER READING

Fahey, L., and Robert M. Randall, *The Portable MBA in Strategy* (New York: John Wiley, 1994).

Goold, M., A. Campbell, and M. Alexander, *Corporate-Level Strategy: Creating Value in the Multibusiness Company* (New York: John Wiley, 1994).

Porter, M. E., *Competitive Strategy: Techniques for Analyzing Industries and Competitors* (New York: Free Press, 1980).

Porter, M. E., *Competitive Advantage: Creating and Sustaining Superior Performance* (New York: Free Press, 1985).

Quinn, J. B., *Intelligent Enterprise* (New York: Free Press, 1992).

PART THREE

MANAGING CHANGE

It has become commonplace to note that one of the hallmarks of today is change. It is our constant. Good management and the management of change are the same thing: how to make sure that what you have in place today will meet the challenges you will face tomorrow. Only 15 years ago, it was fairly easy to predict what that challenge would be. Perhaps the rate of inflation would be different by a few percentage points or perhaps the workforce would pose different training problems, but for the most part, the future was a straight line from the present. Now go into any workplace and you will find managers, and not just the ones born over half a century ago, but managers in their 30s and 40s, struggling to keep abreast of not only the real business they are in and who their competitors are, but also the technology they need to use daily, the structural changes that profoundly affect their relationships and how they go about getting things done, and how they ought to behave as managers and leaders. Are there no constants in this world of change that we can hang on to but change itself?

One constant is a question: "What are we trying to accomplish and what is the best way to do it in our present context?" The analogy of a raft on a river will illustrate how important context is to strategy. In a calm meandering river, you can load up a rubber boat with a lot of people, give each person a paddle, and tell the group to get to the landing 10 miles down. Everyone in the boat has paddled that river many times, and even a newcomer can catch on quickly. There is a helmsman, but everyone in the boat knows what to do at each turn and so even if the helmsman forgets to call out "right oar," it doesn't matter that much. Nothing short of a revolution is going to tip over that boat. Then change the context. The goal is still to get down the river to the next landing. But the river is different. It has tributaries that come in and go out; it has rocks and turbulent churning waters; it has rapids; and sometimes the noise of the water gets so loud you can't hear the helmsperson. Even worse, you're shipping water.

Today's managers and leaders are the people who run the boat concession. They want to get their people down the river to the next landing, but how should they navigate the turbulent business context where the changes are coming so fast and the likelihood of tipping over and sinking, is increasing each minute? Perhaps smaller lighter boats? Perhaps technologically superior earphones so everyone can hear the commands above the roar? Perhaps a different kind of training to start with?

In Chapter 13, "Organizations for the year 2000," William Halal describes the information age of complex technologies, global markets, and intense competition. He suggests that a new model of organization—smaller, quicker, leaner—based on internal markets going completely beyond hierarchy is what will best navigate these waters. In return for their freedom to navigate the river as the context demands, these intrapreneurial units accept controls on performance. Control focuses on outcomes not means.

If the organizations we will work in are these rapidly adaptive internal market units that are judged on performance, what kind of leadership will work best in them? And what is the role of the boat concession owner? In Chapter 14, Jay Conger first reviews the "made or born" debate. Do leaders simply rise to the occasion because of their native intelligence and inclinations or do environment and experience shape their destinies? It is as one might expect, a combination of both, but most telling for the organization of the future, it will be a different combination or mix of qualities that will count. Flexibility and quickness will count as much as vision and patience. Regardless, because the organization we work in will be smaller and more process oriented, the numbers of people who need to take leadership roles will increase as will the importance of understanding how they are created and what nurtures them. Leadership will never go out of style. It is another constant.

13

ORGANIZATIONS FOR THE YEAR 2000: THE TRANSITION FROM HIERARCHY TO ENTERPRISE

William E. Halal

As economies move to an information age of complex technologies, global markets, intense competition, and turbulent, constant change, managers everywhere are struggling to cope with failing organizations. Witness the collapse of central planning in the former Soviet Union, gridlock in the United States Congress, a crisis in the American health care system, and growing demands to reform education. Even IBM, once regarded as the best-managed corporation in the world, recorded the biggest business loss in history during 1993 (which was exceeded shortly after by General Motors).

These are symptoms of a new historic transformation—the information revolution—that is redefining our institutions in roughly the same way the industrial revolution did two centuries ago.[1] Just as the medieval castle, the monarchy, and other institutions of an agrarian era were transformed by the relentless advance of industrial technology into our present corporations and governments, now the relentless advance of information technology is transforming society once again.

This chapter describes the new model of organization that is emerging rapidly to manage business, government, education, and other institutions. We first show how the hierarchy is yielding to a far more fluid network of self-managed enterprises that operate more like a market system. Principles governing the management of such "internal markets" are then described as well as trends

Portions of this chapter are adapted from William E. Halal et al., *Internal Markets: Bringing the Power of Free Enterprise Inside Your Organization* (New York: Wiley, 1993).

toward "teleworking" in "electronic" organizations. Finally, we examine the implications for managers.

THE EVOLUTION OF ORGANIZATIONAL STRUCTURE

Figure 13-1 illustrates the evolution of organizational structure to put today's changes in perspective, and Box 13-1 defines prominent structural forms in roughly the order they were developed.

The Industrial Age: Hierarchy and the Matrix

The hierarchical model emerged during the relatively simple conditions of the industrial age because a "mechanistic" form of management was best for controlling the routine tasks of manufacturing and an uneducated workforce. What could be more reasonable in an age of machines than to manage institutions as "social machines"? But the conditions that gave rise to hierarchy began yielding to a far more complex environment during the 1960s: large organizations, a new breed of demanding workers, more discriminating consumers, foreign competition, the energy crisis, environmentalism, and government regulation.

To handle this complexity, more sophisticated structures such as the matrix were developed to facilitate lateral coordination. As Box 13-1 shows, the matrix creates a second hierarchy that cuts across the functional hierarchy to integrate diverse employees working on different products, projects, and other special needs. Many people condemn the matrix, however, because two sets of managers coordinate the same employees, producing more meetings, paperwork, delays, confusion, and other forms of bureaucracy. If one hierarchy produces bureaucracy, two hierarchies multiply the problem.

Challenge of the Information Age:
Managing Complexity

Recently, the rise in environmental complexity has accelerated with revolutionary advances in computerization, an explosion of knowledge, a unified global economy, the ecological crisis, mounting social diversity, and other global trends that are almost certain to blossom into a far more complex world. These trends are described more fully in the introduction to this book and other specialized sources.[2] The significance of this sudden appearance of a far more turbulent environment cannot be overstressed. It has fundamentally altered the nature of our world, giving rise to a new field of science devoted to the study of complexity, diversity, and chaotic change,[3] and profoundly affecting the work of managers.

FIGURE 13-1   The evolution of organizational structure

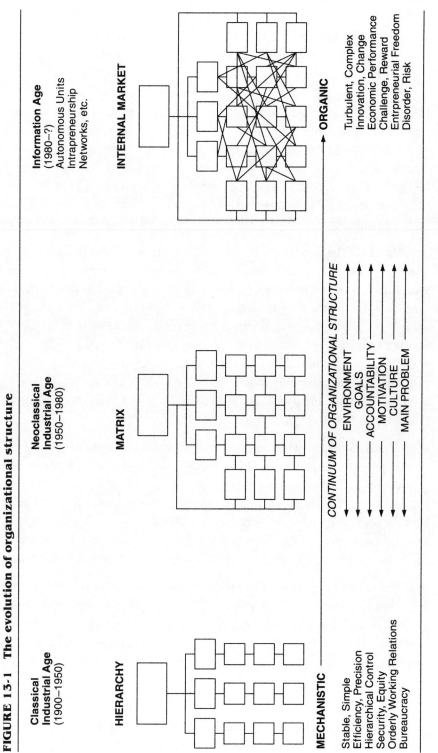

Classical **Industrial Age** (1900–1950)	Neoclassical **Industrial Age** (1950–1980)	**Information Age** (1980–?) Autonomous Units Intrapreneurship Networks, etc.
HIERARCHY	**MATRIX**	**INTERNAL MARKET**

CONTINUUM OF ORGANIZATIONAL STRUCTURE

MECHANISTIC		**ORGANIC**
	ENVIRONMENT	
	GOALS	
	ACCOUNTABILITY	
	MOTIVATION	
	CULTURE	
	MAIN PROBLEM	

| Stable, Simple
Efficiency, Precision
Hierarchical Control
Security, Equity
Orderly Working Relations
Bureaucracy | | Turbulent, Complex
Innovation, Change
Economic Performance
Challenge, Reward
Entrpreneurial Freedom
Disorder, Risk |

Box 13-1
PROMINENT ORGANIZATIONAL FORMS
(Listed in Roughly Their Order of Development)

Hierarchy   This ancient form was used by the early Egyptians, Romans, and the Catholic Church because it offers the most basic structure: A hierarchy of organizational levels controls workers grouped into various "functions": research, manufacturing, marketing, and so on. Implicit in the hierarchy is the complementary principle that authority flows from the top down, creating an "authoritarian" system in which "superiors" control "subordinates."

The Matrix   The matrix appeared in the 1950s and 1960s to facilitate lateral coordination. An aerospace firm, for instance, would create a "project structure," in which functional specialists were assigned to work together on some project and then returned to their departments after completing their tasks. Thus, the matrix creates two hierarchies that cut across one another to coordinate work in two "dimensions": the functional dimension and the project dimension. Today, most large organizations use variations of the matrix because they must organize activities in two, three, or even more dimensions: functional skills, projects, product lines, geographic regions, type of customers, and so on.

Multidivision Form   This type of organization, sometimes called the "M-form," provides large corporations focused management of their various product lines. Each division is assigned the responsibility for managing one product line; it has its own functional groups and operates as a profit center, thereby becoming the equivalent an individual company. Thus, a multidivisional corporation is rather like a holding company that integrates semiautonomous divisions managing different product lines into a cohesive whole.

The Federal Organization   The federal form carries the M-form further by defining a looser form of control. Just as a federal government relinquishes many powers to semiautonomous states, the federal corporation grants its divisions control over all activities they can perform best, creating a decentralized system of semiautonomous business units. The corporate level oversees divisions by holding annual performance reviews, appoints presidents of divisions, and performs other crucial functions.

Networks   The network originated during the 1970s when strategic alliances began linking individual corporations together. Today alliances are common between most corporations and their suppliers, distributors,

(Continued)

governments, and even their competitors. Unlike mergers and acquisitions, which absorb business units into a larger integrated corporation, networks are characterized by temporary business relationships among autonomous partners who agree to work together on some joint venture. Organizational networks are facilitated by information networks, which suggests that the network form seems to be a logical structural model for a knowledge-based economy.

Intrapreneurship   During the 1980s when business needed to become entrepreneurial, most large companies developed systems that encourage ordinary employees to develop creative ideas into new business ventures. These systems typically grant employees release time to pursue their concepts, provide investment capital, and offer advice and support. Intrapreneurship has been a significant development because it introduced market concepts inside corporations. Since then, other market concepts have been used, such as "internal customers," "pay-for-performance," and so on.

Reengineering   Reengineering is part of a broader class of "restructuring" efforts usually called "reengineering business processes," "redesigning organizational architecture," and "reinventing government." This approach integrates scattered parts of some business process into a cross-functional team that delivers a product or service rapidly and efficiently, usually with automated information systems. The result is to restructure an organization into a group of teams that focus on serving clients.

The Virtual Organization   This idea has met with such success that virtually everything is now called "virtual." Because the information revolution is making it possible for any workers to collaborate anywhere, organizations must no longer be *physically* coordinated but can become *electronically* coordinated, creating a global network of constantly changing alliances that draw on the best talent, resources, and knowledge available. The virtual organization is no longer "real" in the sense that people may never even see each other, much less meet every every day; rather it is "virtual," existing primarily as an organized system of electronically mediated working relationships.

Internal Markets   The organizational forms previously described seem to be leading in this direction. As Box 13-2 shows in more detail, the basic concept is disarmingly simple: An internal market system is a collection of self-managed "internal enterprises" that conduct business with one another and outside parties, thereby replicating the features of external markets within organizations to create complete "internal market economies."

One critical instance is the speed-up in product cycles, which has led to an entirely different approach to competitiveness based on rapid response time. For example, Intel has managed to keep ahead of its competitors by introducing successively more powerful microprocessors ever more quickly, even before sales of previous models have matured. In current business terms, the company is "cannibalizing" its older products. Recently, Intel brought to market its much heralded Pentium chip in one year's less time than it had taken them to bring out their previous microprocessors. They did so at lower prices in order to capture the exploding demand for home computers.

Such challenges make it clear that the old form of management based on top-down control of multilayered hierarchies is too cumbersome for an environment that is inherently turbulent and unpredictable. Instead, organic systems are needed that adapt to complexity automatically through numerous small, self-organizing units that engage in continual learning from the bottom-up.[4] A paradigm shift is in progress that raises troubling questions about our most basic management assumptions.

Where corporate Goliaths such as IBM and GM once gained crushing competitive power from their vaunted economies of scale, now size is proving a liability against nimble Davids such as Apple, Microsoft, and MCI—who may in turn suffer the same fate as they grow bigger. Is size now fatal? Must the growth that accompanies success necessarily bring decline? How can small firms manage in a global economy? Can any structure remain useful for long in a world of constant change?

Major corporations comprise economic systems that are as large as national economies, yet most executives and scholars think of them as "firms" to be managed with centralized controls: moving resources about like a portfolio of investments, dictating which units should sell which products at which prices, and setting financial goals. How does this differ from the central planning that failed in the Communist bloc? Why would centralized controls be bad for a national economy but good for a *corporate* economy?

These unorthodox issues have made the old management paradigm obsolete. When Max Weber defined the "theory of bureaucracy" based on principles of hierarchy for an industrial age, the concept was revolutionary because it brought huge gains in rationality, efficiency, and order. Now it means the opposite: irrational adherence to petty rules, inefficient and unwieldy systems, and disregard for mounting chaos. The most damning thing one can say about an organization today is to call it a "bureaucracy."

The 1980s: Downsizing, Networks, Restructuring

With the fall of hierarchy, the move toward organic structures surged forward in the 1980s as corporations struggled to cope with racing technological and economic change. Global competition produced intense pressure to reduce overhead and permit innovation, while new information systems automated blue- and white-collar jobs. Managers were thereby forced to make massive layoffs and eliminate entire layers of management, pruning organizations back to a hierarchical skeleton of flat, decentralized structures. Roughly two million middle-management positions were lost during this wave of "downsizing," about every third manager,[5] wiping out the heart of the corporate hierarchy. Jack Welch described the change at GE:

> We used to go from the CEO to sectors, to groups, to businesses. We now go from the CEO to businesses. Nothing else is in between.[6]

These bare-bones structures were then fleshed out with joint ventures among competitors, partnerships between suppliers and distributors, research consortia uniting entire industries, and other strategic alliances that form "organizational networks." Another new field of science has emerged to explain this unusual phenomenon in which business rivals often cooperate because it is now advantageous.[7] For example, Dell Computer created the "IBM clone industry" by constructing a dynamic network of component suppliers who work closely with Dell's own personnel to bring out top-of-the-line PCs quickly and cheaply. The United States has 200 consortia that pool the efforts of competitors in common R&D efforts. An intricate maze of business alliances began forming in 1993 among companies in the computer, telecommunications, and entertainment industries to build information superhighways offering interactive multimedia.

The most recent innovation focuses on the popular concept of "reengineering," which integrates diverse parts of a business process into a self-managed team that serves clients better. Shenandoah Life Insurance Company installed a $2 million claims processing system but realized no improvements because claims moved through 32 clerks in different departments. After forming autonomous teams of seven people who perform all functions previously done by 32 different staffs, processing time dropped from 27 days to 2 days, and labor productivity rose 60 percent.

These concepts, along with "total quality management" (TQM), "core competence," "organizational learning," and other innovations that focus more on processes than on structure, were widely used as of 1994 because they offered practical approaches to improving operations. There is somewhat of a "faddish" quality to many of these ideas, so some may diminish in time. But they are widely popular largely because most managers now accept major organizational change as unavoidable. *Business Week* described the change in attitude this way:[8]

> Nearly all [management consultants] shun incremental change. They urge managers to think in radical terms, dramatically overhauling entire operations at a single stroke.

The evolution of organizational structure seems destined to continue, however, because even these changes only modify the existing system. That helps explain why they have not been very successful. It is estimated that half to two-thirds of all reorganizations using downsizing, reengineering, and other such strategies are either aborted or produce poor results, usually leaving behind a demoralized workforce.[9] We still lack a well-defined model or theory for the form of organization now emerging, so managers are confused over the enormous task of restructuring operations for a new era.

For instance, theorists have defined the move to flat, decentralized structures as a "federal" model of organization that combines the power of large aggregated corporations with the autonomy of small business units.[10] But this seems a worn-out idea. The old GM structure that is now outmoded was created by Alfred Sloan as a federation of semiautonomous divisions. The question remains, if a decentralized organization is coordinated using hierarchical authority, how can these controls avoid impairing the autonomy that individual units need to produce adaptive change, creative entrepreneurship, and so on?

Even networks and the hot new concept of the "virtual corporation" do not go far enough. Yes, there is a need for temporary working relationships, but these alliances are usually organized by top management, once again incurring many of the same disadvantages of hierarchy. After all, even as GM and IBM floundered in bureaucracy, they were awash in strategic alliances with clever partners such as Electronic Data Systems and Apple Computer. Why would a centrally managed network differ very much from the centrally managed economy that failed in the Communist bloc?

Basically, the problem is that a new era of complex, constant change makes it almost impossible for any type of fixed or centrally controlled organization to withstand the turbulence of today's world. A alternative seems needed that avoids the arbitrary, cumbersome forms of control imposed by authority.

About the Year 2000: Internal Markets

For many years now, a dramatically different approach to organizational structure has been quietly emerging that goes beyond hierarchy completely.

Most Fortune 500 companies have grown so large and complex they are now decentralized into autonomous divisions that constitute large firms in their own right. Many of these divisions would rank in the Fortune 100 if considered separate companies, and some global corporations such as Asea Brown Bovari (ABB) have thousands of such profit centers. These units usually have their own distinct markets, clients, and competitors. At various times, they may sell their products to other divisions within the parent corporation, compete against one another for the same customers, and even award contracts to outside competitors. These practices raise difficult new questions about the nature of enterprise. What is best for the parent corporation as a whole? For the divisions? How do these "collections of small enterprises" differ from an ordinary market economy? Why should they remain together at all? In short, what truly is a modern corporation?

The same confusion exists in the public sector. The concept of educational "choice" is gaining acceptance, in which competition among individual schools is used to improve performance. Should schools be closed if they cannot compete? Should all public agencies allow their clients to select among competing units?

This confusion can be cleared up by seeing that modern organizations are best understood from the perspective of markets rather than hierarchy. Just as the old Communist bloc knows it must adopt markets, so too have leading corporations been moving to market systems. As the evolution of structure in Figure 13-1 suggests, during the past decade many former monoliths, such as AT&T and IBM, have been broken up into autonomous business units, roughly like the privatization of state enterprises in Russia. One of the most striking trends of the past decade was the growing use of "intrapreneuring," "internal customers," and other internal equivalents of markets. Some firms are even using "internal leveraged buyouts (LBOs)" to let managers gain control of their units.[11] Tom Peters urged: "Force the market into every nook and cranny of the firm."[12]

This seminal idea integrates today's structural innovations into a broader organizing framework based on concepts of enterprise rather than authority. Internal markets are *meta* structures that transcend ordinary structures. Rather than fixed hierarchies or centrally coordinated networks, they are *complete internal market economies* designed to produce continual, rapid structural change, just as external markets do.[13] Box 13-2 summarizes this new paradigm in terms of three main principles.

Although only a few leading-edge companies have implemented the internal market concept as yet, a survey of corporate practices in the United States, Europe, and Japan shows wide acceptance of its key features (see Table 13-1). Of 80 executives that were interviewed, 90 percent agreed these changes are necessary, 76 percent felt they would dominate management in the late 1990s, and 85 percent thought that firms that do not adopt the concept will fail or suffer a marginal existence.

Most people initially resist the internal market viewpoint because it breaks so sharply from the traditional hierarchy. At first, the notion seems fraught with conflict, duplication of effort, and other controversial issues, and it is certainly true that internal markets incur the same risks, turmoil, and other

---

Box 13-2
PRINCIPLES OF INTERNAL MARKETS

Transform the Hierarchy into Internal Enterprise Units   The traditional hierarchy is transformed into "internal enterprises" that form the building blocks of the corporation. All internal enterprises, including line, staff, and other units, are accountable for performance but gain autonomous control over their operations, as in any external enterprise. This concept can be carried to the grassroots by decentralizing enterprises into autonomous work teams. Alliances between internal enterprises and teams in different organizations link corporations together to form a global economy.

Create an Economic Infrastructure to Guide Decisions   Rather than manage operations through the chain-of-command, executives design and regulate the infrastructure of this "organizational economy," just as governments manage national economies: establishing common systems for accounting, communications, financial incentives, governing policies, an entrepreneurial culture, and the like. Top management may also encourage the formation of various business sectors that would exist in an economic system: venture capital firms, consultants, distributors, and so on.

Provide Leadership to Foster Collaborative Synergy   An internal economy is more than a laissez-faire market, but a community of entrepreneurs that fosters collaborative synergy (joint ventures, sharing of technology, solving common problems, etc.) among both internal and external partners. Corporate executives are the senior members of this community, so they provide the leadership to guide this internal market by encouraging the development of various strategies.

---

drawbacks of any market system. But that is precisely the point. The concept represents a different mode of organizational logic needed to survive in a difficult world. By grasping the central idea that an internal market replicates the features of an external market, the remaining elements of this perspective become fairly straightforward. Many examples of progressive corporations that have adopted similar systems demonstrate some striking results.

As a corporate community of entrepreneurs launches new products and services, buys and sells, both internally and externally, the same self-organizing, creative interplay occurs that makes all market economies so advantageous. Powerful solutions to difficult problems emerge quickly and spontaneously, spawning

TABLE 13-1   Adoption of various enterprise practices

(Sample = 80 corporate executives in the United States, Europe, and Japan)

Internal Market Feature	Not Practiced	Partially Practiced	Fully Practiced
Pay-for-performance	0%	27%	73%
Employees free to develop new ideas	4	9	87
Autonomous profit centers	30	30	40
Support units accountable for results	21	0	79
Units can buy and sell outside	65	12	29
Networking among all units	45	27	27
Great organizational flexibility	13	30	57
Unit managers decide strategy	0	19	81

Source: William Halal and San Retna, "Corporations in Transition" (work in progress).

a rush of economic growth that could not conceivably have been planned by the most brilliant hierarchical system.

Markets have their drawbacks, but they are spreading around the globe because they excel over the other alternative—central planning—whether in communist governments or capitalist corporations. In both nations and organizations, planned economies are too cumbersome to cope with a complex new era, while free enterprise—either internal or external—offers the only economic philosophy able to produce adaptive change rapidly and efficiently.

Looking back on the evolution of structure over the past few decades, the movement from mechanistic hierarchies to organic enterprises now appears to be one of the most profound changes in management. As of 1994, the old monolithic pyramid had evolved into a flat, decentralized structure, composed of numerous small, self-managed profit centers, connected by networks of strategic alliances. The development of complete internal market economies is likely to form the next major phase in this evolution, and our estimates suggest it should enter the corporate mainstream about the year 2000 when the information age fully arrives.

PRINCIPLES OF THE INTERNAL MARKET MODEL

The beauty of the market model is that it is a simple idea with profound ramifications—hierarchical authority is replaced by market forces. This key idea leads to the possibility of replicating within organizations all the features long used in external markets with good success. The following sections describe this perspective in terms of its three main principles. Examples are taken from the experiences of progressive companies and governments.

Principle 1: Transform the Hierarchy into Internal Enterprise Units

Rather than think of organizational units as "divisions," "departments," and other hierarchical concepts, the logic of internal markets reconceptualizes line, staff, and all other units into their entrepreneurial equivalents—"internal enterprises." This may require creative reengineering of existing structures, but it is usually feasible if an external or internal client can be identified, and that is almost always possible, as we will show.

To provide the advantages of markets, all internal enterprises accept controls on *performance* in return for freedom of *operations.* Hewlett-Packard (HP) is famous for its entrepreneurial system that holds units accountable for results but gives them wide operating latitude. As one HP executive described it, "The financial controls are very tight, what is loose is how [people] meet those goals." This sharply focused understanding enhances both control and freedom to provide two major strengths:

1. Accountability for results is ensured for all units.
2. Creative entrepreneurship is encouraged to flourish.

There is wide agreement that a combination of performance measures is needed to ensure a realistic balance that avoids overemphasizing short-term profit: customer satisfaction, product quality, and the like. Managers are then held accountable through incentive pay, stock plans, budget allocations, or outright dismissal. The ideal situation is to treat each unit as a small, separate company, free to manage its own affairs, while integrated into the parent corporation as described later. It is important to allow all units the freedom to conduct business transactions both inside and outside the firm. In the same way that the Soviets overcontrolled their economy, managers without that freedom are subject to the monopoly and bureaucracy of central controls.

Although the decentralization of line units is well known at AT&T, IBM, HP, 3M, and other companies, the concept is also being applied to support units, manufacturing facilities, information system departments, R&D, marketing and distribution, employee work teams, and even the CEO's office.

Support Units

Control Data converted all its corporate support units into "internal consulting firms" that operated as profit centers serving clients within Control Data and at other corporations.[14] IBM recently converted its Human Resource Development division into an autonomous business, "Workforce Solutions," which is saving millions of dollars each year and selling its services to other companies.[15] Even the federal government is breaking up the monopoly exercised by the General Services Administration and the Government Printing Office by allowing line agencies to patronize other suppliers. Raymond Smith, CEO of Bell Atlantic, described the logic that led his company to adopt this strategy:

> We are determined to revolutionize staff support, to convert a bureaucratic roadblock into an entrepreneurial force. Staffs tend to grow and produce services that may be neither wanted nor required. I decided to place the control of discretionary staff in the hands of those who were paying for them . . . line units. . . . The most important thing is that spending for support activities is now controlled by clients.[16]

Manufacturing

The concept can also solve problems in manufacturing. Modern factories are very expensive, so it is essential to use them effectively. Alcoa treats its manufacturing units as "internal job shops" that produce goods for internal and external clients. IBM, DEC, NCR, and other companies are selling their excess plant capacity by "contract manufacturing" for other firms, including their competitors.[17] Bruce Merrifield at the U.S. Department of Commerce summed it up: "Manufacturing is becoming a service function. Plants are making different products for different companies in different industries."[18]

Information Systems

Rather than have the information systems (IS) department impose its decisions on users, the market model redefines the situation so that line units become clients of the IS office. One corporation was struggling to contain rising IS costs with little success. When it made the IS unit a profit center, however, demand for services dropped by half even though all needed computer work was still performed, complaints from internal customers diminished markedly, and the IS unit brought in revenue from external clients. Many other firms such as Brown-Foreman and Sunoco have realized dramatic gains using this approach.[19] In the U.S. government, the Federal Aviation Agency (FAA), the Department of Defense (DoD), and other agencies are forming "information utilities" that charge internal clients for computer time, electronic mail, and other IS services.[20]

Research & Development

Likewise, R&D can be defined as a service that helps line units develop products. Under competitive pressures to use research funds more effectively, AT&T's Bell Labs, Phillips Electronics, and Esso Canada are converting their

R&D departments into profit centers that sell research services to line units and outside clients.[21] Instead of relying on the debatable allocation of resources from the top of a hierarchy, the value of research should be determined by the willingness of profit-center managers to pay for the results.

Marketing, Logistics, and Service

On the output end of business, marketing, logistics, and customer service units can be reorganized into the internal equivalent of distributorships. Like ordinary distributors, these profit centers handle the full line of a company's products for some region to provide the integrated service that individual business units cannot. Johnson & Johnson established common customer units that provide all sales and distribution services to outside retailers,[22] and IBM's 13 new divisions share a common sales force to provide customers what IBM calls a "single face" that handles all their needs.

Work Teams

Market principles can be carried down to the grassroots by organizing workers into self-managed profit centers. Crown-Zellerbach helped loggers form work teams that simply were paid for the amount of timber they produced. The result was to eliminate the need for job classifications, work rules, performance evaluations, foremen, and other complex systems. Loggers became keenly motivated because they earned more and could "run their own business" as they saw fit, and management was pleased with the higher productivity and lower overhead. GM Saturn, AT&T, and other large companies are forming self-managed teams that control all aspects of their work—choice of co-workers, work methods, supplier relations, quality—and receive substantial incentives for good performance. It is estimated that 70 percent of American companies now use some form of "pay-for-performance" system.[23]

The CEO's Office

The concept can even be applied to the chief executive. When James Rinehart was CEO of Clark Equipment, he redefined the CEO's office as a profit center in which revenue was derived from assets invested in business units (similar to a venture capital firm), and from a portion of sales (like a "tax" of the "corporate government").[24] This concept establishes a logical relationship between the CEO and operating managers. Like any profit center, the CEO must keep the costs charged to managers down and the value they receive up to add value to

FIGURE 13-2   Example of an internal market organization

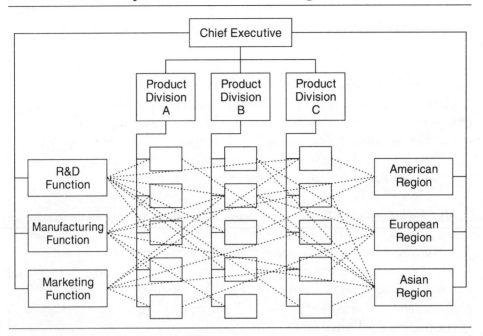

these "clients." Some firms may not want to go this far, but it reminds us of the key principle guiding internal markets: All market functions can be replicated within organizations.

Figure 13-2 illustrates the internal market that results from "privatizing" a three-dimensional matrix organization with product, functional, and area structures. The heart of the system consists of new ventures spun off by product divisions to become independent business units that develop products or services. Functional support units are profit centers that sell their assistance to other units or external businesses. Geographic areas are also profit centers, distributing the full line of products and services to clients in their region. Box 13-3 provides several examples of successful companies that have realized considerable advantages by adopting this central organizing concept.

From this view, the organization is no longer a pyramid of power but a web of changing business connections held together by clusters of internal enterprises, as in any market. This system may appear radically different, but it simply represents an extension of the trend that began decades ago when large corporations decentralized into autonomous product divisions.

Box 13-3
EXEMPLARS OF INTERNAL MARKET ECONOMIES

Cypress Semiconductor   This company is one of the most perfect exemplars of an internal market. Each business unit is a separate corporation with its own board of directors, and support units from manufacturing subsidiaries to testing centers all sell their services to line units. The CEO, T. J. Rodgers, says, "We've gotten rid of socialism in the organization," while Tom Peters claims the company demonstrates "perpetual innovation."

MCI Communications   MCI challenged the AT&T monopoly by designing an organization that operates as a market rather than a hierarchy: new ventures can be started by anyone, resources are allocated to reward performance, and units compete with one another. This entrepreneurial system has brought forth a string of successes—discount phone rates, MCI Fax, Friends & Family—to make MCI the second largest communications company in the United States.

Johnson & Johnson   J&J is organized into 166 separately chartered companies that sell a particular product, such as Tylenol. These internal enterprises are not only permitted, but expected, to pursue their own strategies, relationships with suppliers and clients, and all other normal aspects of an independent business. CEO Ralph Larsen says the system "provides a sense of ownership and responsibility that you simply cannot get any other way."

Clark Equipment   Clark survived a brush with Chapter 11 by requiring all business units—including a corporate staff of 500 people—to become self-supporting enterprises. Even the office of the CEO was converted into a profit center to set an example for managers. Within months, corporate staff decreased by 400 positions, costs were reduced across the company, and sales moved upward.

Au Bon Pain   After struggling for years to run this chain of bakery-cafes in the traditional manner, performance took off with the conversion to an entrepreneurial model in which each store manager became a part-owner of his or her unit and gained wide control over its operations. Sales and earnings spurted up, turnover disappeared, and store managers earned as much as $100,000 a year.

(Continued)

Alcoa Corporation   Alcoa revitalized a out-of-touch bureaucracy by converting all line and staff units into a market system of autonomous internal suppliers and customers that were free to conduct business with outside competitors. This reintroduction of economic reality doubled productivity and sales among line units, and support groups such as R&D began bringing in outside business.

Nucor Corporation   Nucor has become so famous for its management system that it is widely regarded as "The closest thing to a perfect company in the steel industry." Minimills are run by small teams of workers, technicians, and managers who have almost complete control over all operations and receive bonuses that can double their income. Ken Iverson, the CEO, claims, "We're eliminating the hierarchy."

Merck & Company   Merck recently has been rated the top Fortune 500 company four years in a row largely because of its unusually flexible system for organizing scientists into effective project teams. Researchers from 12 scientific disciplines are completely free to pool their efforts in any project they choose, spontaneously merging the intellectual talents and financial resources of various units into a committed team. The CEO, Dr. Roy Vagelos, described the system this way: "Everybody here naturally gravitates around a hot project. It's like a live organism."

Sun Microsystems   Sun hollowed out its nonessential functions by subcontracting chip manufacturing, distribution, and service functions in order to focus its energies on designing advanced computers. Its remaining divisions are independent subsidiaries with contractual authority over these allied business partners, giving them more control while providing the flexibility and focus on core competence that has made the company a leader in the competitive workstation market.

Principle 2. Create an Economic Infrastructure to Guide Decisions

With operational matters relegated to internal enterprises, top management focuses on designing an economic infrastructure of performance controls, financial incentives, accounting and communication systems, an entrepreneurial culture, and other corporatewide frameworks that guide business decisions by market forces instead of by administrative fiat. The behavior of this organizational architecture is then regulated, monitored for weaknesses and market failures, and corrective changes are made to improve its performance.

One of Alcoa's biggest gains in moving to an internal market economy was the realization that management had been making decisions based on inaccurate estimates of costs and revenues. Like many corporations, the finances of operating units was pooled into larger divisions, absorbed by corporate overhead, and otherwise not identified accurately for individual units. When the corporation converted all units into autonomous enterprises with their own profit and loss statements, the newfound awareness of actual costs and revenues immediately altered decisions in more realistic directions.[25] AT&T realized the same benefits when its large groups were divided into 40 or so profit centers to highlight their individual performance. "The effect was staggering," said James Meehan, the CFO.[26]

A striking example of the power of incentives to change behavior can be seen when converting staff units into profit centers. In the typical organization, IS services are provided free to line units, with the predictable result that people waste resources. Stories abound of corporate officers demanding multiple copies of huge computer printouts that are never read, of overseas offices equipped with international phone lines used by clerks to call home every day. But when presented with monthly bills by the IS department, there is a marked change in attitude, causing line managers to select less expensive systems that often provide better service as well.[27] Conversely, giving line units the freedom to choose among competing IS sources causes their internal suppliers to shape up equally fast.

Beyond the incentives of financial systems, there is also a need for the subtle norms of a social system. MCI has learned that an internal market must be augmented by deliberate plans for encouraging an entrepreneurial culture that stresses individual initiative, fighting bureaucracy, embracing change, and supporting employees. Strong corporate cultures are common, but at MCI, these principles constitute what CEO Bert Roberts called a "virtual organization" long before the term became popular in 1993. At MCI, the phrase means a set of commonly understood values and concepts representing an "informal management system" that guides working together effectively. This informal system is far more flexible precisely because it exists in the minds of MCI people as a shared idea rather than in cumbersome written policies. MCI employees and the company are one and the same, allowing instantaneous agreement on difficult undertakings, whether it be a new product, organizational change, or acquisition.[28]

These powerful effects of financial incentives, information, and culture suggest that managers must come to grips with the need to design organizations as complex, interacting knowledge systems. The fact is that modern organizations are information systems used to manage knowledge about market demand, production schedules, employee capabilities, capital assets, and other strategic factors. As Jay Forrester and Peter Senge point out, a central task of managers today is to become organizational *designers,* in addition to organizational *operators,* creating a new class of intelligent, high-performing, adaptive learning organizations.[29]

McGraw-Hill developed an interesting system that illustrates this concept nicely. The company is engaged in industries that all involve various forms of knowledge: publishing, information services, electronic data transmission, and so on. The CEO created a corporatewide information system, incentives, and training programs to unify all units into an "intellectual community," somewhat like a university or research lab. The central element in this strategy was the development of a computerized database that pooled the information gathered by all units, allowing them to draw on a growing central storehouse of valuable knowledge to serve their clients better. This early prototype of an organizational learning system was appropriately called an "information turbine" because it converted raw information from diverse sources into a powerful stream of knowledge that "drives" the organization.

In an industrial age, companies manufactured goods, but in an information age, they "manufacture" knowledge. Developing strategic information systems that facilitate the creation of this vital knowledge is now the key factor that drives economic success.

Principle 3. Provide Leadership to Foster Collaborative Synergy

This new form of entrepreneurial management raises tough questions about the role of executives and the very nature of corporations. If an organization is no longer a fixed, centrally controlled structure but a fluid tangle of autonomous units going their own way, what distinguishes it from the outside marketplace? What gives it an identity that makes it more than the sum of its parts? In short, what is top management really managing?

In addition to designing organizational systems, corporate managers must also provide leadership to integrate the firm into a cohesive community. CEOs may give up much of their formal authority in a market system, but they lead by ensuring accountability, resolving conflicts, and encouraging cooperation, thereby providing a more subtle but more powerful form of guidance that shapes the strategic thinking of this corporate community.

MCI offers a good example in which corporate executives work hard to turn contentious issues into advantageous solutions. Top management understands that the autonomy of operating managers must remain inviolate, so they avoid imposing decisions. Yet the company's entrepreneurial stance often provokes heated controversy over risky ventures. A new product concept like Friends & Family is usually proposed by sales, engineering, or any other group, which then leads to a debate over the merits of the idea. Rather than squelch this conflict, MCI managers embrace it as a stimulant for tough, creative thought; they call it "creative dissonance." From this socially acceptable means for direct, constructive argument among diverse viewpoints, a solid course of action usually emerges that all can support with confidence.[30]

Johnson & Johnson (J&J) encourages coalitions of business units that serve everyone better. Although J&J is organized into three major product groups, its 166 separate companies retain almost complete autonomy because it "provides a sense of ownership that you simply cannot get any other way," says the CEO, John Larsen. But the company's big clients, Wal-Mart, K mart, and other retailers, want to avoid being bombarded by a barrage of sales calls from dozens of J&J units, and this duplication of efforts is costly. The CEO's approach was to urge his operating managers to pool such functions into common "customer support centers" that operate as internal distributorships coordinating sales, logistics, and service for each major retailer.

These leaders have steered a new course between two opposing demands that are often hard to reconcile. To allow operating managers the entrepreneurial freedom that is essential for commitment, creativity, and flexibility, modern CEOs must avoid imposing controls. Yet they must also avoid disruptive conflict, needless duplication, and unnecessary risk.

A market can provide this combination of freedom and control, but not by remaining a laissez-faire system. The internal market model reveals that a sound organization must add net value to its internal enterprises which would not be available to outside enterprises working alone. That is the central role of leadership: to create the synergy that provides a competitive edge. For instance, the Japanese do not think of their keiretsu as internal markets, but the strength of the keiretsu system emanates from this same basic principle. Keiretsu are families of independent companies free to conduct their business as they think best, yet bonded together by their collective ability to assist one another.

It is useful to compare the management of organizational economies with the management of national economies. Effective governments understand that they cannot be limited by either laissez-faire or industrial policies, but must steer a middle course that facilitates collaborative working relationships among autonomous economic actors. Using a similar form of balance, effective corporate management must unite autonomous internal actors into a collaborative corporate community. Unlike a government, an organizational economy is more manageable because it is a smaller system that top executives can influence more easily.

So an internal market system must be shaped into a "guided market," a vehicle for reaching common goals that is more effective than either a laissez-faire economy or an authoritarian hierarchy.

TELEWORKING IN THE ELECTRONIC ORGANIZATION

The trends previously noted are likely to pale in comparison with what should occur soon as the revolution in information technology (IT) short-circuits today's hierarchy. Box 13-4 describes how the cost of teleconferencing and other powerful new IT systems continues to drop by a factor of 10 every few years, causing a form of "teleworking" to increase roughly 50 percent per year. Who can imagine being without a fax machine today? Yet fax was rare just a few years ago. The same wave of popular use may make other forms of IT de rigueur soon as a critical mass is reached.[31]

Teleworking is not for everyone, and it will not eliminate direct interaction because people need personal contact. Studies show that most employees prefer to continue working at their office two to three times per week. Instead, it should become a viable *alternative* to the real thing as IT becomes user-friendly and inexpensive, offering a convenient way to augment face-to-face meetings. White-collar workers would then be able to do their jobs almost anywhere in addition to working in the office, which what we now think of as the "virtual organization."

Rather than the traditional organization of permanent employees working nine to five within the fixed confines of some building, the virtual organization is a changing assembly of temporary alliances among entrepreneurs who work together from anywhere using the worldwide grid of global information networks. *Business Week* described it as "electronic corporations made up of individuals and groups scattered all over the country."[32] Here are a few examples of fledgling virtual organizations that are finding useful ways to "work off the grid."

Companies such as Boeing, 3M, and Hewlett-Packard are using interactive teleconferencing now, reducing the time required to complete a typical project by 90 percent. At other organizations, new employees are no longer issued a company car but a portable computer because everyone remains in contact while working on various projects from locations around the world. The Los Angeles advertising agency, Chiat/Day, turned its offices into a meeting and leisure center for occasional employee gatherings because everyone works out of their homes through computer networks.

As the use of such these powerful new modes of teleworking swells during the 1990s, an electronic maze of lateral relationships should cut across the old

---

Box 13-4
GROWTH OF TELEWORKING

Decreasing IT Costs   IT costs are dropping by a factor of 10 every few years, making far wider usage feasible in the late 1990s. A teleconferencing system that cost $1 million in 1982 could be bought for $100,000 in 1992, and transmission time has gone from $2,000 per hour to $200. The coming "telecomputer," which will combine the functions of today's PC, TV, and telephone, is likely to sell for roughly $1,000 at about the year 2000 or possibly less.

Telecommuting   Nine million Americans were telecommuting full-time in 1994, but the number leaps to 40 million if part-time telecommuters and self-employed people are included. Bell Atlantic now has all of its 16,000 managers telecommuting at least part time, and plans to expand this capability to 50,000 employees. Roughly 60 percent of all office products are sold to lawyers, stock brokers, managers, and other entrepreneurial workers who work at home, traveling, at resorts, and any other location. "Think of almost any job or business, and someone's doing it from home," said the editor of *Home Office Computing*.

Teleconferencing   Various forms of teleconferencing are growing at 40 to 60 percent per year and should be commonly used before the year 2000. As of 1994, there were about 20 million PCs in the United States wired together by 6,000 local networks that are operated by 300 types of groupware, such as Lotus Notes. Internet is expected to have 100 million users around the world by the late 1990s. The installation of telecommunication and fiber-optic networks is growing at 50 percent per year to connect all electronic systems into one great digital soup.

All Functions   IT use now covers the entire span of business and social activity: electronic banking, shopping, education, publishing, supplier-distributor linkages, medicine, and other functions being added to this list daily. Roughly 70 percent of all managers used a PC as of 1993.

Source: William Halal, "Teleworking" (Information Strategies Group Report, 1992).

chain-of-command to dramatically alter the way organizations work. John Hagel, a partner at McKinsey & Company, claimed:

> As the costs of using IT systems fall, we're going to see a widespread disintegration of U.S. business and the emergence of very different corporate entities.[33]

Drawing together the concepts introduced in previous sections allows us to summarize what it should be like to manage in the year 2000. Today's exploding environmental turbulence seems destined to make life far more hectic for managers as they struggle with constant change: racing technological advances, bold new competitors, the death and birth of entire markets, and a rolling series of crises. Fortunately, the wiring of the globe should provide a powerful new set of tools for coping with this turmoil. IT systems will allow managers to remain instantly in touch with far-flung operations involving scores of global partners who all work in real time and with the aid of near-perfect information. And as the growth of market organizations provides the flexibility to cope with all this turmoil, the typical manager is likely to operate like an entrepreneur. Within the constraints of corporate life, managers should have almost sole control over their enterprise, while being accountable for performance, and they may be involved in a variety of different ventures simultaneously. Box 13-5 presents a fictional scenario that projects current trends into the year 2000 to convey the feel and flavor of a typical manager's life working in tomorrow's organizations.

This imminent transformation poses the unavoidable challenge of constructing a new type of organization around the IT that even now forms the central nervous system of the modern firm. Paul Strassman, who has been called the "high priest of MIS," is concerned that most IT systems "take a rigid bureaucratic structure and ossify it further by enshrining it within a layer of computer code."[34] IBM itself used IT to exert tight control, with the results we now witness in the firm's decline.

This interface between organization structure and IT systems has become one of the most crucial issues in management, yet it is so poorly understood that we usually allow the inexorable force of IT to ramble through organizations unguided, with powerful unintended consequences. It's almost as if a robust ivy were growing over a building, destroying its aging mortar and old bricks, and leaving only the vine as a supporting structure.

Business will not be able to use IT effectively without a sound working model of the modern organization, and that model seems to be the market paradigm. From this view, only a few essential standards are needed to ensure compatibility of the hardware, software, finances, communications, and learning systems composing the firm's IT architecture. Even these requirements may fade as open systems make all IT compatible. Most importantly, the way

---

Box 13-5
MANAGING IN 2000
A Day in the Worklife of Vera Pace Asian Regional
Manager, Biotronics Inc.

Vera was awakened by the persistent beep of her computer assistant, Vera-2, lying on the night table. When she asked who it was, Azmi Ibrahim's undulating voice announced that he had a serious problem at the bioplant in Sarawak.

"The Malay Union of Pipefitters has struck the factory, and nothing is getting done because all of the other workers are honoring their stand," he complained. "They are deeply offended at being forced to work on a sacred Moslem holiday."

She asked Azmi to arrange a meeting with the union leaders at 10:00 A.M. over the hotel's video conferencing system and started preparing for the day. "The first thing I'd better do is reschedule that breakfast meeting with Rene Latour," was the thought that jumped to her mind. Before taking a quick shower, Vera asked her assistant, Vera-2, to tell Rene she would have to meet for lunch instead, and to transmit the Biotronics proposal for her to look over in the meantime. "This joint venture with the French is crucial if we're to enter the Thai market for bioengineering products," she worried.

Promptly at 10 o'clock, Azmi was patched through while Vera sat at the desk in her room at the Hong Kong Hilton. "Good morning Ms. Pace," he announced in a formal tone. Looking up at the wall monitor, Vera attributed his unusually diplomatic mood to the three union leaders seated with him at the Biotronics plant in Sarawak, Malaysia. "Please allow me to introduce Mister Seri Anwar, Chief of the Malay Pipe Fitters Union and his associates," he said while bowing slightly.

Although Azmi spoke English fluently, the three union leaders relied on the automatic translation system to convert their Malay for Vera. "Blessed be Allah," they greeted Vera, who replied the same in English as she had learned to do.

"Mister Anwar," Vera continued. "Please explain the cause of your unhappiness, and I will do what I can to resolve it." After an hour of difficult discussion, it was finally agreed to release the workforce for the duration of the 3-day holiday with half pay, and to jointly plan a schedule that would work around Moslem traditions in the future. Vera and the union chief then signed the electronic agreement Azmi had put on the screen using

(Continued)

> pen entry systems at both ends of the video conference. When the Islamic good-byes were automatically translated from English to Malay and from Malay back into English, the screen dimmed.
>
> Vera still had an hour before meeting with Rene, so she called up her New York office to tell the president of Biotronics about the incident. He was out, so she told Vera-2 to locate him, and to transmit a brief report of the union agreement culled from the video conference the machine had been monitoring. She then made a few calls to sort out plans for five other ventures that were at various stages of development in China and Japan. Finally, she called her youngsters in Portland to tell them she would be flying home tomorrow, and to make sure they were using their new IBM Personal Tutor System to go over the lessons assigned by their teacher. Sure enough, they had been goofing off on Virtual Reality.

IT systems are used should be left to the discretion of local units, just as any enterprise is free to use technology as it chooses.

Information technology seems to obey subtle but inexorable laws that we are just beginning to grasp. Information must be guided carefully because it is powerful stuff, but it cannot be contained too tightly either. Although IT systems are still crude in the socialist bloc, attempts to restrict information were largely responsible for the collapse of centrally planned economies. Lech Walesa pointed out the underlying force that powered the revolution he merely guided in Poland: "How did these reforms appear?" he asked. "The result of computers, communication satellites, television." The lesson seems clear: IT is replacing hierarchies with markets everywhere.

IMPLICATIONS FOR MANAGERS

The preceding trends suggest that a revolution is imminent in management thought. In a decade or so, our prevailing notions of hierarchy may seem as archaic as the medieval belief in the divine right of kings. Organizations are no longer pyramids of power controlling employees at fixed locations, but self-organizing groups of roaming intrapreneurs united by electronic market systems. And these internal markets are forming a worldwide web of alliances that will become a seamless global economy. Without conscious planning, a dramatically different system of management is emerging based on principles of enterprise in which power, initiative, and control originate from the bottom up.

Pros and Cons of Market Organizations

Naturally, internal markets incur the same drawbacks of external markets—complex working relationships fraught with risk, uncertainty, inequality, and failure. However, the advantages are usually more compelling.

For instance, economists argue that hierarchies are superior because markets incur transaction costs in searching for alternatives, managing financial transactions, and so on.[35] But the IT revolution is reducing transaction costs, and cost increases can be offset by decreased overhead and gains in innovation. Western Airlines replaced 500 managers with IT systems, saving huge costs and improving performance because of less bureaucracy.[36] Studies by Thomas Malone at MIT show that the decrease in transaction costs made possible by IT "should lead to a shift from [management] decisions within firms to the use of markets."[37]

It is often thought that markets cause conflict as organizational units pursue different goals and compete for resources. Our experience shows that market systems can *resolve* the abundant conflict that persists now. Peter Drucker observed that competition within corporations is much more intense than competition between corporations, and it is a lot less ethical. In a market, however, relationships between sellers and buyers are clearly defined, voluntary, and selected from a range of options. In contrast, hierarchies are usually fraught with misunderstanding, decisions are often imposed by authority, and the choices are minimal, if any. Thus internal markets provide a rational basis for sound working relationships, replacing office politics with openly reached agreements that serve all parties better.

Even the troublesome aspects of internal markets can actually represent useful organizational adjustments. Are some managers unable to staff their units with volunteers? In the outside world this means that working conditions are poor. Are some units suffering losses? A market would let them fail because they do not produce value. Do differences in income exist? Wage inequalities can motivate good performance and they urge poor workers to shape up. Thus, what appears to be disorder in a market is often vital information about economic reality that should be heeded.

Finally, the internal market concept offers a feasible way to manage a new age of complexity. A disenchantment has set in with strategic planning because any form of centrally coordinated planning usually produces more bureaucracy rather than actual change. The organic behavior of market systems, however, goes beyond planning altogether to produce a constant stream of structural change throughout the organization. Instead of having top managers forecast business conditions and force the organization to move in some wholesale direction, the individual units of an internal market feel their way along like the cells of some superorganism possessing a life of its own.

Although the market model is superior under most conditions today, there are no perfect organizational designs. Organic systems can foster creativity, but at the cost of enduring some loss of orderly control. Conversely, hierarchies may avoid disorder, but they inhibit creative freedom. We should hold no illusions about some universal ideal of structure to be applied in an all-encompassing way. Internal markets are no panacea, therefore, because they are not useful in some situations, such as military operations and space launches, that demand the close coordination of thousands of people and complex plans.

Some troubling corporate experiences highlight the difficult problems posed by internal markets. One firm showed a burst of vitality after moving to a market system that spawned numerous ventures, but poor control of the risks resulted in serious business failures. This problem could have been avoided with strong leadership, but it also illustrates both the challenge and the potential that are involved. Organizational freedom unleashes great reservoirs of creative energy, and this energy must be carefully guided into constructive avenues.

So it may always be necessary to trade off the costs and gains of different organizational designs. Although the balance is shifting today toward market systems offering entrepreneurial freedom, the advantages of enterprise can only be gained by tolerating an increase in disorder.

Working and Leading in a Market System

The drawbacks of enterprise seem especially severe now as mergers, bankruptcies, downsizing, and other changes are causing unemployment, ending corporate loyalty, and generally making work life more difficult. Even IBM is laying off workers for the first time in its history. If internal markets introduce more of the same, how will people tolerate working in market organizations?

Corporations are not firing workers to be harsh, but because the world is in the throes of a massive economic restructuring that exerts two major new demands: accountability for performance in order to survive competition, and organizational flexibility to adapt to chaotic change—the same major strengths of internal markets. This explains the new role now emerging for individuals. Whereas it made sense to treat people as *employees* in a hierarchical system, an internal market system requires people to assume the role of *entrepreneurs* (or intrapreneurs). Thus, the old employment relationship in which people were paid for holding a *position* is yielding to a new relationship offering people an *opportunity* to use their talents, with all the freedom, self-reliance, risks, and rewards associated with being an entrepreneur.

This trend toward mobile, entrepreneurial work is highlighted by the growth of a "contingent workforce." Part-time employees, temporaries, subcontractors, and self-employed workers made up one-third of American workers in 1990, and the percentage is far larger in Europe. Some estimates suggest that half of the entire labor force may be composed of contingent workers by 2000 A.D.

To handle the risks better, many worried people are taking charge of their own careers by packaging themselves as self-employed contractors able to move from company to company, consultants working for various firms, and individuals starting their own businesses.[38] About 20 percent of all professionals now work as "temps," including lawyers, doctors, and even executives, and there are signs that professionals may constitute the fastest growing segment of the contingent workforce. Hundreds of temporary personnel firms have sprung up to help engineers, systems designers, and managers change jobs in industries that are going through an economic upheaval. "We're in the mindpower—not the manpower—business," said the CEO of one temporary agency,[39] and another claimed: "The temporary executive [has become] a permanent fixture in American corporate life."[40]

Coping with this turmoil of market systems may always be difficult, but much of it can be ameliorated by cooperative leadership that shares critical policy decisions with organizational members and supports them through trying times. Thus, corporations should become hospitable to creative people by emulating the hundreds of business incubators that have sprung up to nurture new ventures.[41] One of IBM's most successful actions was the Independent Business Unit concept that created the PC in 1½ years. General Motor's new electric car project is spearheaded by a team of 200 people working outside the normal chain of command.

A more complex business environment is evolving in which we must often both compete and cooperate with one another. General Motors, Ford, and Chrysler compete ferociously with Toyota, Fiat, and Renault—while they also work together as partners with these same adversaries. To manage this tension, a new business ethic is needed which handles competition in a constructive way that allows people to work together cooperatively as well. Excessive internal competition can be contained where necessary by agreeing to form consortia, joint ventures, and other internal alliances, just as we do now in external markets.

Ultimately, the relentless force of economic realities will require all of us to assume the responsibility for our own welfare, with the support of a collaborative corporate community.

The New Economic Foundation of Management

These advantages of enterprise stem from structural redesign; it is the first imperative for revitalizing institutions because it builds the economic foundation supporting all other aspects of management. A sound structure does not assure effective behavior, but it is an essential starting point. Talented employees, collaborative leadership, inspired strategies, and other factors are also needed to create excellence. These are secondary factors, however, because people have difficulty working effectively in a faulty organizational structure. *Structure is the first requirement for good management.*

That is the basic problem facing executives today. Capable, well-intentioned people working in corporations, governments, schools, and other organizations are struggling against outmoded hierarchical structures. This impending shift to a new concept of market organization appears to form the single most important change in today's economies, presenting roughly the same challenges and opportunities posed by the restructuring of socialist economies. John Scully expressed it best:

> The command-and-control model of running a large organization no longer works. . . . the single biggest theme in the world of business during the 1990s . . . [will be] the reorganization of work using information systems to compete in the marketplace.[42]

Although many CEOs agree with Scully that the command-and-control approach is now obsolete, it is still being used as the basic foundation for managing large corporations, albeit modified somewhat by innovative concepts such as organizational networks. Forming networks of strategic alliances is certainly a central feature of the new model of organization, but the idea of "networking" says little about how these relationships should work in the absence of central controls. Who should be responsible for forming alliances? What rights and responsibilities do parties share? Who is accountable for the success of a network? And so on.

The enterprise model answers such questions by placing networks within a logical economic framework. Alliances should be formed by the managers of internal enterprise units because they can make working commitments directly on a sound business basis, although CEOs can provide guidance and support. The roles of internal enterprise managers are similar to those of any business in a joint venture, so they share the responsibility for success. And employees in an internal enterprise are used to working with alliances because that is how everyday relationships are managed.

Internal markets are also likely to make reengineering, TQM, organizational learning, and other business processes more successful. Implementation of these concepts often fails because they are imposed on units or they are done in an inappropriate manner. A McKinsey & Company study estimates that two out of three quality programs "stall" because of excessive bureaucracy.[43] Just as any external business must be allowed to manage its own affairs, these important processes are likely to work better if they originate through the voluntary decisions of operating managers held accountable for serving their clients, with corporate management providing advice and support.

True organizational learning, for instance, cannot be "managed" through a hierarchical system, but requires the voluntary involvement of willing learners that entrepreneurial freedom provides. The creative flow of information has always been one of the advantages of markets over hierarchy. Hierarchy restricts information flows to the chain-of-command and distorts communication, while good markets encourage a synergistic exchange of knowledge among autonomous economic actors. Corporate executives must create the IT systems that provide a framework for learning, but the learning itself must be accomplished by entrepreneur-employees operating freely within a market organization.

Our views are almost certain to change as organizations continue to evolve. But whatever happens, it is hard to escape the conviction that enterprise systems provide a logical economic foundation for the organic management now crucial for world competitiveness. The key ingredient is to construct organizations as clusters of internal enterprise units coordinated by market mechanisms, thereby facilitating the use of teams, reengineering, TQM, networks, organizational learning, virtual corporations, and all other fluid organizational practices.

Making the Transition

Similar changes are taking place in other institutions and other nations. An entrepreneurial form of government is emerging in the United States in which agencies compete to serve clients better.[44] As noted earlier, this trend is most noticeable in education where choice is replacing the old educational monopoly with a market system, but a wave of attempts is underway to restructure governments at city, state, and federal levels.

There are even signs that Japanese corporations are also submitting to this same imperative by eliminating layers of middle management, introducing merit pay, and allowing employees to switch jobs. One Japanese executive put the change this way: "The era of waving the company flag to motivate people is over."[45]

Many CEOs are providing leadership by making major reorganizations. In the late 1980s when computer companies had become bloated after years of growth, Hewlett-Packard adopted features of a market system to avoid the bureaucracy that swamped IBM. "We had too damn many committees. If we didn't fix things, we'd be in the same shape as IBM is today," said David Packard. HP dismantled unneeded controls to renew its belief that each division should be a self-managed enterprise no larger than 1,500 people. Former CEO John Young endorsed the development of radical new products—such as HP's first desktop printer, which competed with the firm's existing machines—an undertaking that would have been heresy at IBM. Today the LaserJet line accounts for 40 percent of HP's sales. In 1990, HP was valued at one-tenth of IBM; by providing a skillful blend of freedom and support that enabled this entrepreneurship, HP is now worth roughly as much as IBM.

IBM has been following this same path recently, although the strategy of its new CEO is not yet clear. As the examples mentioned before show, IBM entrepreneurs are now entering each other's once sacrosanct markets and support units are being converted into profit centers. Cheap clones of IBM PCs are even being purchased by some IBM offices. Now, that's an internal market.

Other troubled companies such as General Motors should undertake this same transition. Instead of a few divisions reporting to a top management team that makes major decisions, GM's entrepreneurial managers and engineers should be turned free to start hundreds of creative ventures like Saturn. Many would fail, but many more would thrive because they have met the test of the market rather than hierarchical authority.

Major reorganizations of this type are formidable because they require a profound structural upheaval, rather like the struggle facing the postsocialist bloc. But experiences of prominent companies offer some guidelines. The best approach is to first learn about the idea thus gaining a solid grasp of the possibilities and the problems involved. Then recruit willing, enterprising volunteers who have the ability to see it through. Provide thorough training in the business skills needed to succeed in a market environment. Take care to plan the change collectively and to sketch out a realistic vision of how it would work. Prepare the organization by shaping a culture that fosters enterprise. Most importantly, give the reorganization top priority.

Asea Boveri Brown (ABB) offers a fine, detailed example of how to design a large, global organization along enterprise principles, as shown in Box 13-6. Listen to how Percy Barnavik, the CEO, approached the task of creating a decentralized market organization consisting of 4,500 autonomous profit centers: "We took our best people, the superstars, and gave them six weeks to design the restructuring. We called it the Manhattan Project."[46]

The challenge is enormous but the stakes are also enormous. Managers who develop a market organization should realize the same advantages that inspired the overthrow of Communism: widespread opportunities for achievement, liberation from authority, accountability for performance, creative innovation, high quality and service, ease of handling complexity, fast reaction time, and flexibility for change. This approach seems especially appropriate for the United States because it could harness the American entrepreneurial spirit to create a unique form of management based on the power of enterprise—an "American Keiretsu."

There is no one best way to approach this task because each manager and each institution must devise a solution based on their special needs, talents, and circumstances. Whether the design emphasizes cross-functional teams,

---

Box 13-6
ABB'S ENTERPRISE MODEL OF THE
GLOBAL CORPORATION

Percy Barnavik, the CEO of the Asea Boveri Brown organization, has been portrayed as moving more aggressively than any other CEO to build the new model of competitive enterprise. He provides the following descriptions of the corporation's structural features.

A Confederation of Entrepreneurs   We are a federation of national companies . . . a collection of local businesses with intense global coordination.

Multidimensional Structure   Along one dimension ABB is structured into 50 or so business areas operating worldwide. Alongside this structure sits a country structure of 1,100 local companies that do the work of business areas in different countries.

The Decentralization Contract   Our managers need well-defined responsibilities, clear accountability, and maximum degrees of freedom. I don't expect them to do things that hurt their business but are good for ABB. That's not natural. We always create separate legal entities. Separate companies allow *real* balance sheets with *real* cash flow and dividends. Managers inherit results year to year through changes in equity.

Support Units as Profit Centers   You can go into any centralized corporation and cut its headquarters staff by 90 percent. You spin off 30 percent into freestanding service centers that perform real work and charge for it. You decentralize 30 percent by pushing them down into line organizations. Then 30 percent disappears through reductions.

Small Internal Enterprises   Our operations are divided into 1,200 companies, which are divided into 4,500 profit centers with an average of 50 employees. We are fervent believers in decentralization. People can aspire to meaningful career ladders in units small enough to understand and be committed to.

A Strategic Information System That Unites the Firm   We have a glue of transparent, centralized reporting through a management information system called Abacus.

(Continued)

Employee Entrepreneurs   I don't sit like a godfather, allocating jobs. What I guarantee is that every member of the federation has a fair shot at the opportunities.

Providing Leadership   I have no illusions about how hard it is to communicate clearly and quickly with thousands of people around the world. Real communication takes time, and top managers must be willing to make the investment . . . meeting with the company CEOs in an open, honest dialogue.

Source: William Taylor, "The Logic of Global Business," Harvard Business Review (March–April 1991).

decentralized profit centers, a network of strategic alliances, powerful information systems, or other organizational forms yet to come, the common framework supporting all these structures should be an economic foundation of free enterprise that permeates the institution.

The transition of a new model of organization seems likely to be an accomplished fact by the year 2000, whether we are ready for it or not. Managers can best prepare for this coming upheaval now by learning to make a mental shift from hierarchy to enterprise.

FOR FURTHER READING

Davidow, W., and M. Malone, *The Virtual Corporation: The Structuring and Revitalizing the Corporation for the 21st Century* (New York: HarperCollins, 1992).

Halal, W., A. Geranmayeh, and J. Pourdehnad, *Internal Markets: Bringing the Power of Free Enterprise inside Your Organization* (New York: John Wiley, 1993).

Handy, C., *The Age of Paradox* (Boston: Harvard Business School Press, 1994).

Wheatley, M., *Leadership and the New Science* (San Francisco: Berrett-Koehler, 1992).

14

LEADERSHIP FOR THE YEAR 2000

Jay A. Conger

Few topics generate as much interest and curiosity today as leadership does. At the same time, it is one of the most difficult roles that a manager or executive can effectively play. The pressures of short-term financial targets, the increasing power of shareholders, the active intervention of governments, and the growing resistance in society to formal authority are just a few of the forces that make leading a difficult activity. Yet at no time in recent history has there been such an enormous need for leadership at all levels of management than today. With the entry of world-class competitors from Asia and Europe over the past two decades, business has become a global pressure cooker. Many of the corporate success stories of the 1970s and 1980s such as IBM or American Express or Eli Lilly are now struggling to adapt to more fiercely competitive markets. Leadership, or its lack, is proving to be one of the most important determinants of whether organizations will survive and flourish in this new landscape.

We are witnessing not only a dramatic increase in the need for leadership but also a transformation in what we call leadership. Many of the skills that organizational researchers of the 1960s and 1970s identified as "leadership skills" now seem very out of date. In contrast, a word like "vision," which is so popular today, would have sounded strange to managers of 20 years ago. After all, an effective *planning* process would have anticipated many of the more gradual marketplace changes occurring during the 1950s or even the 1960s. But with today's marketplaces changing at a dramatic pace, visionary skill captures the foresight necessary to grasp a more turbulent future.

This turbulence is in turn changing where leadership is practiced. For example, hierarchies collapsing into flatter pyramids to respond to faster-paced markets are pushing leadership further and further down into the organization. The old model of the chief executive officer as the leader no longer works in a business environment where your competitors change the game rules weekly. To respond effectively, the front line of any organization must have leaders as well. Today's strategic moves of a competitor are more often apparent to the field than to the executive suite. An immediate leadership response may be needed that only the local manager can provide.

In addition, today's flatter organizations mean that most of us will have to manage across more functions and be sitting on more project teams throughout our management careers. Our teammates around the table will no longer be our subordinates. Instead they may be somebody else's subordinates, or peers from other functions, or suppliers, or even our customers. And how do you lead such groups where you have no formal authority to lead? It's a far more complicated task than the old model of the leader as "the boss."

But leadership is now not only being assumed at lower levels and in team settings but also at the very top by the company's board of directors. Strange as it may seem, boards have traditionally been a relatively passive force in corporate governance. Recently, however, boards have begun to awaken to their own leadership role. They are becoming more active—even to the point of forcing out prominent CEOs. So leadership is not only appearing in new forms but also in new places.

This chapter will look at these many changes in leadership to illustrate what readers can learn from them to become effective leaders themselves. We'll start with an overview of the roots of leadership and from there examine how the nature of leadership is changing from times past because of new challenges. With this knowledge, you can begin to discover your own leadership capabilities and liabilities, and how you can tap more deeply into your potential by finding the right developmental experiences.

WHERE DO LEADERS COME FROM?[1]

There are two schools of thought on the origins of leadership ability: One argues principally in favor of childhood experiences (the "born-leader" school); the other argues that later life experiences (the "made-leader" school) are more critical.

Surprisingly, there is some agreement among leadership researchers that genetics and childhood must play a role. Where the debate heats up is in the degree to which they assume a *determining* role. The born-leader school believes that genes and/or childhood are the overwhelming forces shaping a leader. Implicit in this school's argument is an assumption that the "right" genes or the "right" family are generally rare. This rarity in turn explains why we see so few leaders.

There is indeed some support for the idea that genetics may play an important role. Certainly, two qualities often described in leadership studies—intelligence and physical energy—appear to have genetic roots. More interestingly, studies conducted on identical twins separated at birth and reared in different families hint that certain personality traits associated with leadership could be inherited.[2] The principal study of such adult twins was conducted by the University of Minnesota. It was discovered that in the majority of the cases more than half the variation of 11 personality traits was due to heredity. Intriguing from the perspective of leadership is that heredity explained 61 percent of the variation in a particular trait called *social potency*—an individual's ability to be masterful and a forceful leader. A second trait perhaps also associated with leadership had significant ties to genetics. Inversely related to the leader's ability to take risks, this trait—*harm avoidance* (an individual's desire to shun the excitement of risk and danger, preferring the safe route even if tedious)—had 51 percent of its variance explained by heredity.[3]

Beyond these traits, genetics may play other roles. For example, the ability to be a strategic thinker could depend on an innate cognitive ability to think out problems over long time spans and to process and simplify complex information.[4] The ability to motivate people may be tied to what Harvard psychologist Howard Gardner calls "personal intelligences," the capacity to read the intentions and motivations of individuals.[5]

Unfortunately, from the standpoint of providing a conclusive answer to genetics' contribution to leadership, the Minnesota project is only one such study. It has not been duplicated by others as yet. So beyond general speculations, it would still be premature to say with authority that genetics are the key determinant of leadership. And even if genetics did shape leadership ability, experience would still have to play a role. For example, a child is not capable of devising effective strategies for a telecommunications company. While an unformed ability to think strategically may be in place, it cannot be effectively utilized without a base of knowledge and experience. An analogy would be an individual born with the proper musculature to become a successful athlete. Without effective coaching and training, this individual's athletic potential will likely remain forever underdeveloped. On-the-job experiences, education, colleagues, and mentors can provide a foundation of expertise and training that develop and refine the future business leader's native "musculature" of intelligence to think strategically.

Moving beyond genes to the forces of early childhood in the leadership equation, other factors may come into play. For example, in consultations with distinguished child psychologists concerning their views on the "born-leader" issue, Stanford professor and leadership scholar John Gardner described their speculative responses:

> Physical vitality and intelligence (of a leader) are probably primarily genetic, but intelligence is very likely influenced quite substantially by early childhood experience with respect to language usage.
>
> The capacity to understand others and skill in dealing with others has its most striking development in adolescence and especially young adulthood, but the beginnings are in the years before five.
>
> The need for achievement is probably formed by experiences in the first year of life.
>
> Confidence and assertiveness are formed early but they are situation-specific. The child may be confident or assertive in certain contexts and not in others.[6]

So while child psychologists would agree that genes play a role, it is *childhood conditioning* that lays the important groundwork for leadership. Families in essence cultivate the child's intellect, interests, and talents, and they are the first role models for interpersonal skills. As such, their actions may directly affect the future leader's ability to think strategically, to be articulate, and to motivate others.

The family also sets expectations for the child's later achievements and success. Through their demonstrations of love and praise, parents powerfully influence the child's sense of self-esteem. Families that build a child's confidence and desire to take measured risks may encourage latent leadership. Taken together, these actions may address a critical element of the leadership equation—from where springs the motivation to become a leader? On the other hand, certain families may undermine leadership potential by their behavior. For example, families that produce overprotected and spoiled children or those that instill a deep fear of failure in their children and, in turn, an aversion to risk may seriously weaken the ability and desire to lead. Surprisingly, however, a home with incessant high expectations and inadequate love may be just as conducive to producing leaders as one with a strong base of love and well-measured expectations. For example, always striving to be a success to meet the never-ending expectations of a demanding father—and finally to have his esteem—may provide enormous motivational energy for some future leaders while dampening all motivation for others. According to political scientist James David Barber who studied political leaders, two types of individuals are likely to be drawn into leadership contests: "Those who have such high self-esteem that they can manage relatively easily the threats and strains and anxieties involved . . . and those who have such low self-esteem that they are ready to do this extraordinary thing to raise it."[7]

Normally, this striving for self-esteem should create a needy individual with little appeal. Yet since childhood usually occurs within the social system of the family, it is balanced in most of us by a capacity to empathize with others. Our families encourage us to identify our strivings for self-esteem within the strivings of a larger social group. Family dynamics may therefore give life to the quest for leadership by shaping these esteem needs early on in life. But again like the potential athlete, these needs require a context and a baseline of skills to manifest themselves into actual leading.[8]

In addition, other needs related to the desire to lead may be tied to childhood such as needs for *self-actualization* or *individuality*. The self-actualization need may be especially important in enabling leaders to understand their followers, "I suggest . . . it is their capacity to learn from others and the environment . . . . It is this kind of self-actualization that enables leaders to comprehend the needs of potential followers, to enter into their perspectives, and to act on popular needs," proposes leadership scholar James MacGregor Burns.[9] Family dynamics may contribute to such needs with parents who encourage active learning and curiosity.

Individuality needs, on the other hand, may explain why certain people are more willing to assume the risks often associated with leadership such as breaking from conventions or taking bold, visionary stands. Some psychiatrists argue that the unconventionality associated with certain leaders arises specifically from a need to create a special identity that has its roots in specific family situations. William James, an early American pioneer in psychology, formulated a theory to explain the origins of these needs based on upbringing. This theory holds that there are two basic personality types—the "once-borns" and the "twice-borns." Once-borns experience life as reasonably straightforward from the moment of birth. Lives in their families are peaceful and harmonious. For the twice-borns, however, life is a great struggle. Little can be taken for granted. The outcomes of such different childhoods lead the once-borns to feel quite comfortable acting largely within the status quo; twice-borns, on the other hand, feel profoundly separate as individuals. This later develops into a lack of dependence on their organizations and on others. As a by-product, they have few or no compulsions to follow the status quo and instead can become change agents to lead people in new directions.

Yet here again, later life experiences may influence these needs as well. For example, I am aware of at least one leader who was anything but a risk taker until late in life. While his biography is poorly documented, the reformist leader Archbishop Romero of El Salvador spent most of his career as politically cautious priest. It was not until the assassination by government death squads of several priests who were his close friends that he began to take radical stands and become a populist leader. In his case, external circumstances fueled him to take risks. Later life events could well serve as such catalysts for leadership.

At this point, we might draw the following conclusions about the "born-leader" school. Genes appear to play a role in determining certain leadership dispositions and necessary qualities such as personal energy and various intelligences. And in a majority of cases, family environments may well serve as catalysts for the *need* or *motivation* to lead. They may also encourage the development of certain intellectual and interpersonal skills required by leaders. Of the many possible permutations, some family environments could be more conducive to the development of leadership drive and ability than others and could ultimately shape constructive or destructive forms of leadership. I use the plural—"some family environments"—because numerous situations are probably influential. For example, comparing the childhood families of Adolf Hitler and Franklin D. Roosevelt, we find they are diametrically opposed. Hitler's father, a civil servant, was a petty tyrant who bullied and beat his wife and child. Roosevelt's father was a benevolent man who was a risk-taking business tycoon. While Hitler met the difficulties of life head-on, Roosevelt stayed protected within a world of wealth.

As such, we are not likely to find a single "best" family dynamic. Just as there is no one leadership personality, so there can be no one conducive family type. The many different contexts in which leadership occurs demand different types of leaders and in turn different family environments.

As with genes, we might ask ourselves, How rare or common are conducive family environments? Perhaps they are not as rare as we might think. Instead, we may find that a significant proportion of the population has the right genes and family environments. The paradox is why does a potentially larger pool of possible leaders dwindle down to only a few? The "leadership is learned" school answers this question best.

In this camp falls the majority of leadership researchers. For them, leadership development extends beyond genes and family to other sources. Work experiences, hardships, opportunity, education, role models, and mentors all go together to craft leadership. It is assumed that the potential to lead is actually quite widely distributed. Its scarcity is a reflection of neglected development rather than a rarity of certain abilities and families.

Some recent research has been particularly important in shedding light on the "leadership-is-learned" argument. Leadership researchers Morgan McCall, Michael Lombardo, and Ann Morrison studied 191 successful executives to determine the forces behind their success. They concluded that experience was the common denominator in the ability of all these individuals to lead:

> . . . people who emerge as candidates for executive jobs may come with a lot of givens, but what happens to them on the job matters. Knowledge of how the business works, ability to work with senior executives, learning to manage governments, handling tense political situations, firing people—these and many others are the lessons of experience. They are taught on the firing line, by

demanding assignments, by good and bad bosses, and by mistakes and setbacks and misfortune. Maybe executives are blessed with characteristics that give them the edge in learning these things, but learn them they must.[10]

Harvard Business School professor John Kotter surveyed 200 executives at highly successful companies and interviewed in depth 12 individuals demonstrating highly effective leadership. He concluded that early in their careers his leaders had opportunities to lead, to take risks, and to learn from their successes and failures. He specifically identified the following as important developmental opportunities: (1) challenging assignments early in a career, (2) visible leadership role models who were either very good or very bad, (3) assignments that broadened knowledge and experience, (4) task force assignments, (5) mentoring or coaching from senior executives, (6) attendance at meetings outside a person's core responsibility, (7) special development jobs (executive assistant jobs), (8) special projects, and (9) formal training programs. All these forces provided a breadth of perspective necessary to lead effectively as well as the skills of aligning organizations to strategic directives and of motivating subordinates. Successes and failures also taught important lessons about how future actions should be taken.[11]

From these two studies, certain types of work experiences emerge as the primary developmental forces behind leadership. For example, hardship taught personal limits and strengths, whereas success bred confidence and an understanding of one's distinct skills. Challenging and multifunctional work assignments taught self-confidence, persistence, knowledge of the business, managing relationships, and a sense of independence. Diversity of experience developed breadth and perspective on the business and in human relations. Bosses modeled managerial and human values and taught the lessons of politics. This mix of experiences laid the groundwork for leadership ability.[12] In addition, luck and opportunity played a role. A job opening or an unexpected emergency situation might create a chance to demonstrate leadership and to provide visibility ensuring future opportunities to lead. Napoleon, for example, started out as a novelist—a mediocre one at that. It was only after entering the military that his talents as a military strategist emerged. His luck was to be drafted.

In conclusion, the learned-leadership school argues that the many potential leaders dwindle down to a few only because most of us do not have the right opportunities or developmental experiences. Companies undermine leadership development when they do not provide people with challenging assignments early in their careers as well as leadership role models and jobs that broaden experience.

The issue is a bit more complex, however. From my own experience, I believe that some managers simply choose not to use their leadership ability. This includes those with a backlog of the experiences just described. So a critical factor in the equation is the individual's personal level of motivation. This is what dries up the pool of potential leaders even further. If a talented individual is not inclined to become a leader, work experiences and other developmental opportunities are of limited value. In reality and despite our skills, many of us do not want the responsibilities and hardships associated with leadership. Leading others is a demanding and time consuming responsibility filled with difficult and not always pleasant choices. For example, often leaders must break away from the status quo of their organizations to lead. Yet many of us are driven by a need to conform. We do not wish to be seen as too unconventional. Instead, social acceptance and the need to belong are what make us feel secure. Leadership also involves hard choices about people and their careers. We may have to fire and demote others on a frequent basis. To understand where the motivation to undertake such a difficult and challenging role develops, we must probably cycle back to the family.

THE SKILLS OF LEADERSHIP

Given the right motivation and mixture of certain genes and family environments, what does a leader need to do? A decade ago, we would have said that leadership essentially involved being a very good manager. This meant effectively planning, budgeting, monitoring systems, delegating responsibility, ensuring participation in decision making, and so on. Popular theories of leadership at the time very much reflected this perspective. For example, one of the most influential theories stated that leadership clustered around two distinct roles—a people role and a task role. The people-oriented role reflected the extent to which an individual led by developing good interpersonal relations among group members, being sensitive to others' feelings, or promoting mutual trust. The task-oriented role reflected the degree to which a person led by defining the goals that the group was seeking and by organizing the roles and tasks of group members to achieve these outcomes.

By the late 1970s, however, managers and executives begin to recognize that *leading* might be something quite separate from *managing*. Leadership, perhaps, meant more than two simple roles or the degree to which you involved your subordinates in decision making or the level of sophistication in your financial reporting systems.

This distinction between leading and managing began as the result of upheavals that the world of business was facing with the dramatic increase in global competition. North American industry had enjoyed a relatively protected history up through the early 1970s. Following World War II, the United

States had established itself as the supplier of consumer goods for the world—especially automobiles and appliances. Global competitors were few. In addition, only a handful of American companies dominated each sector, and demand for their goods was insatiable at the time. Much of what we called "leading" in those days was really being efficient at getting products out the company door. Today, we would call the 1950s and 1960s the decades of managing. Traditional management skills were paramount—administering, controlling, structuring, and costing. Companies like the massive conglomerate ITT under its CEO Harold Geneen flourished because of their mastery of complex control and planning systems. But then something happened that dramatically challenged managerial efficiency. Competition became global.

To understand the magnitude of changes that occurred in one industry alone, we can take automobiles. In 1958, at the heyday of American dominance in automobiles, a buyer could choose from 21 different makes of cars manufactured by 10 automobile companies. By 1989, the consumer had a choice of 167 different models produced by 25 different car companies. And the vast majority of these new companies resided outside North America.

Ultimately, this intensity of competition translated into one important force—change. Not nicely paced change, but instead a turbulent and never-ending flood of change. In laptop computers alone, Toshiba would introduce 31 different models between 1986 and 1990. Such rapid product innovations wreaked havoc on the traditional management practices that had evolved during the 1950s and 1960s and which, in many companies, had continued to persist into the 1980s. It was no longer enough to have sophisticated control systems if you were suddenly producing outdated products. It was no longer enough to have five-year plans if they had to be scrapped every year because of fundamental market changes that had occurred overnight. It was no longer enough to reward people for being efficient managers if you wanted them to be change agents. The competitive tidal waves of the past few decades began to change fundamentally the complexion of many corporations and how they needed to be led. Companies, business schools, and the popular press suddenly realized that leadership no longer meant just effectively managing people and systems, but more importantly meant effectively leading change. Out of this realization of the new ramifications of leadership came a distinction between managing and leading.

Table 14-1 outlines the essential differences between management and leadership.[13] You will notice that the leadership skills are quite different from the earlier models of the 1950s and 1960s. The terms "vision" (establishing direction), "aligning," and "motivating" now appear, replacing terms such as "planning," "organizing," and "problem solving."

As we will see, the three main activities of leadership that I am about to describe—visioning, aligning, and mobilizing—all have to do with change. We start with the notion of vision.

TABLE 14-1   Comparing management and leadership

	Management	Leadership
Creating an agenda	*Planning and Budgeting* Establishing detailed steps and timetables for achieving needed results, and then allocating the resources necessary to make that happen	*Establishing Direction* Developing a vision of the future, often the distant future, and strategies for producing the changes needed to achieve that vision
Developing a human network for achieving the agenda	*Organizing and Staffing* Establishing some structure for accomplishing plan requirements, staffing that structure with individuals, delegating responsibility and authority for carrying out the plan, providing policies and procedures to help guide people, and creating methods or systems to monitor implementation	*Aligning People* Communicating the direction by words and deeds to all those whose cooperation may be needed so as to influence the creation of teams and coalitions that understand the vision and strategies, and accept their validity
Execution	*Controlling and Problem Solving* Monitoring results vs. plan in some detail, identifying deviations, and then planning and organizing to solve these problems	*Motivating and Inspiring* Energizing people to overcome major political, bureaucratic, and resource barriers to change by satisfying very basic, but often unfulfilled, human needs
Outcomes	Produces a degree of predictability and order, and has the potential of consistently producing key results expected by various stakeholders (e.g., for customers, always being on time; for stockholders, being on budget)	Produces change, often to a dramatic degree, and has the potential of producing extremely useful change (e.g., new products that customers want, new approaches to labor relations that help make a firm more competitive)

Source: Reprinted with the permission of The Free Press, a member of Paramount Publishing from *A Force for Change: How Leadership Differs from Management* by John D. Kotter, copyright John P. Kotter, Inc.

THE LEADERSHIP SKILL OF VISIONING[14]

Despite its mystical aura, vision is a critical aspect of leadership, and it very much reflects the new world of competition. By its nature, vision implies looking ahead and often with a paradoxical twist—seeing with a degree of clarity what may not be apparent to others. Steven Jobs, for example, "envisioned" enormous markets for personal computers in advance of their existence. He could see—before many others—the potential that lay in a small box with a computer chip inside.

Visions can take many different forms. To illustrate, I will use two contrasting examples. James H. Clark, a computer professor at Stanford University, had developed a "visual computing" system. He sensed that this innovation would powerfully shape the future of computing. Unlike the two-dimensional computer graphics of the day, Clark's systems allowed individuals to design moving, three-dimensional graphics on their screens. His goal was to create realistic images that people could manipulate with ease and in turn use to increase productivity whether that be in designing jet engines or creating special effects for movies or devising molecules for biological research. In 1982, he founded a company called Silicon Graphics, which would grow to sales of $1.09 billion and profits of $95.2 million by 1993. It was Clark's "vision" of this technology's future that propelled the company onto phenomenal success. The vision itself was quite simple: The computer screen would become a window onto a virtual world. Silicon Graphics' mission and focus was to make this happen. Like all visions, it was not realized overnight but occurred in increments as the technology itself developed over time. For example, first came three-dimensional graphics in color. Later, technological advances allowed the company to add digital audio and video capabilities. Sensing that the television screen would also transform itself into a virtual world, Silicon Graphics built alliances with Time Warner in interactive digital television and Nintendo in home video games—again enlarging the scope of its corporate vision.

The second example of a vision comes from a company called Zebco whose product stands in stark contrast to complicated computer systems. Zebco is North America's number one producer of fishing rods and reels. It is a company whose existence only a few years ago was threatened by low-cost producers from Asia. But its president Jim Dawson had a vision for the company. He articulated his vision as serving customers better than anyone else and making a profit at it, restoring jobs to American enterprises, and creating an environment of trust between management and employees. You might imagine that it would be difficult to be visionary about fishing reels and about such ideals as restoring national productivity. Yet this vision would propel Zebco into pioneering innovations both in fishing equipment and in production processes that were highly cost-effective and protected American jobs. You might also feel that "being the best" is a vision that most companies claim, but few realize. So what's the difference with Zebco? In Zebco's case, Dawson deeply believed in becoming the absolute best at customer service and employee satisfaction. Operating out of Oklahoma, his vision spoke to the concerns of his heartland and patriotically minded American employees who feared they might lose their jobs to low-cost Asian competitors. It was also a product with which both Dawson and his staff personally identified. Like Silicon Graphics, the vision was backed by the emotional commitment of the leader who had a passionate belief in his company's products and people. At their core, visions have as much to do with personal passions as they do with future goals.

While visions vary between leaders and companies, they share a simplicity built around a positive image of the company's role in the future. Unlike tactical goals, which often aim at a greater return on assets or increased market share or the introduction of a certain number of new products each year, visions involve more abstract and personally satisfying goals. For example, Steven Jobs in the early days of Apple Computer described his company's mission as revolutionizing the educational system of the nation through making computing power widely accessible for young people. He rarely spoke in terms of ordinary goals such as product, revenue, and ROI targets.

Visions essentially play two important roles for organizations by providing, first, a strategic focus and, second, a motivational stimulus. In their first role, they are typically articulated as a statement of purpose. This simplicity of focus offers an important advantage. Company strategic plans are typically too lengthy and detailed for most employees to understand clearly. A well-articulated strategic vision provides clarity and focus. For example, Jan Carlzon, the former CEO of Scandinavian Airlines, was one of the first airline executives to envision the importance of a business class for traveling executives. His vision for the company was built around creating the best business class experience possible. Opportunities or investments unrelated to this vision would never be considered—they distracted from the core focus. Carlzon would often tell the story of a company marketing group requesting funds to attend a vacation travel conference in Las Vegas. Since vacation travel was not directly related to the business class vision, the trip was not approved. In the early days of the new strategy when the company was losing money, resources nonetheless were still channeled wholly enhancing business class.

Just as important is the power of an effective vision to stimulate enormous motivational energy. When an organization has a clear sense of purpose that is widely shared and perceived as highly meaningful, employees find their mission and work more rewarding. Participating in such a highly worthwhile enterprise sparks greater commitment and enthusiasm, as well as the motivation to work harder. It creates a sense of being at a special place where real change and innovation are taking place. Imagine being on the ground floor of the personal computer revolution or a Microsoft or the new Boeing 777 or the turnaround of the Chrysler Corporation.

Given the importance of vision, how do we develop one? There are two schools of thought on the origins of a leader's vision, both of which are myths. The first is that we can develop vision from several days of brainstorming sessions. The second is that vision is something we are born with. In reality, the process of formulating a vision lies somewhere between these two extreme positions.

Visionary leaders rarely if ever start out with a complete vision. Their creativity is not neatly planned and linear, unlike the step-by-step process that we normally associate with a company's planning function. Instead it is much more of an opportunistic, fragmented, and intuitive process. It also depends on external events that the leader may be unable to control, but is sensitive to and in turn knows how to harness. An example would be Fred Smith, the founder of Federal Express. His original vision for his company was to deliver computer parts overnight. At the start-up of this enterprise, computers were mostly mainframes. A breakdown created havoc since all of an organization's computer terminals were dependent on it. Replacement parts and equipment were needed quickly to get all the terminals up and running fast. Hence Fred Smith's original vision of air-shipping these parts overnight. This simple idea, however, would later radically expand its horizons. As Fred Smith recognized the information age's increasing demand for speed of information, Federal Express's vision would enlarge itself to include overnight delivery of packages and letters and in turn ultimately revolutionize the package delivery industry.

But where do these initial ideas come from? Many times, a leader's vision has to do with a personal passion combined with a talent for opportunism. For example, Fred Smith was an avid flyer. Bill Gates, founder of Microsoft, was an impassioned computer software designer. Jim Dawson is deeply emotional about the development of people and creative innovations in fishing equipment and its manufacture. It is not uncommon for visionary leaders to have a history of personal interest in their business or in their particular skill. This depth of interest provides a strategic perspective and expertise that others less deeply involved are unlikely to possess. The visionary leader is therefore in a much better position to spot emerging opportunities. So the more you can immerse yourself in an industry of interest, the greater your chances of seeing underexploited opportunities.

Visionary leaders also tend to be great information collectors, often drawing on seemingly unrelated sources of information. For example, they might be reading an article about the cultural history of the United States and come to a realization that an important demographic trend offers a unique strategic opportunity. They sometimes look for parallels outside their own industry that offer a chance for innovations in their business. At Federal Express, the decision to develop a single nationwide clearinghouse for the company's package delivery system around a hub in Tennessee evolved after Fred Smith studied the banking business. Banking long ago faced a similar dilemma to that of Federal Express. Routing millions of checks between thousands of banks was a potential coordination nightmare. The dilemma was resolved through centralized clearinghouses to receive, sort, and ship out checks to their proper banks. Smith saw this parallel to his package delivery business and built the Tennessee clearinghouse.

In addition to these characteristics, visionary leaders often share certain other background characteristics:

- Early career experiences that provide broad exposure to a particular product or service and industry.
- Personal career experiences that heighten sensitivity to customers' concerns or needs, marketplace trends, and employees' needs/concerns.
- Exposure to other people's or other companies' innovative ideas, tactics, and market strategies from which they learned important lessons.
- Willingness to experiment continually with innovative ideas and processes and to question status quo approaches.
- Enjoyment of and the search for difficult challenges.

ALIGNING OTHERS TO THE VISION

No matter at what level a leader is in a company, one of the most important leadership roles is the aligning of staff to the organization's vision. To be meaningful and effective in the first place, visions must be widely shared throughout an organization. So part of today's leadership process is achieving widespread consensus on the validity of the vision. But even that is not enough; believing in the company vision is not the same as taking the necessary actions to make it happen. We all know that people do not necessarily practice what they preach. So aligning the organization to the vision in both minds and deeds is a critical task. This is accomplished through the leader's own words and behavior and through the careful design of all aspects of the organization to fulfill the vision.

As mentioned earlier, Jan Carlzon's vision for Scandinavian Airlines was to create a customer-driven business class service. On his first day as president, he had to take a flight on his own airline. While in the waiting room at the boarding gate, he realized that it was five minutes to departure and no one had been boarded. He became concerned about a possible delay. He approached the employee at the gate and asked whether something was wrong. She informed him that they were waiting for him to board. She explained that it was the airline's policy for company executives to board first. Amazed, he told her that customers should always take priority, and so he would board last. So boarding began, and in the end, Carlzon found a seat in the back of the coach section. After the flight departed, a steward came down the aisle with a stack of magazines going past everyone in the coach section directly to Carlzon. He asked if Carlzon would like a magazine. Carlzon explained to the steward that customers always came first. If any magazines were left, he would then take one. Word of these two events spread like wildfire throughout the company, and employees realized that Carlzon's vision of customer service was for real. Much of the alignment process has to do with leaders demonstrating commitment to their vision in their own actions—as we say, "to walk the talk."

A leader can demonstrate this kind of commitment in many ways, and sometimes small efforts are surprisingly the most effective because they can be accomplished more quickly and can take on symbolic value. At one organization, the president had called his management staff together on a retreat to brainstorm a new strategy and vision for the company. The managers, however, were somewhat suspicious of the president's sincerity. They felt he often talked about doing things rather than actually doing them, but they were willing to give him the benefit of doubt in light of this important initiative. Except for a few minor issues, most of the ideas and goals proposed during the session were highly significant. One of the lesser problems was actually so minor that it seemed silly in light of the others—a coffee machine used by many of the management staff needed to be moved from its current inconvenient location to a more accessible one. The new location had been decided on at the retreat, and immediate action had been promised by the president along with other initiatives. The next day, staff began to watch whether the president had made arrangements to move the coffee machine. Nothing happened. Days and then weeks went by, and the coffee machine remained in its customary place. For many, this single incident was used to argue that the president himself had not changed; as usual, he did not act on what he preached. It was a simple thing, but it took on enormous symbolic meaning as people tried to predict and test their president's behavior in everyday events. If—on that first day after the retreat—he had moved the coffeemaker himself, his staff might have seen it as a change in behavior and been more supportive of their president and all the changes that had been proposed. Instead, the oversight simply reinforced cynicism about the implementation of the company's new vision.

It becomes critical then that leaders continually demonstrate commitment to their goals. Constant trips to operating units or to customers are often interpreted as signs of personal investment. Involvement in priority projects is another means. An executive I studied in the early 1980s could see the coming importance of personal computers to the telecommunications industry. He wanted to get his own staff aligned to this focus as well. A senior member of his team explained what then happened: "Our boss bought one and called every CEO and consultant who was familiar with them. He literally sucked in every personal resource with great intensity until he thought he knew as much as there was to know. . . . It showed a "hands-on" willingness to get involved himself. . . . We knew from his involvement that this was an important technology and one that we'd each have to understand and build our strategy around." Even something as simple as excitement in a leader's voice when speaking about goals can convey impressions of great commitment.

In addition to words and deeds, leaders may have at their command other mechanisms to foster alignment to the vision. A framework developed at the consulting firm McKinsey and Company called the "7-S" model highlights the elements of an organization that can and should be aligned to the company vision: (1) the specific strategic objectives, (2) the systems, (3) the organizational structure, (4) the staffing, (5) the style of the leadership and the company culture, (6) skills unique to the organization and (7) the shared values.[15] These must be in alignment with the company vision to implement it successfully.

A currently popular company Southwest Airlines, which is based in Texas, illustrates how one leader—Herb Kelleher—aligned these various "S's" to the company vision. Southwest's vision centers around being a direct competitor with automobiles and buses, not other air carriers. It is built around a strategy of being a no-frills, highly efficient, on-time, low fare, high-frequency airline. This is achieved through a pricing strategy on par or below what it would cost to drive to its destinations. Tactically, they use only one type of aircraft—fuel-efficient Boeing 737s. Therefore, parts and maintenance routines are the same throughout the system. To succeed at its low-cost strategy, it has kept its structures (or hierarchy) lean; there is little structural overhead. Unlike the major airlines, which use national reservations systems, Southwest avoids them because their booking fees are too expensive. It does not have connecting flights, so its own booking and baggage tracking systems are simplified. Thus on the system side, they can maintain a low-cost advantage. When it comes to staffing, people are hired on their efficiency skills and on "attitude." Efficiency skills come in everyday activities such as a 15-minute turnaround time for unloading, reloading, and taking off a typical flight, a procedure most major carriers accomplish in triple the time. An employee attitude of "friendliness and cooperation" is based on the widely shared company values to make work fun, to recognize others' accomplishments, and to be a team member. These are modeled by the personal style of Herb Kelleher, who has been known to show up at the break room of the company's aircraft cleaners at 3:00 A.M. handing out doughnuts or donning a pair of overalls to clean a plane. He's also an inveterate prankster who appeared in a hangar one night disguised as a woman; on other occasions he has impersonated Elvis Presley. As a result, his staff share in the sense of fun, with stewardesses wearing turkey outfits on Thanksgiving and reindeer antlers on Christmas.[16] All the company's 7-S's align to support the company vision. On the other hand, when the individual "S's" are out of alignment with the overall vision, successful achievement becomes less likely.

MOBILIZING OTHERS INTO ACTION[17]

The third dimension of effective leadership is the ability to motivate staff to achieve the vision. It is one thing to devise an organizational vision and to get others to believe in it, but the real test comes when staff deeply desire through their own efforts to make it happen. The most useful term that captures such efforts is empowerment. Although empowerment has become a buzz word, when applied properly, this approach can result in enormous motivational energy.

We can think of empowerment as the act of strengthening an individual's beliefs in his or her sense of effectiveness. It is essentially a process of changing the internal beliefs of people. Any leadership practice that increases an individual's sense of self-determination will tend to make that person feel more powerful. From research, we know that there are at least four means of providing empowering information to others: (1) by helping them actually experience the mastering of a task with success (the most effective source), (2) by presenting models of success with whom people can identify, (3) by giving positive emotional support during experiences associated with stress and anxiety, and (4) by offering words of encouragement and positive persuasion.[18]

An example of an effective empowerment strategy comes from the actions of an executive of a large New York money-center bank who assumed leadership responsibility for his company's retail branches. His appointment occurred just after a major reorganization that had transferred away the division's responsibility for large corporate clients. Demoralized by this loss in responsibility and status, the branch managers began questioning their importance. After establishing a new retail banking strategy, our leader set about rebuilding the morale and motivation of his organization. His first step was to focus on the branch managers with a personal canvass of the bank's 175 retail branches. He commented to me:

> I saw that the branch system was very down, morale was low. They felt like they'd lost a lot of their power. There were serious problems and a lot of staff were just hiding. What I saw was that we really wanted to create a small community for each branch where customers would feel known. To do that, I needed to create an attitude change. I saw that the attitudes of the branch staff were a reflection of the branch manager. The approach then was a manageable job—now I had to focus on only 250 people, the branch managers, rather than the 3,000 staff employees out there. I knew I had to change their mentality from being lost in a bureaucracy to feeling like the president of their own bank. I had to convince them they were special—that they had the power to transform the organization . . . All I did

was talk it up. I was up every night. In one morning, I hit 17 branches. My goal was to sell a new attitude. To encourage people to "pump iron." I'd say, 'Hi, how's business?', encourage them. I'd arrange tours of the branches for the chairman on down. I just spent a lot of time talking to these people—explaining that they were the ones who could transform the organization.

By providing a positive emotional environment and words of encouragement, he started to restore the division's motivation. He also role-modeled self-confidence both in the staff and in the new strategy during his visits. But then he took the most important of empowering steps: He began pushing greater responsibility down into the organization and encouraging more initiative. He transformed what had been a highly constricted branch manager's job to a branch "president" concept. The idea was simple: Every manager was made to feel like the president of his own community bank and not just in title. Responsibilities, goals, and compensation were all changed to match this new reality. For example, performance measurement systems were completely restructured. The traditional measurement yardstick had been something called value-of-funds generated, but branch managers had little real influence over this measure since much of it was determined by interest rate fluctuations in the economy. So instead, managers were now measured on something they could control—deposits. Before branch managers rotated every few years. Now they stayed put: "If I'm moving around, then I'm not the president of my own bank, so we don't move them anymore." He then pushed responsibilities that normally resided up in the hierarchy into the branches by allowing them to hire, give money to charities, be involved in advertising. All this delegation soon translated into actual successes—a critical source of empowerment. These mobilizing efforts are in essence the fuel that drives any organization to achieve its vision. In this case, branch deposits doubled from $1 billion to $2 billion within five years, and what had been losses turned into after-tax profits of $85 million.

THE CROSS-FUNCTIONAL AND GLOBAL LEADER: NEW DIRECTIONS OF LEADERSHIP

While we might think of the leadership skills of visioning, aligning, and mobilizing as limited to more senior positions of a company, they are, quite to the contrary, skills that can and must be exercised at all levels of an organization. Earlier in this chapter, I described how speed is now an essential part of the competitive picture. Competitors may change marketplace rules or product offerings on a weekly basis in today's world. If responses to competitor moves must first travel up the hierarchy for approval and then back down for implementation, a company will eventually be unable to compete successfully.

Managers on the front line must now also develop similar leadership skills to those at the top. Though their visions may be of a more restricted version or represent one element of the company's overall vision, individual managers need the focus and meaningfulness of a vision for their own operations. Aligning and mobilizing skills are also just as essential.

But not only is leadership responsibility cascading down throughout organizations, it is also facing two operational imperatives. The first is to have a multifunctional perspective. Since increasingly more work is done on cross-functional teams, leaders of the future will have to possess a broad company view rather than a narrow functional one. Again, this is a by-product of an era based on speed. Japanese automobile producers can go from design to production of a new car in less than 40 to 50 percent of the time that American manufacturers require. In part, this is due to the involvement of cross-functional expertise early on in the design phase. As well, Japanese engineers start their careers by assembling cars on manufacturing lines. Afterward at Honda, for example, they are rotated to the marketing department for another three months and then spend a year rotating through all the different engineering departments before being assigned to an engineering specialty. So they start their careers with a cross-functional perspective.[19]

The coming generations of business leaders will need much of the same orientation if they are to understand fully the essential contributions of each function without being trapped in their own functional expertise and upbringing. The more people can gain multifunctional experiences early on, the better prepared they will be to lead effectively.

The second imperative is to possess a global perspective. The growth markets of the next decade are more likely to be in Asia than in North America. Future financing and banking is just as likely to be through a Japanese or German bank as an American one. So future leaders will have to be well schooled in foreign markets, geopolitical forces, global economics, and local cultures to manage overseas operations and to negotiate business deals and joint ventures with foreigners. But much like developing a cross-functional perspective, the dilemma is that each of us has a home culture as well as a functional silo. This biases our ability to comprehend foreign markets where customs and business tactics may be quite different from our own. In addition, we may have only one or two international assignments in our career or even none. From that limited experience, we may think we can extrapolate to understanding all foreign markets. But this is just as serious an error as being biased by your home country's culture. As we reach senior management positions where we must lead across the globe, we have to develop a transnational vision for our organization while at the same time appreciating the many and critical nuances of each geographic market even though we may only partially understand them. Instead, we must be adept at building strong international teams that can collaborate and comprehend one another rather than compete and be in conflict.

THE BOARD OF DIRECTORS: NEW SOURCES OF LEADERSHIP[20]

Traditionally, the formal leadership of any organization is accountable to its board of directors. In theory, these individuals oversee the activities of senior management and can take actions themselves to address poor executive leadership. That's the theory. In reality, however, boards have had little real power because of numerous forces. For one, corporations have grown to enormous sizes in the twentieth century and now daily face complex issues often demanding immediate decisions. With board meetings every quarter or so, directors have little opportunity or time to be on top of the issues facing the corporation. In addition, most of a board's membership comes from outside the company and its industry. So it is difficult for members to be knowledgeable enough to gauge accurately the effectiveness of a CEO's actions or to take those decisions themselves. So directors can never match a CEO on current information. In addition, the CEO usually determines what information the directors will receive and controls the meeting agenda and the selection of the directors. Due to these and other historical factors, boards of directors in the past normally responded to poor company leadership only after a prolonged period of distress. In many cases, it took time to build a consensus among board members that serious action needed to be taken—after all, the directors were often friends of the CEO or feared they would create shock waves throughout a corporation if they dismissed or reprimanded the CEO. These forces conspired to make boards far less powerful than one might imagine.

The 1980s, however, began to challenge the traditional role of boards and their "boys' club" nature. Global competition and the wave of corporate takeovers and restructurings put into question the effectiveness of quite a number of company managers and CEO's in North America. The junk bond financed acquisitions of the 1980s revealed how susceptible management could be to takeovers and that they could be overthrown with some ease. This set a precedent. By the 1990s when numerous Fortune 500 companies began bleeding red ink as a result of their poor strategic and financial decisions, questions were raised about who was minding the store if the CEO was not. Naturally, attention turned to boards of directors.

By the early 1990s, the speed with which boards responded to leadership problems began to accelerate. In the years of 1992 and 1993 alone, boards pushed out a remarkable list of well-known CEOs: James Robinson III of American Express, Robert Stempel of General Motors, John Akers of IBM, Paul Lego of Westinghouse, Vaughn Bryson of Eli Lilly, Philip Lippincott of Scott Paper, Anthony D'Amato of Borden, and Kay Whitmore of Eastman Kodak, just to name a few.

A great deal of the force behind the newfound activism causing tremors in corporate governance has to do with certain fundamental shifts in who really owns American corporations and with the rise of the business media. Large institutional investors owned some 19 percent of the equity of companies in 1970. Today, that percentage is some 50 percent. Pension funds and mutual funds have over the decades replaced the small shareholder. Naturally, this has concentrated power in the hands of a few investment managers running these funds and has potentially increased their ability to influence CEOs and their boards. I say potentially because only recently have investment managers actually taken an active interest in shaping the direction of the companies they invested in. Instead, investment funds traditionally follow a simple guideline: If a company has poor management, then sell its stock.

There have been many reasons for this approach, but among the most important is the issue of costs. It takes time and money for a fund manager to intervene actively in the affairs of a company. Rarely are the performance problems of a major corporation a quick-fix issue. Yet at any given time, fund managers may have investments in 30 or 100 companies. Actively influencing the policy and actions of a particular CEO and company can require a month or more's worth of attention—costly time that the average fund manager simply could not afford given a small staff, potentially high legal fees, and many other companies to watch. Just as important, investment managers are not trained to be organizational turnaround artists nor is it a great interest to most.

But the growing enormous size of investment funds puts special constraints on institutional investors, especially the giant pension funds. Being somewhat limited in what they can purchase and sell, they generally invest in large blocks of equity, which translates principally into investments in large corporations. As a result, it has become less and less easy to move in and out of such stocks. After all, dumping an underperforming stock would disrupt the markets.

Recently, however, a handful of pension funds have decided to become activists in corporate governance. Among the first to be active into this area was Calpers, the California Public Employees Retirement System. In 1990, the approximately $80-billion-dollar fund decided to become involved in the long-term performance issues of their investments. They hired outside research firms to conduct business audits of poor performers and to share these with company managements. Another prong of Calpers activist strategy was to pressure companies to select more independent directors. Soon a handful of other pension funds followed suit.

An important turning point came in October of 1992 when the board of General Motors ousted Robert Stempel, its chairman. General Motors is 43 percent owned by institutional investors. After the previous chairman Roger Smith retired, many of these investment funds pressured the board to find an outsider to lead the company. But their pleas were ignored when the board, as it normally did, approved the internally selected candidate Stempel. Then into a third year of enormous losses, institutional investors increased their pressure tactics, and the board responded with Stempel's retirement.

But was it just the pressure from institutional investors? In reality, an outspoken individual and the business media had also joined forces in challenging the cozy relationship between boards and their executives. After the acquisition of his company Electronic Data Systems by General Motors, Ross Perot gained a seat on the company board. Within weeks, he began challenging GM management about their ineptitude. The press would follow suit, and the media blitz continued until Stempel's demise.

These events are reshaping leadership at the very head of corporations. CEOs are slowly losing control of the nominating process for their directors. In a recent survey, corporations told the executive recruitment firm of Korn/Ferry that more board vacancies are being filled by candidates nominated by other board members. A recent Conference Board survey showed that compared with 50 percent 10 years ago, two-thirds of the companies responding said they used independent committees.

THE DARK SIDE OF LEADERSHIP[21]

As implied in the previous section, not all the individuals we might consider to be leaders or in leadership positions are effective. Though we normally associate business leaders with positive outcomes, they may sometimes cause more harm than good. The very qualities that distinguish leaders from managers have the potential to create dilemmas and even disasters for their organizations. Typically, several aspects of a leader's behavior can contribute to a dark side. These include their strategic visions, their communications and impression management skills, and their management practices.

As we observed earlier, strategic vision is a crucial element of effective leadership, but visions by their nature of being oriented to an uncertain future contain significant risks. They also require a great deal of ego commitment on the part of the leader to keep the organization focused in the face of obstacles. But herein lies a major problem.

The blind drive to realize a personal vision can cause leaders not to see problems or else to distort their perceptions of marketplace opportunities. We also know from social psychology that the greater the commitment an individual has to something, the less willing he or she is to see competing approaches. For example, Thomas Edison so passionately believed in his vision of direct electrical current (DC) for urban power grids that he failed to see the more rapid acceptance of alternating current (AC) by emerging utility companies in the United States. The company founded by Edison to produce DC power stations soon failed.

So, typically, leaders get into trouble when their visions are based on (1) an exaggerated sense of marketplace opportunities, (2) significant underestimates of the necessary resources and the responses of competitors, and (3) a failure to detect important changes in the market (e.g., fundamental changes in consumer tastes or technological innovations).

A classic example of a derailed visionary leader is Robert Campeau. It is also the tale of how success and a strong ego may ultimately blindside a leader. A highly successful real estate developer from Canada, Campeau decided to enlarge his business empire into retailing with a series of purchases in the mid-1980s of the American chains of Allied and Federated Department Stores. He believed that there would be tremendous synergies between his expertise in commercial land development and the large retailing operations that sat in many of the malls he had or would develop. His plan included building some 50 U.S. shopping malls each anchored by his newly acquired retail stores. He commented to the press: "Most retail managements don't know much about real estate and finance . . . (but) real estate is the gravy on top of these great retailing deals." Also, his newly acquired stores sat on prime land—more possibilities for future deals. With this vision in mind, he would spend some $13.4 billion for his new acquisitions. Bankers' and lawyers' fees alone were some $400 million. Overnight, he became the most powerful retailer in the world. But for his vision, he paid an enormous price in the form of high-interest junk bond debt. In addition, the United States was just entering a slowdown in retailing sales and an emerging glut of shopping malls. On top of this, his two chains, while highly visible names, were known for their inefficiencies.

Quickly within the next few years, Campeau's vision unraveled. By August 1989, his retail operations ran out of operating cash. By January, the entire company stood at the edge of bankruptcy. Forced to sell out, by February 1990, Campeau's own personal fortune of $500 million had all but evaporated. His blind ambition became his undoing.

Another dark side of leadership has to do with what are called impression management skills. This is the ability to create an overall impression of yourself or your goals through the information and behavior you choose to convey. For example, leaders may present information that makes their visions appear more realistic or appealing than they actually are. They may screen out negative information or foster an illusion of control when, in reality, things are out of control. John DeLorean, the General Motors executive who went on to create his own car company, claimed responsibility for projects without acknowledging the contributions of others. His aim was to reinforce impressions of his own ingenuity and expertise. In *Current Biography*, DeLorean is described as owning "more than 200 patents, including those for recessed windshield wipers and the overhead-cam engine." Hill Levin's biography of DeLorean, however, reported that the U.S. Patent Office lists a total of 52 patents in DeLorean's name, none of which are for the wipers or the overhead-cam engine.

DeLorean also went out of his way to fulfill popular stereotypes of the successful businessperson. Because he wanted to convey the image of a youthful entrepreneur, he underwent cosmetic surgery, dieted from 200 pounds to 160, lifted weights, and dyed his grey hair black. He flew only first class, and when he ate out, he obtained only best tables. All of these were designed to reinforce an image of a successful leader. While such impressions garnered him an image of success and perhaps increased his ability to raise venture capital for his new company, poor tactical decisions ultimately undermined and bankrupted the organization.

Finally, leaders often suffer from their own poor day-to-day management practices. Common problems include (1) a failure to manage upward and sideways, (2) an inability to manage the details, (3) poor mentoring of others who may be potential successors, (4) the creation within their organizations of in-groups and out-groups, and (5) an autocratic, controlling style. In one case, the charismatic president of a division of a large corporation used the TV cartoon character Roadrunner as his group's emblem and mascot (you may remember that the Roadrunner was particularly adapt at outwitting a wily coyote). His division managers were the "roadrunners" who were smarter and faster than the corporate headquarter's "coyotes" who laid roadblocks in their path. He also had a habit of ignoring corporate staff requests for information, and he returned their reports with "STUPID IDEA" stamped on the front. Although such behaviors fostered a sense of camaraderie within the leader's division, they ultimately were detrimental both to the leader and the overall organization. In the end, this division president was forced to step down.

One of the greatest dilemmas for leaders is to develop others who are or will be of equal prominence. Many leaders simply enjoy the limelight too much to share it with others. Their egos, as well as the need not to be challenged, encourage these individuals to surround themselves with compliant staff—the "yes-man" scenario. As a result, subordinates end up being more often order takers than leaders themselves. One of the greatest challenges facing any successful leader is to know when to let go of the reins and to have cultivated leadership talent in their staffs all along the way so that they can take over for them.

FOR FURTHER READING

Conger, J. A., *The Charismatic Leader* (San Francisco: Jossey-Bass, 1989).

Conger, J. A., *Learning to Lead* (San Francisco: Jossey-Bass, 1992).

Kotter, J. P., *A Force for Change* (New York: The Free Press, 1990).

McCall, W. M., M. M. Lombardo, and A. M. Morrison, *The Lessons of Experience* (New York: Lexington Books, 1988).

CHAPTER NOTES

Chapter 3: Managing People: The R Factor

1. Comments from a speech for the Conference Board, March 22, 1994.

2. "Recognizing Quality Achievement: Noncash Award Programs," Conference Board, 1992, p. 6.

Chapter 4: Quantitative Tools: Numbers as Fundamental Language of Business

1. For the reader with a background in mathematics or engineering, the normal distribution is defined by the expression

$$\frac{1}{s_y \sqrt{2\,\pi}}\, e^{-(y-\bar{y})^2/2s_y^2},$$

where

$$\pi = 3.14159 \text{ and } e = 2.71828.$$

2. Some analysts prefer to create the adjustment factors using a measure of central tendency other than the mean, such as the median or the geometric mean (the square root of the product of the column elements), since the column elements are ratios and the arithmetic mean of a series of ratios is subject to distortion when the denominator of one or more of the ratios approaches zero. In most real-world applications, use of the mean is acceptable.

3. Steven C. Wheelwright and Darral G. Clark, "Corporate Forecasting: Promise and Reality," *Harvard Business Review* (November–December 1976), reprinted in the *HBR* publication no. 17055, *Planning: Part V,* p. 101. Wheelwright and Clarke's results were based on a survey of 127 U.S. companies.

4. Decision analysis can deal with risk explicitly by assessing the decision maker's willingness to incur risk through a series of questions (e.g., what is the most you would pay to obtain a 50-50 chance of winning $100,000?) and then representing the decision maker's risk preference or aversion with a *utility function.* The decision maker then selects the available course of action that maximizes *expected utility,* rather than expected profits.

5. This formula can be derived by writing the equation

Total costs = Holding costs + Order costs

then expressing holding costs as the product of the average inventory level times the holding cost per unit per year, H; replacing the average inventory level with one half the quantity ordered per order; expressing order costs as the product of the number of orders placed per year times the order cost per order, O; replacing the number of orders per year with the total annual demand divided by the quantity ordered per order; taking the derivative of total costs with respect to the quantity ordered per order and setting it equal to zero; and solving for the quantity ordered per order.

6. As a practical matter, you should be interested in considering whether to change the mix of saws and drills, given projected shifts in demand and in the profit margins of each. We're keeping the problem simple to facilitate understanding of basic principles.

7. Space limitations and the existence of readily available personal computer software make a more thorough discussion of manual solutions to the transportation problem impractical here. The solution procedure presented here does not always produce the optimal solution to the transportation problem, but it is rarely far from optimal and has the virtue of simplicity. For a treatment of transportation algorithms that always produce optimal solutions, you should refer to Russell L. Ackoff and Maurice W. Sasieni, *Fundamentals of Operations Research* (New York: John Wiley, 1968).

Chapter 5: Managerial Economics: Guidelines for Choices and Decisions

1. The geometrical measure of "excess burden" is the area of the triangle bounded by the vertical line at Q_1, the original supply curve, and the demand curve. All commodity taxes are subject to some excess burden; the degree of excess burden depends on the slopes of the supply and demand curves.

2. Just as the unemployment rate measures the rate of utilization of the labor force, the *capacity utilization rate* (as measured by the Federal Reserve Board) reflects the utilization rate of the nation's capital stock. The "natural" or full-employment rate of capacity utilization is in the vicinity of 85 percent.

3. An important element of the sticky price model is the *price adjustment equation:*

$$\eta_t = \frac{P_t - P_{t-1}}{P_{t-1}} = f \cdot \text{YGAP}_{t-1}$$

where η is the rate of inflation between year $t - 1$ and year t, YGAP_{t-1} is the output GAP in year $t - 1$, and f is a parameter (number) greater than zero. This equation says that when output is below potential (YGAP < 0), prices will tend to fall in the coming year, and that when the economy is above full employment, prices will tend to increase. According to the sticky price model, the response of the economy to the decline in AD from AD_0 to AD_1 would be as follows. In the short run (before contracts have expired), the price level remains at P_0 and output falls below potential to Y_0. As time passes, old contracts expire and new ones are negotiated at prices that are below P_0. Prices continue to fall until they reach the value P_1.

4. This follows from the mathematical fact that the growth rate of a product of two variables equals the *sum* of the growth rates of the variables. For example, revenue-price $\times$ quantity, so if price increases 5 percent and quantity increases 3 percent, revenue increases 8 percent.

Chapter 6: Marketing Management: Providing Value to Customers

1. General Electric Company, *1990 Annual Report* (March, 1991).

2. Peter F. Drucker, *The Practice of Management* (New York: Harper & Row, 1954), pp. 37–41.

3. C. K. Prahalad and Gary Hamel, "The Core Competence of the Corporation," *Harvard Business Review,* 68 (May–June 1990), pp. 79–91.

4. Thomas V. Bonoma and Benson P. Shapiro, *Segmenting the Industrial Market* (Lexington, MA: Lexington Books, 1983).

5. Al Ries and Jack Trout, *Positioning: The Battle for Your Mind,* 1st ed.–rev. (New York: Warner Books, 1986), p. 2.

6. Robert C. Blattberg and John Deighton, "Interactive Marketing: Exploiting the Age of Addressability," *Sloan Management Review,* XX (Fall 1991), pp. 5–14.

7. Theodore Levitt, "Marketing Success through Differentiation—of Anything," *Harvard Business Review,* 58, no. 1 (January–February 1980), pp. 83–91, or Chap. 4 of *The Marketing Imagination* (New York: Free Press, 1983), pp. 72–93.

8. Stanley Davis, *Future Perfect* (Reading, MA: Addison-Wesley, 1987); B. Joseph Pine II, *Mass Customization: The New Frontier in Business Competition* (Boston: Harvard Business School Press, 1993).

Chapter 7: Information Technology: The Challenge of Strategic Transformation

1. See especially, M. S. Scott-Morton (Ed.), *The Corporation of the 1990s* (New York: Oxford University Press, 1991); Peter Keen, *Shaping the Future: Business Design through Information Technology,* (Boston, MA: Harvard Business School Press, 1991). The popular articles include F. W. McFarlan, "Information Technology Changes the Way You Compete," *Harvard Business Review* (1984), R. I. Benjamin, John Rockart, Michael Scott-Morton, and John Wyman, "Information Technology: A Strategic Opportunity," *Sloan Management Review* (Spring 1984); John Rockart and James Short, "IT in the 1990s: Managing Organizational Interdependence," *Sloan Management Review* (Winter 1989).

2. *Computerworld* (November 25, 1991).

3. See Max Hopper, "Rattling SABRE—New Ways to Compete on Information," *Harvard Business Review* (May–June 1990).

4. P. Strassman, *Business Value of Computers* (New Cannon, CT: Information Economic Press, 1990).

5. See Richard L. Huber, "How Continental Bank Outsourced Its 'Crown Jewels,'" *Harvard Business Review* (January–February 1993); see also my paper with Lawrence Loh: "Diffusion of IT Outsourcing: Influence Sources and the Kodak Effect," *Information Systems Research* (December 1992).

6. See my paper with Lawrence Loh, "Stock Market Reaction to IT Outsourcing: An Event Study," MIT Center for Information Systems Research Working Paper, November 1992.

7. General Electric Corporation Annual Report, 1993.

8. *Computerworld,* August 6, 1990, p. 70.

9. See my article with James Short, "Beyond Business Process Redesign: Redefining Baxter's Business Network," *Sloan Management Review* (Fall 1992).

10. *Computerworld,* February 19, 1990, p. 81.

11. Details on Otis Elevators are based on primary research interviews with Otis managers, primary documents, and sources such as *Information Week,* May 18, 1987; *Business Wire,* May 30, 1990; *Inbound/Outbound,* (August 1988); and others.

12. Richard G. LeFauve and Arnoldo Hax, "Managerial and Technological Innovations at Saturn Corporation," MIT Sloan School of Management Working Paper, 1992.

13. See Michael Hammer, "Re-engineering Work: Don't Automate, Obliterate," *Harvard Business Review* (July–August 1990); see also his book with J. Champy, *Reengineering the Corporation* (New York: Free Press, 1993).

14. For an overview of the emerging principles of organizing, see particularly, James Brian Quinn, *Intelligent Enterprises* (New York: Free Press, 1992); Tom Peters, *Liberation Management* (New York: Knopf, 1992).

15. M. S. Scott-Morton, *The Corporation of the 1990s* (New York and Oxford: Oxford University Press, 1991).

16. Tom Davenport in *Process Innovation: Reengineering Work through Information Technology* (Boston: Harvard Business School Press, 1993), p. 5.

17. Tom Davenport and James Short, "The New Industrial Engineering: Information Technology and Business Process Redesign," *Sloan Management Review* (Summer 1990); see also Davenport's book, *Process Innovation: Reengineering Work through Information Technology* (Boston: Harvard Business School Press, 1992).

18. This term is introduced by Benn R. Konsynski. For a good overview, see his article with Jim Cash: "IS Redraws Competitive Boundaries," *Harvard Business Review* (March–April 1985).

19. See my paper with Akbar Zaheer, "Electronic Integration and Strategic Advantage: A Quasi-experimental Study in the Insurance Industry," *Information Systems Research* 1 (December 1990).

20. In a different data collection effort, Akbar Zaheer and I demonstrate that the degree of interdependent business processes enabled by the interfacing system is

an important determinant of the level of business channeled by an agent to the focal carrier. See A. Zaheer and N. Venkatraman, "Determinants of Electronic Integration in the Insurance Industry: An Empirical Test," *Management Science* (1993; forthcoming).

21. Reported in *Purchasing* magazine, September 12, 1991.

22. Remarks at *MIT Center for Transportation Studies Seminar* (February 1992).

23. See *Computerworld*, December 9, 1991.

24. See for instance, Quinn's book, *Intelligent Enterprise* (1992); "The Virtual Corporation," *Business Week* (February 8, 1993); William Davidow and Michael S. Malone, *The Virtual Corporation* (New York: Harper Business, 1992); Tom Peters, *Liberation Management* (1992).

25. See Quinn (1992), p. 81

26. *Inbound/Outbound,* August 1988, p. 28.

27. See my article with Ajit Kambil, "The Check's Not in the Mail: Strategies for Electronic Integration in Tax-Return Filing," *Sloan Management Review* (Winter 1991), pp. 33–43.

28. See my article with Jim Short in *Sloan Management Review* (1992).

29. For background discussions on the role of IT in restructuring relationships, see Vijay Gurbaxani and Seungjin Whang, "The Impact of Information Systems on Organizations and Markets," *Communications of the ACM* (January 1991); and Tom Malone, R. I. Benjamin, and J. Yates, "Electronic Markets and Electronic Hierarchies: Effects of Information Technology on Market Structure and Corporate Strategies," *Communications of the ACM* (June 1987).

30. James Brian Quinn, *Intelligent Enterprise* (New York: Free Press, 1992), p. 47.

31. Quinn (1992), p. 49.

32. See, for instance, Hammer and Champy (1993), Davenport (1992).

Chapter 8: Human Resource Management: Competitive Advantage through People

1. Tichy, Noel, and Mary Anne Devanna, *The Transformational Leader* (New York: John Wiley & Sons, 1986).

2. See, e.g., Ackoff, Rusell L., *Creating the Corporate Future* (New York: John Wiley & Sons, 1981) and *Management in Small Doses* (New York: John Wiley & Sons, 1986).

Chapter 9: Operations Management: Productivity and Quality Performance

1. Based on research from the McKinsey Global Institute, reported in the *International Herald Tribune,* October 14, 1992.

2. "Work Simplification Conference Notes," Lake Placid, NY, 1959. See also "Work Simplification," *Factory Management and Maintenance,* July 1958, pp. 72–106.

Chapter 11: Financial Management: Optimizing the Value of the Firm

1. Notes payable and current debt maturities are omitted from current liabilities. Accounts receivable, inventory, and current liabilities are averaged.

Chapter 12: Strategic Management: The Challenge and the Opportunity

1. Because most people are familiar with the automobile and computer industries, we shall use many examples from these two industries in this chapter.

2. A number of the principal bridges between strategy and organization are noted and discussed in the last section of this chapter.

3. This argument has been persistently and effectively articulated by Peter Drucker. See, in particular, *Innovation and Entrepreneurship, Practice and Principles* (New York: Harper & Row, 1985).

4. Most organizations can exercise some degree of influence over some sector of their environment, but rarely can an organization impose its will on all institutional sectors of its environment—customers, suppliers, competitors, community groups, and governmental agencies. Demographic, social, and technological changes also lie outside the control of all organizations.

5. Unfortunately, it is commonplace to find the word *strategy* used differently by managers in different subunits or hierarchical levels within the same organization. The absence of a generally accepted meaning of strategy is reflected in and compounded by its association with all spheres of business activity. Thus, one hears frequent reference to human resource strategy, marketing strategy, financial strategy, product strategy, and information strategy.

6. Entrepreneurial content articulates the need for an organization's strategy to be different from that of its competitors; otherwise, it does not possess any degree of differentiation.

7. The most extensive development of mass customization can be found in B. Joseph Pine II, *Mass Customization, The New Frontier in Business Competition* (Boston: Harvard Business School Press, 1993).

8. The argument here is that strategy is about both means and ends. Means are meaningless without some understanding of goals, and vice versa. Some authors equate strategy with means and thus keep goals distinct from any consideration of strategy.

9. Strategic intent is a term coined by C. K. Prahalad and Gary Hamel, "Strategic Intent," *Harvard Business Review* (May–June 1989), pp. 63–76.

10. See, for example, *Business Week,* October 12, 1993, pp. 156–158.

11. This discussion reflects the emergent nature of strategy.

12. The battle between Komatsu and Caterpillar is delineated in detail in Caterpillar Tractor Co. #9-385-276 and Komatsu Limited #9-385-277, Harvard Business School Cases.

13. A number of authors have recently stressed the importance of identifying and enhancing core operating processes. See, for example, Thomas J. Housel, Chris J. Morris, and Christopher Westland, "Business Process Reengineering at Pacific Bell," *Planning*

Review (May–June 1993), pp. 28–34; Robert B. Kaplan and Laura Murdock, "Core Process Redesign," *The McKinsey Quarterly,* 2 (1991), pp. 27–43.

14. Many of the key questions involved in building and fostering linkages among a corporation's business units and among a business unit's product areas have been identified in the GE example earlier in this chapter.

15. Organizational decision-making processes affect every phase of decision making: the generation and evaluation of alternatives, and the choice and execution of the preferred course of action.

16. The discussion of the difficulties in changing "paradigms" and effecting the reinvention of strategy illustrates why both change within organizations and change in strategy almost always occur *after* the need to change is reflected in such performance criteria as market share, new products developed, margins, and profits.

17. "Can Jack Smith Fix GM?" *Business Week,* November 1, 1993, pp. 126–134.

18. This argument has been extensively documented by Eileen C. Shapiro, *How Corporate Truths Become Competitive Traps* (New York: John Wiley, 1991).

19. The role and importance of outsourcing as a means of developing capabilities and competencies are discussed in some detail in Chapter 8.

20. We return to the notions of renovating and reinventing strategy at the end of this chapter.

21. For further elaboration of this point, see George S. Day and Liam Fahey, "Putting Strategy into Shareholder Value Analysis," *Harvard Business Review* (March–April 1990), pp. 156–162.

22. The point to be emphasized here is that differentiation must be sufficient not just to attract customers but to win and retain them as customers.

23. See also C. K. Prahalad and Gary Hamel, "The Core Competence of the Corporation," *Harvard Business Review* (May–June 1990), pp. 79–91.

24. For further treatment of this topic, see Thomas H. Davenport, *Process Innovation: Reengineering Work through Information Technology* (Boston: Harvard Business School Press, 1993).

25. We emphasize here the *desire* to reinvent strategy as well as to transform the organization. Process reengineering in some organizations has led to efficiency improvements but not to strategy reinvention.

Chapter 13: Organizations for the Year 2000: The Transition from Hierarchy to Enterprise

1. Douglas North, *Institutions, Institutional Change, and Economic Performance* (New York: Cambridge University Press, 1990).

2. William E. Halal, "Global Strategic Management in a New World Order," *Business Horizons* 36, no. 6 (December 1993).

3. The new science of complexity is described by M. Waldrop, *Complexity: The Emerging Science at the Edge of Order and Chaos* (New York: Simon & Schuster, 1992) and D. Freedman, "Is Management Still a Science?" *Harvard Business Review* (November–December, 1992).

4. Margaret Wheatley, *Leadership and the New Science* (San Francisco: Berrett–Koehler, 1992).

5. See Douglas Hall and Judith Richter, "Career Gridlock: Baby Boomers Hit the Wall," *The Executive* (August 1990).

6. Welch is quoted from Mark Potts, "GE's Management Vision," *Washington Post* (May 22, 1988).

7. Robert Axelrod, *The Evolution of Cooperation* (New York: Basic Books, 1984).

8. "Management's New Gurus," *Business Week* (August 31, 1992), p. 46.

9. Ronald Henkoff, "Getting Beyond Downsizing," *Fortune,* (January 10, 1994).

10. See Charles Handy, "Balancing Corporate Power: A New Federalist Paper," *Harvard Business Review* (November–December 1992).

11. G. Bennett Stewart, "Remaking the Public Corporation from Within," *Harvard Business Review* (July–August 1990).

12. Tom Peters, "Get Innovative or Get Dead," *California Management Review* (Fall 1990).

13. See Jay Forrester, "A New Corporate Design," 7, no. 1, *Industrial Management Review* (Fall 1965), pp. 5–17; Russell Ackoff, *Creating the Corporate Future* (New York: John Wiley, 1981); and William E. Halal, Ali Geranmayeh, and John Pourdehnad, *Internal Markets: Bringing the Power of Free Enterprise Inside Your Organization* (New York: John Wiley, 1993).

14. Pourdehnad, *Internal Markets,* Chapter 10.

15. "IBM Has a New Product: Employee Benefits," *Business Week,* May 10, 1993.

16. Rosabeth Moss Kanter, "Championing Change: An Interview with Bell Atlantic's CEO Raymond Smith," *Harvard Business Review* (January–February 1991).

17. Pourdehnad, *Internal Markets,* Chapter 8.

18. Susan Walsh Sanderson, "The Vision of Shared Manufacturing," *Across the Board* (December 1987).

19. Also see Brandt Allen, "Making Information Services Pay Its Way," *Harvard Business Review* (January–February 1987).

20. Pourdehnad, *Internal Markets,* Chapter 17.

21. See Pourdehnad, *Internal Markets,* Chapter 14, and "In the Labs, the Fight to Spend Less, Get More," *Business Week,* June 28, 1993.

22. Pourdehnad, *Internal Markets,* Chapter 2.

23. Shawn Tully, "Your Paycheck Gets Exciting," *Fortune,* November 1, 1993.

24. Pourdehnad, *Internal Markets,* Chapter 9.

25. Pourdehnad, *Internal Markets,* Chapter 8.

26. Shawn Tully, "The Real Key to Creating Wealth," *Fortune,* September 20, 1993.

27. See William E. Halal, *Fee-for-Service in IS Departments* (An International Data Corporation Report, 1992).

28. Pourdehnad, *Internal Markets,* Chapter 7.

29. Pourdehnad, *Internal Markets,* Chapters 3 and 5.

30. Pourdehnad, *Internal Markets,* Chapter 7.

31. John Walsh, "Videoconferencing Comes of Age," *Telecommunications*, November 1989; Gail Runnoe, "Videoconferencing Set to Soar," *Network World*, July 3, 1989; and Roberta Furger, "The Growth of the Home Office," *InfoWorld*, October 9, 1989.

32. "The Portable Executive," *Business Week*, October 10, 1988, p. 104. Also see William Davidow and Michael Malone, *The Virtual Corporation* (New York: Harper, 1992).

33. Thomas A. Stewart, "Boom Time on the New Frontier," *Fortune*, Autumn 1993, p. 160.

34. Strassmann is quoted from "Information Strategist Paul Strassmann," *INC.*, March 1988, p. 27.

35. See Oliver Williamson, *Markets and Hierarchies* (New York: Free Press, 1975).

36. David Clutterback, "The Whittling Away of Middle Management," *International Management* (November 1982), pp. 10–16.

37. Thomas Malone et al., "The Logic of Electronic Markets," *Harvard Business Review* (May–June 1989).

38. For instance, see Kenneth Labich, "Take Control of Your Career," *Fortune*, May 1992, and "I'm Worried about My Job!" *Business Week*, October 7, 1991.

39. Jerry Flint, "A Different Kind of Temp," *Forbes*, February 28, 1994.

40. "Part-Timers Are In," *The Conference Board's Monthly Briefing*, March 1988; "And Now, 'Temp' Managers," *Newsweek*, September 26, 1988.

41. Harvey Wagner, "The Open Corporation," *California Management Review* (Summer 1991).

42. "John Scully," *Forbes*, December 7, 1992.

43. R. Krishnan et al., "In Search of Quality Improvement," *Academy of Management Executive* 7, no. 4 (1993).

44. David Osborne and Ted Gaebler, *Reinventing Government* (Reading, MA: Addison-Wesley, 1992).

45. "Japan, Wracked by Recession, Takes Stock of Its Methods," *The Wall Street Journal*, September 29, 1993.

46. William Taylor, "The Logic of Global Business," *Harvard Business Review* (March–April 1991).

Chapter 14: Leadership for the Year 2000

1. J. A. Conger, *Learning to Lead* (San Francisco: Jossey-Bass, 1992).

2. Tom Bouchard, "All about Twins," *Newsweek*, November 23, 1987, p. 69.

3. Daniel Goleman, "Major Personality Study Finds That Traits Are Mostly Inherited," *New York Times*, December 1, 1986, C1.

4. T. Owen Jacobs and Elliot Jacques in their article, "Military Executive Leadership," in K. Clark and M. Clark, *Measures of Leadership* (Greensboro, NC: Leadership Library of America, 1990) analyze the ability of military leaders to think

out strategy over long time spans. They identify this ability as a temperament or proclivity and believe its development occurs early in life.

5. H. Gardner, p. 239.

6. John W. Gardner, "Leadership Development," *Leadership Paper 17*, Washington, DC, Independent Sector, June 1987, p. 10.

7. J. M. Burns, *Leadership*.

8. Ibid.

9. Ibid, p. 117.

10. W. M. McCall, M. M. Lombardo, and A. M. Morrison, *The Lessons of Experience* (Lexington, MA: Lexington Press, 1988), pp. 3–5.

11. J. P. Kotter, *A Force for Change* (New York: Free Press, 1990).

12. McCall et al., *Lessons*, p. 145.

13. Kotter, *A Force for Change*.

14. J. A. Conger, *The Charismatic Leader* (San Francisco: Jossey-Bass, 1989); W. Bennis and B. Nanus, *Leaders* (New York: Harper & Row, 1985).

15. R. T. Pascale, and A. G. Athos, *The Art of Japanese Management* (New York: Simon & Schuster, 1981).

16. B. O'Brian, "Flying on the Cheap," *The Wall Street Journal*, October 26, 1992.

17. J. A. Conger, "Leadership: The Art of Empowering Others," *Academy of Management Executive*, February, 1989.

18. The theory behind these ideas comes from the work of Stanford psychologist Alfred Bandura who conceptualized the notion of self-efficacy beliefs and their role in an individual's sense of personal power.

19. J. P. Womack, D. T. Jones, & D. Roos, *The Machine That Changed the World* (New York: Harper Collins, 1990).

20. D. W. Linden and N. Rotinier, "Good-bye to Berle & Means," *Forbes*, January 3, 1994; B. McMenamin, "Help Wanted," *Forbes*, November 22, 1993.

21. J. A. Conger, "The Dark Side of Leadership," *Organizational Dynamics*, Fall 1990.

ABOUT THE AUTHORS

Allan R. Cohen is Academic Vice President and Dean of Faculty at Babson College where he is responsible for academic activities including undergraduate and M.B.A. programs, the School of Executive Education, and the development of 120 fulltime faculty. Previously, he was a chaired Professor of Management at Babson and the University of New Hampshire, teaching organizational behavior and negotiations.

In the spirit of continuous learning, Cohen persists in conceptualizing about management. His books include: *Managing for Excellence* and *Influence Without Authority* (both coauthored with David Bradford); *The Portable MBA in Management* (Editor); *Alternative Work Schedules* (coauthored with Herman Gadon), winner of the 1978 ASPA best book prize; and six editions of a textbook, *Effective Behavior in Organizations* (written with Fink, Gadon, and Willits), that introduced the Classroom-as-Organization to teaching organizational behavior.

Cohen's consulting clients have included General Electric, Digital Equipment, Polaroid, and Lafarge Coppee. His education includes an A.B. in English literature from Amherst College, M.B.A. and D.B.A. from Harvard, and an Applied Behavioral Science Internship from NTL.

Jay A. Conger is Professor of Management at McGill University.

The author of over sixty articles and four books, Dr. Conger researches executive leadership, the management of organizational change, and the training and development of leaders and managers. His most recent book, *Learning to Lead* (1992), is the culmination of a two-year research effort examining the field of leadership training.

423

In 1994, Professor Conger was invited to join the Harvard Business School as a visiting professor to help redesign their M.B.A. curriculum around leadership issues. In addition, he is actively involved in executive education at INSEAD, a European business school located in France. For his contributions to education at McGill, he is the two-time recipient of McGill University's Distinguished Teaching Award.

He received his B.A. from Dartmouth College, his M.B.A. from the University of Virginia, and his D.B.A. from the Harvard Business School. Prior to his academic career, he worked in government and as an international marketer for a high-technology company.

Mary Anne Devanna, before her recent death, was Associate Dean and Director of Executive Education at the Graduate School of Business, Columbia University. She was the coauthor (with Noel Tichy) of *The Transformational Leader* (John Wiley & Sons, 1986) and co-editor (with Charles Fombrun and Noel Tichy) of *Strategic Human Resource Management* (John Wiley & Sons, 1984). Her articles appeared in *The Journal of Applied Behavioral Science, Organizational Dynamics,* and the *Sloan Management Review.* Dr. Devanna was editor of the *Columbia Journal of World Business* and had done extensive research and writing on the role of women managers in American corporations. Dr. Devanna was a senior consultant for "Workout," a major change program at General Electric. Earlier in her career, Dr. Devanna was director of advertising at Longines. Her doctorate was from Columbia University.

Liam Fahey, an Adjunct Professor of Strategic Management at Babson College and Visiting Professor of Strategic Management at the Cranfield School of Management (U.K.), has received awards for his teaching, research, and professional activity. The editor of *Planning Review,* a bi-monthly magazine on strategic management and planning, he also serves as co-chairperson of an annual strategic management conference sponsored by The Planning Forum. He consults for a number of leading North American and European firms in the areas of competitive strategy and competitor analysis and is a frequent speaker in executive education programs and business management conferences. Dr. Fahey is the co-editor of *The Portable MBA in Strategy.*

Brain Forst is Associate Professor at the American University School of Public Affairs. Previously he was Professor at the George Washington University School of Business and Public Management (1989–92). He received his Bachelor of Science degree in statistics from the University of California, Los Angeles; his M.B.A. degree from U.C.L.A.'s Graduate School of Management; studied managerial economics in the Ph.D. program at Cornell University; and was a fellow at the Massachusetts Institute of Technology. He has also lectured at the U.C.L.A. Business School. Dr. Forst is an experienced management consultant, with 20 years of experience in analyzing and improving the performance of business and public organizations.

William E. Halal is Professor of Management at George Washington University in Washington, DC. An authority on emerging technologies, strategic management, and institutional and economic change, he has conducted research and consulting projects for General Motors, IBM, AT&T, Blue Cross/Blue Shield, MCI, International Data Corporation, Japanese firms, the National Science Foundation, the DoD, NASA, the National Institutes of Health, the federal courts, Saudi Arabia, and the Center for Soviet-American Dialogue.

Halal's publications have appeared in journals such as *The California Management Review, Business in the Contemporary World, Long-Range Planning, Business Horizons, Human Relations, Systems & Cybernetics*, and *Technological Forecasting & Social Change*, as well as popular media like *The New York Times, The Christian Science Monitor, USA Today, Advertising Age*, and *The Futurist*. His book, *The New Capitalism* (Wiley, 1986), outlined the transition to a new system of business and economics for the Information Age. Professor Halal's most recent book, *International Markets* (Wiley, 1993), describes how dynamic organizations are replacing the hierarchy with internal market economies.

Frank R. Lichtenberg is a Professor of Finance and Economics at the Columbia University Graduate School of Business and a Research Associate of the National Bureau of Economic Research. He received a B.A. with Honors in history from the University of Chicago and an M.A. and Ph.D. in economics from the University of Pennsylvania.

He has conducted research on a variety of subjects, including productivity, corporate control, technological change, research and development, and information systems. His articles have been published in numerous scholarly journals and in the popular press. His book *Corporate Takeovers and Productivity* has been published by MIT Press.

He has been awarded research fellowships and grants by the National Science Foundation, the Fulbright Commission, the Alfred P. Sloan Foundation, the German Marshall Fund, and other organizations. He is an academic advisor to the consulting firm of Princeton Economic Associates and a member of the Consortium on Productivity in the Schools.

He has served as a consultant to private organizations and government agencies including the Securities Industry Association, the Community Preservation Corporation, the RAND Corporation, the Bureau of the Census, the New York City Water Board, Touche Ross and Co., and the American Federation of State, County, and Municipal Employees.

Previously Mr. Lichtenberg taught at Harvard University, the University of Pennsylvania, and the University of Adelaide (Australia), and worked at the Brookings Institution, the Congressional Budget Office, the Department of Justice, and the Bureau of Labor Statistics.

John Leslie Livingstone directs a nationwide management consulting practice headquartered in West Palm Beach, Florida. Dr. Livingstone is a CPA, and earned M.B.A. and Ph.D. degrees at Stanford University. He is a former Chairman of the Division of Accounting and Law at Babson College, and was previously a senior partner in the "Big 6" international accounting firm of Coopers & Lybrand, and then a principal in THE MAC GROUP, a management consulting firm with offices in Boston, Chicago, San Francisco, London, Paris, Rome, Madrid, Munich, Hong Kong, Tokyo, and Buenos Aires. Dr. Livingstone, a frequent speaker at conferences and seminars, is the author or coauthor of ten books, fifty articles in professional periodicals, and chapters in several authoritative handbooks. He has also held endowed professorial chairs at Ohio State University, Georgia Institute of Technology, and the University of Southern California.

Leonard A. Schlesinger is Senior Associate Dean, Director of External Relations, and Professor of Business Administration at the Harvard Business School. He has, since February of 1993, chaired the M.B.A. program curriculum redesign effort and is now leading the design and development of a new M.B.A. Foundations program. Since 1988, his teaching and research have focused on the management of service firms and the organizational challenges of a rapidly changing business environment. He has taught M.B.A. elective courses on *Service Management, Field Studies in Service Management* and *Not-for-Profit Management,* and has served as faculty chairman of the *Achieving Breakthrough Service* executive program. He holds an A.B. in American civilization from Brown University, an M.B.A. in corporate and labor relations form Columbia University, and a doctorate in organizational behavior from Harvard University.

From 1985 to 1988, Professor Schlesinger served as Executive Vice President and Chief Operating Officer of Au Bon Pain Co., Inc., a rapidly growing chain of French bakery cafés which has pioneered the adoption of numerous human resource and service innovations. Prior to joining Au Bon Pain, Professor Schlesinger served as a member of the Harvard Business School faculty from 1978 to 1985. During this period he served as head of the required M.B.A. course in *Organizational Behavior* and as faculty chairman of the executive program in *Human Resource Management* while conducting research activities in both areas.

Professor Schlesinger is the author of over 40 articles and eight books (among them *The Real Heroes of Business . . . and Not a CEO Among Them* (with Bill Fromm, Doubleday Currency, 1994) and *Out in Front: Achieving Breakthrough Service by Putting People First* (with James L. Heskett, Harvard Business School Press, 1995)), he is Associate Editor of *Human Resource Management* and a member of the Editorial Board of *Journal of Management Inquiry.* He has also served on the Editorial Boards of the *Academy of Management Review* and the *Academy of Management Executives.*

Linda G. Sprague is Professor of Operations Management at the Whittemore School of Business and Economics, University of New Hampshire, and Professor at the Manufacturing Management Centre, School of Industrial and Manufacturing Science, Cranfield University in England. She is Founding Director of the Manchester Manufacturing Management Center at the University of New Hampshire. Dr. Sprague has also served on the faculties of IMD (International Management Development Institute) in Switzerland, the Tuck School (Dartmouth College), and the Graduate School of Business at Stanford University. She was a Founding Professor of the National Center for Industrial Science and Technology Management Development at Dalian, China.

Professor Sprague received her doctorate in Production/Operations Management from the Harvard Business School. She holds an M.B.A. from Boston University and an S.B. in industrial management from the Massachusetts Institute of Technology. She is a Fellow of the Decision Sciences Institute, a Fellow of the British Production and Inventory Control Society, and a Certified Practitioner in Inventory Management. Mrs. Sprague is an Associate Editor of *Decision Sciences,* a member of the Editorial Advisory Board of the *Journal of Operations Management,* and Chair of the Publications Committee of the Operations Management Association. Professor Sprague is a Past President of the Decision Sciences Institute, Past Chair of the Production/Operations Management Division of the Academy of Management, and is President-elect of the Operations Management Association. She is a member of the Systems and Technology Committee of the Certification Council of the American Production and Inventory Control Society.

N. Venkatraman, a Professor in the School of Management at Boston University, conducts research and teaches in the area of the formulation and implementation of business strategies, with particular emphasis on the emerging impact of information technology on the scope of business strategies. He has published extensively in several scholarly and managerial journals such as *Management Science, Strategic Management Journal,* and the *Sloan Management Review.* Previously he was at the Sloan School of Management, M.I.T. Professor Venkatraman holds a Ph.D. degree in business administration from the University of Pittsburgh (his dissertation was awarded the 1986 AT Kearney Award for Outstanding Research in General Management), an M.B.A.

degree from the Indian Institute of Management, and an undergraduate degree in mechanical engineering from the Indian Institute of Technology.

James E. Walter was Professor of Finance at the Wharton School of the University of Pennsylvania. he was the author of many books including *Financial Strategy: A Guide for the Corporate Manager* (John Wiley & Sons, 1989) and *Dividend Policy and Enterprise Valuation* (Wadsworth Publishing Company, 1967). Dr. Walter's many articles appeared in such publications as *Financial Management Journal, Journal of Finance,* and *Accounting Review.* He was also an Associate Editor of *The Journal of Finance.* Dr. Walter held a Ph.D. from the University of California (Berkeley).

David Warsch writes a column on economics and related topics for the *Boston Globe,* which appears regularly in the *Chicago Tribune* as well. He has been a newsman for more than 30 years. He is the author of *The Idea of Economic Complexity* (Viking, 1984). A collection of his columns appeared as *Economic Principals: Masters and Mavericks of Modern Economics* (The Free Press, 1993).

Frederick E. Webster, Jr. is the Charles Henry Jones Third Century Professor of Management at the Amos Tuck School of Business Administration at Dartmouth College, where he has been on the faculty since 1965. His research and teaching focus is on marketing strategy, industrial marketing and procurement, and social and ethical issues in marketing.

Mr. Webster earned his doctorate at Stanford's Graduate School of Business, and was on the faculty at the Graduate School of Business at Columbia University before he returned to Dartmouth, where he had earned his bachelor's and master's degrees. At Tuck, he served as Associate Dean in 1971–72 and again from 1976 to 1983. He has also served for several years as Faculty Director for Executive Education.

He has been a visiting professor at the International Management Institute in Geneva, Switzerland and at the Harvard Business School. From 1987 to 1989 he served as the Executive Director of the Marketing Science Institute in Cambridge, Massachusetts.

His research in marketing strategy, industrial marketing, sales force management, corporate culture, and buyer behavior has resulted in the publication of over 50 journal articles and book chapters and a dozen books. His article "The Changing Role of Marketing in the Corporation" received the Alpha Kappa Psi Award from the *Journal of Marketing* as the best paper in 1992 for its contribution to management understanding of the marketing profession. His most recent books are *Market-Driven Management* (Wiley, 1994) and the third edition of *Industrial Marketing Strategy* (Wiley, 1991).

INDEX